Einstein on the Beach

Philip Glass and Robert Wilson's most celebrated collaboration, the landmark opera *Einstein on the Beach*, had its premiere at the Avignon Festival in 1976. During its initial European tour, Metropolitan Opera premiere, and revivals in 1984 and 1992, *Einstein* provoked opposed reactions from both audiences and critics. Today, *Einstein* is well on the way itself to becoming a canonized avant-garde work, and it is widely acknowledged as a profoundly significant moment in the history of opera or musical theater. *Einstein* created waves that for many years crashed against the shores of traditional thinking concerning the nature and creative potential of audiovisual expression. Reaching beyond opera, its influence was felt in audiovisual culture in general: in contemporary avant-garde music, performance art, avant-garde cinema, popular film, popular music, advertising, dance, theater, and many other expressive, commercial, and cultural spheres. Inspired by the 2012–2015 series of performances that re-contextualized this unique work as part of the present-day nexus of theoretical, political, and social concerns, the editors and contributors of this book take these new performances as a pretext for far-reaching interdisciplinary reflection and dialogue. Essays range from those that focus on the human scale and agencies involved in productions to the mechanical and post-human character of the opera's expressive substance. A further valuable dimension is the inclusion of material taken from several recent interviews with creative collaborators Philip Glass, Robert Wilson, and Lucinda Childs, each of these sections comprising knee chapters, or short intermezzo sections resembling those found in the opera *Einstein on the Beach* itself. The book additionally features a foreword written by the influential musicologist and cultural theorist Susan McClary and an interview with film and theater luminary Peter Greenaway, as well as a short chapter of reminiscences written by the singer-songwriter Suzanne Vega, among others.

Jelena Novak is Researcher at the Centre for the Study of the Sociology and Aesthetics of Music (CESEM) at NOVA University of Lisbon. Her publications include *Opera u doba medija (Opera in the Age of Media)*, *Postopera: Reinventing the Voice-Body*, and *Operofilia*.

John Richardson is Professor of Musicology at the University of Turku in Finland. His publications include *An Eye for Music: Popular Music and the Audiovisual Surreal*, *Singing Archaeology: Philip Glass's Akhnaten*, and *The Oxford Handbook of New Audiovisual Aesthetics* (eds. Richardson, Gorbman, and Vernallis).

Ashgate Interdisciplinary Studies in Opera
Series Editor:
Roberta Montemorra Marvin, University of Massachusetts, USA

The *Ashgate Interdisciplinary Studies in Opera* series provides a centralized and prominent forum for the presentation of cutting-edge scholarship that draws on numerous disciplinary approaches to a wide range of subjects associated with the creation, performance, and reception of opera (and related genres) in various historical and social contexts. There is great need for a broader approach to scholarship about opera. In recent years, the course of study has developed significantly, going beyond traditional musicological approaches to reflect new perspectives from literary criticism and comparative literature, cultural history, philosophy, art history, theatre history, gender studies, film studies, political science, philology, psychoanalysis, and medicine. The new brands of scholarship have allowed a more comprehensive interrogation of the complex nexus of means of artistic expression operative in opera, one that has meaningfully challenged prevalent historicist and formalist musical approaches. This series continues to move this important trend forward by including essay collections and monographs that reflect the ever-increasing interest in opera in non-musical contexts. Books in the series are linked by their emphasis on the study of a single genre - opera - yet are distinguished by their individualized and novel approaches by scholars from various disciplines/fields of inquiry. The remit of the series welcomes studies of seventeenth-century to contemporary opera from all geographical locations, including non-Western topics.

For more information about this series, please visit: www.routledge.com/music/series/AISO

Einstein on the Beach

Opera Beyond Drama

**Edited by Jelena Novak and
John Richardson**

LONDON AND NEW YORK

First published 2019
by Routledge

2 Park Square, Milton Park, Abingdon, Oxon OX14 4RN

and by Routledge
605 Third Avenue, New York, NY 10017

First issued in paperback 2021

Routledge is an imprint of the Taylor & Francis Group, an informa business

Publisher's Note
The publisher has gone to great lengths to ensure the quality of this reprint but points out that some imperfections in the original copies may be apparent.

British Library Cataloguing-in-Publication Data
A catalogue record for this book is available from the British Library

Library of Congress Cataloging-in-Publication Data
A catalog record has been requested for this book

ISBN 13: 978-1-03-208260-8 (pbk)
ISBN 13: 978-1-4724-7370-7 (hbk)

Typeset in Times
by Deanta Global Publishing Services, Chennai, India

MIX
Paper from
responsible sources
FSC
www.fsc.org   FSC™ C013985

Printed in the United Kingdom
by Henry Ling Limited

Contents

Figures

Music examples

Series editor preface

Ashgate Interdisciplinary Studies in Opera provides a centralized and prominent forum for the presentation of cutting-edge scholarship that draws on numerous disciplinary approaches on a wide range of subjects associated with the creation, performance, dissemination, and reception of opera and related genres in various historical and social contexts. The series includes topics from the seventeenth century to the present and from all geographical locations, including non-Western traditions.

In recent years, the field of opera studies has not only come into its own but has developed significantly, going beyond traditional musicological approaches to reflect new perspectives from literary criticism and comparative literature, cultural history, philosophy, art history, theater history, gender studies, film studies, political science, philology, psycho-analysis, and even medicine. The new brands of scholarship have allowed a more comprehensive and intensive interrogation of the complex nexus of means of artistic expression operative in opera, one that has meaningfully challenged prevalent historicist and formalist musical approaches. Today, interdisciplinary, or as some prefer cross-disciplinary, opera studies are receiving increasingly widespread attention, and the ways in which scholars, practitioners, and the public think about the artform known as opera continue to change and expand. *Ashgate Interdisciplinary Studies in Opera* seeks to move this important trend forward by including essay collections and monographs that reflect the ever-increasing interest in opera in non-musical contexts.

In *Einstein on the Beach: Opera beyond Drama*, Jelena Novak and John Richardson have assembled a rich collection of essays that re-examine in timely and fascinating ways a major musical-theatrical work that from its premiere unsettled widely held assumptions about opera, theater, music, and dance. The volume is enriched by a wide range of important and original critical perspectives that contribute to the literature on this now significant work in the history of opera. Overall, the studies form a pretext for far-reaching interdisciplinary reflections including views on aesthetics and politics of the production, performance, and reception of *Einstein on the Beach* to consider the manner in which the opera balances between modernism and postmodernism.

Roberta Montemorra Marvin
Series Editor

Foreword

Music and culture in the wake of *Einstein*

The history of music usually unfolds in a relatively orderly fashion, with composers accepting and working within the precepts of the previous generation. But occasionally a composition – Peri's *Euridice*, Beethoven's *Eroica*, Stravinsky's *Sacre du Printemps* – changes the ground rules once and for all. Musicologists may try to uncover a backstory to make such cataclysms seem less traumatic, explaining them as the natural results of energies long brewing under the surface of an apparently homogeneous style. Yet no one could have anticipated the shock of any of these innovations, nor could they have imagined the ways that not only music but the broader culture itself would turn as a consequence in new, uncharted directions. Historian of science Thomas S. Kuhn calls such moments paradigm shifts.[1]

In 1976, *Einstein on the Beach* joined the ranks of those game changers, and we are still coming to terms with the tremors set off by that explosive premiere, which took place more than 40 years ago. Today when film composers draw without thinking twice upon Philip Glass's musical idiom, when opera houses pay fortunes to have Robert Wilson direct even the most traditional of Puccini's works, when the *New York Times* features a retrospective of Lucinda Childs, we may have trouble recalling or comprehending just how flabbergasted audiences and critics were at the audacity of this collaboration. Yet watching the excerpts posted on YouTube never ceases to astound. For all that elements of *Einstein* have trickled down over the years, the viewer/listener can never quite prepare for the radical strangeness of this work.

Einstein changed the cultural terrain in countless ways. Since the essays included in this collection examine and assess many of these, I will mention only a few. First, *Einstein* made opera itself a viable medium again for new music. To be sure, a few twentieth-century composers had tried to keep the flame alive, and Benjamin Britten even contributed masterpieces that have endured in the canon. But most of these hewed closely to the models inherited from nineteenth-century

---

1   Thomas S. Kuhn, *The Structure of Scientific Revolutions*, Chicago, University of Chicago Press, 1962. Greil Marcus explores a series of similar moments in popular culture in his *Lipstick Traces: A Secret History of the 20th Century*, Cambridge, MA, Harvard University Press, 1989.

dramaturgy; they stood far apart from the avant-garde, which scorned such efforts as middle-brow at best. Alban Berg's daring experiments, *Wozzeck* and *Lulu*, seemed to represent the last submissions to a genre that had long since been dominated by museum pieces from former eras.

With *Einstein*, the operatic stage became once again a potential site for radical experimentation. I teach a seminar titled "Opera After *Einstein*" every two years, for the flood of new music-theater pieces that followed that landmark event shows no sign of ebbing. Sometimes we find ourselves studying operas that had not yet premiered when the semester began. Artists such as John Adams, Thomas Adès, George Benjamin, Olga Neuwirth, David Lang, Unsuk Chin, Nico Muhly, Osvaldo Golijov, Kaija Saariaho, and director Peter Sellars rushed through the gate blown open by Glass, Childs, and Wilson. Even Olivier Messiaen (teacher of Boulez, Benjamin, Saariaho, Chin, and others) finally yielded to the siren song in his last decade with the magnificent *Saint François d'Assise*. No other genre of concert music holds nearly the prestige of the new operas ushered in by *Einstein*.

Einstein also threw down the gauntlet before the guardians of high modernist styles. Although the innovations of Wilson and Childs disrupted the status quo within theater and choreography (see the discussions in this volume), I will comment here only on the music. Philip Glass had studied within the academic institutions that understood their duty as holding a hard line against the encroachment of popular genres; they compelled students to regard serialism as the only sanctioned option, and they forged a narrative for Western music history that led from Wagner to Schoenberg and Webern to Boulez and Babbitt, with the explicit assumption that the next generation would produce ever more esoteric devices.

Although some artists of my generation bit the bullet and churned out the kind of music demanded for their professional advancement (while many brilliant would-be composers simply dropped out), Glass turned decisively against what he derided as "that creepy music." Channeling the kinds of energies he heard in sources such as Indian ragas, La Monte Young, and sixties rock, he forged a musical language that aggressively violated the enforced taboos against repetition and triads. And although many of us cherish Glass's early improvisations at the keyboard, it took an extended work of gargantuan proportions – moreover, one that had taken European opera houses by storm – to turn the tide.

University composers and the musicological holders of their flame exploded in indignation. Ten years after *Einstein*'s premiere, I spoke in a panel after a performance of Glass's *The Photographer* at the Walker Art Center, and I nearly lost my tenured job at the University of Minnesota as a result. The department chair called me in and chastised me for having besmirched the honor of the school for even acknowledging Glass. Although some younger scholars now question its power, the Serialist Mafia ruled with an iron hand.[2] Glass confronted and defied

---

2   This kerfuffle inspired my "Terminal Prestige: The Case of Avant-Garde Music Composition," *Cultural Critique* 12 (Spring 1989), 57–81. But see also my return to the topic 25 years later, "The Lure of the Sublime: Revisiting Postwar Modernism," in *Transformations of Musical*

that power bloc, making it possible for subsequent composers to pick and choose eclectically from the whole range of musical sources. Whether or not their music actually resembles Glass's, they owe much of their artistic freedom to his courageous stance. Musicologists like me who try to deal with music since *Einstein* only reflect the revolution he brought about.

Glass's most significant innovation, however, concerns the shaping of temporality. We usually account for major shifts in musical style by focusing on pitch, in large part because we can point to pitches right on the page. But I would argue that alterations in temporality drive not only musical but, more broadly, cultural change. Pitches only serve as raw materials that follow the exigencies of ways of being in time – something not visible in scores and therefore ignored or else written off as subjective. Yet it was not the dissonances in Monteverdi's madrigals that set off the thorough-going upheavals in seventeenth-century music but Peri's casual way of declaiming text, which he had developed through his experience as an improviser and which Monteverdi only too happily latched onto. Nor was it Prog Rock that altered the ways we understand our bodies and emotions but dreaded Disco, especially as deepened and enriched by musicians such as the late Prince.

Of course, multiple experiments with time occur constantly in music. But only some of these catch on such that they become the way a generation perceives itself. No one – not even Glass – could have envisioned how his music would come to saturate our cultural soundscape, in concert music and also in popular media such as cinema.

Hollywood rarely takes chances, as is clear from its long-time reliance on the gestures and sonorities of late Romanticism, then the Americana of Aaron Copland or the brutalism of Carl Orff's "O Fortuna." The fact that Glass's idiom now appears in film after film means not that it was easily appropriated but rather that it has become a lingua franca. So close are the imitations that I frequently stay to the end of the credits to ascertain whether I had heard real or pseudo-Glass. Millions of viewers now accept this style quite simply as the ways their feelings operate. So accustomed are they to those procedures that they may not even register hearing them, though this only reinforces the power of Glass's innovation: it has become like the air we breathe.[3]

Needless to say, Glass did not bring about this transformation in sensibilities single-handedly. Popular music underwent a similar sea change around the same time with the emergence of hip-hop, with its emphasis on high-energy repetition. It would appear, in other words, that both the minimalists and rap artists picked

Modernism, ed. Erling Guldbrandsen and Julian Johnson, Cambridge, Cambridge University Press, 2015, 21–35.

3   See my "Minima Romantica," in *Beyond the Soundtrack: Representing Music in Cinema*, ed. Richard Leppert, Lawrence Kramer, and Daniel Goldmark, Berkeley and Los Angeles, University of California Press, 2007, 48-67. In the ten years since I published this account, Glass-inspired soundtracks have become ever more prevalent.

up on, gave voice to, and amplified crucial cultural currents barely discernable as such in the 1970s.

It may take decades for historians to untangle the links between these musicians, their contexts, and – especially – the reasons millions of listeners have chosen to identify with these new ways of construing time.[4] Whatever their answers, they will necessarily acknowledge *Einstein on the Beach* as a major turning point in Western culture.

Susan McClary
Case Western Reserve University

---

4   See my "Rap, Minimalism, and Structures of Time in Late Twentieth-Century Culture," in *Audio Culture: Readings in Modern Music*, ed. Christoph Cox and Daniel Warner, New York, Continuum/The Wire, 2004, 289–98.

Contributors

Johannes Birringer is a choreographer and media artist; he co-directs the DAP-Lab (with Michèle Danjoux) at Brunel University where he is a Professor of Performance Technologies in the School of Arts. He has created numerous dance-theater works, video installations, and digital projects in collaboration with artists in Europe, the Americas, China, and Japan. The digital oratorio *Corpo, Carne e Espírito*, premiered in Brazil at the FIT Theatre Festival (2008). DAP-Lab's interactive dance-work *Suna no Onna* was featured at festivals in London (2007–2008), and the mixed-reality installation UKIYO went on European tour in 2010. His last production (2014), a dance opera, *for the time being*, was created as a homage to the 1913 futurist Russian opera *Victory over the Sun*. He also writes. His last monograph was *Performance, Technology and Science* (2009), and he has spearheaded new transdisciplinary dance-research projects, including the books *Dance and Cognition* (2005) and *Dance and Choreomania* (2011), and *Tanz der Dinge/Things that dance* (2019).

Zeynep Bulut is a Lecturer in Music at Queen's University Belfast. Prior to joining Queen's, she was an Early Career Lecturer in Music at King's College London (2013–2017), and Research Fellow at the ICI Berlin Institute for Cultural Inquiry (2011–2013). She received her Ph.D. in Critical Studies/Experimental Practices in Music from the University of California at San Diego in 2011. Situated in the fields of experimental music, voice, and sound studies, Zeynep's scholarly and creative work examines the emergence, embodiment, and mediation of voice as skin. She is currently completing her first manuscript, entitled *Building a Voice: Sound, Surface, Skin*. Her articles have appeared in various volumes and journals including Perspectives of New Music, Postmodern Culture, and Music and Politics. Alongside her scholarly work, she has also exhibited sound works, and composed and performed vocal pieces for concert, video, and theatre. Her composer profile has been featured by British Music Collection. She is sound review editor for *Sound Studies: An Interdisciplinary Journal*, and project lead for the collaborative research initiative "Map A Voice."

Bojan Djordjev is a performance maker from Belgrade, educated in theater and art theory in Belgrade at Faculty of Drama/University of Arts and Amsterdam at

DasArts. Apart from Belgrade, his works have been shown in Berlin, Brussels, Amsterdam, New York, Vienna, Zurich, Zagreb, Rijeka, and Ljubljana. Directing credits include performances based on: H. Guibert, E. Jelinek, J. Joyce, G. F//ercec, I. Sajko, and three operas including *Les enfants terribles* by Philip Glass. He is a member and co-founder of the editorial collective TkH (Walking Theory) platform and *Journal for Performing Arts Theory* (editor of TkH issue 2 dedicated to *Einstein on the Beach*). As an artist he is interested in using theater as a place for collective thinking, a machine for processing complicated discursive propositions such as economy, art history, politics, and critical theory. His recent works revolve around finding artistic and theatrical public formats for Marxist thought as well as research into artistic heritage of the Left in Yugoslavia and elsewhere.

Robert Fink focuses on music after 1965, with special interests in minimalism, popular music, post-modernism and the canon, and the intersection of cultural and music-analytical theory. He has published widely in musicological jour-nals, and is the author of *Repeating Ourselves* (2005), a book-length study of the minimal music of Steve Reich, Philip Glass, John Adams, and others as a cultural reflection of American consumer society in the mass-media age. More recent work on minimalism includes "*Klinghoffer* in Brooklyn Heights," a critical reception-history and defense of the controversial opera, and the deconstructive exploration of Steve Reich's attitude towards singing, speech, and writing in "Jewish" works like *The Cave*. His co-edited collection, *The Relentless Pursuit of Tone: Tone and Timbre in Popular Music*, is scheduled for release in 2018, and he is a general editor for the University of Michigan Press's "Tracking Pop" monograph series.

Professor Fink is a recipient of UCLA's Distinguished Teaching Award and Graduate Mentorship Award (both 2014). He currently chairs the UCLA Herb Alpert School of Music's program in the Music Industry, and is a past President of the US Branch of IASPM. He works as a practicing forensic musi-cologist, and has been a frequent public speaker on contemporary art and popu-lar music in Los Angeles, presenting lectures at UCLA's Royce Hall, Disney Hall, the Getty Center, and the Los Angeles Museum of Contemporary Art.

Kyle Gann is a composer and was the new-music critic for the *Village Voice* from 1986 to 2005. He is the author of *Charles Ives's Concord: Essays After a Sonata*; *The Music of Conlon Nancarrow*; *American Music in the 20th Century*; *Music Downtown: Writings from the Village Voice*; *No Such Thing as Silence: John Cage's 4'33"*; *Robert Ashley*; *The Arithmetic of Listening: Tuning Theory and History for the Impractical Musician* and the introduction to the 50th-anniversary edition of Cage's *Silence*, along with dozens of scholarly arti-cles on contemporary music. Gann studied composition with Ben Johnston, Morton Feldman, and Peter Gena. Of his hundred-plus works to date, many are microtonal, using up to 58 pitches per octave. He is the Taylor Hawver and Frances Bortle Hawver Professor of Music at Bard College, where he has taught since 1997.

Tom Johnson, born in Colorado in 1939, received BA and MMus degrees from Yale University, and studied composition privately with Morton Feldman. After 15 years in New York, he moved to Paris, where he has lived since 1983. He is considered a minimalist, since he works with simple forms, limited scales, and generally reduced materials, but he proceeds in a more logical way than most minimalists, often using formulas, permutations, predictable sequences, and various mathematical models.

Johnson is well known for his operas: *The Four Note Opera* (1972) continues to be presented in many countries. *Riemannoper* has been staged more than 30 times in German-speaking countries since its premier in Bremen in 1988. Often played non-operatic works include *Bedtime Stories, Rational Melodies, Music and Questions, Counting Duets, Tango, Narayana's Cows*, and *Failing: a very difficult piece for solo string bass*. Johnson received the French national prize in the Victoires de la musique in 2001 for *Kientzy Loops*. The latest project is *Knock on Wood*, a sound installation in collaboration with Martin Riches, which began at Circuit in Lausanne (2019).

Pieter T'Jonck is an architect and art critic in the field of theater, dance, architecture, and occasionally fine arts. From 1986, he has run his own architectural firm. From 1980, he has written on (performing) art(s), architecture, and urbanism for various media such as the national newspapers *De Standaard* (1985–2000), *De Tijd* (2001–06), *De Morgen* (since 2006) and journals such as *Etcetera, DWB, De Witte Raaf, Tanz), Corpus AT,* (H)Art and *A+*. He also works regularly for *Klara Radio* since 2006. He has contributed to many books and wrote all of the surveys on dance in Flanders for the *Flemish Theater Institute* (now *Kunstenpunt*). Between 2015 and 2017 T'Jonck was editor in chief of the Belgian architectural review *A+*. Apart from that, he has led an architecture studio at the University of Ghent (1994–2001), and still teaches architecture history at the academy of Ghent. Between 2007 and 2013, he was an advisor at DasArts, Amsterdam. He has run workshops on dance criticism in Amsterdam, Brussels, Istanbul, Vienna, and Bucharest. In 2010–2012 he was curator of the triennial for visual art, fashion, and design, *Superbodies* (an exhibition running from February–May 2012) in Hasselt. He lives in Leuven.

Petri Kuljuntausta is a composer, improviser, musician, and sonic artist. He has performed music for an underwater audience, improvised with birds, and made music from whale calls and the sounds of the northern lights. As an artist he often works with environmental sounds and live-electronics, and creates sound installations for galleries/museums. Kuljuntausta has performed and collaborated with Morton Subotnick, Atau Tanaka, Richard Lerman, David Rothenberg, and Sami van Ingen, among others. He has made over 100 recordings for various record labels in Australia, Colombia, Finland, France, Germany, India, Sweden, UK, and the USA. Star's End and Inner Space radio shows selected Kuljuntausta's *Momentum* as one of the most significant CD releases of the year. Kuljuntausta has published three books on sound art and electronic music. In 2005 he won The Finnish State Prize for Art from the Finnish government, recognizing his position as a distinguished national artist.

Sander van Maas is Assistant Professor at the University of Amsterdam and Utrecht University College, and Senior Lecturer at the Amsterdam Conservatory. He held positions at Utrecht University (Endowed Professor of Contemporary Dutch Composed Music) and Codarts University for the Arts in Rotterdam. In 2010–2011 he was Visiting Associate Professor of Musicology at Boston University and visiting scholar at Harvard University. He authored *The Reinvention of Religious Music: Olivier Messiaen's Breakthrough toward the Beyond* (2009) and edited several volumes including *Thresholds of Listening: Sound, Technics, Space* (2015) and *Contemporary Music and Spirituality* (2016, with Robert Sholl).

Jelena Novak works as a researcher at CESEM (Center for Studies of Sociology and Aesthetics of Music), FCSH, Universidade NOVA de Lisboa. Her fields of interests are modern and contemporary music, recent opera, musical theater, singing and new media, capitalist realism, voice studies, and feminine identities in music. Exploring those fields, she works as a researcher, lecturer, writer, dramaturge, music critic, editor, and curator focused on bringing together critical theory and contemporary art. Novak holds a PhD in the Humanities (Amsterdam School for Cultural Analysis).

She has been a founding committee member of the Society for Minimalist Music and a founding member of the editorial collective TkH [Walking Theory]. In 2013 she won the Thurnau Award for Music-Theatre Studies from the University of Bayreuth, Germany. Her most recent books are *Postopera: Reinventing the Voice-Body* (2015) and *Operofilia* (2018).

Juhani Nuorvala is a composer and Lecturer in Composition at the Sibelius Academy in Helsinki. A notable variety of influences – microtonality, minimalism, neoromanticism, popular music such as techno – has been regarded as a special feature of Juhani Nuorvala's idiom. Born in 1961, Nuorvala studied composition in the 1980s and 1990s in Helsinki, Paris, and New York; his teachers include Eero Hämeenniemi and David Del Tredici. He has composed chamber, orchestral, and electronic works. He has also created the music and sounds for several stage plays, and written an opera based on the life of Andy Warhol. Starting from the 2000s, Nuorvala has written most of his music in alternative tuning systems.

John Richardson is Professor of Musicology at the University of Turku. He is the author of *An Eye for Music: Popular Music and the Audiovisual Surreal* (Oxford University Press 2012) and *Singing Archaeology: Philip Glass's Akhnaten* (Wesleyan University Press 1999). He is additionally co-editor of *The Oxford Handbook of New Audiovisual Aesthetics* (eds. Richardson, Gorbman, and Vernallis 2013), *The Oxford Handbook of Sound and Image in Digital Media* (eds. Vernallis, Herzog, and Richardson 2013), *Music, Memory, Space (*eds. Brusila, Johnson, and Richardson 2016) and *Essays on Sound and*

Vision (John Richardson and Stan Hawkins 2007). Richardson is an active songwriter and composer. His first solo album, *The Fold*, was released in 2017 (Svart Records) and is the subject of an ongoing study in the field of research-creation. His second solo album, *The Pine and the Birch*, is scheduled for release in 2020.

Avra Sidiropoulou is Assistant Professor at the M.A. in Theatre Studies Programme at the Open University of Cyprus, and a stage director. Her main areas of specialization include the theater of the director-auteur, adaptation and the ethics of directing, and theory of theater practice. Avra has contributed articles and chapters to several international peer-reviewed journals and edited volumes. She has published two monographs: *Directions for Directing. Theatre and Method* (Routledge 2018) and *Authoring Performance. The Director in Contemporary Theatre* (Palgrave Macmillan 2011). She has also conducted practical workshops, and delivered invited lectures in different parts of the globe and was a visiting researcher at the Institute of Theatre Studies, Freie University, in Berlin and the City University of New York (Martin E. Segal Theatre Center), as well as at the Universities of Surrey, Leeds and Tokyo (in the last case, as a Japan Foundation Fellow). As a director, she directed performances internationally (both independently and with Athens-based Persona Theatre Company).

Pwyll ap Siôn is Professor of Music at Bangor University, Wales, UK. His publications include *The Music of Michael Nyman: texts, contexts and intertexts* (2007), *Michael Nyman: Collected Writings* (2013) and *The Ashgate Research Companion to Minimalist and Postminimalist Music* (2013), the latter co-edited with Keith Potter and Kyle Gann. In 2014 he co-edited with Lauren Redhead a special issue of *Contemporary Music Review on Musical Borrowing and Quotation in the Twentieth and Twenty-First Centuries* and *Rethinking Reich*, which he is co-editing with Sumanth Gopinath, is due out in Oxford University Press in 2018.

Miško Šuvaković was born in 1954 in Belgrade. He received his PhD from the Faculty of Fine Arts at the University of Art in Belgrade in 1993. He has been Professor of Applied Aesthetics, Faculty of Music in Belgrade (1996–2015). Currently he is a Professor of Applied Aesthetics and Theory of Art and Media, at the Faculty for Media and Communications, Belgrade, where he is also a dean. Šuvaković is a member of Slovenian Society of Aesthetics and a member of the Society for Aesthetics of Architecture and Visual Arts, Serbia. He is also President of the International Association for Aesthetics (IAA). His books include *PAS TOUT – Fragments on art, culture, politics, poetics and art theory 1994–1974* (1994); *Impossible Histories* with Dubravka Đurić (2003; 2006); *Epistemology of Art* (2008); *Neo-Aesthetic Theory* (2017); and *Diagram Aesthesis* (2018).

Suzanne Vega emerged as a leading figure of the folk-music revival of the early 1980s when, accompanying herself on acoustic guitar, she sang what has been labeled contemporary folk or neo-folk songs of her own creation in Greenwich Village clubs. Since the release of her self-titled, critically acclaimed 1985 debut album, she has given sold-out concerts in many of the world's best-known halls. (…) Suzanne's neo-folk style has ushered in a new female, acoustic, folk-pop singer-songwriter movement that would include the likes of Tracy Chapman, Shawn Colvin, and Indigo Girls. In 1997, Suzanne joined Sarah McLachlan on her Lilith Fair tour which celebrated the female voice in rock and pop. She was one of the few artists invited back every year. Suzanne was also the host of the public radio series "American Mavericks," 13 hour-long programs featuring the histories and the music of the iconoclastic, contemporary classical composers who revolutionized the possibilities of new music. The show won the Peabody Award for Excellence in Broadcasting. (Extracts from the official Suzanne Vega website biography, www.suzannevega.com/biography/)

Frits van der Waa (1954) studied musicology at Utrecht University. From 1982 he has worked as a music critic, mainly for the Dutch daily *de Volkskrant*. He was the editor of a book about Louis Andriessen (*De Slag van Andriessen*, 1993), and translated books about Bach, Beethoven, Mick Jagger, and several non-musical subjects.

Leah G. Weinberg completed a BA at Wesleyan University and a PhD in Historical Musicology at the University of Michigan, where her dissertation drew on archival documentation and oral history to track *Einstein on the Beach*'s reception as a landmark opera. Her work focuses on minimalism and the performing arts in New York's downtown scene, as well as music in film and television. She has presented research at meetings of the American Musicological Society, the Society for American Music, the Society for Minimalist Music, and Music and the Moving Image, and her work appears in the 2nd edition of the *Grove Dictionary of American Music*.

Acknowledgements

The initial impulse for creating this book came during the international symposium *Einstein on the Beach: Opera after Drama*, which Sander van Maas and Jelena Novak organized at the University of Amsterdam (UvA) in January 2013. The symposium was made possible by the support of the Amsterdam School for Cultural Analysis (ASCA), the musicology department of the UvA, and the Centro de Estudos de Sociologia e Estética Musical (CESEM), Universidade Nova de Lisboa. This took place at the same time as *Einstein* was performed at the De Nederlandse Opera, and Philip Glass generously supported the event by taking part in a public talk moderated by John Richardson. Discussions continued over the next few years, an important landmark along the way being the conference *Minimalism Unbounded! The Fifth International Conference on Minimalist Music* in September 2015, organized jointly by the University of Turku and the Sibelius Academy in Helsinki and chaired by this publication's co-editor John Richardson.

Following the electrifying atmosphere of the premiere, intense symposium encounters, vivid discussions, and the palpable interest of a wider audience, it became clear that there was a need for a book that would take *Einstein* as its central concern. Above all, we are grateful to Philip Glass and Robert Wilson, who supported this idea and helped by providing materials, generous advice, and a positive cooperative spirit. Thank you also to Lucinda Childs for her support, materials, and discussions about dance. We are extremely grateful to all participants of the symposium and their respective institutions. It is great that all of them continued on this voyage together with us, along with several new crew members whose later contributions enriched the book immensely. Emma Gallon and Annie Vaughan from Routledge, and the series editor at Ashgate, Roberta M. Marvin, also deserve our heartfelt appreciation for helping to bring this book to realization.

There are a number of people and institutions that helped along the way in all kinds of different ways: Eloe Kingma from Amsterdam School for Cultural Analysis, now late video archivist pioneer Jack Henry Moore, who was present at the symposium round table discussion and gave unforgettable insights into what the first *Einstein* performance in Avignon looked like, Christopher Knowles who granted permission to publish the spoken text, Alisa Regas and Linda Brumbach from Pomegranate Arts, Noah Khoshbin, Thom Donovan, and Clifford Allen from Watermill Center, Drew Smith from Dunvagen, Louie Fleck from Brooklyn Academy of Music, Archiv der Akademie der Künste in Berlin who all helped with materials and permissions, photographers that made possible to use their images, directors and artists Achim Freyer, Berthold Schenider, Veronika Witte, Leigh Warren, Mary Moore, and Kay Voges, who provided materials and made it possible to analyze their new views on *Einstein*, Stuttgart and Dortmund Opera houses and the State Opera of South Australia staff, who sent materials on their *Einstein* productions, and Atte Häkkinen, who assisted with transcribing John Richardson's interview with Philip Glass.

Thank you also to Jim Samson, Dejan, Luka and Pavle Marković, Mirjana and Tomislav Novak, Katarina Kostić, Rita Marques, Danijela and Valentin Šendula, Mário Vieira de Carvalho, Manuel Pedro Ferreira, João Pedro Cachopo, Cristiana Vicente, and Vera Inácio Cordeniz.

Finally, thanks to the International Institute for Popular Culture (IIPC) at the University of Turku for funding the compilation of the index.

Introduction

John Richardson and Jelena Novak

At a recent conference on the issue of the "operatic," the question arose, is there any opera that is *not* operatic? This immediately brought to mind *Einstein on the Beach*. There are many ways in which you could argue that it is not operatic – it includes no conventional operatic voices, no divas, nor is there a consistent narrative to follow; there is no conventional libretto, and the title character appears only as a figure. But what, if anything, remains of the category of "opera" that would justify calling this an opera? There is, of course, the general spectacle of singing, dancing, acting, and talking, which are prerequisites in the traditional opera canon, even though *Einstein* stretches the boundaries of these categories almost to breaking point. One of the authors (Jelena) once asked Philip Glass if *Einstein* had changed the world of opera. He responded that it had not, since opera in its traditional forms still exists within its institutions and is probably as vivid an experience as it has ever been.[1] What *Einstein* actually brought about was the drifting away of the world of new opera from almost everything conventional opera represents.

Philip Glass and Robert Wilson's most celebrated collaboration was premiered at the Avignon Festival in France in 1976. During its initial European tour, the Metropolitan Opera premiere and revivals in 1984 and 1992, *Einstein* evinced diametrically opposed reactions from audiences and critics. Embedding repetitive structural principles in a spectacle reflecting the late-capitalist media age, the work problematized commonly held assumptions about opera, music, theater, and dance. Today, *Einstein* is well on its way to becoming a canonized avant-garde work, widely acknowledged as a profoundly significant moment in the history of opera or musical theater, whichever of these terms is considered more fitting, but apparently not – after all – *repeatable*, at least not in such a way that continuity between this work and what followed in the history of the genre would have seemed unavoidable: the result of a linear progression from one stylistic development to the next. Being *sui generis*, as some have called this work, would seem

1   Jelena Novak, "Philip Glass tvillingpar – opera och film" in Nutida Musik 1, 2008/03, pp. 26–32. ("Opera and Film as Twins," Philip Glass interviewed by Jelena Novak, Lisbon, June 24, 2007, unpublished manuscript in English).

almost by definition to rule out any notion that this was a watershed moment in the traditional sense. *Einstein* nevertheless created waves that for many years crashed against the shores of traditional thinking about the nature and creative potential of audiovisual expression. Its influence was not, therefore, restricted to opera but could be felt in audiovisual culture at large: in contemporary avant-garde music, performance art, avant-garde cinema, popular film, popular music, advertising, dance, theater, and many other expressive, commercial, and cultural spheres.

Notwithstanding its powerful impact, *Einstein* has thus far not been the subject of close critical reflection. Inspired by the 2012–2015 series of performances that re-contextualized this unique work as belonging to the present-day nexus of theoretical, political, and social concerns, the editors and contributors of this book take these new performances as a pretext for far-reaching interdisciplinary reflection and dialogue. Debates about the cultural conditions and politics of reception encourage an examination into how and why *Einstein*'s status changed over the years. Its resonance with Hans-Thies Lehmann's concept of postdramatic theater provokes discussion about the work's place in music theater "beyond opera." After Wagner's *Opera and Drama* and Joseph Kerman's *Opera as Drama*,[2] *Einstein* appears as "opera beyond drama": postopera that is postmodern and postdramatic at the same time. The shift from the self-reflexive sound structures of Glass's early minimalist pieces to the representational mechanisms of repetitive music in an opera that makes references beyond circumscribed ideas of the aesthetic – as posited in strict minimalism – provokes new questions.

This book mixes together a broad and inclusive range of views of the subject – academic, journalistic, artistic – but here we will take as our starting point the role of memory in an opera that recycles widely known imagery of an historical icon. In our view it is worth contemplating what it means to take this particular man, the scientist Albert Einstein, and his legacy as the subject of an opera at the dawn of the digital age. We reflect on the opera's surrealist vocabulary of disjunct sights and sounds and how this creates a perceptual divide between the represented past and the unfolding present. We review how the opera's pulsating music and shape-shifting imagery raise new questions about our experiences of time, in much the same way as the scientific theories of Albert Einstein himself overturned existing knowledge of time and space.

A more specific aim of the book is to promote interdisciplinary debate on the questions, how and why *Einstein on the Beach* still problematizes conventions of the art world; and how this work could be considered a prism through which current performance practice and theory might be seen more clearly. Our contributions range from those focusing on the human scale and agencies involved in productions to the mechanical and posthuman character of the work's expressive substance. The chapters cover perspectives and frames of reference ranging from the relationship of the opera's music to the dominant structures of feeling

---

2   Joseph Kerman, *Opera as Drama*, Berkeley and Los Angeles, University of California Press, 1988.

of advanced capitalism; a mode of expression in music and dance that has been compared (by Philip Glass and others) to Baroque aesthetics; work that focus on the music, dance, acting, the quasi-architectural design of the *mise-en-scène*; work that disentangles the reception of the opera from the myths that surround it; and the responses of contemporary cultural agents (a songwriter, a director of film and stage works, and two composers) who came into contact with the opera when it exploded onto the avant-garde scene in the 1970s.

Why Einstein? A hero for the postmodern age?

An essential question that some of our authors touch upon is why choose Einstein in the first place as the opera's protagonist? In an expressive medium and style (minimalist music and theater) that has often been defined as abstract and non-representational, what does it mean to pick a protagonist who is a widely known contemporary cultural icon guaranteed to evoke a wide range of associations in the minds of audience members. Opera is traditionally a setting where one encounters colorful and unashamedly dramatic characters: heroes, villains, and victims. The idea of heroic subjectivity is inextricably bound up these days with Romantic ideas about individuality, bravery, genius, combative masculinity, and a slew of related ideas that postmodernism, which this work is often considered to be an exemplar of, implicitly called into question. However, heroic actions require narrative cohesion in order to be recognized as such. The minimalists are perhaps best known for the break they made in the 1960s with conventional narrative approaches to composition, and since the modes of expression we associate with heroism are often embedded within narratives of conflict and triumph, one might reasonably expect the term to have no relevance to this work. This quotation from Philip Glass demonstrates his determination to steer clear of the quasi-programmatic agendas of concertos, where the "journey" of the music's melody is easily mapped onto the life story of an imagined (heroic) subject.

> [W]hat sets the music apart is the fact that it's non-narrative, we don't hear it within the usual time frame of most musical experiences. As I look at most other music, I see that it takes ordinary time, day-to-day time – what I call colloquial time – as a model for its own musical time. So you have story symphonies or story concertos – even the modernist tradition continues that to a certain extent. There's still almost a compulsion to deal with themes and treatment of themes. The themes become the focus of the listener's attention, and what happens to the theme happens to the listener via a certain psychological trick of identification. This happens in the great concertos of the nineteenth century, with the tortuous journey of the violin and so forth, with happy endings and sad endings.[3]

3 Glass interviewed in Cole Gagne and Tracy Caras, *Interviews with American Composers*, Metuchen, N.J., Scarecrow Press, 1982, 214.

And yet, those of us who have studied Glass's postminimalist oeuvre are aware that it is not quite as denuded of these traditional narrative means as some of its more committed commentators have maintained. We can see this most clearly when it comes to the choice of characters in music theater works. Glass rejected several of Robert Wilson's contenders for "portrait opera" protagonists because they didn't meet his ethical criteria – Hitler, for example, was too "loaded." Protagonists in all three portrait operas turned out to be "powerful personalities," in fact *men* who changed the world for the better. Rooted in post-Brechtian theater and the experimental Artaudian tradition, Glass's operas portrayed real historical figures rather than fictitious archetypes. This does not necessarily mean that the characters in question are not every bit as mythical as Orfeo or Tristan; Einstein and Gandhi have both taken on mythical proportions in modern life (channeled by media culture). Indeed, Glass openly admits that "the almost saint-like" inventor of the theory of relativity was "one of [his] heroes" when he was growing up.[4] It's quite apparent when witnessing performances of *Einstein*, however, that this is no *ordinary* biographical representation. It is abstract and image-centered, composed from loosely connected materials, resembling the deconstructive iconography found in Andy Warhol's screen-prints or the absurdist works of the surrealists more than the dominant heroic archetypes of Western culture.

Glass's music arguably works in a similar way. The opera is made up of streaming and mutating eighth- and sixteenth-note figures performed on heavily amplified organs and woodwinds, accompanied by singers who mindlessly (or mindfully?) recite numbers and solfeggio symbols – all of the above are interrupted by coolly recited texts. Underlying these elements are harmonic formulas that toy with listeners' expectations; shifting eerily between competing tonal centers that don't resolve as you would expect. This is a far cry from the traditional means of Romantic heroism, although one might equally point to traits the music shares with Romantic music: melodies performed in unison (but also counterpoint); epic scale and an emphasis on spectacle; strong rhythms briskly articulated; "massive, simple sonorities that eschewed intricate polyphony or complex structures"; constant pulsing rhythm, and so on, all of which Michael Boyles lists among the conventional musical means of the heroic in Beethoven's influential middle period.[5] Eero Tarasti similarly lists the following characteristics of the heroic-mythical style: grandiose scale, long crescendos (albeit in steps and plateaus in postminimalism), rhythmical sharpness and vigor, the use of bright sonorities, unison in instruments, and so on.[6] Some of these traits are admittedly not relevant to the present discussion, but some do seem to resonate in unexpected ways with postminimalist aesthetics. It might seem perverse to view

4   Philip Glass, *Music by Philip Glass*, Cambridge, Harper & Row, 1987, 11.
5   Michael Boyles, Beethoven: *The Emergence and Evolution of Beethoven's Heroic Style*, New York, Excelsior, 1987, 123–125.
6   Eero Tarasti, *Myth and Music: A Semiotic Approach to the Aesthetics of Myth in Music, Especially that of Wagner, Sibelius And Stravinsky*, Helsinki, Suomen Musiikkitieteellinen Seura, 1978, 91–97.

Glass's *Einstein* in reference to principally Romantic theories of the heroic, but is the scientist's depiction in this opera really the antithesis of traditional heroism, in the same sense as John Adams's Nixon (*Nixon in China*) might be understood as being? Are more complex negotiations perhaps going on here, in which heroism is not discarded altogether; it is simply rendered opaque; it is *rendered*.

Several writers have followed the French philosopher Jean-François Lyotard in classifying Glass's style during this period as representing a non-representational sublime or "countersublime" – another Romantic concept going back to Kant and Burke that is closely related to heroic sensibility.[7] Anyone who has attended a performance of *Einstein* will perhaps recognize that there is *something* heroic about this opera, even if it is mediated through a powerfully constructivist sensibility (happening in quotation marks or by negation); and even if heroism is ultimately located in the audience, who, if they stay the full course of the opera, will end up sitting for almost five hours. Glass himself has displaced the heroic on to the performers, who are required to undergo rigorous training in order to memorize all of the vocal lines coupled with Wilson's elaborately synchronized mimic gestures. This is a common narrative that emerges in the accounts of performers: the element of endurance bonding performers with peers, signaling a transcendence of their ordinary circumstances. Perhaps the specter of the composer as hero, too, has some relevance, although this is undoubtedly something different to the Bohemian heroic artist of Beethoven's time. We can recognize this perhaps in the almost mythic figure of the downtown avant-gardist composer, challenging the modernist establishment and famously driving a cab in order to pay his debts while *Einstein* was being performed at the Met.

Postmodern neosurrealism

When *Einstein* was first performed in the mid-1970s, it was celebrated among critics, some academics, and performers as crystalizing emerging postmodernist aesthetic. Even Glass has described the work using this term. This notion gained attraction through the advocacy of leading thinkers on poststructuralism and postmodernism, such as Julia Kristeva, following the first European tour, and later, Fredric Jameson.[8] When Glass writes of postmodernism, he refers in particular to the work's open-endedness; a work after the decline of the work concept – the post-Cagean idea that our experiences are not fully determined by compositional intentionality. The reflexive relationship of *Einstein* to Romantic spectacle, to the Wagnerian "total art work," to consumer culture, and the contemporary technoscape are all features that resonate with ideas about postmodernism. *Einstein's*

---

7   For more on the sublime in Glass's music and minimalism, see John Richardson, "Resisting the Sublime: loose synchronization in La Belle et la Bête and The Dark Side of Oz," in Steven Baur, Raymond Knapp, and Jacqueline Warwick (eds.), *Musicological Identities: Essays in Honour of Susan McClary*, Aldershot, Ashgate, 2008, 135–48.

8   Fredric Jameson, "Postmodernism and Consumer Society," in *Postmodern Culture*, ed. Hal Foster, London, Pluto Press, 1985, 111.

post-Brechtian constructivism is a further feature that Linda Hutcheon strongly emphasizes in her writing on postmodernism.[9]

Among the most productive ideas is Fredric Jameson's description of postmodernism as "surrealism without the unconscious",[10] although that formulation could be modified so as not to rule out the unconscious altogether (or perhaps the idea of collective memory, which is entangled with the unconscious). We might also bring in the prefix "neo" to form "neosurrealim," which serves a similar function to the prefix in Peter Bürger's idea of the neo-avant garde.[11] Neo not only denotes a reflexive awareness of the shortcomings of previous avant-garde projects, but it also signifies a difference that allows us to view the opera in the light of the dawning information age and the rise of global capitalism. A problem with postmodernism is arguably that the concept blinds us to alternative genealogies and periodization, while overemphasizing the uniqueness and temporal isolation of phenomena and artistic movements. When we talk about postmodernism, the writers of this chapter contend, ~~that~~ we're often talking about traits that might be subsumed under neosurrealist aesthetics.

There is plenty that is surrealist about *Einstein*: most notably the opera's reliance on non-connective, dream-like logic where metaphorical associations replace narrative exposition. As Glass has put it, the entire opera could have been a dream that Einstein had. Indeed, one of the opera's key scenes focuses on a bed, which some commentators have understood as commenting obliquely on the role that imagination played in Einstein's life-work (others have highlighted gender issues).[12] The scientist was known to be a lateral thinker: he used metaphors and visual imagery to circumvent established ways of thinking about scientific problems. He is said to have been dyslexic and, more surprisingly, number blind. These aspects come out in Glass and Wilson's treatment. Academic readers will be familiar with formulations of postmodernism as a kind of collective "schizophrenia."[13] Yet the association of psychological conditions with artistic sensibility and revolution goes back further than this. André Breton, the founder of the surrealist movement and writer of several manifestos, was infatuated with his psychologically unstable lover Nadya, whose random observations seemed, in his eyes, somehow symptomatic of Parisian cultural life in the interwar years. Other leading surrealist thinkers suffered themselves from psychological illness, including Bataille and Artaud. In fact, Freud characterized the whole surrealist movement, which he partly inspired, as pathological because it denied the reality

---

9   Linda Hutcheon, *The Politics of Postmodernism*, 2nd edition, London and New York, Routledge, 1989.

10 Fredric Jameson, *Postmodernism or The Cultural Logic of Late Capitalism*, Durham, NC, Duke University Press, 1991, 67. See also John Richardson, *An Eye for Music: Popular Music and the Audiovisual Surreal*, New York, Oxford University Press, 2011, 34.

11 Peter Bürger, "Avant-Garde and Neo-Avant-Garde: An Attempt to Answer Certain Critics of *Theory of the Avant-Garde*," *New Literary History*, 41, 4, Autumn 2010, 695-715.

12 On the role of dream logic in surrealism, see Richardson 2011, 39–40.

13 Fredric Jameson, "Postmodernism and Consumer Society," in *Postmodern Culture*, ed. Hal Foster, London, Pluto Press 1985, 118-20.

principle. In *Einstein* we have Christopher Knowles, whose disconnected stream of consciousness reflections form the verbal center of Wilson's conception of the opera – and Wilson himself worked as his therapist. Artaud's theater was similarly a theater of pre-linguist signs, enigmatic hieroglyphs, and pulsing noises whose inspiration came largely from non-Western (Balinese) theatrical forms. Its direct descendent was Richard Foreman's ontological hysterical theater and the idea of theater as embodied movement that came out in the dance moves of Balanchine and Cunningham – this inspired Wilson in particular. Other surrealist elements include the use of collage techniques in written texts and projected images, and something resembling automatic writing in the libretto. All of these aspects are found in the various manifestos and other writings on surrealism (although popular definitions typically hinge almost exclusively on the unconscious and sexuality).[14] Fundamentally, surrealism is about diverting attention away from conventional ways of thinking and being through acts of displacement and disjunction that reshuffle reality. On another level, it is about attending to the disjunctive nature of reality and elevating experience over narrative substance and meaning.

Experience and temporality

In comments from the time of *Einstein*'s making, Glass differentiates the "everyday" or "narrative" time of symphonies from the extended timeframe of his music and music theater. Narrative time is classified as "everyday time" presumably because it resembles or imitates classical realist modes of representation. This can be seen in Glass's sarcastic comments about the "tortuous journey" of the violin in the above passage. This is the mode of narrative exposition familiar to us from symphonies, novels, and popular entertainment, including film and television. But Glass's music (and equally, Wilson's staging and the choreography of *Einstein*) steps outside of classical narrative-based modes of framing experience as temporalized. Instead it directs attention towards the unfolding present. More than that, the constant pulse and temporalized buzz of Glass's music imply a continuous flow that is embodied in actions, even while it intimates patterns that extend beyond the present moment towards a potentially infinite past and future. This dreamscape which extends beyond the present moment is indexical of eternal time.

Merleau-Ponty's writes:

> Eternity is the time that belongs to dreaming, and the dream refers back to waking life, from which it borrows all its structures. Of what nature, then, is that waking time in which eternity takes root? It is the field of presence in the wide sense, with its double horizon or primary past and future, and the infinite openness of those fields of presence that have slid by, or are still possible.[15]

---

14 See Richardson 2011, 32–53.
15 Maurice Merleau-Ponty, *Phenomenology of Perception*, Translated by Colin Smith, London and New York, Routledge, 2005, 492.

What happens, then, when you mark out clock time and divide it additively into loops and cycles? One way of apprehending such experiences is to submit to the relentless flow of materials. In this mode of apprehending, the perceiver focuses constantly on the unfolding now: experience as pleasure. Another mode is more selective and involves dipping in and out of the temporal flow. Glass himself in his comments in the interview transcribed in the volume, chooses to emphasize attention, suggesting a mode of focused listening in which the overlapping temporalities that surround us are suspended in favor of musical and dramatic actions. This would lend support to the idea of *Einstein* as "formalist" and "literalist" in its principal modus operandi. Another possibility is to conceive of the experience of time as overlapping layers, temporal frames of reference that alternate or take shape in different ways depending on the orientation of the viewer-listener. On the one hand, this is a musical and presentational style that encourages attentiveness; on the other, this attentiveness is formed within layers of experience, memory, and anticipation. What seems clear is that experiences of *Einstein* are not without affective resonance. Memories and prior experiences play a part.

If there's a dominant mood or tone in *Einstein*, it might be called "neutral" or "mechanical" – perhaps implying something hidden behind the carefully controlled exteriors that remains unexpressed or which *cannot* be expressed. Meaning or meaninglessness in this understanding derives from the depersonalized character of the music, physical movements, and vocalized texts. This depersonalization results from the stalwart imperviousness of the music's temporal and design, and from corresponding dance gestures. Relentless and unyielding, these carry the listener on a wave of pure energy that finds allegorical support both in the plot of the opera and in society at large. The notion of the *posthuman* is perhaps best epitomized in the numerous carbon copy Einsteins who inhabit the stage in performances. *Einstein* is in a very real sense *unknowable*; in the absence of actual information, audiences at some point are compelled to confront their own lack of knowledge concerning the opera's protagonist, or to bring to the work speculative or real knowledge concerning the historical person that was Einstein, or of the intentions of the opera's creative team.

Incomplete memories and collage aesthetics

Because of the opera's juxtapositioning of incomplete fragments, memories, and images that are affective more than informative, *Einstein* again approaches surrealist aesthetics. The opera is haunted with images that never quite connect to the originating spirit or historical contexts that first generated them. These images combine to form loose assemblages that do, however, tell us something about the life and experiences of the creative parties involved in the production (see Robert Fink's discussion of radio playlists and how these influenced Christopher Knowles's texts), and might resonate with the fragmentary experiences of audience members too. The cultural theorist Walter Benjamin was intrigued by how the French surrealists would frequent the flea markets of their native Paris in search of disjunct objects – objects that had been cast adrift from the consumer culture that had created them decades earlier. Such objects were invested with a new uncanny afterlife by the very act of repositioning them in contemporary culture, resulting in a sense of enchantment, but also loss as the objects' original functions and meanings. *Einstein* is on one level a work of collage – an assemblage of objects and images that loosely reference prior experiences. Their detachment from the culture that once nourished them gives them a resonance that resembles how we connect with objects recognized from more distant history. The historian Jan Assmann calls such objects "figures of memory";[16] memories that trigger associations but nevertheless carry with them a ritualized sense of detachment and transcendence, simultaneously elevating the performative present of actions while poignantly drawing attention to the distance between actions and historical origins. This "mnemonic energy," as Assmann calls it, activates and enlivens the imagery of *Einstein*, even while we are left to speculate why and how exactly the imagery affects us.

When Glass and Wilson speak of the participatory role of audiences, this comes close to Assmann's notion of "cultural memory." The emphasis on participation admittedly comes across more strongly in Wilson's comments than in it does Glass's. It is present above all in the quasi-ritualized use of images of Einstein himself, in the image of the Patty Hearst character, in textual allusions to popular songs. But it is present in the music, too, in Glass's "archaeological" approach to musical materials when working on the portrait opera trilogy. Glass's music of this period started to re-sound with the echoes of earlier styles – Baroque ground bass and chaconne figures would emerge in *Einstein*, although they are more transparently present in his second and third portrait operas, *Satyagraha* and *Akhnaten*; Mozartian Alberti bass, harmonic procedures that resemble root movement harmony but work differently. All of these elements are clearly present in the music and dance of *Einstein*, counted out in gestures that leave little doubt about the constructivist tenets of this new aesthetic form. Assmann evaluates the underlying motivations for deployments of cultural memory as follows: "One group remembers the past in fear of deviating from its model, the next for fear of repeating the past ... 'Those who cannot remember their past are condemned to relieve it,'" Assmann writes, quoting George Santayana.[17] In this act of remembering there is surely an element of reflection that allows the person remembering to deviate from the model of past actions, and perhaps to recognize these actions for what they are; a move that resembles what Benjamin has called a leap into the "open air of history." *Einstein* occupies a reflective halfway point between remembrance and amnesia. We remember or half remember opera history, music history, the actions of the opera's protagonists, but at the same time we are jolted into the unfolding present where actions can be reconceived.

16   Jan Assmann, "Collective Memory and Cultural Identity," *New German Critique*, 65, Spring–Summer 1995, 125–133.

17   Assman, 133.

The structure of this book pays homage to the structure of its theoretical object – *Einstein on the Beach*. As in *Einstein*, there are knee plays that serve as "portraits": five of them, where attention is directed towards speaking dancers. Knee Chapter I is a kind of prologue, ongoing already before the audience enters the hall. Further knee chapters separate acts, and the final one functions as a kind of epilogue. The book refers to the portrait function of *Einstein*'s knee plays, and knee chapters accommodate non-academic texts: interviews, portraits, and reviews, which frame the remainder of the book's structure.

The first knee chapter includes material taken from a recent interview with composer Philip Glass, where he reflects on his intentions when writing the opera, his views on how it turned out (what it "means" and how it is experienced), and how it has changed in its various incarnations in different productions. The second knee chapter is a conversation between Robert Wilson and theater director Bojan Djordjev. Lucinda Childs' talk with Jelena Novak is Knee Chapter 3. Knee Chapter 4 provides five instances of fellow creative artists who reflect on the influence of Philip Glass and *Einstein on the Beach* on their own creative work in a series of short essays and interviews. The influential singer-songwriter Suzanne Vega discusses in a beautiful yet characteristically succinct (in some ways minimalist) essay how she was not only influenced by Glass, including *Einstein on the Beach*, but went on to collaborate with him in several projects and now considers him a valued friend. The two contemporary Finnish composers Petri Kuljuntausta and Juhani Nuorvala show how this influence was not only close to home, in New York City, but how it also fundamentally changed how musicians thought about their craft, even in geographically and culturally remote locations where *Einstein* was not performed; one of the pioneers of minimalism in music and written word about it, composer Tom Johnson, remembers the unique atmosphere in which *Einstein* was created and rehearsed; the director, artist, and creative visionary Peter Greenaway, for his part, uses his early encounters with Philip Glass, *Einstein on the Beach*, and minimalist and postminimalist music as a springboard for reflections on the aesthetic premises of his own work, which because of its emphasis on structure, manneristic style and immanence, non-narrative exposition and historical reference (Baroque, Rococo, Renaissance), has a great deal in common with Glass's approach in *Einstein*. It seems that the trajectory of many lives and careers were irrevocably altered as a result of contact with this opera and compositional style. In Knee Chapter 5, the architect and art critic Pieter T'Jonck undertakes a close reading of Lucinda Childs's choreography for *Dance*, a piece that was Glass and Childs's first collaboration after *Einstein*. T'Jonck throws light on how the opera influenced *Dance*, but also how later productions of *Einstein* choreographed by Childs were influenced by *Dance* in certain respects. Knee Chapter 5 closes with an overview of reviews of *Einstein*. Amsterdam-based music critic Frits van der Waa offers a historical portrait of critical responses that were and still are changing.

The longer chapters of this volume form different "acts," beginning with one called "Einstein on the Shores of Culture." This section of the book shows how *Einstein* can be understood as being "stranded" on the shores of different cultures, whether that culture is North American, West European, or East European. Robert Fink, in turn, investigates the world of Christopher Knowles and the pop references he used in *Einstein*'s spoken texts. In his chapter, "Einstein on the Radio," Fink arrives at a surprising discovery: that Knowles's interest in listening to the radio mirrors itself significantly in the texts he typed for *Einstein on the Beach*, which were then incorporated in the opera's tissue as spoken monologues. Fink's musicological discussion shows that Knowles had literally memorized some of the spoken texts in *Einstein* from radio broadcasts. Fink discusses new layers of meaning that this discovery brings to *Einstein*. Johannes Birringer, in his chapter "Sous les pavés, la plage," reads *Einstein* from the context of French Situationist theory, his own revolutionary youth, and Western European theater. The slogan of the Situationists "Sous les pavés, la plage" resonates with the beach in *Einstein*, providing a fascinating sense of friction. Following those two North American and West European perspectives, an East European perspective is offered in the writing of aesthetician and art theorist Misko Šuvaković, who is the only contributor of this volume to have attended a performance of *Einstein* in 1976. This took place in Belgrade (Yugoslavia) during the first tour. Šuvaković embraces his position as witness when considering the geopolitics of the East in a unique reading of *Einstein* which bears witness to the relevance of cultural context in interpretations of this work.

The book's second act, "From Repetition to Representation," opens with Kyle Gann's detailed analysis of *Einstein*'s score, where he argues that the rigid repetitivity of Glass's early minimalistic style transformed into something more intuitive and even romantic, an argument that elaborates on a claim Tom Johnson made some years ago.[18] Musicologist Pwyll ap Siôn investigates how *Einstein*'s universe could be understood in the light of theory on musical affect, which he undertakes by analyzing the experimental theater scene represented by groups such as the Mabou Mines company, with a particular focus on the knee plays and their role. This act of the book closes with Avra Sidiropoulou's chapter, "Creating Beauty in Chaos: Robert Wilson's Visual Authorship in *Einstein on the Beach*." Her discussion concentrates on the authorial role of director Robert Wilson, especially his idea of "beauty" and the impact this has had on the work and its aesthetic.

In the third act, "Beyond Drama: Surfaces and Agencies of Performance," Zeynep Bulut's chapter, "Anonymous Voice, Sound and Indifference" delves into the intriguing realm of *Einstein*'s vocal sphere and captures through various perspectives from the field of voice studies what the opera's voices tell us beyond the words and bodies involved in its staging. In "Heavenly Bodies: The Integral Role of Dance in *Einstein on the Beach*," Leah Weinberg provides an exciting account of two of the opera's choreographies: one by Andy de Groat, the other by Lucinda

---

18 Tom Johnson, "Maximalism on the Beach: Philip Glass", February 25–March 3, 1981, See: http://tvonm.editions75.com/articles/1981/maximalism-on-the-beach-philip-glass.html, Accessed: August 22, 2017.

Childs. Elucidating the roles of De Groat and particularly Childs in different productions, Weinberg describes how the whole opera has changed through time and how the role of dance and choreography has evolved in this piece.

The book's final act is "Operatic Machines and Their Ghosts." This part of the book offers an analytical listening of *Einstein*, as well as a critical glance at a possible "afterlife" of the opera beyond and after Wilson's staging. In the chapter "Leaving and Re-entering: Punctuating *Einstein on the Beach*," Sander van Maas writes about how strategies of listening are changing in relation to different performances of *Einstein*, but also how the opera itself is affected by those strategies. Van Maas analyzes the inaudible in *Einstein*: the series of intentions and decisions that made the opera sound and be heard in a unique way. He pays attention also to how these strategies are audible in *Einstein*'s video recording. Closing the volume with the chapter "Einsteinium: From the Beach to the Church, via Theater and State Bank," Jelena Novak reviews the different realms of productions mounted by directors other than Wilson: Achim Freyer (1988), Berthold Schneider and Veronika Witte (2001, 2005), Leigh Warren (2014), and Kay Voges (2017). She discusses *Einstein*'s inevitable transformations, keeping in mind other directors' perspectives. Novak analyzes *Einstein*'s climactic scene, *The Space Ship*, attempting to capture how different authors read it and how their visions of the end of the universe as we know it might illuminate *Einstein on the Beach*'s future.

It is as if two parallel opera worlds exist today. The conventional one with opera houses, subsidies, traditional operatic voices, a star system of singers, and another, in a sense alternative world, with performances that often take place outside of opera houses – on streets and highways (*Hopscotch* conceived and directed by Yuval Sharon in 2015 in Los Angeles), in botanical gardens (*Operrrra is a Female*, conceived and directed by Bojan Djordjev in Belgrade in 2005), in dismantled factories (*De Materie* [1985–88] by Louis Andriessen, directed by Heiner Goebbels in Duisburg in 2014), galleries (*The Opera of Prehistoric Creatures* by Marguerite Humeau, 2012), and other unofficial spaces. Those two worlds of course sometimes intersect. More and more frequently, it is possible to encounter unconventional stagings in opera houses, or, on the other hand, sometimes traditional operas are staged or imagined in new innovative ways (like La Monnaie/ De Munt 2014 production of *Orfeo e Euridice* by Christoph Willibald Gluck, directed by Romeo Castellucci). While this first, mainstream world maintains and cherishes opera history, the second is preoccupied with opera's present and future. *Einstein on the Beach* stands proudly as a denominator for the beginning of opera's future, a foundation stone for a different type of musical theater.

Knee chapter 1
Paying attention to *Einstein*

Philip Glass interviewed by John Richardson[1]

Thinking back to last night's performance, I don't think there's any other work that so successfully captures what it felt like to live on the cusp of the digital age, an accelerated world in which ideas about time and space are constantly revised. But Einstein *is a piece whose essential elements are more fixed than some of your other operas, where producers can influence how the work is expressed visually. This seems fitting; we want to see it as it was originally conceived. But I was wondering, what it means for an avant-garde piece to be revisited in this way.*

Those are all interesting questions. I think we have to be careful when thinking of it as a revival, because it was a piece that was written 37 years ago. Now, it's surprisingly fresh today. Surprisingly because it's older than some of you in this room. I think Robert Wilson and I pondered this question: Why? How did that happen? It's not that it makes reference to the music being made today. Composers, myself included, are working in different ways. What is interesting is that it still feels relevant in some way. The performers we're working with today are far better than the ones we had in the past. When we began doing this we didn't have a *corps de ballet*, we didn't have a separate group of singers. We had young men and women who could sing a bit and dance a bit. And the performances were amateurish in a certain way. The piece was revised several times. By 1984 we had separated [the performers] into two [groups]: the chorus and those who were dancing. By the time we did it this time, we had a dancing group who could really dance. They have wonderful technique – they all come from ballet. They have that training, and the same with the singers. In terms of the performance, I can't say that these are the performances we imagined. The thing to remember is that in 1976 there was no known performance practice that went with this form. And as everyone here will know, the performance practice comes with new ideas. If you can play a piece in the same old way that you play everything else it's incomplete.

---

1 The interview took place on January 6, 2013 at the University Library of Amsterdam as part of the conference *Einstein on the Beach: Opera after Drama*. This is an edited and slightly abridged version of the original interview.

Part of [inventing] a new language is finding a way to play it. What has happened is that, in the intervening years the ensemble is pretty much the same, but we've actually learned to play the music now. We can actually play it! The first time we did it, at Avignon festival July 1976, the first performance was the first time we played through the piece without stopping. We didn't even know how long it was. [*Audience laughs*] We were struggling with Bob [Wilson] and Lucinda [Childs] – there was another [choreographer] at that time, so it was done jointly. Lucinda began by actually doing a pair of individual dances and ended up doing the long dances later on. But we had worked on them for months and months. I'd even say that we didn't have a really clear idea what the piece was. Over the last 35 years or so, we've come to understand how the music has to be played, and the dancers know how to dance it now, the singers can sing it now. People don't get angry with us anymore when we start to work. So what you heard last night is what we would have done, and could have done, if we knew that that was what we intended ... In January of [last] year [2012], I went to the first [performance] of the new production in Ann Arbor, Michigan. I had played in all the performances until then. So that was the first time I sat down and watched the whole thing. That only happened in January. We looked up all the recordings first. That's just to give a little background to it.

Now I want to get back to that essential question, which is, the reason I think the piece is relevant now is not that it has anything to do with what's going on today. It's a strange thing that happens to certain pieces of music when we look at them they seem like they were inevitable – like they had to have happened *then*. Einstein was one of these pieces. That doesn't speak to the quality of it as [something] transcendental. It just says that, as most of the people in this room will know, that there are social and psychological, and all kinds of factors that bring artforms to a kind of a crisis, which we were definitely at in the 1960s. That was one factor.

But there was another thing: the way that opera was done at that time. In the world of theater, and I had worked a lot in the theater. I had been working in the theater since I was 20, so by the time I began working on *Einstein*, I'd been working in the theater for about 15 years, but I was working in experimental theater. The theater that we were the godchildren of, Peter Brook and The Living Theater. We were the generation that came after that. [In] experimental theater, a work's authorship can be shared between numerous people. One company that I belonged to for a long time, The Mabou Mines, did new work and that was like a religion for us at the time. We did new works of Genet, who was also alive at the time. That kind of work was unknown to people in the opera world. They didn't even know that it existed.

Bob came out of that world too. Bob didn't come out of the world of opera. He came from a completely different place. He was an architect; he also worked as a therapist with deaf people, retarded people. He had a whole other [background]. What was surprising to the opera people was that there was a whole form of theater that had gone on for decades, and this was unknown to people in the opera world. What was shocking was that we were in opera houses, so everyone's thinking it's going to be an opera. But we didn't care whether it was an opera or not. He said, and we had different answers, the word opera meant "work" in the Italian sense, in that it's just a work. My view was somewhat different. It looked to me like you needed a flat space, wing space, you needed an orchestra pit, you needed people that could sing, people that could dance, people that could play. You could call it anything you wanted to, but the only place you could ever perform it was in an opera house. It's the only place it would fit. Since then, when I look at the music theater pieces I've done, I define them now as operas because that's where they're done. So pieces that are done in opera houses are called operas. The first tour we did was all in opera houses. The only places we did it were opera houses, even when it was part of international theater festivals. But when it came to *Einstein* we had to find places it would fit into, so that's how it worked.

This idea of the inevitable – of course, it's absurd. There's no such thing. However, part of the job of the people in this room is to make things appear like they're inevitable. That's part of what we do. Composers not that much older than us, like the whole group at IRCAM. They were shocked and totally dismayed that we were taken seriously at all. Because we were not part of that plan. But that was part of the crisis that happened. And when I say that it was inevitable, well look at it this way, John. I first began working in this way in 1969, and there are pieces from that time that we still play. Seven years later we're at the Metropolitan Opera House. In order for that to happen so quickly, it must have been waiting to happen. If I hadn't done it, someone else would have done it differently. And people did do it differently, like here in Holland, Louis Andriessen, all kinds of people were doing things. For reasons that I don't completely [understand], my work ended up being more prominent. But when you think that my first concert in New York was at the Queens College auditorium and there were six people in the audience and one was my mother – I didn't know whether to count her as an audience member or not. She had to come all the way from Baltimore to see that piece and get back on the train straight home. Seven years later, she goes to the Metropolitan Opera House to see the opera there. For that to happen so quickly, it must have been matters that were so urgent that they couldn't be put aside at all.

This is actually a joint work and [that] became a very important part [of it]. As you can see the dancers are …, it was our intention that there were two big poles holding the tent up. That's the dancers, holding up the piece. But it wasn't always like that. When we first did it, the dancers were considered less important in parts of the work. It became important when we entered into the collaborative work with Lucinda Childs. So the piece is really a joint work by three people at this point. Bob and I started work on it and we haven't changed that [part of it]. Now a very well-known German director, Achim Freyer, did do an *Einstein*, and there have been a few done. Bob and I agreed to that because we wanted to see it happen. I was less disturbed by it than Bob. Bob didn't like it very much. If you were to ask Bob Wilson what he thought of that version, he probably wouldn't say very much. But we have a problem with this piece. Until this year it wasn't even filmed [as a whole]. The present version, Pomegranate, Linda Brumbach and Alisa Regas were a part of it; they made sure it was going to be filmed. And I don't know what's going to happen to that film. To me it doesn't really matter what happens to it because I'm not going to be here anyway. I think that actually there could be other productions, and they may make reference to the structure that we articulated in this piece or maybe not. My feeling is that we've done it as well as we can and now we've done the thing.

So, is it important to have a document of it now that you're all involved?

Now here's the thing. Operas are usually associated with composers. This is not really like that. You know who the composers are because it makes a great difference to the work. This has been a process that it's been difficult for film makers and theater people to really come to terms with. The impact of the music is so compelling that the authorship shifts over to the composer at some point. Though, in fact, this piece didn't begin like that at all. It didn't begin like many other operas, where I begin with an idea, I pick a director and it works like that. This really began with a very level playing field for Bob and I. However, at one point we had to decide what we would do about the rights. There are two ways to do this: we can say that both of us need to agree to have it done, or we can say that only one of us has to agree. We chose the latter. By doing that there were greater possibilities for what would happen. And we didn't even know who would be invited. For example, I can license it and someone else can do it, and Bob can do the same. It actually didn't happen that way. We saw an openness in terms of the future, and I'm not sure if we'd be able to participate in that future. What happens very often with writers is that when they die the estates take over and they usually ruin the chances for new productions. That happened with Becket and Jean Genet. It was very difficult to do those works, because nephews and nieces, people not connected with the work at all, began having control over the work which nobody else would be able to have. We're not going to let that happen.

What do you think about the idea of Einstein on the Beach as a kind of tipping point, about it changing the nature of opera or music theater?

Well, I think that's sometimes misunderstood. Nobody copied it. People did their own things.

It didn't then change the state of the art in music theater in the way that people thought it might have at the time?

What happened is that the theater became progressively more conservative. And what no-one anticipated, which turned out to be true. The overwhelming effects of television and movies, and video games for that matter, had become more important influences on people than any works we might have completed. That's a fact. There are no imitations of *Einstein* and maybe there didn't need to be. I think we might have been a little bit disappointed about that, but in the end, I said, well, I guess it's *suis generis* or a one-of-a-kind work. And yet, the history of music is *full* of works like that. They're not necessarily done by great composers or artists. Think of the works of César Franck. There are three important pieces. But no-one really cares about them all that much. The D minor symphony, the piano quartet, and the choral piano. There are about three pieces for him. And for many composers there'll be two or three pieces. The lives of Bach and Beethoven are a different matter. With them we know everything. But those are very rare. Then again, writing an important work, you don't necessarily have to be a great genius to do it. You really have to have enough talent and to be in the right place and the right time to figure out what needed to be done. And with some clarity, a lot of work and a bit of luck, which counts, it's possible to do an important work, but whether it will become part of history is another matter. I would say that it's even too soon to talk about that. The rule generally is, that in order for the work of a musician or a painter or a writer to be fairly evaluated in history, every person that he [sic] knew has to be dead. It's very simple – it's a very simple mathematical formula, and that hasn't happened for a lot of people we know. And as long as there's a publisher making a nickel off of somebody else's work, you're not going to know them. The works have to stand alone totally, and if they're still standing, then you can talk about it. And not many pieces will be like that.

You mentioned the influence of film, video games, and digital culture. Einstein seems quite prescient in that respect. The extended timescale but also how the dances and the live action are synchronized to the music, sometimes tightly, sometimes quite loosely. This mode of interaction is common today in cinema, gaming, and new media, but it wasn't in the 1970s. When you began working on non-literary theater, did it seem inevitable the music would drive the visuals, or did it just happen that way?

It's the mixture of the piece and the way it works. Anyone on the television circuit can also figure that out. If you change the music and leave the same pictures, the music doesn't change. It's a very simple experiment and anyone can do that. And, of course, this is very distressing to people in the film world, because usually the composers are assigned to a very low place in the process. And it turns out to be so important. I see this happening to so many contract victims, there's almost nothing that can be done about it.

For some reason music has a hold on us. We respond very directly to music and less directly to images. Images are surprisingly neutral in terms of their emotional content. We can change them very easily by changing the music, but it doesn't work the other way around. And that's why I think we're involved in music front-running. I have to apologize for saying this, but you can't really talk about this in Hollywood. People really get extremely distressed. And yet, if you spend your life working in collaborative forms, as I have done and many people have done, people are very concurrent of what's going on.

Could I ask you to expand on why you think it is that the musical language of minimalism had such an impact on cinema and visual forms in general?

There are several other angles to this that have to be mentioned. One is, and we should talk a little about John Cage now, and the precepts that he felt were so important, the main one being that the completion of the work happened with the audience – that it was incomplete until the audience took part by listening.

That was a very radical idea. Books like *Silence* and *A Year from Monday*, you all know those books. He always thought that people don't like the music but they like the books. He hated that, because he was very attached to the music too. But when you talk about postmodernism, if it's about anything then it's about that. It's about [the fact] that the artistic content doesn't exist independently from the perceived work and its listener. In fact, it's the relationship that is the crucial matter: the fact that the work is conveyed in that there's someone to listen to it, and that the audience is fundamental in the social process even if you're on your own. When you're alone, there's someone listening to it, even if it's yourself or just a few friends. What John [Cage] was interested in … and I've talked to him, we liked each other, but he didn't like my music very much. I used to play it for John and he'd say "too many notes, too many notes" [*audience laughs*]. So we would have differences, but one question where there was not: the completion of the work happens when it's performed and when it's listened to.

Now we can talk about what that consists of, what we want from that relationship. Now I've never done teaching at all. I was offered one teaching job and I was 72, and I turned it down, I didn't need it. When I talked to [a conservatory-based colleague] and I said in this conservatory you have a library, and in that library there are books with dots on paper. I said what do you think that is? He said that's music, and I said no, it's not music. It's books with dots in them and lines; the music is what we hear. The transaction that happens between the performer, and before that the composer, and sometimes the composer has to perform it. I did it with Ravi Shankar and it worked well; and I've done it with a number of jazz people too, for whom the performer and the composer became the same person. That's always inspiring, and that's one of the reasons why I became a performer very soon after I finished conservatory, because I understood that that was a crucial relationship. The transaction that happens is where the work is completed.

Now let's take a film, for example, and let's take an image from a film, and how we are perceiving it. You can speak about it in a metaphorical way. You can say there's a distance between you and the audience. The thing that carries you towards the image is actually the music. It becomes a vehicle by which we arrive at the picture. That movement through space or time, or however you want to describe it, becomes the moment at which we personalize the work, where it becomes ours, whether it's Glenn Gould playing the *Goldberg variations* or Nat Cole playing in a club. That transaction, as I call it, is a real thing, and it happens in time and it happens in space, in a metaphorical space, but it happens, nevertheless. Now when we learn to love a work it's because we travel that distance, bring ourselves into that object, and that distance no longer exists anymore. I'm just trying to give you a clinical picture of how I see that happening. And it happens all the time.

What you're describing sounds a lot like phenomenology, the idea that …

[Mr Glass interrupts the interviewer at this point, apparently frustrated that the discussion has taken a philosophical turn. The interviewer then backtracks to what was being discussed before.]

Continuing with this idea of the audience completing the work, to what extent is Einstein on the Beach *dependent on what we know about Einstein?*

It doesn't matter. It's a dog and you just don't know the name of a dog. It's still a dog.

It still means something.

Absolutely. Now there's another part of this too, which is a very important part, and it actually has to do with the language itself. It has to do with structure and how we perceive structure and language. You know the expression, new wine in old bottles? The old bottles are the structures. And we can be stuck with those, and put different names on them though we're actually doing the same thing. Now I've spent a lot of time with people who never went to music school, though they're musicians, and they have another background than I have. And I've learned a lot from that, and one of the things I've learned is that a lot of the things that I've learned about language are not particularly shared by a lot of people. Music can be made in different ways. The actual language of music and the building blocks of music can be different. I've studied with Indian guys and played the drums. I wasn't trying to be a *tabla* player, I just wanted to figure out how they put the pieces together. And I discovered that on the *tabla*, the music was always divided up into groups of twos and threes. I was kind of improvising and it occurred to me that the tals that you play are always combinations of twos and threes, whether it's 16 or 15 or 21 or 6 or 7 it always comes down to twos or threes. I said it's kind of like a binary system; is that right? He didn't really know what I meant, so I said plus, minus; zeros, ones, that's what it is. He said, yeah, that's right. He said basically, we're talking about a rhythmic system which is a binary system, which is actually the way computer language is written. And he said, that's right.

And then it occurred to me that the way we use binary language to carry information, to make information, so to speak, is very similar to music – there's a whole system of music that's based on the same system. I learned to work in that system in 1963. And it became the basis of everything I did for a long, long time, and it continues to this day. I'd say that if you want to take a look at *Einstein*, think of it as a binary music system. I don't know if anyone's ever done that, but I did it. When I wrote it I was thinking that. And then it occurred to me, because I always wondered why do people like this music. All these young people listen to this music, and I never listen to it or expected that. What usually happens is that your audience grows old with you: when you're 50, your audience is 50; when you're 30, your audience is 30; when you're 70, if anyone's left around, they'll be 70 – they'll be older. It didn't happen with this piece. A lot of young people got involved in music, and it occurred to me that, whether we know it or not, the music has a very similar binary way of thinking.

When I start to look at the language the younger people I know are using. I used to have two or three people helping me in the studio, and they're much better with computers than I am, so I write by hand and have these younger people putting it on the computer for us, and when I correct it, they correct it to the computer. So for a long time I've had people working in the studio, so I kind of know what they do, or I'm thinking about what they're thinking, and a lot of their way of thinking is similar to the way that I began thinking, because of my encounters [with Indian music], but not only that, it comes up in African music, Australian music, music of the Far East. It comes up everywhere. Let's talk about the Western Art Music system that we are the children of. Rightfully so, that's what we learned; if you learn harmony by studying Bach, that's what you know. And songs are made up of that, popular music is made up of that, but it's not the only way we can start. Those people that have opened themselves up to these other ways of doing things, they're doing a lot more music and art, whether it's Meredith Monk, or Steve Reich, or other people. I just mentioned a couple of Americans that I know. Getting back to the music of today, a lot of it is based on the way we convey information, the binary languages that we use. And it doesn't have that much to do with functional harmony, or the kind of stuff we learnt from our composition teachers when we were younger. It doesn't have very much to do with that at all. Where *Einstein* fits in, it may be a strange cousin to things that are happening today, in ways that we didn't anticipate.

In the past you've spoken about your music as a different way of experiencing time to conventional narrative thinking.

Well, the difficulty with this topic is that people need to get talking about books, and it's really not about that at all. The fact of the matter is that to play this music you have to be completely alert and attentive to what you're doing. I'm not sure what you mean by the experience of time. I like to talk about it in a different way. Let's talk about paying attention. Paying attention comes up in a lot of practices that people do, whether they're doing yoga or they're doing meditation, it's basically paying attention. When you're writing, or whatever you're doing, your ability to pay attention is a measure of how well you're going to do. One of the simplest things we do is to pay attention. When we think about time, these questions are far too serious for me.

Can we get on to another serious question then? [audience laughs]

Please

Your use of harmony. The harmony in Einstein *is quite distinctive, you've spoken about pivot chords and how the voice leading works in a different way to what listeners might expect, and obviously you've had some very distinguished teachers and maybe that's influenced what you've done in different ways.*

Sure

So, I was wondering to what extent you reflect on that when you're composing, or whether it's less conscious; whether you think of the music spatially, according to where your fingers are on the keyboard; or whether it's in part a motoric process?

That's interesting, I was recently thinking about [a painter, unclear]. He died not too long ago. And what he used to do in paintings, he used to put something in the painting that didn't belong there. And he would try to see if he could make it work. One of his important practices was the inclusion of the unexpected, something that didn't belong. And he was extremely successful with that, if you know his work. I've thought about that in music sometimes. Now the difficulty with that is that it can be very hard to hear that stuff. And sometimes we don't know what we're hearing. One of the biggest problems about writing music is hearing it. Yet the most fundamental activity of the musician is to listen, and it's the hardest thing to do.

I was working on an opera recently and I had four pairs of eyes looking at this score and something wasn't right, we were proofreading this piece, and we still couldn't get it right. It's the damnedest thing to get all the notes right. Yet it's the simplest thing. I used to work for a sculptor [presumably Richard Serra]. For two or three years, I worked for him because I didn't have any money. And I said "Richie, I can't draw, I wish I could draw. I love painting but I can't draw." And he said, "I can teach you to draw." I said, "what do you mean. How could you do that?" He said I'll teach you to see, and if you can see then you can draw. And I saw immediately that painting was about seeing, that dancing is about moving, that poetry is about speaking, that music is about hearing. It's the most fundamental thing that we have to do, and to get it right is the hardest thing that we have to do. I explained this to somebody once. He said, "how do you hear music?" I said, "with great difficulty."

I studied with a great teacher, Nadia Boulanger. One thing she did, and I progressed to a pretty good state where I could do this, was to visualize sounds, and this took several hours of work a day and it went on for years. I wasn't particularly gifted at that kind of thing but I got good at it after a while. I'd write things down, and they'd say, no, no it wasn't that, so I tried to go back to what I was thinking when I wrote it down. Now one of the things I have learned to do is I keep all my sketches, and I number them. I number the pages, so I can find them. But sometimes I go back and that's wrong too. So with a tremendous effort I can conjure up in a certain way what I was listening to at the time. And I was explaining what that's like; it's like when you get up in the morning and it's very foggy and you can't see very much, but if you look long enough you start to see the outlines of a building. And if you keep looking you'll maybe see a barn, and if you keep looking you'll see a window, and if you keep looking you'll eventually see everything. And this is a lot like paying attention. Paying attention and listening are very much the same thing. I was in a rehearsal the other day in Madrid, and we were looking at a tuba part and he said it's a C, and I said it's a D. And he said, no, no, you're right it's a D; it's not a C it's a D. How the hell did that C get in the tuba part? It's right below the staffs, it's all by itself. It was a D the damn thing. Four pairs of eyes saw that and never saw that something was wrong with it. And he said, I think that's a wrong note and he was right – it was the wrong note. [Generally], the voice leading will tell you what the harmony should be.

In a work like Akhnaten, *of course, that's difficult to ascertain, because you're dealing with different tonal centers.*

Now that's an interesting question, where you purposely create an ambiguous situation, where the listener will speculate somewhat, and they don't know exactly what they're hearing. You can provide this through the story. It's a different kind of bitonality. It's not the kind that Milhaud would do. I knew Milhaud, I used to study with him. They would combine different triads together and it's not like that.

But there is the major/minor clash in that piece.

That's a different matter, because it's all in one line. But with a bit of practice you can write pieces that in one line suggest different tonalities. I've been doing a lot of violin music and cello music that's about that. But then again, the works of Bach and Mahler do that. And people will say, that's a Baroque technique, and, of course, it is. I was writing a piece of music this morning on the piano and I saw that it could happen in F flat or F natural and I didn't know where it was going, and I could do it twice, once each way. I decided that was a cheap way to do it. I had to be more definitive than that. I finally decided, I made the decision based on where it worked on the piano I was playing, because I write at the piano, and that's how I made the decision.

Well that answers the question I asked earlier, about how much the creative process depends on the instrument and how things work out when you're playing.

Ah, it's a lot about that. That's something about the composer who is close to playing. You know I read something recently, I don't know if it's true or not, that when Beethoven played when he was stone deaf, he would put an ear trumpet into the piano and bang the pedals. He misheard the sounds so much, he just wanted to hear it.

We've spoken already about the tradition that influenced Einstein. *Perhaps there's another line, which goes back to earlier avant-gardes, Dada/surrealism, and some of the people who influenced your generation of artists: Duchamp, Satie, Cage, Artaud, The Living Theater, and Richard Foreman, and so on.* Einstein on the Beach *incorporates some approaches we recognize from this tradition.*

I listened to them a lot. Of the older generation, John [Cage] was very close to dance, through Merce [Cunningham], and Bob Wilson was also very close to dance, Wilson through Jerome Robins. They weren't classical. We were at that time in our twenties and thirties. Bob and I met at a whole different place but we were living in New York at the time. That was the kind of stuff that we talked about. And those issues at that time seemed very urgent. Whether the dancers were improvising, whether they were working in structure, all of those things were hotly and earnestly debated. And we worked with each other on those things.

And you reconnected with that avant-garde tradition in your work on Cocteau, for example. Well, Cocteau was a different matter. I liked Cocteau because he was a classicist really. He was one of the best film theater writers that I had come across, for knowing how to bring a character into a piece; how to tell a story. He was a master of storytelling. Don't forget, that was coming from a tradition where you didn't tell stories. I always knew Cocteau's work, I knew it from the time I was 15. I eventually did three operas based on his work based on pieces that I'd heard when I was 15 or 15, and I wrote those pieces almost 35, 40 years later. But what I liked about him was his classicism; he wasn't a great experimenter apart from that. There wasn't a lot of money and he had a lot of tricks that were cute – they were good tricks.

I'm doing an opera now about Walt Disney; a funny character, right? Disney was obsessed with the same things that Cocteau was obsessed with. Cocteau was worried a lot about eternity, life and death, about the eternity of art, about the mortality of life. Disney was worried about exactly the same things. Disney would say things like, 50 years from now – this was in 1960 – people will scarcely believe someone called Walt Disney was actually alive, but they'll all know Donald Duck in the pieces. It was painful for him to think that his work could survive him. It would live and he wouldn't. It's a curious thing, the damndest thing! A little bit later he would say that the only thing that matters is the work and nothing else really matters. Cocteau was doing the same thing. At the end of *Orphée* – you all know that piece, I'm sure –, Heurtebise is talking to Death, and Death is going to turn backwards, and Heurtebise said "you can't do that, that's not allowed." And she says to him, in order for a poet to become immortal, a sacrifice needs to be made. That's a profound and interesting statement. The sacrifice she was referring to was her own death, reminding us of Shakespeare, the sonnet "And death once dead, there's no more dying then." And that's what Cocteau advised us; it comes straight from Shakespeare. And that idea comes up in an opera just finished a couple of weeks ago. So, the thing about Cocteau is not in terms of his iconoclasm, but his classicism.

Continuing on the same theme, but getting back to Einstein on the Beach, *I was surprised by some of the Dance sequences last night, how classical they seemed, both the music and the dance.*

Thanks for noticing that, but don't you find it also a bit on the Baroque side?

Yes, it's all of those things. And experimental and postmodern. But now to my final question: how do you think your work on Einstein *relates to what you're doing today?*

Well, I haven't really been able to take it in as a whole piece yet, only in rehearsals. But probably, for Wilson and I, the language of the work hasn't changed all that much but its position has shifted. Things that were in the foreground are now in the background; things that were intense become socialized. So there is a process of inclusion and extension.

Part 1

Einstein on the shores of culture

1   *Einstein* on the radio

Robert Fink

My name is Christopher Knowles. And I do typings. I type designs. I type songs.
And I type lists of songs of top hits. I type space needles. And I typed in colors of
designs and space needles. I type words, and I type songs with words. I type lists
and crosses and squares. And I do drawings. I draw with felt markers. I draw with
many colors. I draw houses and flowers. I draw cars and trees. And I draw clocks,
and I draw traffic lights. I draw designs, and I do is, and I tape records of songs. I
record records of songs. And I make tapes on a tape recorder. And I record people.
I record programs. And I make tapes of people's names. And I listen to radios, and
I listen to songs on a radio, but when a song comes on. That I hav a same song on
tape, and play a same song. tape recorder, and radio, same song. I do is tape people.
I have light-brights. I make pretty things with pegs, it has eight colors. So I make
tapes, and I do typings and drawings.

– Christopher Knowles, *Untitled (My Name*
Is Christopher Knowles), ca. 1980[1]

In the 1987 film *Sunshine Superman*, Harvard undergraduate Richard Rutkowski
documented the life, personality, and art practice of Christopher Knowles, a tal-
ented man in his late twenties whose organic neurological deficits placed him on
the high-functioning end of what would later be known as the autism spectrum.
The short film takes its title from the 1967 pop hit by Donovan, whose full name,
"Donovan Leitch," becomes the material of a minimalist spoken word performance at the end of the film, when Knowles recites it, letter by letter and then as
a phrase, over and over again, into a Panasonic portable tape recorder. Earlier, he
tells us that he has 500 favorite songs on individual tapes, each numbered, and that
tape no. 78, "Everything Is Beautiful (In Its Own Way)," by Ray Stevens, is special: "Back in 1970, that went to number one, so, that's my favorite."[2] It is clear
from the film, and other documentary evidence, that commercial AM radio, with

---

1   In the collection of the Museum of Modern Art, New York City. Accessible online at www.moma.
    org/collection/works/96407. Spelling and orthography as in original. Accessed: January 25, 2016.
2   Richard Rutkowski, *Sunshine Superman* (16mm film, 1987), https://vimeo.com/33455851,
    Accessed: January 25, 2016.

its continuous flow of hit songs, advertising, and fast-talking vocal personalities, was what autism researchers call a "circumscribed interest" for Knowles, a physical phenomenon he followed with single-minded intensity, and that gave rise to characteristically repetitive and systematic modes of behavior, some of which we see in the film.[3]

Interacting with AM radio has consistently been one of Knowles's dominant interests. As he himself noted in the self-descriptive "typing" reproduced as the epigraph to this chapter, in the 1970s he engaged with the radio in obsessive, yet creative and unusual ways: he repetitively typed out names of songs and lists of top hit songs; he taped songs, and sometimes entire programs off the radio, and from records; he made tape recordings of himself saying the names of people he heard and heard about on the radio; he memorized the entire broadcast schedule of his favorite stations; he carefully cataloged and organized his tapes; and when he heard a song on the radio which he already had taped, he liked to play his tape back to the radio, "tape recorder and radio, same song." It's not clear Knowles thinks of it this way, but it has not proved difficult to map his circumscribed interests onto the customary disciplines of the art world; his production of typings and drawings about media and consumer culture count either as poetry or as visual art, his tape recordings of songs and song facts as a kind of sound art.[4] When Knowles brings his interests to his collaboration with Robert Wilson, as he has done off and on since the age of 13, his writing, speaking, and actions, bearing the strong imprint of the commercial mass media, insert the history of Top 40 radio as a commercial medium into the history of postmodern performance art.

Thanks to Wilson's collaboration with composer Philip Glass, AM radio, Knowles's most passionately circumscribed interest, has also become part of the history of twentieth-century opera. Wilson was in the first wave of artists and caregivers to acknowledge basic neurodiversity as an ethical and aesthetic principle, and Knowles's contributions to the "libretto" for *Einstein on the Beach* were fully credited and acknowledged as the autonomous creative work of a neuro-diverse individual. (Stephanie Jensen-Moulton has begun to document the Wilson-Glass-Knowles collaboration within the context of music, disability, and postmodernism.)[5] But, as Telory Davies Arendell notes in her recent study of *The Autistic Stage*, Wilson perhaps too easily enlisted Knowles's geometrical, repetitive, and non-narrative way with language into his own project for a postmodern

3   Lauren Turner-Brown, et al., "Phenomenology and measurement of circumscribed interests in autism spectrum disorders," *Autism* 15-4 (2011), 437–456.
4   On the website of his agent, Gavin Brown, Knowles is positioned as an artist who has, mostly, exhibited physical work in galleries and museums; http://gavinbrown.biz/artists/christopher_kno wles/works, Accessed: January 26, 2016. Telory Davies Arendell, on the other hand, characterizes Knowles at the time he met Wilson as "a young autistic poet." *The Autistic Stage: How Cognitive Disability Changed 20th-Century Performance*, Rotterdam, Sense, 2015, 1.
5   Stephanie Jensen-Moulton, "Disability as Postmodernism: Christopher Knowles and *Einstein on the Beach*." Unpublished typescript, 2012.

theater of abstraction.[6] Although he championed Knowles as a linguistic non-conformist, and used his formally innovative typings as the basis for extended sections of *Einstein*'s libretto, in constructing the opera's scenario Wilson seems to have taken little interest in what Knowles was writing *about*, that is, the autistically circumscribed interest, involving detailed tracking of information about radio programming, advertising, pop singers, and hit songs, that actually motivated Wilson's young collaborator to set words down on paper.

What would an analysis of *Einstein on the Beach* look like that placed Christopher Knowles's passionate interest in AM radio at the center? Posing the question, I am not advocating for a distinctively "autistic" perspective on the opera, or claiming to speak for Knowles as a person on the autism spectrum. But, as a musicologist who has consistently attempted to read pulse-pattern minimalism through the lens of the post-war consumer society and its cultural forms (Fink 2005, 62–119) – especially popular music and the mass media – I share a certain degree of Knowles's obsession with the details of mass media and how they flow. Although he wouldn't have put it this way, something essential about the phenomenology of radio as a commercial medium is captured in Knowles's fast-paced, repetitive, constantly self-interrupting texts for Einstein. As a highly perceptive, socially isolated child growing up in the 1960s and 1970s, Knowles was, even more than most of his generation, "raised on radio." Knowles's poetic voice is not just formally unusual, in the way that much neuro-diverse art and writing is; it shows the strong imprint of the specific media environment in which it was developed, and, as it happens, Knowles's formative media environment can be reconstructed with some precision. His deep love for 1960s-style AM radio is typical for an American baby boomer, and thanks to the curatorial nostalgia his generational cohort still feels for the radio of their youth – in particular, the high-energy "Top 40" programs beaming out of New York City in the 1960s and early 1970s – it's not hard to track down specific media and advertising references in the Einstein libretto, and to experience for oneself through preserved "airchecks" (condensed recordings designed to capture a station's distinctive "flow" by cutting out songs and longer commercials) the stream of mellifluous, fast-paced announcing, noisy jingles, earnest advertising copy, and obsessive counting of "the hits" that dominated both AM radio and Knowles's imagination during the time he worked with Wilson and Glass.

For clinicians, the "obsessive" nature of circumscribed interests like Knowles's marks them as repetitive behaviors, one of a triad of impairments (social, linguistic, conceptual) characteristic of persons on the autism spectrum. As medical humanist Stuart Murray reports, these impairments are imagined by researchers – often backed up by the autobiographical accounts of people with autism – as consequential to failures in perceptual processing: "Because, the logic goes, the brains of autistic individuals process experiences differently, they then struggle with the consequences of such processing – speech and communicating, understanding

6   Arendell, *The Autistic Stage,* 6.

and generalizing, imagining outcomes etc."[7] Murray is sometimes skeptical of the "just so" nature of these explanations, but he does note one of the most influential theories of autism as a processing disorder, that autistic people, unable to fuse perceptual parts of their environment into a whole, experience the world with "weak central coherence."[8] For Murray, this provides both a plausible reason for repetitive behaviors – the collecting and organizing an almost prosthetic attempt to compensate – and a link between those behaviors and some very marked repetitive tendencies in modern art:

> Although never diagnosed, Andy Warhol easily fitted many of the criteria that are now used to determine Asperger's Syndrome, especially in terms of obsessive and patterned behavior. In his art, of course, such patterning was explored to an extent that changed the nature of twentieth-century painting. If we agree that Warhol's paintings are "repetitious" to any degree, and if we allow ourselves to see him within a frame of…autistic creativity, then it is clear that the repetition is no deficit. As part of Pop Art's renegotiation of the idea of the artwork and examination of consumer culture, Warhol's "restrictions" are in fact highly significant cultural statements.[9]

There was, as it happens, an art-world network that linked Warhol and Wilson – and some of it ran through the family of Christopher Knowles – but few commentators would, today, identify *Einstein on the Beach* as an example of Pop Art.[10] (Music critics attuned to high modernism have long disparaged Glass's music as "pop music for intellectuals," a quite different claim.)[11] But there has been since the late 1960s a strain of art criticism that insists on the formal similarities between pop and minimalism. This "hard-edged" reading of American Pop emphasizes lack of ego and a willingness to "avoid tasteful choices."[12] An Asperger's-like posture of weak central coherence, the unwillingness or inability to filter out details, becomes a new way of seeing:

> The Pop artist who documents the most ordinary scenes from daily life views the world as a total and inclusive unity in which all parts have total relevance – not just some relevance to the whole. Thus, for the Pop artist, there are no

7   Stuart Murray, *Autism*, New York, Routledge, 2012, 25.
8   Uta Frith, *Autism: A Very Short Introduction*, Oxford, Oxford University Press, 2008, 95.
9   Murray, *Autism*, 33.
10 As a strikingly attractive gay artist in 1960s Manhattan, Wilson certainly moved in Warhol's circle. Knowles's father, Ed Knowles, was a fellow student of Robert Wilson's at the Pratt Institute of Design in the 1960s; the elder Knowles was prompted to bring Christopher's first tape recordings to Wilson's attention by a family friend, George Klauber, who also knew Andy Warhol from their joint apprenticeship at Pittsburgh's Carnegie Tech and preceded him into New York's illustration business (Als & Elms 2014).
11 Samuel Lipman, "From Avant-Garde to Pop" [*Commentary*, 1979], in *The House of Music*, Boston, Godine, 1984, 48.
12 John Russell and Suzi Gablik, *Pop Art Redefined*, New York, Praeger, 1969, 18.

irrelevant details. Objects are particularized, often isolated rather than juxta-posed, in a non-associative and abstract way which has the effect of convert-ing the familiar into the monumental.[13]

Thus Warhol and the minimalist color-field painter Kenneth Noland "are like men who set off in opposite directions and yet arrived at the same destination";[14] the same might be said of Warhol and Wilson, except that in Wilson's case, the focus on repetitive formal structures based in the unfiltered content of popular mass media was not entirely first-hand: some of it came through the ears and (typing) fingers of his neuro-divergent teenage collaborator. Christopher Knowles was not perceptually equipped to make "tasteful choices" when he began his characteris-tic typings-out of song lyrics, radio patter, and advertising copy – as a response, Wilson recalled in later accounts, to his own repeated question, "Chris, who is Einstein?"[15] Like Andy Warhol, he allowed the commercial aesthetic to pass right through him, presenting it without the critical distance expected from a sophisti-cated member of the creative class. Hilton Als, co-curator of a recent exhibition of Knowles's work, notes that Knowles, like many people on the autism spec-trum, developed language, and an attendant sense of self, largely by repeating ambient voices he heard on radio and TV; Als hypothesizes that in the earliest Knowles tape recordings like "Emily Likes the TV" (1973), one can hear this echolalic, media-spawned voice "looking for an 'I'."[16] The autistic self does not "tune out" advertising media; it is constructed out of the sounds of that media, out of advertising-saturated sounds which Knowles's texts transmit directly into *Einstein*, to mingle there with the repetitive looping music and static images. It can thus be argued that, although neither Glass nor Wilson thought of themselves as "Pop" artists, Knowles truly was one, whether he thus self-identified or not. By the evidence of his recent work, he remains one to this day. Thanks in part to him, *Einstein on the Beach* possesses some of the quotidian monumentality and "toughness"[17] of the most impressive Pop Art.

As we shall see, the commercial radio influences in Knowles's typings for *Einstein* are neither scarce nor subtle; how is it, then, that this strong admixture of Pop Art has largely gone unremarked in critical discussions of the opera? Absent a discourse of neuro-diversity, it has been easy to mistake an autistic conscious-ness for no consciousness at all; fortunately, we are well past the time when pub-lished accounts of the opera elided Knowles's role altogether, assuming that the

13   Ibid, 14.
14   Ibid, 38.
15   This anecdote appears in a number of interviews and retrospectives. Wilson provides a vivid, two-handed reenactment in his documentary, *Einstein on the Beach: the Changing Image of Opera* (Direct Cinema Limited, 1985).
16   Hilton Als and Anthony Elms, "Christopher Knowles: In a Word," Philadelphia, Institute for Con-temporary Art, 2015, http://static.icaphila.org/pdf/gallery-notes/2015_fall/christopher_knowles_galleryguide.pdf, Accessed: January 20, 2016, pp. 3–4.
17   Russell and Gablik, *Redefining Pop Art*, 18.

words spoken by the actors were either meant to be unintelligible gibberish, or improvised on stage, or both.[18] Some of Knowles's AM references have always hit home, of course: calling out singers like David Cassidy and the Beatles, or hits like "Mr. Bojangles" and "I Feel the Earth Move" were as obviously topical in the early 1970s as seeing Patty Hearst's beret and machine gun onstage. But the distinctive form of radio from which these details were abstracted has – in a fate hard to imagine with Warhol's soup can labels or Lichtenstein's ben-day dots – escaped sustained critical analysis. The present chapter will attempt to remedy this by surveying media and advertising references in the *Einstein* texts in light of the phenomenology of 1960s AM radio. I'll then focus on a close reading of a scene ("Trial 2/Prison") in which Knowles's contribution is particularly prominent.

"It could be Franky": Christopher Knowles as Radio Listener

How did we miss this? It has been plainly obvious that Lichtenstein and Warhol copied details and entire formal structures from print and package advertising; but that the libretto of *Einstein on the Beach* bears the same relation to the sounds of Top 40 radio is a fact that might well be lost without some musicological analysis. Of course, 1960s radio broadcasts have become more ephemeral than print advertising, comic strips, or product packaging; they were also more class-and-age-targeted at the time. It's one thing to have seen a Campbell's soup can on the shelf at the local market; it's another to be the kind of person who leaves an AM radio on all day. Most critics who experienced *Einstein* would have despised the noisy radio broadcasting Knowles obsessively loved; and those subjected involuntarily to it during their day-to-day life would have taken pride in their ability to tune it out. (Visitors to Wilson's summer house at Water Mill, NY, learned to ignore the multiple simultaneous streams of AM radio emanating at high volume from Knowles's alcove off the main kitchen.)[19] For even its most enthusiastic neurotypical listeners, Top 40 radio quickly receded into a unitary gestalt, a "bath" of familiar chatter in the background at work or play; memories of it are highly filtered, often colored by the emotional memories which it indexes. But Knowles listened to the radio in a very unusual way, focusing, as the "weak central coherence" thesis might predict, on specific aspects of the flow rather than its overall "feel." Those within the Wilson circle report that Knowles has always had a very strong emotional connection to AM radio programming. But he also, because of his autistically circumscribed interest, still remembers *everything* about it:

---

18 See Samuel Lipman, "*Einstein*'s Long March to Brooklyn" [*The New Criterion*, February 1985], reprinted in Hilton Kramer, ed., *The New Criterion Reader: The First Five Years*, New York, Free Press, 1988, 334.

19 Hilton Als and Anthony Elms, "Conversation: Hilton Als and Anthony Elms on Christopher Knowles." October 7, 2015, Institute for Contemporary Art, Philadelphia. Video accessed at https://vimeo.com/151703149, Accessed: February 3, 2015.

It's, you know, AM radio, you know, a very loud, I mean very *frenetic*, kind of voice, and pop tunes coming through and if you say, "Christopher, what [number] was that Rolling Stones [song] in 19...?" he can tell you, because he's in his body in a way that's very deep and also he can recall a feeling – or a relationship, rather, I should say – to a record or a sound. That's the performative aspect of it, of emotional memory; it's a kind of emotional shorthand for him.[20]

Almost no one outside the industry itself and a few nostalgic critics have thought much about the structural techniques that gave rise to the flow of AM music broadcasting. It's doubtful that Knowles did, either; but his intense focus on, high tolerance for, and quasi-eidetic memories of early-1970s Top 40 radio equipped him to reproduce its distinctive structural features with almost clinical accuracy in the typings that so attracted Robert Wilson.

"On Musicradio 77 W-A-B-C!"

Chris Knowles, like most New York kids in the early 1970s, listened to WABC, "Musicradio 77," whose non-directional, 50,000-watt signal blanketed the NYC metropolitan area and large portions of the East Coast with AM broadcasts at 770 kHz. Originally the flagship NYC station of the American Broadcasting Company, WABC switched to a popular music format in 1960, sprang into Top 40 prominence in the middle 1960s as "W-A-Beatles-C," and dominated the local airwaves as "Musicradio 77" through the 1970s, until the rise of FM, retreating to an all-talk format in 1982. In the early 1970s it was the most influential radio station in the United States, with a peak broadcast audience of almost 8 million spread across 38 states and a staggering 90% share among teenagers in its local market, which stretched from Springfield, Hartford, and New Haven in the north; to Scranton and Allentown in the west; to Atlantic City, Wilmington, and Philadelphia in the south.[21]

20 Ibid.
21 A terminological note for those unfamiliar with the US commercial radio system: radio stations in the United States are privately owned, but license bands of frequency spectrum from the US government through the Federal Communications Commission (FCC). There is one band (approx. 500–1600 kHz) for amplitude modulated signals (AM) and another (88–108 mHz) for frequency modulated (FM) signals. FCC naming conventions for terrestrial radio go back to the 1920s, when stations assigned a specific frequency were also given three to four letter "call signs" akin to those already in use by individual shortwave radio enthusiasts, government installations, and ships at sea. (Stations east of the Mississippi had call letters beginning with W; stations west of the Mississippi began with K.) These call signs have been retained even as ownership and format change; WABC, as its primeval letters imply, is one of the oldest call signs in North America. A commercial radio station might refer to itself by its official call letters ("W-A-B-C"); by its assigned frequency ("770 on the AM dial"), or by its own trademark format ("Musicradio"). During the 1970s, WABC tended to call itself "Musicradio 77," dropping a zero from its licensed frequency to match the shortened AM frequency designations on the tuning dials of car and portable

At the time he wrote the texts that would become a part of *Einstein on the Beach*, Knowles had lived a good part of his life under the wide penumbra of WABC's signal; he knew the station's routine well enough to type out, with a few stumbles, its entire weekly deejay line-up from memory, in a text entitled "I Feel the Earth Move," which would be recited verbatim at the end of *Einstein*'s second Trial scene (Act III, scene 1) by dancer Lucinda Childs:

JAY REYNOLDS from midnight to 6 AM.

HARRY HARRISON from 6 AM to 10 AM.

RON LUNDY from 10 AM to 2 PM.

DAN INGRAM from 2 PM to 6 PM.

GEORGE MICHAEL from 6 PM to 10 PM.

CHUCK LEONARD from 10 PM to midnight.

JOHNNY DONOVAN from 10 PM to 3 AM.

STEVE-O-BRION from 2 PM to 6 PM.

JOHNNY DONOVAN from 6 PM to 10 PM.

CHUCK LEONARD from 3 AM to 5 AM.

JOHNNY DONOVAN from 6 PM to 1OPM.

STEVE-O-BRION from 4 30 AM to 6 AM

STEVE-O-BRION from 4 30 AM to 6 AM

JOHNNY DONOVAN from 4 30 AM to 6 AM[22]

transistor radios. In the text that follows, I will refer to "WABC" and "Musicradio 77" interchangeably, as the station itself did. "Top 40" radio started off as a trademark format of certain Midwestern stations owned by the Storz family (see below), but later became a generic name for hit-oriented, high-energy commercial radio; I will use it here to designate all radio stations using that commercial format in the 1960s and 1970s. During this time, most "Top 40" stations broadcast in AM, since the AM signal could be picked up on the widest range of receivers, particularly the cheap ones favored by youth audiences. Thus in many listeners' minds, "AM radio" and "Top 40 radio" are synonymous; I will try to distinguish between the two, using AM radio as the more general term, although many accounts of radio listening in the 1970s do not. (WABC began as an AM station, but did not become a Top 40 station until the 1960s. It continues to broadcast in AM, but in a news and talk radio format.) Capitalized phrases surrounding the call letters or format name ("Music Radio 77 Top Ten") are trademarked slogans of WABC from the period, which I reproduce as they appeared in contemporary sources (see musicradio77.com).

22   The orthography, spelling, punctuation and line breaks of all Knowles's texts discussed in this article follow the published *Einstein* libretto (http://culturebox.francetvinfo.fr/ sites/default/files/ assets/documents/eob_text_for_libretto.pdf)" http://culturebox.francetvinfo.fr/sites/default/files/ assets/documents/eob_text_for_libretto.pdf.), which, in turn, directly transmits Knowles's typings, which Wilson deliberately did not "clean up" for performance. Stephanie Jensen-Moulton notes, based on her own archival research, that Wilson selected the texts for *Einstein on the Beach*

It is possible to match this list of WABC on-air personalities with the program-ming schedule that went into effect on September 9, 1974, when George Michael replaced "Cousin Brucie" Morrow in the 6 to 10pm weekday evening slot. Knowles would have known about the change, since the new line-up was dra-matically recited in an interstitial jingle introducing the new evening deejay to the local audience. Thanks to the curatorial fervor of WABC listeners, who have pre-served and uploaded an aircheck from that evening, it is possible to listen through Knowles's ears to the actual sound of Johnny Donovan turning the airwaves over to George Michael for the first time:

> J. DONOVAN: "Band on the Run," Musicradio 77 helps you remember that one…
>
> INTERSTITIAL: [heavy echo, slight overlapping of antiphonal announcers]
>
> HARRY HARRISON
>
> JAY REYNOLDS
>
> RON LUNDY
>
> JOHNNY DONOVAN
>
> CHUCK LEONARD
>
> DAN INGRAM
>
> [drum roll, single voice]
>
> GEORGE MICHAEL from 6 to 10pm
>
> [both together]
>
> *on Musicradio 77, W-A-B-C!*[23]

from a larger set of Knowles's typings on the subject, and appears to have rewritten some por-tions (See Jensen-Moulton, "Disability as Postmodernism," pp. 26ff.). Various performers, under Wilson's direction, have chosen to recite different portions of the *Einstein* texts in performance, but on all recordings I have surveyed, both official and bootlegged, they take care to preserve as much as possible the unusual spelling, inconsistent typing, and departures from conventional syntax in what they do recite.

23 Transcribed by the author from the station's aircheck recorded on September 9, 1974 and saved by listener Chip Ordway (musicradio77.com/airchecks.html, Accessed: March 21, 2016). This 13-minute clip is one of hundreds archived by musicradio77.com, covering the entire period of WABC's Top 40 history. As its curator, Allen Sniffen, notes, "you can learn a lot about the evolu-tion of WABC if you listen to the airchecks chronologically," since "the jingles, the music flow and the overall sound of the station changes with time." As we will see, this "flow" was structur-ally complex, and carefully designed to be rhythmically compelling; the texts that Knowles cre-ated for *Einstein on the Beach* are a testament to its power.

What might look like repetitions and mistakes in the *Einstein* text above are, in fact, Knowles being careful to list, after the new weekday rotation, the different personalities that WABC used to fill out its weekend shifts, when the less favored deejays worked some odd combinations of hours. (WABC schedules from the early 1970s can be accessed at musicradio77.com/sked7175.html.)[24] We can thus assume that Knowles's written texts for *Einstein* transmit his circumscribed interest in tiny details of WABC's broadcast schedule starting in late 1974, just as Robert Wilson started serious work on the visual sketchbook that would be the basis for *Einstein*'s "libretto."[25]

What else can we learn by putting *Einstein*'s texts in dialogue with WABC's programming, under the detail-oriented spotlight of autistic perceptual processing? Let's begin with one of the opera's best-known moments. The first recognizable pop culture reference in Knowles's *Einstein* text is in the opening knee play, at the third line, which begins, "It could Franky it could be Franky." This phrase almost certainly invokes the lead singer of the Four Seasons, who returned to WABC's rotation after the better part of a decade with no Top 40 hits, under his own name, "Frankie" Valli, on January 14, 1975. (Appendix A correlates milestones in the Wilson-Glass-Knowles *Einstein* collaboration with playlist positions held by Frankie Valli or the Four Seasons on WABC.) At the end of *Einstein*'s second knee play – in a rarely heard passage omitted from all extant recorded performances – the text calls out both the singer and the group again. As we see him do above, Knowles the typist held down his CAPS LOCK key to transcribe the reverb-drenched, bass-rich "radio" sound of Musicradio 77's announcers:

SWEARIN TO GOD WHO LOVES YOU

FRANKIE VALLI THE FOUR SEASONS[26]

Although the first line makes sense as a kind of found poetry, one needs to read from top to bottom, not right to left, to appreciate how literal Knowles's mirroring of WABC's broadcast stream really was. Exactly as in his text, these two disco-flavored hits followed one another into the Musicradio 77 Top Ten during the second half of 1975: first "Swearin' to God" (top) by Frankie Valli (bottom), from May to September; then "Who Loves You" (top) by The Four Seasons (bottom),

---

24 Elaborate deconstructionist takes on the verbal text of *Einstein* have thus been undermined by a lack of familiarity with WABC's weekly schedule commensurate with Knowles's own. For example, critic Arthur Holmberg quite misses the point when he seizes on such "errors" in Knowles's text as a pretext to exalt the free play of the signifier: "We are told that Donovan is on from 6 to 10 and that O-Brion is on from 4.30 to 6. But language then proceeds to contradict itself. It makes two mutually exclusive propositions. If we listen in at 4.30, whose smiling voice will greet us, Donovan's or O-Brion's? We cannot rely on language to inform us. Language can say whatever it pleases: reality does not keep it on a leash." (Holmberg, *The Theatre of Robert Wilson*, Cambridge, Cambridge University Press, 1996, 57).

25 Philip Glass, *Music by Philip Glass*, New York, Harper & Row, 1987, pp. 31–32.

26 *Einstein* libretto, 6 (Knee Play 2).

from late October into December. By the time Frankie's second hit was riding the top of the charts in the fall of 1975, *Einstein on the Beach* was deep in rehearsals, where, as Philip Glass recounts, texts by Knowles (and others) were being layered over the solfége syllables and beat numbers chanted by the chorus.[27]

Stephanie Jenson-Moulton has uncovered in Wilson's archive an unused chapter of Knowles's *Einstein* typings titled "Pick Out Ten Songs of 1975."[28] Using WABC chart positions as evidence, it doesn't seem unreasonable to date the production of Knowles's *Einstein* typings specifically to the final months of 1975, since there is no mention in any of them of the two even bigger hits that bracketed Knowles's pairing: neither Frankie Valli's "My Eyes Adored You," which had already peaked in February–March 1974, nor The Four Seasons' "December 1963 (Oh What a Night)," which would first enter WABC's playlist on February 20, 1976. Recall from the testimony above that Knowles could recite, decades after the fact, the dates and chart positions of every favorite song ever played on WABC. For him, it could indeed be Franky – but not just *any* Franky.[29]

I feel the earth move

Other names of pop songs and their singers are sprinkled throughout the texts for *Einstein*. In two places, Knowles combines his own name with three of the Beatles to create a new pop group – Knowles, Lennon, McCartney, and Harrison – while mixing in punning, rhyming references to *Sgt. Pepper's Lonely Hearts Club Band* ("lucky as the sky") and "I Am the Walrus" ("Piggy in the sky"). WABC was not an oldies station, so it was not playing the Beatles, and certainly

---

27 Glass, *Music by Philip Glass*, 44.
28 Jensen-Moulton, "Disability as Postmodernism," 27.
29 Other signifiers in Knowles's work can, in sometimes surprising ways, be dated to this specific three-month period. The opening scene's reference to Frankie Valli is followed directly by an unrelated image of childhood ("It could be a balloon"), and then by another apparent non-sequitur seemingly based in popular music of the late 1960s: "All these are the days my friends and these are the days my friends." However, this latter turns out *not* to be a mangled quotation of British folksinger Mary Hopkins's 1968 hit for Apple Records, with its mournful refrain, "Those were the days, my friend." That song did indeed chart on WABC, reaching the #1 position in October–November of 1968, but Chris Knowles was probably too young to have noticed it then. His reference was more likely to a short-lived cartoon series entitled *These Are the Days*, an animated look back at the way technology changed early twentieth-century rural America. The series, developed by the Hanna Barbera studios as educational television, and broadcast on ABC between September 7, 1974 and September 27, 1975, was filled with the kind of machinery and transportation systems in motion that have been hypothesized as particularly attractive to male teens on the autism spectrum (Baron-Cohen & Wheelright 1999). The second-to-last episode, aired on September 20, 1975, was entitled "The Balloon." It seems to have been on Knowles's mind as he typed out the texts that would later appear at the opening of *Einstein on the Beach*. Further research is needed to determine how much of the transportation imagery in *Einstein*'s Knee Play 1 – getting wind for sailboats and finding a railroad for workers – can be traced back to plotlines from this Saturday morning children's show. (The series has never been re-released, and no information exists in standard reference works about the balloon-themed episode.)

not these psychedelic album cuts, in 1975. Evidently we must look further back; was there an earlier moment when Knowles was particularly susceptible to radio influence? Aside from one passing cryptic reference to teen-pop hits of the late 1960s – "It could be cry like a baby i'll be there" (The Box Tops from 1968 and the Jackson Five from 1970, respectively), the other songs and artists mentioned in the *Einstein* texts can all be traced back to the ten-month period between late February and early December 1971 (see Appendix B). The Nitty Gritty Dirt Band's version of Jerry Jeff Walker's 1968 hit, "Mr. Bojangles," extensively referenced in *Einstein*'s two Trial scenes, charted on WABC briefly in February–March 1971, reaching #4 on the playlist – but Carole King's *Tapestry*, released in April, was a phenomenon: a WABC "action" album for over 30 weeks, it threw a series of singles, album cuts, and cover versions onto the station's charts. "I Feel the Earth Move," specifically called out by Knowles in *Einstein*, was a WABC favorite, appearing somewhere on its rotation for 26 of those weeks.[30] The track's slow fade off the NYC airwaves then overlapped with the rise of David Cassidy's first single under his own name (as opposed to the fictitious Partridge Family) during November and December of 1971. It may be pure coincidence that these three radio memories – Mr. Bojangles, Carole King, and David Cassidy – appear in *Einstein on the Beach* in the same order that they did on WABC – in the spring, summer, and fall of 1971 – but I wouldn't want to bet *against* such specificity and ordering appearing in Knowles's lifelong production of typed texts about his circumscribed interest.

What was so special about the summer of 1971? Knowles was born in 1959, so he turned 12 that year. Most media studies of music preference begin with 12-to-14-year-olds, since that is when children take control of their own listening habits, and begin to orient themselves towards popular media.[31] It was also about this time that Edward Knowles, Christopher's father, was given a portable tape recorder by one of his architectural clients, and, having no interest in it, passed it

---

30 Peculiarities in the way WABC categorized records, and an unusual release strategy from Ode Records, make the chart positions of tracks from *Tapestry* a little hard to pin down. WABC's music surveys for 1971 (musicradio77.com/surveys/surveys1971) distinguish between a 30-item "singles" rotation and another set of "album cuts," while also maintaining a list of so-called "action" albums, from which additional tracks could be drawn. Both sides of King's first single, "It's Too Late/"I Feel the Earth Move" were designated as A-sides, so the name under which the record was listed in the charts was somewhat arbitrary. For several weeks, "It's Too Late" was a number-one "single," while "I Feel the Earth Move" was the top "album cut." But we can assume that *both* sides were being played many times a day in the spring and summer of 1971.

31 Some of the most passionate nostalgia for Top 40 radio comes from Knowles's direct contemporaries. Mark Fisher's *Something in the Air: Radio, Rock, and the Revolution that Shaped a Generation* (New York, Random House, 2007) begins with a paean to the power of WABC for another 12-year-old in the summer of 1972: "I kept the radio tuned to Musicradio 77 because I was twelve, this was America, and that was what I was supposed to do....In the voice of my favorite deejay, Dan Ingram, in his six-second antics sandwiched between ads and pop songs, I heard freedom and passion, everything a kid wants to think is out there somewhere, just beyond his reach" (xi).

on to his teenage son, fostering an obsession that would last a lifetime. By 1973, Chris Knowles had two tape recorders, which allowed him to create "Emily Likes the TV," the repetitive, looping vocal composition that brought him to the attention of Robert Wilson.[32] Wilson's interest probably saved Knowles from a life of institutional confinement: "Emily Likes the TV" was made at the Oswald D. Heck Developmental Center in upstate New York, a residential facility for the mentally disabled, where Knowles spent the better part of 1973 and 1974.[33] After impulsively inviting a visiting Knowles onstage to perform "Emily" with him during the December 1973 performances of *The Life and Times of Joseph Stalin*, Wilson convinced both Knowles's parents and his psychiatric case manager to let Wilson house him and fold him into activities at the communal live-work space occupied by Wilson's Byrd-Hoffman School at 147 Spring Street in Manhattan. (In "I Feel the Earth Move," just before the line-up of deejays on WABC, Knowles typed out another list of the people he was now living with: "This would be some all of my friends. Cindy Jay Steve Julia Robyn Rick Kit and Liz.")[34]

The O.D. Heck Developmental Center was located in suburban Niskayuna, just outside Schenectady, NY. Living there, Chris Knowles, for the only time in his life, was outside the daytime broadcast range of WABC. (He might sometimes have been able to pick up its signal at night, if atmospheric conditions were right.) It also seems unlikely that he would have been allowed free access to AM radio in a state-run therapeutic environment focused not on fostering creativity, but on making inmates conform to neuro-typical standards of language and behavior.[35] The layers of pop music reference in the texts for *Einstein* now start to make temporal sense: a strong emphasis on music from the second half of 1971, corresponding to Knowles's entry into radio listening and his first love affair with the tape recorder; then a two-year gap, correlated with his enforced upstate absence from the WABC "family"; then a new explosion of excitement about WABC's programming starting in 1974, when, thanks largely to Wilson, Knowles moved back within range of the station's daily flow, taking advantage of his new-found freedom to immerse himself in it, and to put it at the center of a major avant-garde theater piece in workshop development. In this context, the repeated invocation of WABC's call letters at the end of Knowles's "I Feel the Earth Move," while certainly evidence,

---

32 Bill Simmer, "Robert Wilson and Therapy," *The Drama Review: TDR* 10-1, Theater and Therapy (March 1976), 106.

33 The Heck Center is now closed, the last residents having been relocated in 2015. By all accounts it was not the worst such facility, but suffered from the basic contradictions involved in segregating and warehousing the neuro-atypical in bureaucratized, tax-supported mental institutions. See Hammond 1990 for a local journalistic report on the grimness of life at Heck in the late 1980s. Simmer (*op. cit.*, pp. 104–105) recounts Robert Wilson's intuitive rapport with other, more severely brain-damaged patients who were being badly served by the Center; absent Wilson's bold intervention, one can easily imagine Christopher Knowles wasting years of his life there.

34 *Einstein* libretto, p. 9 (Act II, scene 1). Not all these names can be matched to resident members of Wilson's company in 1974, but the references to Cynthia Lubar ("Cindy"), Robyn Brentano ("Robyn"), and Elizabeth Pasquale ("Liz") are clear.

35 Arendell, *The Autistic Stage*, 7.

interwoven with the ever-expanding list of deejay names and time slots, of his strong circumscribed interest, also takes on the character of a declaration of creative independence, of what can happen when the walls (of the institution, of neurotypical demands on language) come "tumbling down tumbling down":

So this one in like on WABC New York ...

JAY REYNOLDS from midnight to 6 00.

HARRY HARRISON

So heres what in like of WABC

JAY REYNOLDS from midnight to 6 AM

HARRY HARRISON from 6 AM to L

I feel the earth move from WABC[36]

"Tighten Up": *Einstein* and the Rhythms of Top 40 Radio

> The rhythm of my voice at that time was pretty fast, because rock and roll was pretty fast.
>
> (deejay Gary Owen in Fong-Torres, *The Hits Keep On Coming*)[37]

Like many listeners to Top 40 radio, Chris Knowles derived pleasure from being part of an imagined community in which the daily rotation of the station's on-air personalities and the weekly procession of hits up and down the station's playlist helped organize the passage of time. But as we attempt to push deeper into the textual logic of *Einstein on the Beach*, we need to put the station's minute-by-minute broadcast flow *itself* under an analytic microscope, for its verbal and musical rhythms were woven into Knowles's writing at a structural level. Robert Wilson's immediate attraction to Knowles's texts was based not in their content, but in the level of formal and rhythmic control the director perceived in both the tapes and the typings: "I began to realize that the words flowed to a patterned rhythm whose logic was self-supporting. It was a piece coded much like music. Like a cantata or fugue it worked with conjugations of thoughts repeated in variations."[38] Not so important to Wilson, perhaps, but obvious to others in the art world, was how Knowles "came to the inventive rhythms of language through everyday means

36 *Einstein* libretto, pp. 9–10 (Act III, scene 1).
37 Ben Fong-Torres, *The Hits Keep On Coming: The History of Top 40 Radio*, San Francisco, Backbeat Books, 1998, 73.
38 Robert Wilson, unpaginated 1986 review of Christopher Knowles, *Typings, 1974–1979* (New York: Vehicle Editions, 1986) Accessed March 26, 2016 at www.vehicleeditions.com/Site/Robert_Wilson.html.

– television, radio, records, and advertisements."[39] Cynthia Lubar ("Cindy"), who spent a lot of time with Knowles in the 1970s, confirms that he listened structurally to AM radio, paying close attention to its formal patterns:

> Despite or because of his celebrity, Christopher is extremely reluctant to talk. One communicates with him, if at all, through Cindy, his companion. According to her, he spends most of his time working and listening to the radio, usually to at least two stations at once. "Not for the words or the songs or whatever, but for the rhythms of communicating. They're in his work."[40]

How can we get to know these communicative rhythms? Luckily for the musicological analyst, the curators of Top 40 radio stations like WABC had pretty much the same priorities as Knowles, and have been quite articulate about them in interviews and memoirs.[41] It would be going too far to claim that they didn't care about "the words or the songs or whatever," but by the 1970s, AM radio had become, in the words of one disillusioned chronicler, "a sleek system designed to snare listeners as much with pace as with content."[42] Station managers understood quite well that, since they were all playing the same records, running the same kind of promotions, and hiring the same deejays (often from each other), it was the abstract, formal perfection of a station's broadcast rhythm that kept it at the top of the ratings book.

The hits just keep on coming

Even within the highly disciplined world of Top 40 broadcasting, WABC was infamous for its on-air relentlessness. At their peak, in the late 1960s and early 1970s, its broadcasts perfectly realized the fundamental aesthetic goal of Top 40 radio, which was to "hook" listeners with a dense, branded stream of sound and never let them go. As formulated in the 1950s by the Midwestern independent stations of the Storz Broadcasting Company, the Top 40 radio format had three imperatives: to make it clear to listeners that they were continually hearing the most popular records; to make sure that listeners associated this stream of "hit" records with the call letters of the station; and to keep the association strong across all types of content (jingles, advertisements, song intros, announcements, news). The most successful Top 40 station was thus the "tightest"; the thrust of the format was, over time, to shorten or eliminate anything on the air that did not directly serve

39   Als & Ems, "Christopher Knowles: In a Word," unpaginated.
40   John Ashbery, "Christopher Knowles," *New York Magazine*, September 19, 1978, 88.
41   Two quite different sources that make this clear are the gossipy WABC insider's account in Rick Sklar, *Rocking America: How the All-Hit Radio Stations Took Over*, New York, St. Martin's Press, 1984, and the scholarly overview of post-war radio broadcast practices in Richard W. Fatherly and David T. MacFarland, *The Birth of Top 40 Radio: The Storz Stations' Revolution of the 1950s and 1960s*, Jefferson, NC, MacFarland & Company, 2014.
42   Fisher, *Something in the Air*, 98.

those three linked goals. Chronicling the heyday of AM radio, journalist Ben Fong-Torres recounts how a veteran disk jockey replayed for him a typical management oversight call to the "hot line" at the studios of KHJ, then the dominant Top 40 station in Los Angeles: "Ring... 'How's it goin', man?' 'Fine.' 'Tighten up!' Click."[43] At the end of the 1950s, this type of "tighter, faster, and more formalized" radio broadcast was already dominant in most urban markets;[44] by the end of the 1960s, Top 40 radio had become ruthlessly reductive, "a format which is basically 'play those hits, get into them, get out of them.' Get in and get out, do the three major elements, do the time, the call letters, and your name. Over and over again."[45]

The sonic environment of Top 40 was designed to be both seamless and acoustically engrossing. Early Top 40 stations, broadcasting on the less powerful frequencies not controlled by the major networks, made liberal use of audio compression to ensure their signal was always smooth and subjectively loud; WABC's common practice of sweetening the broadcast stream with reverb and punching up key phrases for subliminal effect also goes way back: "By 1962, WQAM [in New Orleans] was using echo to highlight the position of a record on the station's playlist or survey. A typical sentence might sound like this: 'Here's survey song number **FOUR** FOUR *four* four,' with each succeeding 'four' being slightly lower in volume."[46] Riding this stream of sonic energy, the hits, as the saying went, just kept on coming. Top 40 radio's fixed playlist of songs was an autistic's dream: carefully cross-referenced by intensity, genre, and popularity, with nothing, literally nothing, left to chance: "The records were labeled with title, artist, and length. They also carried a color code, and a tempo designation. The color codes differentiated each record by style: general pop, teen-appeal, rhythm 'n' blues, country, and album-oriented rock; and by tempo: up-tempo, moderate-up, moderate, moderate-down, and down."[47] In the early 1970s, Christopher Knowles's WABC had one of the shortest and tightest playlists on air, rotating through no more than 25 songs, so that the top hits repeated every 70–80 minutes. They had to, because the average listener tuned in to WABC for no more than 10–20 minutes at a time. Satirist Harry Shearer's 1967 dissection of Top 40 radio for the underground magazine *Cheetah*, "Captain Pimple Cream's Fiendish Plot," overflows with venom at the "depressing" effect of an evening "when you just left the radio on, tuned to a Top 40 station pouring out the hits while you studied, or wrote, or whatever," and gradually realized that the songs on WABC's playlist were repeating in the same mechanical order every hour and a half.[48] Moments like this, when the enormous amount of repetition in commercial broadcasting becomes directly perceptible, create, in "normal" people, a queasy feeling that

---

43   Ben Fong-Torres, *The Hits Just Keep on Coming*, 174.
44   Fatherly & McFarland, *The Birth of Top 40 Radio*, 104.
45   Fong-Torres, *op. cit.,* 240.
46   Fatherly & McFarland, *op. cit.,* 142. Orthography in original.
47   Fatherly & McFarland, *op. cit.,* 140.
48   Harry Shearer, "Captain Pimple Cream's Fiendish Plot," in Jonathan Eisen, ed., *The Age of Rock: Sounds of the American Cultural Revolution*, New York, Random House, 368.

I have identified elsewhere as "the media sublime," based in terror at seeing (or hearing) something no one is supposed to, that is, all the repetition necessary to make advertising-supported media work in a distracted culture of mechanical reproduction. The thrill of discomfort we feel at extremely repetitive works of art like *Einstein on the Beach* can be read as a restaging of this media sublime.[49]

But the highly structured repetition of mass media might also be comforting, especially if one's mental makeup predisposes one to find environmental change stressful.[50] Persons on the autism spectrum often value radio and TV for just this endlessly iterative aspect, reassured that the experience of a favorite program will remain precisely the same, no matter how many times it is aired or viewed. For Knowles, the fact that, after listening for a while, one could begin to predict when a favorite song would recur in WABC's rotation, was not a reason to turn the radio off; it was an opportunity to celebrate, sometimes, by cueing up a taped version and playing along. For Knowles, unlike Harry Shearer, WABC was not sublimely terrible; it was beautiful, in its own (repetitive) way.

Forward momentum and the imperceptible overlap

WABC's playlist was so short in the early 1970s because the eight or nine hit songs it played per hour jostled for space with a bewildering assortment of interstitial matter: a matching suite of sung jingles in various lengths for the station, the host, and, during countdowns, each top hit song; frequent call-outs of the time and weather; chimes and stingers; and six to eight advertisements per hour, sometimes on tape but often read out live on the air by the host. The temporal flow of AM radio was so complex that Top 40 disk jockeys and engineers relied on a "hot clock" – a graphical representation of the broadcast hour as a clock face – to organize the dozens of taped segments needed to put together a smooth, professional show.

Gluing it all together was the primary job of the on-air personality. A distinctive "radio voice" – usually smooth and mellifluous, but always rhythmically fluent – was the backbone of every Top 40 show, providing a constant flow of talk to weld all the complex agglomerations of sound called for by the station's hot clock into a coherent, jazzy flow. It was easy to make fun of the non-stop vocal bop "Its-three-o-clock-in-*BAWWS*-SAN jew-luss-on-the reeyul-don-steeyul SHOW-im holdin-goldens-in-the-spirit-dont- try-to-*STOP*-me-Hiii!"),[51] but sympathetic observers noted how hard deejays had to work as they "built smooth bridges between songs, patter, and commercials":

49 Robert Fink, *Repeating Ourselves: American Minimal Music as Cultural Practice*, Berkeley, University of California Press, 2005, pp. 161–66.
50 This aspect of childhood autism was highlighted in its very first clinical description. See Leo Kanner, "Autistic Disturbances of Affective Contact," *Nervous Child* 2 (1943), 245–246.
51 For those not fluent in Top 40 radio-speak, this moment of patter from KHJ in Los Angeles (impressionistically rendered by Shearer, in Eisen *op. cit.,* p. 357), translates as: "It's three o'clock in Boss Angeles on the Real Don Steele show. I'm holding goldens in the spirit [sic] – don't try to stop me. Hello."

"Soul and Inspiration" by the Righteous Brothers is fading, and [Paul] O'Day comes on. The voice is strong, measured, medium-tempo:

"Number One in Seattle, this is KJR, and is that great? 'Soul and Inspiration,' the Righteous Brothers, 75 degrees from All-American, All-Request Radio. My soul and inspiration is Jerry Kaye, who, on a warm day like today, he's in the news room, he's taken all of his clothes off. He's sitting on the teletype, and the machine is printing the farm news on his behind. Let's see if I can read it. It says: There's a difference between fryers, and that's why Washington Fryers are easily the freshest of all chickens."

In thirty seconds, he'd done an outro that identified the record, plugged his station, gave the most basic weather, tied into a mention of a fellow deejay, as well as got off a joke that triggered a silly visual image and that led seamlessly into a piece of live commercial copy.[52]

The program director's ultimate goal was "imperceptible overlap," the ability to thread linking sentences with pinpoint precision through the jumble of conflicting beats created by whatever mix of jingles, ads, promotions, and song intros were called for on the hot clock. If a deejay could master that, then the station's broadcasts would have what producers called "forward momentum," the Platonic ideal of Top 40 radio: "all the basics, everything tight, no dead air, everything kick-ass, perfect music. Everything perfect, perfect, perfect."[53]

Knowles's textual references to Frankie Valli, the Beatles, Carole King, and the overnight schedule at WABC are clear enough, and they let us know he listened to the station. But it's only by keeping in mind the fractured transitional logic that ensured WABC's forward momentum that we can appreciate just how deeply he internalized its rhythms, and how saturated *Einstein on the Beach* is in the quotidian vocal stylings of Top 40 radio's on-air performers. Like the deejays whose schedules he obsessively tracked, Knowles's writing often shifted instantaneously between musical references ("it could be Franky") and what sounds like advertising copy ("it could be very fresh and clean"). Some of the most spectacular passages in the libretto reproduce the forward momentum of the bridging voice with eidetic precision; note, in Knee Play 2, how the text spins away from its original call-out to Frankie Valli through a series of free-associated images and then, as smoothly as Jay Reynolds or Harry Harrison, into a classic moment of WABC live advertising, undoubtedly taken directly from the radio,[54] like dictation:

52   Fong-Torres, *The Hits Just Keep On Coming*, 77.

53   Ibid., 169.

54   Wilson described at the time how Knowles's typings evolved directly from radio speech: "He would take anything on the radio – he would hear an announcement, or anything – and he just started to see the words distributed on the page" (Simmer, *op. cit.*, 109).

It could be Franky, it could be.
Back to the rack and go back to the rack. It could be some workers so.
It could be a balloon, it could be Franky, it could be.
Which one are the ones for. So if you know. So i you take your watch off.
They're easy to lose or break. These are the days my friends and these are
the days my friends. It could be some of th ... It could be on your own.
It could be where of all. The way iron this one. So if you know you know.
this will be into where it could be. So look here.
Do you know they just don't make clothes for people who wears glasses. There's
no pockets anymore. So if you take your glasses off. They're easy
to lose or break. Well New York a Phonic Center has the answer to your
problem. Contactless lenses and the new soft lenses. The Center gives
you thirty days and see if you like them. And if you don't. They could refunds your
money. So this could be like into a satchel in the sky. A batch
of cookies was on the for these are the days. This could be into
a satchel.
It could get the railroad for these works

In performance, these texts generated their own species of "forward momen-tum." Wilson had already developed a distinctive style of quick, rhythmi-cally stylized stage patter while working with Knowles on a series of intricate two-person vocal fugues collectively called *DIA(log)*, and he appears to have instructed his actors – whom he often deployed in contrapuntal pairs – to move just as briskly through Knowles's texts, using the studied inflections of the pro-fessional radio announcer, who knew how to "punch up" station identifications, clumsy advertising copy, and mundane recitations of the time and weather by self-consciously varying vocal pitch and stress. As a result, *Einstein*'s texts often come out sounding like standard AM "radio-ese": "All these are the days my *friends* and these are the *days* my friends" (shifting emphasis mine, follow-ing Lucinda Childs).

Talk-ups and "hitting the post" (text-music relations on the AM dial)

Thus far, we have seen that Christopher Knowles's texts for *Einstein on the Beach* transmit an obsession both with the music played on WABC (through the tracking and naming of hit records) and, separately, the distinctive way its dee-jays spun out words (through imitating the bridging function of their patter). But what about the *relation* of words and music on WABC – and, for that matter, in *Einstein*, which is, after all, an opera, with a composed score that "accompanies" the on-stage recitation of Knowles's typings? To be clear, there is no evidence that Philip Glass took any aspect of Knowles's texts into account when compos-ing *Einstein*; as he tells it, he was not interested in setting the typings to music, and convinced Wilson that Knowles's contribution was best treated accord-ing to what he called, borrowing a term from radio announcing, a "voice over procedure."[55] During rehearsals, Wilson freely distributed voicings of Knowles's texts (and others) over the work's already-composed musical numbers. (Glass's 2013 published full score of *Einstein* contains no information about the disposition of the opera's spoken texts.)

We can therefore dismiss any intention to create determinate musical relationships between Knowles's voice-over text and Glass's music. But this does not mean no such relationships exist. In fact, the music-text relation in a 1970s-era theater where *Einstein on the Beach* was being performed was structurally similar to that obtained on a 1970s-era Top 40 station like WABC: in both, a stream of rhythmic, repetitive music met a stream of allusive, rhythmic, only indifferently signifying speech, the music and the talking each an independent creation, meant to be layered together only at the point of performance. On WABC, as in *Einstein*, the most distinctive moments were when the talking was layered *on top of* the music. In the post-Beatles era, as Top 40 radio became tighter and tighter, the primary job of an announcer was to avoid "dead air" and maximize forward momentum, and the most effective method turned out to be the most notorious. Rather than slow down the rhythm of the station's broadcast by showing off their personality *between* records, deejays were encouraged to "talk up" each record, slipping in jokes and zingers over its instrumental introduction.[56] The best radio talents would effortlessly "hit the post" every time, finishing their improvised patter as close as possible to the precise beat where the vocals came in. A fastidious craftsman like WABC's George Michael even used a stopwatch, timing intros to the split-second, so he could create "adlibbed walk-ups spoken over the introductions to each song, masterfully timed so his mini-drama ended exactly as the song's vocal began."[57] Michael was going for emotional connection, but sometimes this high-wire search for the most imperceptible overlap became a subject for self-referential performance art:

> But, once, when [Reynolds] messed up, he immediately turned it into a bit. The song was Brenda Lee's "I'm Sorry," and Joey spoke over its languid opening, ending just a beat before Brenda began singing. That wasn't good enough. "Think we can hit the cue a little better than that," he said, signaling the engineer to restart the cartridge. He did, and Joey tried again:

> "Hitting a cue meaning I talk over the instrumental portion of the song until the vocalist begins, and, uh, by the time she starts singing, I should have shut up with what I have to say, and the closer you are, the better a disc jockey you are, and now, ladies and gentlemen, Brenda Lee sings 'I'm...'"

> *I'm sorry...*

> "Agggh! Two tries! I'm gonna try it again, pal!"[58]

55 Glass, *Music by Philip Glass*, 44.
56 Sklar, *Rocking America*, 168.
57 Fisher, *Something in the Air*, 202.
58 Fong-Torres, *The Hits Just Keep On Coming*, 121.

With this practice in mind, let us return one last time to the beginning of *Einstein on the Beach*. The longest talk-up George Michael ever attempted – and it was a stunt, the kind of thing only a top-ranked AM deejay could get away with – was during the 28-second instrumental prelude to Harold Melvin and the Blue Notes' six-and-a-half-minute soul epic, "The Love I Lost." (He had enough time to tell the entire story of his first marriage.) The opening 15 minutes or so of *Einstein* present a bass line, an organ "intro" which begins, in performance, well before the audience has settled itself in to watch "the show." As with the radio, we tune in to a program already in progress. By the time the chorus enters, singing beat numbers and then solfége syllables, two onstage figures have been talking at the audience for quite some time. Although they are both women, they are dressed as men; they each sit at a desk; their voices are highly amplified.[59] Who are they supposed to be? Well, Albert Einstein was a man, of course, and thus most commentators have interpreted them as Einsteins, and their busy hand motions as calculation. Certainly one of the women (in every one of Wilson's productions so far she has been African-American), whose text consists entirely of numbers, is miming the use of an adding machine. The other might well be typing – which would be appropriate, since the text she is reciting was actually typed out by Christopher Knowles:

> It could be Franky it could be very fresh and cleann. So it could be
> those ones. So if
>
> You cash the bank of world traveler from 10 months ago.
> Doo you remember! Honz the bus driver... , Well put the red
> ball blue ball two black and white balls. And Honz pushed on his brakes
>   and
>
> the four balls went down to that. And Honz said. "Get those four
> balls aw ay from the gearshift."[60]

This may be one of the longest "talk-ups" ever heard in New York City; George Michael was using a stopwatch to time his intros in 1976, but one hardly needs a sweep second hand to measure out the immense timespan that these two "announcers" have to fill. Like Joey Reynolds, but much, *much* more slowly, they spin out a self-reflexive repeating cycle of words that has the effect of filling up every second of the "dead air" before the first "song" comes in. Around their text, Glass's music follows its own additive logic, which is clearly *not* that of the American Top 40. But there are some interesting parallels in sound. We already know Knowles's emotional connection to doo-wop and vocal harmony groups: the Box Tops, the Jackson 5, the Nitty Gritty Dirt Band, and, especially, Frankie Valli and the Four Seasons; all of these groups sang in close harmony over simple repeating bass lines

59 Maria Shevtsova, *Robert Wilson*, New York, Routledge, 2007, 92.
60 *Einstein* libretto, 2 (Knee Play 1).

– none as minimal as the bare bones six-five-one progression that underpins Glass's Knee Play 1, but in the same ball park, at least. *Einstein*'s nimbus of accompanying numbers, recited on stage and sung in the pit, refer to the math that underlies theoretical physics, of course, but also have their direct analog in the constant counting down of hit records and chart positions (**"FOUR** FOUR *four* four") that so fired Christopher Knowles's AM radio imagination. Even the use of SATB chorus chanting numbers and syllables has its counterpart in the flow of Top 40 radio, which was articulated by repeated choral jingles that delivered the station's name, number, and call letters; a deejay's name; or one of the station's advertising slogans *("more music! on W-A-B-C!")* in the style of up-tempo, harmonized vocal jazz.[61]

Analysis: *Einstein on the Beach,* Act III, scene 1 (Trial 2/Prison)

We are now ready to consider *Einstein* as an aesthetic whole, putting Knowles's textual fascination with the sound of AM radio in counterpoint with Glass's music and Wilson's staging. Listening to this robustly commercial third voice (or voice-*over*, as it may be) often frustrates epistemic closure; it can pull our decoding of the opera's "message" away from Wilson and Glass's tendency, as reflexively left-of-center avant-gardists, to mythologize their alienation from consumer capitalism and instrumental rationality.[62] Such interpretive tension is strong in the reading I will propose of the opera's most overtly "political" section, the trial sequence in Act III, scene 1. This scene, designated in Wilson's plan as "Trial 2/Prison," is designed to rhyme visually and thematically with the previous Trial in Act I, scene 2. In both, a lawyer, played by Sheryl Sutton in the original production, addresses the judge and jury using sections of a text from Knowles titled "Mr. Bojangles." In the second Trial scene, a witness, Lucinda Childs, also testifies, using a text of her own creation, "The Air-Conditioned Supermarket," giving the whole the character of an extended cross-examination. After both the witness and the lawyer act out a complex series of symbolic behaviors, the witness takes her place behind a set of prison bars, reciting another Knowles text, "I Feel the Earth Move."

Who is on trial in Act III, scene 1? Certainly not Albert Einstein, whatever some critics of the opera might believe.[63] In the 1976 production, the witness, sporting a revolutionary beret and trench coat while brandishing an assault weapon, was a dead ringer for Patty Hearst, whose kidnapping, arrest, trial, and conviction

---

61   The sound of Top 40 radio jingles can be traced back to one company, Production Advertising Music Service (PAMS), based in Dallas, TX. Producer Bill Meeks effectively invented the station jingle in the 1950s, and by the 1960s, the symbiotic relationship between PAMS and WABC, which had first call on all new PAMS jingles, dominated the sound of AM radio. WABC broke off its relationship with PAMS in late 1975, and started using a new set of station jingles in October 1975 created by a Dallas competitor, JAM Creative Productions. JAM now owns the rights to all PAMS jingles, and sound samples and a detailed company history can be found at www.pams. com. For the relationship of WABC, PAMS, and JAM, as well as dozens of station jingles, see www.musicradio77.com/jingles.html.

62   Lipman, "Einstein's Long March," 335–336.

63   See Lipman, *op. cit.,* 336, and Holmberg, *The Theatre of Robert Wilson,* 56.

neatly framed the two-year span during which *Einstein* was conceived, written, rehearsed, and premiered. But it appears that Wilson's indictment is more general than that. During the first part of her "testimony," the witness, dressed in a white silk dress, is instructed to writhe on and around a large, glowing white platform that serves, during this sequence, as a bed. The text, written by Lucinda Childs, is thus transformed from anti-consumer anecdote into erotic reverie:

> I was in this prematurely air-conditioned supermarket
> and there were all these aisles and there were all these bathing caps that you could buy
> which had these kind of Fourth of July plumes on them
> they were red and yellow and blue
> I wasn't tempted to buy one
> but I was reminded of the fact that I had been avoiding the beach.[64]

As I have noted elsewhere, the air-conditioned supermarket was in fact ground zero for consumption as a new state of consciousness in post-war America; market researchers reported as early as the mid-1950s that women tended to drift through store aisles in a "mild hypnoid trance," the repetitive abundance of consumer objects – plumed bathing caps in a range of attractive colors, for instance – having the same tranquilizing effect on them as the new class of benzodiazepines (Librium, Valium) doctors were just starting to prescribe for anxiety and depression.[65]

Childs's character actually struggles against this reading – she is anxious to assure us that she was *not* tempted by all those products on display – but by the 1970s, the linkage between overconsumption, mass media, and curdled sexuality within the (fading) society of affluence had become a staple of leftist social critique.[66] Wilson's campy staging plays up the free-floating eroticism of consumption; in this sequence the lanky Childs resembles no one so much as debauched bombshell Ann-Margret writhing in ecstasy on the same lily-white bed in Ken Russell's 1975 film version of *Tommy* by The Who, a pop-operatic text precisely coeval with *Einstein on the Beach*. Like Nora, Tommy's abusive mother, the witness is judged for her fantasies and found wanting, as Wilson's *mise-en-scène* takes a rare turn to the didactic. In short order, the dancer-witness: 1) rises from the bed, and begins to imitate the gestures of two stereotypical prisoners in striped uniforms; 2) puts on a long A-line skirt, and executes a quick soft shoe with a male partner; 3) dons a trench coat, discarding the skirt underneath for pants; 4) picks up

---

64 *Einstein* libretto, 8 (Act III, scene 2).

65 Fink, *Repeating Ourselves*, pp. 75–79.

66 The most dramatic examples come from Wilson Bryan Key's floridly paranoid investigations into "subliminal seduction" in advertising imagery – in titles like *Subliminal Seduction*, New York, Prentice-Hall, 1973, and *The Clam-Plate Orgy*, New York, Signet, 1980, he scoured printed advertisements that depicted seemingly innocent things like plumed bathing caps, looking for (and, of course, finding) an overload of hidden turn-ons like penises, naked women, and copulating couples.

a carbine and threatens the audience with it, again moving in sync with the prisoners behind her; 5) drops the trench coat in favor of a tailored blouse; 6) puts on and then takes off a set of manacles; and 7) finally produces a large, brightly colored lollipop and walks offstage. It is hardly a surprise when she reappears behind the prison bars – she has just made the case against herself, in mime: within the consumer society, sexualized fantasies of abundance (1) undermine the authentic self, which we are encouraged to put on and take off like a series of costumes (2) (3) (5); trapped in a meaningless dance (2), we are prey to spasms of "liberatory" violence (4), yet fundamentally unfree (1) (3) (6); attracted to things that are instantly gratifying but bad for us, we regress to the infantile (7).

Let's stay with this admittedly blunt reading for a moment. Wilson's staging demands that the witness repeat her single paragraph of testimony over 30 times; the iterations are not identical, but build systematically, peaking in speed and intensity when the assault weapon appears in her hands. Underneath, Glass's

Music Example 1.1   Additive process in *Einstein on the Beach*, Act III, scene 1 (Trial 2/Prison), underpinning Lucinda Childs's speech, "I was in this prematurely air-conditioned supermarket…" Credit: *Einstein on the Beach* by Philip Glass ©1976 Dunvagen Music Publishers Inc. Used by Permission.

ensemble cycles four times through a complex additive melodic process (see Music Example 1.1). It is difficult not to interpret this overdose of musical repetition and accumulation as the *how* underpinning Wilson's staged diagnosis of *what* is wrong with a technological society that fashions malleable, empty human figurines like Patricia Hearst, *aka* the witness. From this perspective, the daily barrage of advertising-driven repetition in the mass media seems little different than the exotic brainwashing techniques that reputedly turned the heiress into a revolutionary. If that sounds a little melodramatic, it's not out of line with the way people talked in the mid-1970s; sample, for instance, the absolutist position taken by former advertising executive Jerry Mander in his *Four Arguments for the Elimination of Television*, published in 1978:

> No matter who is in control, the medium remains confined to its cold, narrow culverts of hyperactive information. Nothing and no one can change this, nor can anyone change how television's technical limits confine awareness. As the person who gazes at streams becomes streamlike, so as we watch television we inexorably evolve into creatures whose bodies and minds become television-like.[67]

Mander doesn't say anything about AM radio, which is, of course, quite different as a medium from television. But in the 1970s, both epitomized the repetitive structures characteristic of advertising-supported broadcasting, in which hypnotically flowing program segments were rhythmically interrupted by "technical events" like cross-cutting, zooming, voiceover, and special effects – the televisual equivalent to the elaborate techniques of audio montage developed by Top 40 radio in service to its own commercial-driven aesthetic of imperceptible overlap.[68]

Is that it, then? Is it the media and consumer society that are on trial in *Einstein*'s Act III, scene 2? Wilson, when asked by an interviewer from the French literary magazine *Tel Quel* to explain *Einstein*'s scenario, snapped, "I do not have a message. What I do is an architectural arrangement."[69] Like most avant-gardists in post-war consumer society, Wilson and Glass have consistently positioned epistemic openness in their work against the closed, manipulative structures of advertising and mass media: "If you didn't have that space there...there wouldn't be anywhere for the viewer to place himself. In that case, it's like what you end up with on commercials. That's why commercials end up looking more like propaganda than art."[70] But it is, paradoxically, thanks largely to Knowles – a naïve devotee of the most relentlessly manipulative commercial

67 Jerry Mander, *Four Arguments for the Elimination of Television*, New York, Quill, 1978, 355.
68 Mander, *op. cit.*, 303.
69 Shevtsova, *Robert Wilson*, 52.
70 Philip Glass in Richard Kostelanetz, *Writings on Glass. Essays, Interviews, Criticism*, New York, Schirmer, 1997, 141.

medium ever devised, so immersed in Top 40's flow that his typings transcribe with fanatic, literal-minded precision the way deejays talked up the hits and read ad copy – that the second Trial scene of *Einstein* avoids becoming the same kind of propaganda, but on the anti-commercial side. It avoids this fate by *not* making, or at least, not making with one, unified voice, what Gablik would correctly have disparaged as the "tasteful choice" to disparage media, advertising, and (a feminized) consumer society.

Notably, Wilson continues Act III, scene 1 by assigning portions of Knowles's "Mr. Bojangles" typing to Sheryl Sutton's lawyer, even though she is repeating Childs-the-witness's elaborate play with clothing, gun, and lollipop:

> This song wear a black and white then this has been
> This about the things on the table
> This will be counting that you allways wanted has been very very tempting
> So stop
> Hey Mr. Bojangles
> Hey Mr. Bojangles
> Hey Mr. Bojangles

This disjointed text's vocabulary of desire, temptation, and abundance echoes Childs's (that's undoubtedly why Wilson placed it here), but Knowles, of course, does not intend to present himself as resistant to the mediated blandishments of the consumer society. In fact, the rest of this particular typing is filled with classic commercial AM radio material, including call-outs to WABC staples like the Beatles ("that major star/Paul McCartney") and some niftily styled song dedications ("This has been addressed to all those girls/All this one has been very American"). Even the repeated injunctions to "stop" function less as semantic negation of desire and more like the performative articulation at the end of a deejay voiceover, followed directly by the vocal hook of a familiar pop song. Wilson could not have been unaware how perfectly the textual image of "Mr. Bojangles," an old man Jerry Jeff Walker met in a New Orleans jail cell who would "dance for you…with silver hair, a ragged shirt, and baggy pants/The old soft shoe," could be made to match the dramatic action of the scene. (He used this special effect very sparingly.)[71] In modern performances, the lawyer begins her soft shoe dance, partnered by a male dancer in the default Einstein costume of shirt and baggy pants, precisely where the downbeat at the end of the talk-up ("So stop/Hey Mr. Bojangles") would suggest.

---

71 "Usually in theater the visual repeats the verbal…I don't think that way…Once in a while I let the visual align with the verbal, but usually not." Wilson in Holmberg, *The Theatre of Robert Wilson*, 53.

Thus the stage is set for a direct clash of values: either the witness and (her?) lawyer are guilty – they *have* been avoiding the beach – or they are, like Christopher Knowles, completely innocent, caught up in the joy of belonging to a huge, if imaginary community of willing listeners, the WABC "family" that was as real to him as his new friends at the Byrd-Hoffman School. Knowles's final text for the opera, "I Feel the Earth Move," brings the two together, listing both the deejays on WABC and some of the actual performers he had worked with in workshops and productions over the preceding two years, mixed up, as they doubtless were in his imagination, with the artists and hit songs whose comings and goings he tracked so carefully:

So this could be where if the earth moves or not. So here we go.
I feel the earth move under my feet. I feel the tumbling down tumbling down.
I feel if
Some ostriches are a like into a satchel. Some like them. I went to the window and wanted to draw the earth. So if David Cassidy tells you all you when to go into this on onto a meat. So where would a red dress. So this will get some gas. So this could This would be some all of my friends. Cindy Jay Steve Julia Robyn Rick Kit and Liz. So this will get some gas. So this would get any energy. So if you know what some like into were. So
[…]
So about one song.
I FEEL THE EARTH MOVE
CAROLE KING
So that was a song this what it could in the Einstein On The Beach with a trial to jail. But a court where it could happen. So if David Casidy tells you all of you to go on get going get going get going. So this could be in like on WABC New York
[…]
JAY REYNOLDS from midnight to 6 AM.
HARRY HARRISON from 6 AM to 10 AM.
So heres what in like of WABC
[…]
JAY REYNOLDS from midnight to 6 AM.
HARRY HARRISON from 6 AM to 10 AM.
RON LUNDY from 10 AM to 2 PM.
DAN INGRAM from 2 PM to 6 PM.
I feel the earth move from WABC
[…][72]

---

72 *Einstein* libretto, 9 (Act III, Scene 1).

It should be easy to recognize that almost every phrase in this text bears the imprint of what we can now identify as the characteristic "AM radio voice": note the pervasive interstitials, including periodic station announcements, some clearly designed to move out of a song ("I feel the earth move from WABC") and some to lead in ("So…So about one song/I FEEL THE EARTH MOVE"). Knowles even captures a bit of the quick, caustic wit for which popular WABC deejays like Dan Ingram were famous, deftly turning a paean to sexual satisfaction into a joke about male inadequacy by adding two well-chosen syllables: "So this could be where if the earth moves *or not.* So here we go").[73] The text exhibits exemplary forward momentum at all times, moving easily between pulverized fragments of ad copy ("So this will get some gas. So this would get any energy") and the echolalic whipping up of verbal excitement around top artists and their music ("So if David Casidy tells you all of you to go on get going get going get going"). If we think of the opera as a Top 40 radio broadcast, Glass's music functions perfectly, if unintentionally, within it: Knowles's chatty "I Feel the Earth Move" is recited over a four-chord instrumental vamp ending on a local dominant, which allows it to function in the work's larger structure as an extended talk-up to the dramatic entrance of the full ensemble, led by a solo vocalist, to kick off the next scene, the very rocking and rolling Dance 2 (see Music Example 1.2).

Signing off

To think of *Einstein on the Beach* as a Top 40 radio broadcast is not, of course, to undermine any pretentions it might have as a critique of consumerism and mass media. But it must, at the very least, make those pretentions more complex and nuanced. Both Glass and Wilson have self-identified as reductionists, their minimalism gainfully employed in keeping open an aesthetic space where audiences, freed from the manipulative over-signification of mass art and popular media, can be given back the freedom to construct meanings for themselves. Carl Andre justified the "blankness" of his readymade sculptures by noting that, in the society of affluence, *any* art required "some space that suggests there is a significant exhaustion. When signs occupy every surface, then there is no place for the new signs."[74] Wilson and others have conscripted Knowles into this formal program, but that seems to me to be only half right. Knowles's contributions to *Einstein* are indeed, as language, formally radical, but they have an immersive, not ascetic (*askesis*, "emptying out") character. Knowles's seamless flow of radio chatter helps *Einstein* enact what for Frederic Jameson is *the* characteristic mutation of space in contemporary art. Abandoning the empty, Cartesian grid of modernism, with a detached, measuring subject at the center – a pretty good description of

---

73   Emphasis added, of course. According to program director Rick Sklar's memoir of WABC's glory days, *Rocking America*, Ingram, "whose sharp sense of satire could be set off by a record title or a line in a radio commercial," was responsible for more station complaints than all the other deejays combined (1984, 169).

74   Quoted in Christopher Lasch, *The Minimal Self*, New York, Norton, 1985, 149.

Music Example 1.2 "I Feel the Earth Move" text as talk-up: Instrumental "vamp" (end of scene 1) followed by highlighted entrance of solo female vocalist (beginning of scene 2) in *Einstein on the Beach*, Act III. Credit: *Einstein on the Beach* by Philip Glass ©1976 Dunvagen Music Publishers Inc. Used by Permission.

both Einstein's world and *Einstein*'s stage pictures of it – the new, postmodern space is filled to overflowing by "barrages of immediacy" that shatter distance, overwhelm subjectivity, and foreclose perspective. For Jameson it is the unseen and un(re)presentable forces of global capital that warp and ultimately destroy the legibility of shared human space.[75] But for persons on the autism spectrum, the

75 Fredric Jameson, *Postmodernism, Or the Logic of Late Capitalism*, Durham, Duke University Press, 1991, 410.

"illegibility" of the social is not just an artifact of life under capitalism. It is a fact of mental life itself.

Jameson traced the "cultural logic of late capitalism" through a diverse collection of confusing, often overwhelming postmodern aesthetic structures: the flatness of Andy Warhol's silkscreened canvases; the careening plot of David Lynch's neo-noir thriller, *Something Wild*; most famously, the incomprehensibly shaped atrium between the four identical glass towers of the Westin Bonaventure Hotel, in downtown Los Angeles. In art music, he pointed to the listener's experience of "John Cage, but also the synthesis of classical and 'popular' styles found in composers like Phil Glass and Terry Riley."[76] The alchemy of *Einstein on the Beach* thus rests in a basic dialectical conflict between modern and postmodern ideals of representation. Wilson's neo-modernist *mise-en-scène*, which, as Maria Shevtsova notes, is akin, in its pellucid visual clarity, to "an architectural arrangement in space and time," is counterbalanced by Glass's funky underscoring, which uses repetition and process to construct a postmodern sound space filled with whirring immediacy and disorienting tricks of harmonic perspective.[77] Although Wilson sponsored Knowles's participation in *Einstein*, his young librettist's radio-derived texts of the 1970s, as spoken aloud in *Einstein*, shift the work's center of gravity. Knowles's words and Glass's music blend together into a simulacrum of "the steady beat of the car radio," Jameson's shorthand aural trope for postmodern media flow, into which, thanks to the "semiotic bombardment" of "sheer repetition," modern art's "textual referent has disappeared."[78] In effect, although *Einstein* has rarely been on the radio, the radio is always "on" in *Einstein*. Sometimes, when the signal is particularly strong, its sound can drown out the work-character of the whole assemblage.

Sometimes, you can hear the earth move.

So that was one song this what it could in the Einstein On The Beach with a trial
to jail. But a court were it could happen. So when David Casidy tells you all of you to go on get going get going. So this one in like on WABC New York.

So heres what in like of WABC…
I feel the earth move from WABC …
This could be true on WABC…

76 Jameson, *Postmodernism*, 1.
77 Shertsova, *Robert Wilson*, p. 53; Fink, *Repeating Ourselves*, pp. 120–28.
78 Fredric Jameson, "Reification and Utopia in Mass Culture." *Social Text* 1 (Winter 1979), pp. 138-39.

Appendix A: "It Could Be Franky": *Einstein*'s creative genesis and the reign of Frankie Valli on WABC, 1974–1975. Chart data from musicradio77.com and Hoffmann 2015; *Einstein* chronology from Glass 1987

Einstein on the Beach	*WABC*
Spring 1974 – Wilson and Glass begin meetings about a new theater piece (Knowles is there, sometimes). Wilson shows Glass writings by Knowles; Glass demurs, unable to imagine creating vocal lines out of them	
	6 September 1974 – George Michael replaces Bruce Morrow in the evenings, creating DJ line-up referenced by Knowles in *Einstein,* Act II, scene 2
Late Fall 1974 – basic structure of *Einstein on the Beach* is set; Wilson begins work on visual "libretto"	
	14 January 1975 – Franky Valli, "My Eyes Adored You" enters WABC rotation at position 30
	4 February 1975 – "My Eyes Adored You" reaches WABC top ten at position 8
Spring 1975 – Wilson completes visual sketchbook; Glass begins composition of *Einstein* score	*26 February – 11 March 1975* – "My Eyes Adored You" holds #1 position on WABC playlist
	13 May 1975 – Valli's "Swearin' to God" enters WABC rotation at position 17 (though not in numbered rotation, "My Eyes Adored You" is still being played as a "recurrent" chart hit)
	17 June 1975 – "Swearin' to God" reaches #1 position on WABC playlist
	***July–September 1975* – "Swearin' to God" remains in WABC rotation**
	***28 October 1975* – The Four Seasons' "Who Loves You" enters WABC rotation at position 8**
November 1975 – Glass finishes score for *Einstein*	*25 November 1975* – "Who Loves You" reaches position 5 in WABC rotation
December 1975 – *Einstein* rehearsals begin; chorus's numbers and solfége syllables become sung text, while texts by Knowles and others are incorporated into opera as "voice-overs"	*9 December 1975* – "Who Loves You" still in rotation, but dropping; Frankie Valli, "Our Day Will Come" enters rotation at position 20
	20 February 1976 – The Four Seasons' "December 1963 (Oh What a Night)" enters WABC rotation at position 30

(Continued)

Einstein on the Beach	WABC
	March 1976 – "December 1963 (Oh What a Night)" holds #1 position on WABC playlist for entire month
May–June 1976 – break in *Einstein* rehearsals	*June 1976* – No songs by Frankie Valli or the Four Seasons in WABC rotation after this point
25 July 1976 – *Einstein* premiere at Avignon Festival	

Appendix B: Key popular music references in Christopher Knowles's texts for *Einstein on the Beach*

Scene	Text	Pop music reference	WABC context
Knee Play 1	It could be Franky	Frankie Valli/The Four Seasons	See Appendix A
Act I, scene 1 (Train)	I could be cry like a baby I'll be there	(?) The Box Tops, "Cry Like A Baby" (1968) (?) The Jackson 5, "I'll Be There" (1970)	March–May 1968 September–December 1970
Act I, scene 2 (Trial 1)	Mr Bojangles	The Nitty Gritty Dirt Band, "Mr. Bojangles" (1971)	February–March 1971
	So this could be reflections for Christopher Knowles-John Lennon Paul McCartney-George Harrison	The Beatles	
Knee Play 2	SWEARIN TO GOD WHO LOVES YOU FRANKIE VALLI THE FOUR SEASONS	Frankie Valli, "Swearin' to God" (1975) The Four Seasons, "Who Loves You" (1975)	See Appendix A
Act III, scene 1 (Trial 2)	The song I just heard is turning (The song in where) … Tis thing This will be the time that you come This has been addressed to all those girls All this one has been very American So stop	The Nitty Gritty Dirt Band, "Mr. Bojangles" (1971)	February–March 1971

(Continued)

Scene	Text	Pop music reference	WABC context
	When you see when it was it has been When you Hey Mr Bojangles Hey Mr Bojangles Hey Mr Bojangles Say this That call you Piggy in the sky Like up in the … This is written John Lennon for from Christopher Knowles' actions where that (major) star Paul McCartney George Harrison The peoples Where I this has also worked This has been reflections Has been lucky as the sky so Christopher Knowles and the Beatles so so	The Beatles, "I Am the Walrus" (1967) The Beatles, "Lucy in the Sky with Diamonds" (1967)	
Act III, scene 1 (Trial 2), con't.	I feel the earth move … I feel the tumbling down tumbling down … This will be doing the facts of David Cassidy of were in this case of feelings. That could make you happy. So this could be where if the earth move or not. So here we go. I feel the earth move under my feet. I feel tumbling down tumbling down. I feel if I FEEL THE EARTH MOVE CAROLE KING So this one in like on WABC New York … JAY REYNOLDS from midnight to 6 00. HARRY HARRISON So heres what in like of WABC … JAY REYNOLDS from midnight to 6 AM HARRY HARRISON from 6 AM to L I feel the earth move from WABC …	Carole King, "I Feel the Earth Move" (1971) David Cassidy, "Cherish" (1971)	June–December 1971 November– December 1971 WABC weekly schedule (as of 9 September 1974)

(*Continued*)

Scene	Text	Pop music reference	WABC context
	JAY REYNOLDS from midnight to 6 AM. HARRY HARRISON from 6 AM to 10 AM. RON LUNDY from 10 AM to 2 PM. DAN INGRAM from 2 PM to aga9 JAY REYNOLDS from midnight to 6 AM. HARRY HARRISON from 6 AM This could be true on WABC. JAY REYNOLDS WABC. JAY REYNOLDS from midnight to 6 AM. HARRY HARRISON from 6 AM to 10 AM. RON LUNDY from 10 AM to 2 PM. DAN INGRAM from 2 PM to 6 PM. GEORGE MICHAEL from 6 PM to 10 PM. CHUCK LEONARD from 10 PM to midnight. JOHNNY DONOVAN from 10 PM to 3 AM. STEVE-O-BRION from 2 PM to 6 PM. JOHNNY DONOVAN from 6 PM to 10 PM. CHUCK LEONARD from 3 AM to 5 AM. JOHNNY DONOVAN from 6 PM to 1OPM. STEVE-O-BRION from 4 30 AM to 6 AM STEVE-O-BRION from 4 30 AM to 6 AM JOHNNY DONOVAN from 4 30 AM to 6 AM		

2 Sous les pavés, la plage

Johannes Birringer

Après Mai/Something in the Air

When the reviews came out after Olivier Assayas's *Après Mai* (2013), they stated that the filmmaker looks back at the days following the events of May 1968 – and at his own youth – with a fine-tuned, delicate wit but ideas about the revolution, and the explosive tendencies that were "in the air," get lost in a nostalgic, elegiac glow. Looking back at the late 1960s and early 1970s may generate the same dilemma for me, as the distinctions between revolution and avant-garde art get blurry. I had only just begun to concern myself with performance, hearing and reading about it, so how do I remember the theatrical avant-garde that stretched our imagination; how do I connect the dots between living, in history in the making, and The Living Theatre? Between Grotowski's poor theater and Tadeusz Kantor's theater of death, or between the Judson Church in Greenwich Village and other downtown New York artists such as Robert Wilson and Philip Glass, following in the footsteps of the adventurous Cage-Rauschenberg-Cunningham generation – Rauschenberg having just mounted, alongside Billy Klüver, one of the most exorbitant and scintillating cross-over events in the history of art and technology, *Nine Evenings: Theatre and Engineering* (at the 69th Regiment Armory, 1966)?[1]

How do we reflect back on something we did not witness in the first venues or fields, when performance, sculpture, or cinema for that matter, had moved into the "expanded field" and become infinitely malleable, hybrid, and scrambled?[2] And do failed revolutions inevitably generate nostalgia and an elegiac mood? I imagine I was like Gilles, *Après Mai*'s protagonist, an earnest 17-year-old in the final years at a suburban *lycée* and on the way to art school. But I'm not sure. I

---

1 Collaborations included Steve Paxton, Deborah and Alex Hay, John Cage, Yvonne Rainer, Lucinda Childs, Robert Whitman, David Tudor, Öyvind Fahlström, and numerous engineers. See Johannes Birringer, *Performance, Technology and Science*, New York, PAJ Publications, 2009, 75–83.
2 Rosalind Krauss's influential essay, "Sculpture in the Expanded Field," October 8 (1979), 30–44, begins with a reference to an earthwork and wonders about the surprising things that during the 1960s and 1970s had come to be called sculpture.

was too young to even understand the notion of a theatrical avant-garde, to ponder scientific-technical, synesthetic experiments of the kind the *Nine Evenings* of multi-media art, dance, film, sound, sculpture, and performance set in motion. When I saw the retrospective exhibition *9 Evenings Reconsidered: Art, Theatre, and Engineering, 1966*, mounted by the MIT List Visual Arts Center (in 2006) as a critical homage to the original event (featuring records of 1966 and the testimonies of many contributors, collected in the catalogue edited by curator Catherine Morris), I was mesmerized and agitated in ways that I had not imagined possible, regarding the matter of such archeological arrangements. That record of avant-garde live art quite likely offers a compensatory role for me. It carries me back, after many years of having worked in performance art, to my adolescence – to confession time and a perverted religious upbringing, to necessary dreams of unfulfilled yearning. And, of course, wouldn't one want to know what those yearnings were, exactly?[3]

As an exploration of my unconscious, the theatrical avant-garde may not be the best guide, but I recall the repressions of guilt slowly unravelling when my oldest brother dragged me out to demonstrations in Frankfurt, where Joseph Beuys happened to perform in front of the city hall with a horse, orchestra cymbals, and a tape recorder, and on to occupied university halls where Adorno, Marcuse, Sartre, and Lenin were debated while Robert Wilson, unbeknownst to me, created *The Life and Times of Sigmund Freud* (1969), a few years prior to *The Life and Times of Joseph Stalin* (1973) and some other undefinable, muted operas, *The King of Spain* (1969), *Deafman Glance* (1970), and *KA MOUNTAIN* ... (1972), the latter quite literally staged in the mountains of Shiraz. Interestingly, this excursion into pre-revolutionary Iran hardly ever gets mentioned in the expanding literature on Wilson's oeuvre. It's gotten lost in the haze.

And however puzzled I may have been about the comparison, Beuys and Andy Warhol were indeed contemporaries. Superficial pop art and consumer capitalism, however, were the enemy and the US imperialist war in Vietnam a constant cause for protest. I certainly associated Beuys, when I first witnessed him in performance, with a political-artistic vanguard suffused with the phantasmagoric aftermath of 1968 (which for me was also Woodstock, sexual revolution, and in the German context, a painful rupture with the country's post-war trauma about its fascist past – what came to be known as *bleierne Zeit* [leaden time]). Beuys, ex-pilot, war survivor, and shaman of action art, pointed out the significance of energetic presence, and of the symbolic potency of materials, even if his preferred substances – fat, felt, honey, margarine, iron, copper, and so on – seemed quaint to us. All the same, his shamanism played dangerously with

---

3   Frank Witzel's disturbing new novel, *Die Erfindung der Roten Armee Fraktion durch einen manisch-depressiven Teenager im Sommer 1969* [*The Invention of the RAF by a manic depressive teenager in the summer of 1969*] (Berlin, Matthes, and Seitz, 2015), is taking me right back into the emaciating realm of the hallucinatory but of course not only imaginary claustrophobia of revolutionary terror as well as teenage angst.

the phantasmagorias – *Show your Wound* (1974–75) was one of the pertinent titles of his installations.

Classificatory terminologies of "post-," are troubling, and of course I remember the post-World War II era in Europe as a complete mess, my protected childhood a lie built on denial and the Marshall Plan, the Cold War soon becoming the overbearing existing-real. Old and new wounds opened up. The defeat of the Paris Commune caused some deep leftist traumas, and yet there was a stubborn revolutionary militancy in the air, in Germany, Italy, France, and other places (if no longer in Prague). The texts of the Situationist International were passed around in my school, tactics of the *dérive* were passionately debated, graffiti slogans sprayed onto walls. The entire hallucinatory rebel side of it more or less dissolved a few years later with the suicides of the Baader-Meinhof-led Red Army Faction (RAF) in the Stammheim prison (1977). The cobblestones of the uprising, so poetically evoked in the Situationist slogan *Sous les pavés, la plage*, had been torn up from the street but the police, the state machine, and the courts had held their line.

"The beach," then, for me was not associated with Einstein but with uprising, and also of course with the power of imagination, with a vision promising that such an uprising was possible. The revolutionary 1960s, though now largely forgotten, embraced utopian energies that manifested themselves in perplexing architectures and audio-visual cultural spaces, including the "theatre of images," which had not been heard or seen before (just think of Xenakis's polytopes), and could not be perceived in existing terms of theater, opera, and dance.[4] How can "the beach" be reclaimed as radical cultural memory or myth if, as I now realize, it may already have been too late to reconnect the trance opera with the political and cultural context I evoked above? By too late I mean 1984, when I encountered *Einstein on the Beach* at the Brooklyn Academy of Music (I didn't attend the original 1976 Avignon version but the recreation) *after* already having watched the various fairy-tales Wilson directed/assembled for his incomplete 12-hour Olympic *the CIVIL warS,* in the early 1980s. By the time I saw *Einstein*, I had already dismissed Wilson and labored to comprehend the emphatic and uncanny impact Pina Bausch's tanztheater had on my generation of performers.

Knee Play: Les Revenants

I patiently watch a video of the 2012–13 recreation of *Einstein on the Beach*, (performed and filmed at Théâtre du Châtelet in 2014). I am 20 minutes

---

4   The expression "theatre of images" was originally coined by Bonnie Marranca in her book of the same title (1977) which revolves around artists who exemplified a new direction – Robert Wilson (with *A Letter for Queen Victoria*), Richard Foreman (Ontological-Hysteric Theater), Lee Breuer (Mabou Mines) – their work suggesting a decisive move away from having theater founded exclusively in theatrical traditions and ideas, to a theater more interested in visual arts and dance. For Xenakis's work on musical design and multi-media architectures, see Brandon LaBelle, *Background Noise: Perspectives on Sound Art*, New York, Continuum, 2007, 183–93.

into the prolog – "And these are the days my friends and these are the days.....65...37... 9...2..." – when I notice the slow arrival, one at a time, of the chorus. They are just like *les Revenants* (The Returned), the walking ghouls, right out of the chilling French drama written and directed by Fabrice Gobert, now shown on British television. The chorus zombies move onto the downstage area, one with a contorted smile, the other with a wrist turned in a twisted way, the third with oddly angled shoulders, the next with an arm extended out; their faces mimic a parade of the strangely curious undead. Looking in different directions, they gaze at the audience which has not settled down yet, still chatting. They will soon sing numbers and solfège syllables for close to five hours, jutting their elbows, twiddling their fingers, walking off and on in strange goose steps.

I'm prepared now to question rigid assumptions about Wilson's apolitical formalism and the widely admired, extraordinary painterly directorial craft with which he has created the vernacular American sublime of his grandiose *kabuki* fairy-tales, servicing bourgeois spectacle audiences that flock to opera houses to be titillated. I also wonder about ways to re-imagine Glass's late minimalist music and the intricate rhythmic machine he composed (after *Music in Twelve Parts* [1971–74] and during *Another Look at Harmony* [1975–1977], when he began combining harmonic progression with the additive rhythmic structure he had developed to produce a new overall structure) through the speed and volume of the sound travel and tempi conjoined to Wilson's theater of expansive *tableaux vivants*, and Lucinda Childs's ice-cold, austere mathematical minimalism, the concentrated movement along the "three diagonals" which Wilson had suggested to Childs.[5]

What does this psychedelic trance machine tell us about its surfaces or its spatial volumes, its "field dances," train and court scenes, its weightless dream scenes, its spiraling flux of movement, its drowning by numbers? How strange that a photograph seems to capture relative motion trajectories – Lucinda Childs traveling on a vertical, slightly diagonal axis down and backwards up the stage as if evoking the arrival of an oncoming (or departing) train, yet a train struck in the groove like a needle, the smoke/light corridor on her right

5   In Rachel Donadio's review, "Paris Embraces 'Einstein' Again" (*New York Times*, January 3, 2014). Lucinda Childs is quoted as saying that she recalls Wilson's original direction: "His instructions were very free. He said, 'Can you just use those three diagonals?'" I should point out that the 1976 choreography was done by Andrew de Groat; at that time Wilson and Glass worked with a mixed ensemble of singers/dancers/performers, whereas the 1984 revival at BAM had Childs involved, writing a monolog, dance and doing the choreography for her professional Dance Company; the music was performed by the Philip Glass Ensemble, along with professional soloists and chorus (the original 1976 cast consisted of a mix of amateurs and professionals, with singers dancing and dancers singing, a testimony to the collaborative culture of New York's 1960s and 70s downtown avant-garde scene). For an intricate reading of the 2012–13 re-performance focusing on musical/spatial temporality in *Einstein*, see Susan Broadhurst, "Einstein on the Beach: A Study in Temporality," *Performance Research* 17:5 (2012), 34–40.

flowing away into a different diagonal, the actual lateral theater train not having appeared yet from stage left (it will slowly emerge and re-emerge three
times, or was it six times)? How could *Einstein* have wanted us to enter into it
back in the 70s, or later on during its revival history (1984, 1992, 2012–14)?
(Figure 2.1)

I wish to briefly review the directing of the temporal object of this experimental
opera under the light of the strange paradance or paradox of motions both abstract
and narrative. The surrealist dream and abstraction of space-time, the addition and
repetition, the mutation and irresolution, are unmistakable and have been pointed
out invariably by commentators. The non-linear narrative, I venture to suggest,
however, is also a silent progression towards a "beach" that can be figured politi-
cally, backwards and forwards. The beach, here, needs to be examined as a utopic
space, or outer space, even if the spirit of revolution, in a socio-political sense, or
the spirit of the space age (with its Sputnik and Apollo moon flights), is largely
unrecoverable now, which makes the recent recreation of *Einstein on the Beach*
(2012–14) a puzzle, as I believe it can only generate a kind of perplexed sadness
at the incongruity of its *kabuki* aesthetic in the current posthumanist era. On the
other hand, looking at the undersides, or other sides, of Wilson's early operas, and
especially their presumed formalist poetic architectures and dislocations of the
corporeal, this essay wants to probe the aesthetic politics of Wilson's stagecraft
and Glass's composition to re-imagine the perceptional context of the operas and
their cybernetic character (and thus the language of technologized motion and
control) (Figure 2.2).

Figure 2.1 Choreographer and dancer Lucinda Childs in *Einstein on the Beach*, 1976.
Photo Copyright © Philippe Gras.

Figure 2.2 "A Journey from A to B" from the film *Live – Supersurface*, Superstudio 1971. Courtesy of Adolfo Natalini, Cristiano Toraldo di Francia, Gian Piero Frassinelli, Roberto Magris, Alessandro Magris, Allessandro Poli.

Deafman Glance, Molecular Gaze

Woe to those who, to the very end, insist on regulating the movement that exceeds them...

(George Bataille, *The Accursed Share*)

1968 was the year in which the ICA (Institute of Contemporary Arts) in London staged *Cybernetic Serendipity: the Computer and the Arts*, hailed as the first major exhibition of electronic and computer-driven art, attracting huge attention. Cybernetics and systems theory were gaining influence, in much the same way as Marshall McLuhan's media theories. The larger picture of course was half a century of extraordinary creative developments in mathematics, science, technology, and modern art, with "the common trend toward abstraction and new forms of visuality turn[ing] out not to be serendipitous," as Arthur I. Miller argues in *Einstein, Picasso: Space, Time and the Beauty that Causes Havoc.*[6] The completely unconventional (non-theater like) happenings during *Nine Evenings: Theatre and Engineering* indicated a particular range of possibilities for the invention of a dialectical exchange between human action and technology. That exchange was a kind of machining, with both human and machinic finding their

---

6   Miller adds, "That art and science should have progressed in a parallel manner in the twentieth century is abundantly clear from the intellectual struggles of Einstein and Picasso," See *Einstein, Picasso: Space, Time and the Beauty that Causes Havoc*, New York, Basic Books, 2001, 8.

cognitive-perceptual agency extended as well as compromised by the gain and the cost of "technics."

Bernard Stiegler uses "technics" (*la technique*) as a general term for techni-cal systems suggesting that every civilization constitutes itself around a technical system, defined as a stabilizing element within the technical evolution based on previous achievements.[7] The projection of new forms, orientations, and mappings – for example in Cage's aleatoric processes, Rauschenberg's science-art collab-orations, or Constant's cybernetic architectonics for his New Babylon – offers challenges as to what might otherwise be foreseeable in a stabilized economy of representation (for example the naturalism of theater), and in an empirical, gravity-bound world in which one had assumed to know what it means to be, or to have a body, or perceive a body.

The question of how technics act upon the body and human movement in an unforeseen manner might also evoke the *long durée* of postdramatic forms that Alan Read locates in many kinds (archeological, theological, historical, mythi-cal, technological, and so on) of metamorphic performances, ranging, for exam-ple, from Inigo Jones's masques to Gertrude Stein's poetic "landscape plays" to Wilson's operas or the visual theater art of Societas Raffaelo Sanzio. In Wilson's stagecraft, Read finds echoes of liturgical ceremonies, the baroque theater of effects, the stage machineries of the Jacobean masques, the effects of Victorian spectacles and modern variety shows, "all of which have always irreverently and effectively incorporated the depths of myth as much as the attraction of mythi-cal clichés into their vocabulary."[8] This understanding of the *postdramatic* in fact deflates the current hype around the term considerably, which can only be welcomed. Importantly, Read mentions the centrality of dance to masques and the "new images of the postdramatic body," and I think Wilson's and Glass's use of polyrhythms, temporal lines, and repetitions, contrasting tempi and chan-nels (visual, aural) requires special attention if we are to grasp the counting or the mathematics in *Einstein on the Beach*, and thus the work's specific culture of space, or ideological perspective. Unlike Cagean aleatory, unpredictable pro-cesses, Wilson's and Glass's scores reject random chance completely and choreo-graph each visual and aural gesture absolutely precisely.

Such high-technology of control seems counterintuitive; I will address spe-cific instances in which perceptions and proprioceptions[9] are confronted in such numerical performance. Wilson's directing method, after all, is controversially contradictory as it tends to favor cold precision through a mechanical and math-ematical approach while he himself is said to have criticized, in rather strong words, the imposing "fascist theater" of directing the actor's effort and emotional

---

7   Cf. Bernard Stiegler [1994], *Technics and Time, 1. The Fault of Epimethus*, trans. Richard Beards-worth and George Collins, Stanford: Stanford University Press, 1998.

8   Alan Read, *Theatre in the Expanded Field: Seven Approaches to Performance*, London, Blooms-bury, 2013, 56.

9   Editors' note: proprioception is a sense of bodily position, movement, and equilibrium that is not dependent on the other sense, or stimuli from the exterior world.

affect.[10] Rehearsals I attended were illuminating, as indeed was the emphasis on strictly counting and on repetitive clarity of minutely executable gesture (*gestus*). In regard to performance history, of course it must have occurred to Wilson that he was closer to Nijinsky and Schlemmer than to Artaud and Grotowski, though the Artaud of the "moving hieroglyphs" (the Balinese theater) seems rather more pertinent. Wilson's masques are constructivist and hieroglyphic (and remind me of El Lissitzky's designs). I also sense a scientific underside, and certainly an interest in the counter-logical (evidenced in Wilson's collaboration with Christopher Knowles, and the gentle care he took to embrace both the autistic Knowles and the young deaf teenager, Raymond Andrews, whom he adopted). The results of science, and what Suzanne Anker and Dorothy Nelkin have called the "molecular gaze," at the same time offer provocations to prevailing rationalist and anthropocentric visions of the body as the measure of all things, of mind, of life's reproducibility, from the prospects of genetic engineering (trans-speciation, cloning) and nanotechnology's neuro- and bio-medical applications to other advances in industrial engineering, the animation of artificial bodies, and time manipulation.[11] *Einstein on the Beach* strikes me as an immensely ambitious time-manipulation experiment; in this sense it is to the performing arts what CERN's Large Hadron Collider is to particle physics.[12] It is a neo-mythical time machine.

Pierre Boulez found in Cage's indeterminism a big challenge, at first, as the musical event became entirely unforeseeable. Moreover, electronic instruments could be considered transgressive; they exceed the limits of what one can do with traditional instruments, unleashing new possibilities for performance and the spatialization of sound. On the other hand, Boulez disagreed with a complete reliance on chance, faulting Cage for his abandonment of the tools of composition, the logic of grammar, and the logic of organization. The Cagean silence had dislocated Boulez's logic, as much as Duchamp's ready-made had dislocated the traditional art object, or Brecht's epic theater had sought to dislocate the theatrical illusions of reality through methods of interruption, later reformulated by leftist filmmakers such as Jean-Luc Godard or Chris Marker. Brecht's epic method was based on an episodal narrative structure interrupted by titles, films, songs, and

---

10   Cf. Erik Berganus, "Robert Wilson: Entrevista por Erik Berganus," in *Robert Wilson* [exhibition catalog, IVAM Centre del Carme], Valencia: Institut Valencia d'Art Modern, 1994.

11   For an overview of the intersections between art and science in the developing arena of genetic research and engineering, see Suzanne Anker and Dorothy Nelkin, *The Molecular Gaze: Art in the Genetic Age*, Cold Spring, NY, Cold Spring Harbor Laboratory Press, 2004. For Boulez's comments on John Cage, see Rocco Di Pietro, *Dialogues with Boulez*, London, The Scarecrow Press, 2001, 27–34.

12   The Large Hadron Collider is a gigantic scientific instrument near Geneva, where it spans the border between Switzerland and France about 100m underground. It is a particle accelerator used by physicists to study the smallest known particles – the fundamental building blocks of all things. Two beams of subatomic particles called "hadrons'" – either protons or lead ions – travel in opposite directions inside the circular accelerator, gaining energy with every lap; physicists use the instrument to recreate the conditions just after the Big Bang, by colliding the two beams head-on at very high energy.

other factors; an active separating out of the other elements of the drama from the narrative; and a detached style of acting (in "quotation marks"). Brecht explicitly advocated a science of the theater, thinking that the theater of the scientific age was in a position to make dialectics a source of enjoyment, and he proposed that the present-day world could only be described to present-day people if it were described as capable of transformation.[13] Such transformational politics represent the core of his dramaturgy.

In order to produce a revolutionary theater, Brecht argued for a separation of the elements. In his *Mahagonny* notes, he distinguishes his separation of words, music, and scene from the Wagnerian *Gesamtkunstwerk*, which fused the elements into one seductive and overarching whole in which drama, music, and scene work together to engulf the spectator in the aesthetic totality. Conversely, in his separation of the elements, each aesthetic component retains its autonomy and thus can comment on the others, often in contradiction, to provoke critical insight. The measures to be taken, Brecht believed, are rehearsals for the production of revolution, learning the dialectics of historical change by educating ourselves, carrying through certain behaviors. Half a century later, in Heiner Müller's *Hamletmachine*, the idea of self-education is reduced to radically condensed matter, a few shrunken heads, an actor playing Hamlet who thinks he is a data bank of past failures and false moves, and now refuses to act. The machine: a few pages of surreal imagery, hypertextual samples, re-mixes, with strongly entropy-dependent material properties – Müller's relativity theory, in other words (staged by Wilson in New York, 1986).

While the promise of revolution (always) remains to be fulfilled (cf. *Les Revenants*, returning in the twilight, *entre chien et loup*, as the director explains. The dead are the living and the living are the dead), not surprisingly the notion of indeterminacy (based on Heisenberg's uncertainty principle) proved to be as fertile to the artistic and philosophical imagination of the twentieth century as the second law of thermodynamics. Entropy – the tendency of organized systems to disintegrate over time – came to be of central interest in Robert Smithson's earthworks, mirror displacements and "non-sites," but especially in his comments on the "monuments" of synthetic mathematics in art obsessed with the fourth dimension. Mathematician Brian Rotman, reflecting on the equally unnerving fascination with metaphors of the "virtual," added his own entropic vision:

traditional mathematics' syntax-driven discourse of symbols, notation systems and formulas organized into linear, alphabetic chains of logic (pictureless first-order languages, axiomatization), is confronted by a discourse that is performative and driven by digital – screen-visualizable – images for which proof and logical validation are secondary. This is not to say that the classical, infinitary agent will disappear, but rather its ideality, its ghost ontology,

---

13   *Brecht on Theatre*, edited and translated by John Willett, New York, Methuen, 1978, 131.

cannot but be revealed and ineluctably altered when confronted by the materializing, de-infinitizing action of digital computation.[14]

For Rotman, the contemporary virtual, within the technological matrix of the digital, is to be seen as re-structuring the domination of text-based culture and its systems of symbolic reference, a process likely to affect most of those entities which are the product of written mediation – either transforming them or introducing phenomena foreign or antagonistic to them. Our cognitive abilities and subjectivities are not only collective, Rotman suggests, but dispersed across heterogenous arenas, smeared across multiple sites as, ever more connected, we navigate through an expanding universe of virtuality and encounter innumerable digitized traces, anticipations, proxies, avatars, representations, and doubles of ourselves. We'll never walk alone, we are all Humpty Dumpty, Wilson's chorus of *revenants*.

It may well be misleading now to think of algorithmic aesthetic ideology as avant-garde, as progressive and politicized in the sense in which Brecht understood his rejection of opera and the proscenium. Wilson's breakthrough occurred in 1971, when he staged his seven-hour *Deafman Glance* in Europe and entranced his audiences, including surrealist writer Louis Aragon, whose review, published as an open letter to André Breton, drew attention to the director's compositional synthesis of "gesture and silence, of movement and the extraordinary." Aragon's astonishment can still be felt when we read his attempt to describe a performance ("I have seen nothing more beautiful in this world") which seemed to resist interpretation: "because it is at once both wakeful life and life with its eyes closed, the confusion that arises between the everyday world and the world of every night, reality mixed with dream, the totally inexplicable in the gaze of the deaf."[15] Aragon succumbed to the psychedelic side of Wilson's hypnotic spectacle, and I am sure I had a similar response to *Einstein* since it transported me back to the whole experience of a long-durational rock festival, lying on the ground for many hours, listening to voices, to the organ, guitar, drums, the vocals slowly becoming indistinct and blurry as they would for me during an extended Jefferson Airplane jam session....."it could get some wind for the sailboat...it it, it is, it could... be could be frankly fresh and clean...the red ball, the blue ball...two black and white balls...and these are the days my friends, these are the days my friends..."

14   Brian Rotman, "Ghost Effects," Lecture at Stanford Humanities Institute, 2004, quoted with permission. See also Birringer, "Gestural Materialities and the Worn *Dispositif,*" in *Digital Movement: Essays in Motion Technology and Performance*, ed. Nicolas Salazar Sutil/Sita Popat, Basingstoke, Palgrave Macmillan, 2015, 162–85.
15   Louis Aragon, "Lettre Ouverte à André Breton: sur *Le Regard du Sourd. L'art, la science et la liberté,*" *Les Lettres Francais*, no. 1388 (1971), quoted in Miguel Morey and Carmen Pardo, *Robert Wilson*, Barcelona, Ediciones Poligrafa, 2002, 23. I am indebted to the illustrations and commentaries in Morey and Pardo's book, an extraordinary resource for anyone interested in the computational logic of Wilson's *mise-en-scène*.

The architectural and painterly vocabularies of Wilson's *tableaux vivants*, his specific treatment of the visual and the aural scores through heightened attention to the choreography of lighting, rhythm, and duration, with a slowed-down, dilated, and abstracted choreography of the body in movement, create the distinguishing vocabulary, which in its *visual excess* I have repeatedly compared here to Japanese *kabuki* (even if this is meant in a tongue in cheek way). We could dwell on the verbal emissions, but they are actually sonic elements rather than semantic language, they are dada, incomplete and unresolved iterative antiphonies to the imposing additive fluidity of Glass's rhythmic music structure which is in fact overwhelmingly present, quite unlike in the earlier muted Wilson operas. I try to construct a small layout of Wilson's technology of visual persuasion, his abstract machine, based on my diagram of a set of his architectural compositions and structural principles ranging from *Deafman Glance* to *Einstein* and beyond. I enumerate these principles to suggest a template of Wilson's formal techniques which might help to construct a small data base or arithmetic of such a rhetorical and iconographic apparatus, leading us to the New Babylon.

0. Wilson is an action painter who does not pour out curved gestures onto the canvas. Early compositions – *Poles, The King of Spain, The Life and Times of Sigmund Freud, Deafman Glance, I was sitting on my patio* – are like black and white Barnett Newmans, cool and austere color fields, light fields with darkness, structured silence. Clear straight lines (geometries). Surface without depth.
1. The first approach to performance is drawing. The stage is a flat plane, framed. Wilson's stage is always the proscenium. The Italian-style proscenium supplies an immense space for minute, intimate movements. The literary model of theater, and illusion, is dismissed. Scale is attractive. There are no "four saints in three acts" (Gertrude Stein); or rather, there are no historical figures that matter.
2. The first principle: space (mental space). Drawing is the diagram, the language for painting which is also a mathematical language. Painting the space for performance is to compose it, to organize the plane with basic elements. Lines, geometric forms, light, and color.
3. Acts and scenes are numbered. Actors are numbered. Steps are numbered. Movement of the actor is envisioned as an algorithm. Precise counts, for each line (gesture), each motion (step), each position (figural) in the landscape.
4. The drawing is *chiaroscuro*. Light and dark, strong contrast and clear architecture. Pictorial space can become cinematic space of black and white film (film noir). In later works (after *Einstein on the Beach*), the palette changes and theatrical lighting is used for color. Wilson's virtuosity as a lighting artist creates an increasing rhetoric of luminescence. Color sensations are explored in slow motion, from dark blue to paler blue to white ("I can do anything with those three lights").[16] *Einstein* tends to happen *entre chien et loup*.

---

16 Robert Wilson discussing his color palette, quoted in Morey and Pardo, *Robert Wilson*, 55.

5. From drawing to lighting, Wilson adds and subtracts. Giving light to generate the scene, creating passages, squares, windows, corridors, lines, grids, geometric shapes. Geometric contours are outlined, objects are illuminated as if from within, the actor is in silhouette. Light is an actor. Objects become actors, chairs are sculptures designed to draw attention to their surreal form and their "role" as a character. A conch shell becomes a character taking us to the "beach," the sea.

6. Actors receive their separate light that identifies them. Their hand or their face is spotlighted. Body-lines become gestures, the hand or the arm is immobilized, and light traces the imperceptible movement of stillness and displacement. If the actor moves, the space seems to move with him or her and stillness is experienced or dreamt as moving immobility.

7. The length of the performance (many hours) guarantees that immobility is also movement, slow duration, slow space. Time is time-line but we are confused. Subjective and objective time differ. Geometries (vertical light) introduce the fourth dimension; choreography of lines, light, and movement are felt as durations, with rhythms based on a dense structure of stillness, movement, repetition, variation, mutation, and contrast (Figure 2.3).

8. The sound of the performance can be spoken language, recorded language, distributed/amplified sound (of language and music and sound effects), live or recorded music, light. The light in the later productions (of the 1980s and 1990s) is attuned to the musical libretto of the operas and gives it emotional

Figure 2.3 Light bar, *Einstein on the Beach*, ACT4-Sc2C-Bed by Robert Wilson and Philip Glass, 2012. Photo: Courtesy Lucie Jansch

weight. Light becomes quasi-Wagnerian, more chromatic and transcendental (*Parsifal*), yet sometimes it defies gravity. In order to choreograph and
express the (musical) content within the context of the abstract formal stage
paintings, Wilson adopts the Wagnerian rhetoric, slows the tempo, and to
maintain the continuity of sound he makes tonal compensation. Wilson's
color of the sound becomes symmetrical and repetitive, he adds trance-like
weight to the sound. Glass's music for *Einstein* is relentless, mathematical-
transpositional. He composed each section, over a period of six months, like
a portrait of Wilson's drawings that he had put on the piano before him.
The additive process used is very complex, including cyclical structures
that superimpose different rhythmic patterns which slowly but progressively
diverge before gradually converging again.[17]

9. Wilson's grail: the spatialization of time. "The time is a vertical line and the
space is horizontal. This time-space cross is the architecture of everything,
and it is the tension between these lines that interests me."[18] Of course we
don't know what this means, yet we can't figure the ideological side of it.
Except that the sublime orientation (unlike the Situationist *détournement* and
the sublime disorientation of New Babylon) of Wilson's work is modernist,
aesthetically and ideologically. It is pure plasticity of abstraction, tinged with
surrealist distortions.

10. The stage score has two main elements – the visual and the auditory – and
is composed of the visual elements, the way they are painted and their stage
presence, along with the textual elements, and lastly the music. In Wilson's
diagram for *Einstein on the Beach*, the mapping is written in the following
code (Figure 2.4):

I, II, III, IV; A, B, C, D; 1, 2, 3, 4, 5 ... Well, that is how I make an opera.
First I decide to make a work called *Einstein on the Beach*. I start with
the title. Then I decide to make four acts with three themes and all the
possible combinations of these three themes: A and B, C and A, B and
C, and finally the three themes together. Then I introduce the interludes,
which I call knee plays (kind of articulations). Then I define the duration,
I decide that this part is going to last 22 minutes, that one 21. All together
I have 4 hours and 40 minutes. By this time I know the form, the structure,
and the duration. Then I decide what I want to put in A. This is the next
phase. Einstein talked about trains, so I show a train that comes on stage
... Einstein said that when you fly over a train, all you would see is a line.
Then, when the train has crossed a quarter of the stage, it is interrupted
by a vertical line of light. Then the train continues its route. The line of
light disappears. The train gets to the middle of the stage and is interrupted
once again by a vertical line of light. Then the train starts up again and gets

17 Cf. Philip Glass, *Music by Philip Glass*, ed. Robert Jones, New York, Da Capo Press, 1995, 58–59.
18 Quoted in Miguel Morey and Carmen Pardo, *Robert Wilson*, 71–72.

Figure 2.4 Fielddance with object, ACT3-Sc2B. *Einstein on the Beach*, by Robert Wilson and Philip Glass, 2012. Photo: Courtesy Lucie Jansch.

three quarters of the way across the stage, where there is another vertical line of light.[19]

11. The breadth of the horizontal is interrupted by the vertical line that gives depth and also implies, opens up, and expands time-movement. This breadth allows for the breathing of the space and the gaze. Scales, disproportions (the huge Abraham Lincoln tree in *the CIVIL warS*, the tall Cycladic statue in *Alcestis*, the enormous chairs in *The Black Rider*), oblique angles (the tilted doors in *The Golden Windows*, the crooked expressionist houses in *The Black Rider*), layering of different planes, shadows, the repetitions and shifts in perspective (the rotating stage configuration in *Hamletmachine*), and 3-D illusions (the floating shoe and bicycling boy on the penny-farthing in *Monsters of Grace*): continuous movement from simplicity to complexity.

12. The deafman glance is always the apparent, deceivingly simplistic figure of silence, inarticulate tone poems of mundane language (*A Letter for Queen Victoria*, the *Einstein* chorus, and knee plays), the childlike fairy tales (the knee plays in *the CIVIL warS*), the miming of an abstract formal choreography (the actor counts to 50, turns left, and slowly walks ten steps to stage right). The *musique concrète* of the early libretti creates extended loops of vowels and consonants, molecular word reverberations and oscillations,

19   Ibid., 72.

making the voice audible and physical, creating voice-lines and delays, oscillographs without semantic meaning.

13. The ephemeral oscillographs are like a dance, the stage a recording machine of visual and aural time lines, non-sequiturs. Lucinda Childs's choreography for the "Field Dances" is such a non-sequitur, just as her oft-repeated/modulated and slightly inflected knee play monologue:

I was in this prematurely air-conditioned supermarket
and there were all these aisles
and there were these bathing caps that you could buy
which had these kind of Fourth of July plumes on them
they were red and yellow and blue
I wasn't tempted to buy one
but I was reminded of the fact that I had been avoiding the beach.

The dancers are identically clad men and women in white costumes, who circulate the "field" like subatomic particles, follow their own exact but constantly shifting pathways. They go in and out of sync with each other. Their steps are simple – *chassé*, *sauté arabesque*, *soutenu* turns, slow single *pirouettes*, loping leaps. Yet they travel a space, constantly, cleanly, and rigorously mechanically. As in Childs's most well-known work, *Dance* (1979) and the recently recreated *Available Light* ([1983] featured at Berlin's Tanz im August Festival 2015), the movements lead nowhere and thus have a distinct sense of circularity. They are the visual counterpart to Glass's musical loops.

14. The chorus (*les revenants*), during one of the knee plays, performs a vastly complex chorale. They alternate between staccato numerical sequences (1-2-3-4, 1-2-3-4, 1-2-3-, 1-2-3-, etc.) and legato *solfège* (la-si-do), which they perform in counterpoint, with unexpected changes in tempo. The words have no meaning, they are music, frequencies, repetitions; *tessituras* of voices.

15. Counting is the Wilsonian algorithm for the automaton actor. No intention, no psychology, no emotion. Movement itself is movement of the deafman, animated lines, crossing the stage laterally, as if listening to inner counting. 1, 2, 3, 4, 5, 6, 7, 8, 9. The surface of the senses is in the gaze focused on the drawings. The listening of the deaf follows the drawn line, movement in stillness and stillness in movement.

16. The code is restricted by its lack of indexicality. What is seen is, perhaps, nothing. But as in dreams, the movement appears internal, imagined, fantasized, open to speculation and thought experiments. How do thought experiments become persuasive?

17. In Wilson's choreography, the model actors are deaf, listening to their inner scores. They furnish the gaze with a scenario enacted by the viewer's proxy. The automaton actors in Wilson's *tableaux vivants* are agents of what we would experience through our glancing at the silhouettes in the architecture. The glance is self-persuasion.

18. The arithmetic of Wilson's choreography is performed according to an order of operations: addition (+), subtraction (−), multiplication (Å~ or ·), division (÷ or /), acceleration, deceleration, abbreviation, zero. Wilson's performance logic is perfectly reductive and infinitely expansive at the same time. Each gesture could be described as a potentially alienating *mudra*, an abstract stylization that crosses Western painting and modern dance with Indian dance, *Noh* theater, and *kabuki*.

19. As the *mudras* mean nothing, the movement (based on arithmetic counting) exists, lives, breathes in the abstract geometries of these visual worlds, and in the long duration, they may change from physical reality to supernatural. In *Monsters of Grace*, an abstract opera with no actors on stage but live music by Philip Glass and 3-D computer animation, Wilson finally reaches the full digital stage of such performance.

20. *Einstein on the Beach* models its digital-baroque structure on an additive process (four acts: A+B, A+C, B+C, ABC, and five knee plays) and on structures repeated in cyclical succession. The sound material is reduced to the most minimal terms (numbers and syllables), the repetition of very brief rhythmic and melodic modules, and a rhythmicization based on the sequence of small units. The visual process, such as the appearance of the train in Act I, Act II, and Act IV, follows the same formal abstraction culled from arithmetic and geometry. The Einstein figure plays the violin; the gestures of the musicians a continuous drawing of lines.

21. The deafness of the body in Wilson's performance is the condition for resonance, for listening to such vision, to the virtual and the supernatural. A chair very very slowly descends from the ceiling, a tortoise crosses the stage in 35 minutes, other movements happen in a polyrhythm of graphic writings and drawings, in the midst of vocal litanies, repetitions, and echoes, a dog barks in the distance, King Lear abdicates and a small boy approaches on a bicycle, as if from a very great distance, closer and closer, until you can almost touch the digital image. The supernatural envelops the realm of parables: in *Les Fables de La Fontaine* (created with La Comédie Française in 2004), the stage is populated with lions, foxes, and various birds.

22. Molecular language, intoned and distributed (amplified via loudspeakers), ebbs and flows in the architecture of modulated light. Texts in Wilson's auditory book are sampled, mixed and remixed, repeated and re-repeated, becoming sound points or echo-traces in the space. Film projections appear as geological layers or sediments of the landscape. Visual libretto (stage), sound libretto (music, language samples), film libretto: all elements can be combined, modulated, held in tension, separated. Different screens. A fundamental formalism is used to set in motion a whole range of operations we now call digital.

Knee Play: Les Revenants 2

Wilson's and Glass's New Babylon carried a utopian energy that seemed to thrive into the fabulous realms of psychogeography (science fiction), while at the same time remaining locked into a tight cybernetic machine, an abstract control machine of repetition and mutation. The machinic concatenation, and especially the lifeless living chorus of *les revenants*, make it difficult to ascertain the political subtexts of this opera – "the beach" may indeed refer to nothing, nothing but a mathematics bound to the limits of time, incapable of imagining moving forward, riding on a beam of light, into a reversal of the future.

The returns of the *Einstein* opera to the stage (in the twenty-first century) of course remain a puzzle. The abstract modernist fable may now be mistaken for a hymn, its antiquated mathematical style a strange example of a dadaist poetic machine dissociated from its time, from something that was in the air – revolutionary revelation, critical gains in consciousness, potential triggers of action, social transformation, the coming community (*la communitá que viene*), the electric stimulation imagined by McLuhan and the Situationists. And yet, one might argue that retrospectively *Einstein* perfectly captured a moment of vast expansion of perception (in the history of performance ideas), and a space of uncanny compulsion to stare at the object of an enigma, hearing voices. The "beach," then, was a hypnagogic event, a drifting by of a distant early warning system of changes to come, changes in our conception of history, time, technological information, and control systems. Its monumentality now looks less mythical, and more domestic.

3 *Einstein on the Beach* in Belgrade

A critical testimony

Miško Šuvaković

The tactics of memory: socialism, BITEF, and public opinion

In this chapter I offer an eyewitness account of a performance of Robert Wilson and Philip Glass's *Einstein on the Beach* at the 10th Belgrade International Theater Festival (BITEF) in 1976. This testimony will be recontextualized in relation to my recollections of the event itself and the Cold War socio-political framework of socialist era Yugoslavia which I belonged to at the time.

When I say the society "I belonged to at the time," I mean a vague convergence of the following factors: (1) the acute manifestations of the Cold War[1] division between the European political East and West; (2) the decision of socialist Yugoslavia's leadership after 1948 to pursue a social and cultural politics located between the East and the West, and (3) my uninhibited cosmopolitan desire for a position in the complex map of international art and culture outside the borders of the political East. For me and for the people I spent time with then, or with whom I took part in experimental art practices in Belgrade, Zagreb, or Ljubljana, there was a sense of belonging to an international Western history of "new art," comprising neoDada, Fluxus, minimalism, post-minimalism, conceptual, performance, and video art. Unlike most of my colleagues and peers in the East of Europe – Hungary, Czechoslovakia, Poland, and the USSR – who worked in self-

---

1   TheColdWar(Rus.Холоднаявойна)wasapolitical,economic,andculturalconflictbetweentheUnited States and the Soviet Union between 1946 and 1991. On April 4, 1949, the Western allies launched the North Atlantic Treaty Organization (NATO) headquartered in Brussels. The Warsaw Treaty of Organization of Friendship, Cooperation and Mutual Assistance was created on May 14, 1945. After the political split with the USSR, Yugoslav politics was marked by the introduction of two concepts that at the time were considered innovative: the concept of socialist self-management and that of political non-alignment. A turn was made from Bolshevik-style revolutionary state Marxism towards a state which proclaims and implements a direct form of democracy within the organization of the production process. As a "state in-between," Yugoslavia gravely needed an "effective" position within the Third World which would enable and create room for manoeuvre in political, economic, and cultural terms. The core of the Non-Aligned Movement was formed at the UN General Assembly, consisting of the states of Yugoslavia, Ghana, Guinea, Ethiopia, India, Indonesia, Mali, Sudan, and Egypt. The first conference of the Non-Aligned Movement was held in Belgrade on September 1–6, 1961.

organized and unprotected private spaces, in other words, in the "other" public sphere of dissident or underground art, we found ourselves in protected spaces, reserves of sort, which the state's cultural politics provided by creating student and youth culture centers, and hosting Yugoslav and international art, theater, and film festivals. The programs of Belgrade's festivals, for example, BITEF (theater), FEST (film), or *Aprilski susreti – Festival proširenih medija* (*April Encounters – Festival for Expanded Media*) allowed for the presentation of theater, film, and art cultures of the First, Second, and Third Worlds, but also the positioning of the official Yugoslav cultural politics as an intermediary between East and West, and an ally of the Third World.

BITEF – The Belgrade International Theater Festival, Belgrade[2] was launched in 1967 and, along with the Avignon theater festival, it became an important European focal point of the neo-avant-garde and, subsequently, postmodern theater. BITEF was founded on December 26, 1966, on the basis of a decision by the City Assembly of Belgrade. It was constituted as an independent organization with the task of organizing the international festival's approach to new theater. The central concept of the festival was formulated by Mira Trailović, director of the theater Atelje 212, in cooperation with her associate and co-organizer, drama- turge Jovan Ćirilov. The first BITEF festival was produced by the theater Atelje 212 in September 1967.[3] The festival was propelled by two fundamental inten- tions. The first was to present to audiences in socialist Yugoslavia the new and experimental international trends in theater and inform Yugoslav theater profes- sionals about contemporary international artistic practices and theater networks in the First, Second, and Third Worlds. The second was to reconstitute Yugoslav cultural politics (and, thereby also state politics) from the cultural politics of a closed, real-socialist society into the cultural politics of an open society of self- management socialism. The cultural liberalization leading from a closed to an open culture was an expression of political will that communicated the special and exceptional position of socialist Yugoslavia in West-East political relations. On the other hand, by creating defined (in other words, legal) institutions dedi- cated to promoting contemporary and experimental performing arts, the state demonstrated that through the mediation of these institutions, it actually kept the new artistic practices under control. They were granted space, but in a context of permanent managerial "surveillance." This double game of liberalization and control was a specific feature of the Yugoslav progressive path. The character of the "double game" is clearly visible in the fact that no censorship constrained the program decisions made by BITEF's management and selectors. However,

---

2   Vladimir Stamenković, *Kraljevstvo eksperimenta – 20 godina BITEF-a*, Belgrade, Nova knjiga, 1987.

3   Bojan Đorđev, 'Pozorišna (neo)avangarda pedesetih i šezdesetih godina – Atelje 212', in: Miško Šuvaković (ed), *Istorija umentosti XX vek: Radikalne umetničke prakse*, Belgrade, Orion Art, 2010, 367–374.

cultural bureaucrats deliberately turned public opinion against the festival's more radical or transgressive performances.

Finally, this kind of social behavior demonstrated and argued that culture and art matter in Yugoslav society. Some leftist intellectuals saw this complex dialectic within Yugoslav society as part of an optimistic project of "socialism with a human face." For example, Georg Schöllhammer saw BITEF, and (through BITEF) Yugoslav society in general, in the following terms:

> In the post-war history of European avant-garde theater, since the 1970s Belgrade has been considered a canonic place – among other things, because of BITEF, which has become, since 1967, one of the most significant experimental venues of the international scene. ... By the mid-1970s Yugoslavia was a theatrical Mecca, a laboratory of late-modernist architecture, the point of crystallization of unorthodox Marxism and one of the internationally best-connected points of the avant-garde art in Europe.[4]

A more pessimistic picture of the festival was painted by Natalia Vagapova, a regular BITEF guest:

> Its task was to demonstrate to the world the openness of the cultural politics, the tolerance of the Titoist leadership, and their split with the theory and practice of socialist realism in art. In fact, the festival, as did the overall Yugoslav culture, survived in the circumstances of, in essence, primitive and cruel political censorship cunningly hidden from the eyes of the public.[5]

The tactics of memory: **Einstein on the Beach**

Accompanying the 10th BITEF festival, an exhibition was mounted at the Gallery of Happy New Art at Belgrade's Student Cultural Centre. The exhibition was held from the eighth to the eighteenth of September 1976, featuring artists from Yugoslavia, including myself.[6] During the exhibition we were affiliated with the 10th Belgrade International Theater Festival. It provided a connection between

---

4   Georg Schöllhammer, "An Ontologist Observes," *Springerin*, no. 1 – 'Other Modernities,' Vienna, 2007, www.springerin.at/dyn/heft_text.php?textid=1900&lang=en, Accessed: May 9, 2008.

5   Ana Vujanović, 'Nove pozorišne tendencije: BITEF/Beogradski internacionalni teatarski festival', in: Miško Šuvaković (ed): *Istorija umetnosti XX vek: Radikalne umetničke prakse*, Belgrade, Orion Art, 2010, 377.

6   These included the composer and performer Miroslav Savić (Belgrade); the conceptual artists Jovan Čekić (Belgrade), Braco Dimitrijević (Sarajevo and Zagreb), and Goran Trbuljak (Zagreb); the post-minimal artist and former member of the neo-avant-garde group Gorgona, Julije Knifer (Zagreb); the analytical painter Gergelj Urkom (Belgrade and London); the conceptual artist and performer Raša Todosijević (Belgrade); the Belgrade-based conceptual artists, Zoran Popović, Neša Paripović, and Goran Đorđević; the film director and visual experimental artist Slobodan Šijan, from Belgrade, and myself.

visual artists and the festival of experimental theater and its program. In some indirect way, I was part of this project, which involved performances of the opera *Einstein on the Beach.*

From the time of its founding until the late 1980s, BITEF meant a festival of theater for audiences in Belgrade and Yugoslavia, theater professionals and accidental accomplices, lasting a couple of weeks. Along with the performances, Belgrade's urban life in clubs, kafanas (local bistros), and private apartments carried on as usual. In 1976 the tenth BITEF was held under the title *Theatre of Nations* from September 9–27. Some 20 performances were put on and I watched four of them: the Soviet *Hamlet* directed by Yuri Lyubimov, the Spanish production *Divinas Palabras* (*Divine Words*) directed by Victor García, the Danish performance by Odin Theatre, *Come! And the Day Will Be Ours*, directed by Eugenio Barba, and the American opera *Einstein on the Beach* conceived by Robert Wilson and Philip Glass. *Einstein* was performed on September 21 and 22 in the Yugoslav Drama Theatre (Jugoslovensko dramsko pozorište) in Belgrade. I missed the premiere. I had a ticket for the second night. Twenty-four hours later – as the first performance was already proclaimed a cult event – seemingly the whole of Belgrade was in attendance. The house was exceptionally full. People came with and without tickets. They entered from all sides. There was no police presence. The chatter from the auditorium and the theater foyer during the performance objected to Glass's cold, repetitive music.

Not without shame – I can now testify that what I really remember is some chaos. The bodies of spectators/listeners were all around. It seemed to me that people crawled over each other. Bushy female and male heads bobbed in expectation of the beginning. These were still late hippy days and in Belgrade everybody had long hair. Nobody sat in their seats. Some kind of *rhizomatic* chaotic movement went on in the auditorium. This chaos in Belgrade may perhaps be compared to the chaos aroused in Avignon. One of the accompanying articles in the catalogue of the tenth BITEF described the atmosphere at the premiere in Avignon:

> Bob Wilson and Phil Glass triumphed in Avignon. Much earlier than the city theater opened its doors, all tickets for the premiere of their opera *Einstein on the Beach* were sold out. And when the doors were opened, the audience burst into the auditorium in an indescribable scramble. The rule of the survival of the fittest applied in the audience because the seats were unnumbered, and perhaps because some non-existing seats had been sold. However, after some spectators wandered in search of a seat with a better sightline, everything ended peacefully and without incident; and, after four and a half hours, that mass of people gave a grandiose ovation.[7]

I tried with considerable effort to see at least part of the stage. Dim lights and unbearable heat – then came Glass's music and it all started. For those of us

---

7   BITEF 10, 1976.

unaccustomed to minimalist music, Glass's score resembled blast of sounds – one after another. The monotony was unbearable. The chaotic, motley audience was confronted with the cold and restricted order of an audiovisual event which demanded almost five hours of attention – concentration on the image, the sound, and the movement. Rigid figures and mechanic motion on the stage. The audience slowly began to quiet down. Some of them left. Some of them arrived only then. I remember the repeated vocal chant: *one, two, three...* primary structures shaken to complete instability. I was familiar with the music of Cage and Stockhausen, but this sounded completely different. It was quite close to my own concept of visual syntactic structures, something I was working on at the time, and which I certainly knew from the works of the American minimalist and post-minimalist artists Donald Judd and Sol LeWitt. Sound structures took place in time.

I could say that I remember the music quite well, but the stage event is now remote and blurred – made unclear by the trajectory of my gaze traversing the mass of spectators towards the stage, where the almost mechanical bodies of the performers moved. I liked the lack of plot immediately. One of the lynchpins of the erstwhile "new art" was anti-narrativity – event rather than story. I recognized the logic of the index as opposed to the iconic reference in the narrative. This was perhaps the most important point of fascination for me and the "kids" from Belgrade, who were pretty much like me. Opera or theater did not matter. What mattered was beyond opera or theater, and it made way for the poetics of the event – fundamentally it was about performativity.

No, I am not a good witness! Although I find pleasure in testifying:

> We may perceive Wilson's focus on the "simple surface" and the recollec-tion (indexing) of "complex depth" as a pragmatic gesture (behavioral order) which allows for an almost radical post-structuralist conclusion that, instead of the things themselves, we only see their contours and surfaces.[8]

To see and to hear the contours, surfaces, and hard edges formed by sequences of sounds in the music, and the rigidly artificial figures-bodies in motion or lack thereof – this was quite a different experience from watching/listening to the other festival productions, which claimed identity between the theater and its transgres-sions, para- and anti-theater. The opera by Wilson and Glass was not a vitalist game, the result of the liberating impulses of post-1960s artists who still craved for the forms of a new political sensibility. Here was an "opera" that was meant to be looked at and listened to in the manner of a minimalist performance that arbitrarily combined three events: the stage event, the dance event, and the music event. These events were somewhat detached, as if three different performances were going on at the same time in the same place. This was something com-pletely different from what I knew thus far about Western theater according to

---

8   Miško Šuvaković, "Razoriti (ili) čitati teatar. Pisanje o pisanju o teatru – slučaj *Ajnštajn na plaži*," *TkH* Journal no. 2, Belgrade, September 200, 82.

Lessing's reading of Aristotle's *Poetics*; implying unity of place, time, and action. Instead we are offered detachment, disunity, parallel flows – tripolarity instead of monopolarity in the theater. This caused some discomfort; the simulation of a split personality. Spectators were confounded in their attempts to connect the parallel actions of the stage movement, the progress of the repetitive music structures, and the works' referential semantics. This was a long night.

In subsequent days, I talked about and listened to talks about *Einstein* – each talk slipped into the realm of an urban myth. Minimalism was radicalized in talk about this opera that was not an opera, at the place of a theater which was not only a theater, but a relationship between music, the stage, and dance that was present within us. Everybody was talking about *Einstein*. Only the occasional uninformed person would ask about the scientist Einstein, references to his life, the speed of light, the theory of relativity, his violin, or private life. The conversation would always return to the fascinating appearance of the surfaces, contours – the rhetoric of music and body in space. Semantic-free rhetoric was a mythical structure in *Einstein on the Beach*.

Time passed quickly.

The next September – it was 1977 – I participated with Group 143 in the 10th Paris Biennale of young artists.[9] I arrived in Paris at the end of October. The exhibition marked the moment of demise of analytical and critical conceptualism and it announced the postmodern in its eclectic configurations. This was one of the rare occasions when my desire for cosmopolitism was granted – the other exhibitors were Laurie Anderson, Marc Devade, Francesco Clemente, Anselm Kiefer, John Hilliard, Adrian Piper, Mladen Stilinović, Andraž Šalamun, Jarosław Kozłowski, Mary Lucier, Bruce McLean, Gerhard Merz, Anette Messager, the art collective General Idea, and others. Group 143 mounted a theoretical installation including diagrams and hand-made books. This was a time when the RAF (Rote Armee Fraktion) or their followers performed terrorist actions in Paris. It represented a war against the state(s). Paris was full of armed gendarmes. The parks were yellowish from yellow chestnuts. I made a short film which reflected my understanding of Godard's shooting of films with a hand-held camera. There was a state of emergency. One could hear the roar of police sirens. No one could pass by the Paris Opera. I was roaming the city. In a small gallery on 40 Rue Mazarine,[10] I found some records by the American minimalists. I asked for the record of *Einstein on the Beach*. The shop assistant replied that they did not have the record yet. She asked how come I knew about Glass's *Einstein*. Probably she could tell from my accent that I was East European. She wondered how someone from behind the Iron Curtain actually knew about Glass's work. I told her about the Belgrade performance of *Einstein* at the BITEF. She looked at me in awe. I do

---

9   *10e Biennale de Paris*, 1977, 138–139.

10   The art gallery on 40 Rue Mazarine in Paris was founded by Chantal Darcy and Daniel Caux. It was associated with a record label promoting post WWII avant-garde music. The label *Shandar* released the works by Albert Ayler, Karlheinz Stockhausen, Steve Reich, Sunny Murray, Philip Glass, Richard Horowitz, Charlemagne Palestine, La Monte Young, Alan Silva, Pandit Pran Nath, Terry Riley, Cecil Taylor, and Sun Ra, among others.

not think she initially believed me. I bought Glass's LP *North Star*, Steve Reich's LP *Four Organs, Phase Patterns*, and the LP *The Theater of Eternal Music* by La Monte Young and Marian Zazeela. The shop assistant's awe amused me. Those of us from the former Eastern Bloc countries were typically regarded as suspicious. I walked on. I felt good. I strolled around. I perused the stands of small and large bookshops. I filmed with a Super 8 camera. I left Paris soon afterwards.

Twenty-six years after seeing the performance of *Einstein*, together with a group of students and recent graduates of the Faculty of Music and Faculty of Dramatic Arts in Belgrade, I realized the project *Beyond Einstein on the Beach*. It was published in the then recently launched journal for theoretical research on new theater and performance art, *TkH – Teorija koja Hoda* (*Preko [beyond] Ajnštajna na plaži*, 2001, 6–96). The project based on *Einstein* was ideological in tone. Its purpose was to critically theorize the contemporary performing arts in the context of the theory-phobic art world in Belgrade. The choice of *Einstein* set what we were doing apart from the "warm" or "organic" theater alternative of the 1990s and early 2000s, and the more intuitively conceptualization of dance, opera, and theater at the beginning of the new century. Our intention was to use *Einstein on the Beach* to demonstrate the potential of the urge for critical thinking as opposed to the intuitive blends found in the alternative theater of the 1990s. This was a rather utopian intervention and an act of theoretical excess in the context of Belgrade's stale moderate-postmodernist artistic practices (Figure 3.1).

I missed the performance of *Einstein* at De Nederlandse Opera (The Amsterdam Music Theater Venue) on January 10, 2013. A longtime collaborator and colleague Jelena Novak invited me to the conference on *Einstein* convened for the occasion of its restaging. I was somewhere else at the time, telling other stories – so I missed the live performance of the new *Einstein*. Sometime later, I watched the broadcast of the "new" *Einstein* from Paris.[11] At this point, certainly, one detail should be discussed: the problem of recycling historical performances in the present. Some works of performing arts in the twentieth century are simply not repeatable pieces in the manner of the dramatic arts, the opera, and ballet. These are performance art events, by which I mean live unrepeatable performances occurring in a singular moment and place, with very specific individualized performers aspiring to authorship. Formally speaking, the difference between the repeatable and the unrepeatable work pertains to the source text: a play, a libretto, a musical score, or a choreographic script. Repeatable works are performed representations of the source authorial text. Unrepeatable works are events which do not stem from a play, a libretto, a musical score, or a choreographic script. Some avant-garde, neo-avant-garde, and contemporary pieces of performance art belong to a category between repeatable and unrepeatable works – they may be repeated but it is not just another text-based performance, but rather a media or performance-based "recycling" of memories and documents, media records of the

11   http://culturebox.francetvinfo.fr/einstein-on-the-beach-au-theater-du-chatelet-146813, Accessed: June 10, 2013.

Figure 3.1 Cover, *TkH journal* (Walking Theory) no. 2, Belgrade, 2001. Courtesy Miško Šuvaković Archive.

original performance. Recycling here implies reconstruction of a piece from the past as an actual live event with all the conceptual and media imprints of the present. And this means that the contemporary stage technology is put to work and a high level of professionalism accomplished, including a turn from "historical authentic gestuality" to the "contemporary spectacular production and postproduction" of the art piece. If that is the case, we may claim that, on the one hand, this recycling represents a return from the unrepeatable act of performance to the traditional framework of the potentially endless performability of the stage piece. On the other, it is a turn to the totalizing realm of spectacle, which was in technological terms unthinkable at the time of the first performance(s). The impression of the historical *Einstein* was innovatively enchanting (a miracle happened), while the impression of the contemporary recycled *Einstein* is obsessively astounding: the result is a hybrid mix of spectacle and nostalgia on the *battlefield* of theater/opera production, exchange, and consumption – two different esthetical regimes.

These were my encounters with *Einstein*. After this brief reflection, I have the feeling that I have always been somewhere outside – in the outer space surrounding that piece. Does it suffice to occupy the domain of this outer Other in order to be qualified to testify? Perhaps it does.

A reconstruction of facts and ideological dispositifs

The stage for Robert Wilson's appearance at the BITEF had been set since 1970. Wilson had a presentation at the 5th BITEF in 1971. He had a talk in Atelje 212's Theater in the Cellar and the Student Cultural Centre on September 21 and 25, 1971. Both events would nowadays be called "lecture performances"; not merely talks about the theater, but performances of the theater discourse with the director's speech and behavior. The event at the Student Cultural Centre took place at midnight on September 25, 1971. After an hour of concentration, Wilson performed the talk. The message "Start the discussion" was written on the floor. A number of local theater professionals understood this invitation to discussion as an invitation to attack Wilson himself. Sitting behind the curtain, he asked the audience for one more hour of silence for concentration. Part of the angry audience left the auditorium at about 3:30 am. Wilson came out in front of the stage and started to talk with the audiences. Some kind of a workshop was going on.[12]

The terrain for Wilson's return was cleared.

On September 19–22, 1974, the opera *A Letter for Queen Victoria* was performed in Atelje 212 at the 8th BITEF. The music was written by Alan Lloyd and the choreography was conceived by Andrew de Groat. The performance was produced by the theater company Byrd Hoffman School of Byrds from New York.[13] With this piece, Wilson became the talk of the town.

But, let us return to *Einstein*.

---

12   BITEF/40 godina, 125–126.
13   *BITEF 8*, 1974, 42–46

The premiere of *Einstein on the Beach* was held at the Avignon Festival on July 25, 1976. The opera toured that summer, in Hamburg, Paris, Belgrade, Venice, Brussels, and Rotterdam, and in November 1976 it was performed in the Metropolitan Opera House in New York.

The presence of this opera at the Belgrade International Theatre Festival[14] was made possible thanks to The Byrd Hoffman Water Mill Foundation. Robert Wilson founded the BHF in New York (1969) to encourage multidisciplinary research in the theater and professional development of theater artists. According to the credits stated in the BITEF catalogue, the opera was conceived by Robert Wilson and Philip Glass.[15] (Figure 3.2)

At the 10th BITEF in Belgrade, three productions were awarded prizes: Yuri Lyubimov's *Hamlet*, Peter Brook's *The Ik*, and Robert Wilson's *Einstein on the Beach*. The atmosphere at the festival was triumphant and, in some ways, the BITEF assured the citizens and the state that Belgrade had become a world metropolis. What was new from the artistic point of view was ascribing an exceptional creative importance to the role of the director. A French critic wrote in her report on the 10th BITEF in *Le Monde* about the "directors' coup" at the Belgrade festival.[16]

Observed from the American perspective, Wilson and Glass's *Einstein* marked the peak of the gradual dissolution of modern theater, from the neo-avant-gardes (Living Theater, La Mama, and others) to postmodern theater and its multi-mediated spectacularization, involving the transdisciplinarity and multiculturalism of the contemporary performing arts. In the European context, *Einstein* may be identified as an ideal transfiguration of theater into spectacle, or opera as a new ideal of the reconfigured stage event. Much later, German theatrologist Hans-Thies Lehmann would use the term "postdramatic theater." Both the American and the European insights into *Einstein* had the character of confrontation by emphasizing the hybridized immanence of the work in performing arts. This implied some exceptionality as regards the autonomy of the aesthetic space as a field of exploration challenging the borders of the theater space through directors', composers', scenographers', and choreographers' experimentation, in other words, the opera. The Western conception of *Einstein* was based on ideas of immanence of the artistic creation/research as the ideal continuum of art. In the Yugoslav context, interpretation of the opera *Einstein* as performed at the 10th BITEF in 1976 was an index of the external contradictions present in Yugoslav cultural politics in relation to the Cold War zones of identity, power, influence, and games between

14 'Ajnštajn na plaži', *BITEF 10* catalogue, Belgrade, 1976.
15 The choreographer was Andrew de Groat. The music and sung lyrics were written by Philip Glass. The opera contains writings by Lucinda Childs, Samuel M. Johnson, and Christopher Knowles. The set design was conceived by Robert Wilson and Christian Giannini. The costumes were designed by D'Arcangelo-Mayer. The lighting was designed by Gene Rickard, and the sound by Kurt Munkacsi. Among the performers were Lucinda Childs, Samuel M. Johnson, and Sheryl Sutton.
16 Natalija Vagapova, *Bitef: pozorište, festival, život*, Belgrade, Bitef teatar, 2010, 115.

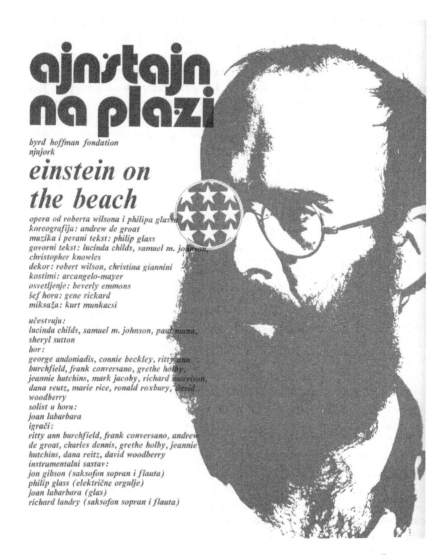

Figure 3.2 Page from Catalogue BITEF 10, Belgrade, 1976. Courtesy Miško Šuvaković Archive.

the East and the West. The Yugoslav cultural politics confronted the demands for liberalization of culture and art, for socialist self-management, and for cultural autonomies outside of state control, with the system of actual bureaucratic use of "Western liberalism" an instance of the pragmatic *state* politics of Yugoslavia, rather than its cultural politics. That is why the opera *Einstein*, in all its asestheti-cal immanence, signified a political intervention that would only have the specific impact I have described in the context of the Yugoslav political contradictions.

Einstein could assume different meanings and pragmatic functions, regardless of the ungraspable beauty of the staging and the music itself. But, *for us*, what mattered was that Belgrade's performance of *Einstein* actually preceded New York's. In those grey, late Cold War times, this was a statement of mediation both to the East and to the West.

Knee chapter 2
Einstein on the Beach is not radical, it is classic

Robert Wilson interviewed by Bojan Djordjev[1]

Einstein on the Beach *was staged and re-staged in four very different decades and contexts. The world of 1970s and the world today are different, artists are different, politics is different… What kind of reaction did you get from the audience this time around? Did something surprise you? Is today's audience surprised by the world of* Einstein?

I think when we first made *Einstein*, at least in New York, there was much more experimentation and cross-over between music and theatre. We were coming out of the 1960s which were a kind of renaissance period, with people like John Cage, who was a composer, but also a painter, a philosopher, writing books; and Robert Morris who made sculpture, but he was also a performer… There were so many things happening at that time, *Einstein* was sure unusual but maybe not quite so unusual, it was different from other things happening.

You are known for reclaiming the proscenium theatre for the avant-garde. After experimentation with space in the 1960s, what did it mean to reconquer this space, the traditional opera house? What were you drawn by?

In 1969 and 1970 I made a radical departure from what I had been doing. I was usually performing in alleys, churches, and galleries, rooftops… I went to see a major retrospective at the Whitney Museum of American Art in 1969. It was called *Art Without Illusion* [eds. *Anti-Illusion: Procedures/Materials*] – there were all the people that I admired: Yvonne Rainer, Trisha Brown, John Cage, a whole school of people who were doing works that "did not deal with illusion." So in 1969 I made a work called *The King of Spain* in which I went to a proscenium theatre that had nineteenth-century décor. After that I made a work called *The Life and Times of Sigmund Freud* and I did that at an opera house in Brooklyn. You could not even see strings pulling the drops, everything was happening behind the proscenium arch, it was a kind of two-dimensional space, one side was hidden and the other side was viewed. So much of what had been happening in the performance art and the visual arts at that

1   This is a transcript of a conversation conducted on June 7, 2015, in between two perfor-
    mances of *Krapp's Last Tape* at Stadsschouwburg, Amsterdam.

time was dealing with a very different space. Rauschenberg painted a goat
and put it in the middle of the floor so you can see it 360 degrees. Merce
Cunningham made dances in gymnasiums, so the dancers' bodies were
viewed from all sides – this is very different from the ballet George Balanchine
was doing, in a two-dimensional space, in the proscenium arch. And I was
attracted to this box and the magic of the box. It was radical to come back to
the box. Marina Abramović wanted me to work with her – she asked me to do
the Venice Biennial with her and I said: Marina, I am not going to sit in a basement room with all that smelly meat for three months. I am not going to do it.
If it's plastic and you paint it red, I might do it, but I am not going to sit there.
She wanted things to be very real. When I did the piece [*The Life and Death
of Marina Abramović*] here [Stadsschouwburg Amsterdam] with her, there is a
scene with her sitting on a block of ice. She said – it's made of plastic, I want
it real – and I said – the dress fits better if the block of ice is made of plastic.
So I went in a very different direction. And *Einstein* was a part of that. For
example, Lucinda Childs never wore make up, she never wore a dress when
performing. In *Einstein* she wore a dress, she was putting make up on. In that
way it was a radical departure from what was going on in the New York scene,
but there was so much activity going on. I think there is far less today. Warhol
had made his film *Sleep* and *The Empire State Building [Empire]*, I had made
a play that was seven days long, I made a 24-hour *Overture*, so a five-hour
opera was not so strange.

*Many of your early pieces work with extreme durations. Is this luxury of time pos-
sible in today's theatre and performance?*

I hate naturalism in theatre, to me what is interesting is that theatrical time is also
plastic, you can stretch it, you can compress it, and you construct it. It's the
time-space decisions that are most important.

*Einstein can also be about time – the time the pictures/scenes need to develop,
the time that is stretched, relativized, and transformed by repetition in both
music, dance, and staging, the duration of the piece – there is a clock in the
court scene without hands (but actually an Arabic decorative plate) …*

Sure it is; the whole thing is about time. The second scene, the *Trial*, looks like
nothing is happening, but actually, it is very baroque. There are kids who
perform hand gestures that are counts, they are counting: *this-times-fourteen*,
this-here-times-twelve, and *this-here-times-sixteen*, and the counts of the
music are totally different from the gestures, it's 24 times *Do-So*. They used to
call it the minimal opera but it's actually baroque.

Do you relate to this label of minimalism at all?

It's just a label… You take anyway that Trial scene, which is quite static, and then
next to it is a scene with people moving in space [Dance/Field]. One supports
the other because they are so different. I divided the space according to the
classical tradition: portraits, still life, and landscape. So if I see my hand here
it's a portrait; if I see it there it is part of still life, but if I go to the end of the block
and look at it – it is a part of landscape. There are Knee Plays at the beginning, which are very close to the audience – I thought of them as portraits. The

Train and Trial scenes were further away so they were still life, and the dance sections were deepest in space, so they were like landscapes. It is structured time and space, it is four acts and three themes: act one is *a-b*, act two is *c-a*, act three is *b-c*, and in Act Four they are all together for the first time, *a-b-c*. All of that was considered even before we knew what we were doing.

What were the sources and what are the topics of Einstein? *Where does the imagery come from? What was the significance of* Einstein *for your artistic practice? What kind of questions and interests made you do it? What kind of answers and directions did you get from it, what kind of fields did it open up for you?*

I started with light. Without light there is no space. Einstein said "Light is the measure of all things." So I always start with light. I was very fortunate to see Louis Kahn when I was a first-year student of architecture in New York. I heard him at a presentation in Philadelphia – he was just talking about light. I was amazed – my teachers at school never mentioned light. Later when I lectured at UCLA, Stanford, at the University of Texas, the Architectural School in Copenhagen, I was shocked that almost no-one, none of the architectural students were starting with the light. Kahn said – start with light. So I started with light. It was a way of structuring. In the first act in Scene 1a you have a train going across a field – Einstein talked about trains in his theories. Einstein said – if you see the train from your perspective, you'll see it one way, like we normally see it, but if you see it from the bird's perspective, you'll see a straight line. There is a train moving across the stage, and when it is interrupted by a vertical line of light, the train goes offstage and the light goes out; when it comes back for the second time it is half way across the stage when it is interrupted by the vertical line of light. The third time, it comes two-thirds across the stage and it is interrupted by the vertical line of light. The next scene, Act 1b starts with a horizontal bar of light which is a window high up in the court room, then the light comes in on the edge of the bed, so there are two horizontal bars of light. To me, time is a line that goes through the center of the earth and goes to the heavens. Time is a vertical line, space is a horizontal line and this is the basic architecture of everything. If you look at the Vermeer painting – it's that drip of milk, if you look at Barnet Newman's painting – it's that stripe down the middle of the canvas. It's how you play Mozart on a piano – the finger goes down the key and up and out on the string, it is always the tension between the vertical and the horizontal that makes the difference in the sound. There are only two lines – there is the straight line and there is the curved line. In the first Knee Play there are two women sitting – one does little hand gestures on a grid of *two-five-and-seven* and the other one is repeating *three*, so you have geometry and calculus. It is not a kind of work that you are going to read in a history book on *Einstein*, it is a work by two artists who made a poetic work, so it is full of associative images. For years people have been trying to figure out what this bed from the piece is – why do you have a bed in the middle of a courtroom? Well, I don't know, every time I see it I think about it differently: science is on trial, Einstein dared to be a dreamer, it's full of meanings. There are references to time traveling, to time and space, things that Einstein talked about in his theories. I don't want to be like a bad teacher at high school who is trying to lecture on Einstein. It is about what you see and something you hear.

How did you choose your collaborators? How much did the piece change from the original 1976 version? The choreographer changed – how much did that influence the piece? Was there a difference in training and professional background of the performers from the original version and the subsequent versions, and what did that bring to the piece?

I have known Philip's music before I knew him personally. I made a work called *Life and Times of Joseph Stalin*, it was 12 hours long – it started at seven in the evening and ended at seven in the morning – Philip came to see it and he stayed the entire time. Afterwards he came backstage, we talked and had breakfast together, and that morning we decided we would make a work together. We started meeting on Thursdays and we'd have lunch. I realized that Phil and I thought alike. I made diagrams of my work and he made diagrams of his work – it was exactly how I structured work in time and space, theme and variations. *Einstein* was not really as radical as people said – it just didn't tell a story. *Einstein* was based on theme and variations – and there is nothing radical about that, it is a classical music construction – all the possible combinations of *a*, *b*, and *c* put together.

I met Lucinda Childs by chance, when I was performing with Christopher Knowles in New Haven. I knew about her from before, we met one evening and started talking, and I asked her that evening if she would like to be in *Einstein*. She asked what she would do, and I said – you would be Einstein. Really, everyone was Einstein, and she said – yes. Then I asked Andy de Groat to do the choreography. At that time I was really not so interested in the display of skills on stage, and I still very much like the work Andy did because he did it for "natural" dancers, kids from the street. I have loved the ballet, and I love Balanchine, but I didn't necessarily want someone who could jump in the air and land on their toe in the piece. The ordinary was maybe extraordinary. What was most important is that someone is comfortable with themselves and they can relate to the public. So Andy did the original dances and most of the performers were not trained dancers. Later for the revival, we asked Lucinda to bring her company in and to do a new choreography. In this last revival Lucinda did not perform. She and I together found someone that she can hand her role to.

Before Einstein *you have called many of your pieces OPERA. And* Einstein *is considered the most important avant-garde opera of the twentieth century. After* Einstein *and until today, the creation and staging of operas are the most significant parts of your practice. What does opera as a format mean to you? What significance did this format have for you in early 1970s NYC, and how do you relate to the cultural and even national charges opera has in some European societies? And was* Einstein *in dialogue with those as well?*

My first major work – we did it also in this theatre in 1971 – *Deafman Glance* was seven hours long and silent. The French called it "the silent opera." In a sense, it was structured silences. John Cage said to me – that's a very good way to describe your work. But they called it an opera. If we go back to the Latin meaning of the word "opera" – it comes from "opus," which means "work." When I did *Sigmund Freud* and those early works, people said it's not theatre, it's not really dance, it's very visual, but it is not a painting – it seemed to me, one way you could refer to it, was that it is an opera. Because it brought together painting, light, sculpture, movement, architecture, all those elements and eventually, words, texts, sounds were incorporated, so it was like an opus. An epic theatre. Today we think of opera as music that is sung, but the ancient meaning of the word, the roots of the word are much broader.

What's the difference for you now between creating an opera "from scratch" and taking an already existing work and staging it, if there is any difference?

It is always a collaboration. *Einstein* was a collaboration with other artists. You compromise, they take you in a different direction; you have to respect your collaborators, partners, whether it is Wagner or Mozart or Philip Glass, or Lucinda Childs, and now I am working with CocoRosie. They are visual artists. They don't only write music, they have ideas about make-up, they have ideas how you dress somebody, what the stage looks like... You have to respect your partners... One season I did Heiner Müller, Chekov, Virginia Woolf, William Burroughs, Shakespeare... I once did Lou Reed with Luigi Nono back to back. Nono is all about quiet and *piano, piano*; Lou just has to be loud. I have learned to appreciate loudness of sound because of Lou, and also because I was just coming from working on Nono. I did *Hamlet* – and I can't rewrite *Hamlet*. It's the greatest play ever written, so you have to respect it – but at the same time, I had to find my own way of doing it. Everything is in finding the balance, respecting your partner.

Who are the younger artists that intrigue you? Who would you like to collaborate with, who do you feel is driven by similar passions in their practice?

Right now I am working with CocoRosie. How old are they, 30 or something? They are super great, they are fresh, they are young, they have new ideas, other ideas from mine... I invite close to 200 artists, young kids, to The Watermill Center during the course of the year, people with totally different aesthetics than mine. One of them is working at Stedelijk Museum right now on a piece he developed at The Watermill Center. He is a dancer, but he also writes music, and he is only 20 years old. Yes, there are a lot of young artists that I am meeting and working with. I don't want to have a school, I don't want to have a Robert Wilson way of doing things. What I did was right for me, would not be right for you necessarily.

I was walking down a street in 1967 and I saw a policeman about to hit a black kid over the head with a club and I stopped it. I asked why do you hit him and he said it's none of your business, and I said, but it is, I am a responsible citizen, why do you hit the boy? It turned out he was deaf and I learned he was going to be institutionalized because they thought he couldn't learn. He has never been to school. We didn't know where his parents were. I went to court and adopted him. That was Raymond Andrews and I wrote my first play with him. I didn't learn theatre by going to Yale University, by reading a book... By chance I met Christopher Knowles in the early 1970s and he spent a number of years of his life in an institution and suddenly *A Letter for Queen Victoria* was written with Christopher. He was composing text mathematically and based on geometry. This was totally fascinating to me. He could see big patterns quickly and it was by chance I met him, just by chance one night. These and similar encounters helped form my theatre.

In the last decade, performance in museums and galleries made a big come back. Not only producing new work but also re-enacting historical pieces. The visual arts world seems to have re-discovered performance, as if recovering from amnesia. How do you feel about this? You are active in both fields. Why are they still so divided and why is everyone so surprised and fascinated when, from time to time, these re-discoveries occur?

Lincoln Kirstein said in the late 1950s, "Modern dance will have no tradition." It was a shock for me when I read it. Now I think he was right. The work we were doing in happenings and galleries, streets, will never happen again, the *Deafman Glance*, a seven-hour silent play, *Overture*, a 24-hour play I did only once at the Opéra Comique, were events of their time, they were shooting stars... I had homeless people from the street performing, I had Christopher Knowles, these events were not meant to be repeated. You knew when you were going to it that it was an event that was never going to happen again. Marina's exhibition at MOMA – I love Marina, and we are very close friends, and I admire her tremendously – to be very honest, to go and see her recreate what she did 30 years ago to me no longer had the same power. What was interesting was to see her sitting in that museum – there the power was. Because that was the real thing. These pieces from the past, when they are re-created, they lose something. Of course, they gain something else. I think so much of performance art, dance, will have no tradition as Kirstein said it. Perhaps 200 years from now we will be doing Balanchine's ballets, because they are classically constructed and they were meant to last, we'll still be playing Shakespeare, but *A Letter for Queen Victoria* – it will never happen again. It was a product of the time, and that's the beauty of it. It exists in memory and disappears and that's that. It was never written or meant to last.

Socrates said a baby is born knowing everything, and life is just the uncovering of the knowledge. We are always rediscovering what we were born knowing – and that is the classics. I wrote an article for the *Village Voice* about Donald Judd when he did 100 stainless steel cubes [*100 untitled works in mill aluminum*] in Marfa, Texas. It was ridiculous, the *New York Times* was asking if it is sculpture or what is it – just 100 steel boxes? For me, 500 years from now, it will be as interesting as it is today. It is classical, the form is classical, it is like the pyramids, it is classical architecture. But we are always rediscovering the classics. *Einstein* is a classic, but we had to rediscover it. When we did it in 1976 – read the English press, read the German press – they were totally confused, they were trying to make a narrative where there was no narrative.

Now the *London Times* says it's the masterpiece of the twentieth century; so 35 years later, it is looked at differently.

Do you think they understand it better or it's just 35 years old, so it must be a classic?

I think that people got used to the idea that music theatre could be structured this way. And they got used to Philip Glass.

Part 2

From repetition to representation

4   Intuition and algorithm in *Einstein on the Beach**

Kyle Gann

Some of us are old enough to remember the public impression that minimalist music made before the premiere of *Einstein on the Beach*. Minimalism in its first manifestation was a strict, objectivist style. We thought of it, pretty much, as gradual-process music. Philip Glass's *Music in Fifths* and *Music in Contrary Motion* (both 1969) offered us perceptual exercises in additive process, and taught us to hear the gradual expansion of a time frame. Steve Reich's out-of-phase tape loops amplified microscopic phenomena of the human voice. The similarly phasing 12-note pattern of *Piano Phase* (1967) created its own objective geometry, as did the change-ringing patterns of Jon Gibson. La Monte Young's sine-tone installations were comfortingly based in mathematics. Charlemagne Palestine's piano improvisations conjured up overtones. Only Terry Riley seemed a little loopy, pardon the pun, but even in *In C* (1964) we heard the echoes of melodies as a strict canonic process.

It is odd to remember at this distance how important this criterion of objectivity seemed at the time. We had come out of a period of serialism and strict chance processes, glorifying mathematics and the natural world. In the conditioned milieu of 1960s avant-garde music, mere expression of emotion seemed at the time unworthy of serious study; subjectivity was distrusted. The worship of science was rampant, and music had become scientific. For many musicians involved in the avant-garde it accelerated the acceptance of minimalism, I think, that it seemed to be about natural and or logical phenomena. Some of us weren't yet ready to return to intuition, art, shading, eccentricity, and the unsteady foundation of personal preference. The gradual going out of phase of otherwise identical phrases in Reich's *Come Out* (1966) and *Piano Phase*, and the additive processes (A, A+B, A+B+C, A+B+C+D) in Glass's works for his own ensemble, reassured us that we were listening to natural, or at least mathematical, phenomena.

There were enough hints of gradual process in *Einstein*, I think, that it was accepted as fitting this paradigm at the time. The use of numbers and solfege syllables as text facilitated this impression. So did Glass's liner notes to the original

*   All the music examples of this chapter refer to the following credit line: Einstein On The Beach Words & Music by Philip Glass & Robert Wilson © Copyright 1976 Dunvagen Music Publishers Incorporated. Chester Music Limited. All Rights Reserved. International Copyright Secured.

Tomato recording. Of the lightning-fast patterns in the Building scene (Act IV, scene 1), Glass states that "the repeated figures form simple arithmetic progressions," and he refers to a figure in the Trial scene which, he writes, "slowly expands and contracts" "through an additive process."[1] While this is arguably true of the Trial scene (Act I, scene 2), I will show that the progressions of the Building scene are far from arithmetically simple, and also that many of the other scenes are devoid of predictable algorithmic thinking.

Looking back in retrospect, *Einstein* seems a far more intuitively written work than we thought at the time. For several decades the score wasn't available, and to transcribe these lightning-fast patterns would have taken a lot of patience; those of us accustomed to the earlier minimalist works thought we had a pretty good idea what we were hearing. Eventually a score became available via links on Glass's website, and I bought it in 2008. Upon opening it I was immediately struck by how much more unpredictable the music was than I had remembered it, how circuitous its forms were, how difficult it often was to pinpoint the musical logic. I was struck by how compositionally *playful* the piece is. In particular it offers some striking examples of *recomposition*, of writing through the same parallel succession of motives and harmonies several times within one piece and doing it a little differently each time. It is this playful, intuitive technique of recomposition in the composed musical scenes of *Einstein* that I want to focus on in this chapter.

Einstein is written in four acts separated by "Knee Plays" which connect them (as the knee connects the calf with the thigh). Certain scenes are recapitulated, with variations, in more than one act: the trial material, for example, appears in Act I, scene 2, and again in Act III, scene I. Dance 1 (Act II, scene 1) and Dance 2 (Act III, scene 2) are very similar, though the addition of the violin soloist (Einstein) in the latter necessitates certain changes in the form. The layout below comes from the liner notes to the original 1977 Tomato recording:

Knee Play 1
Act I: Scene 1: Train
          Scene 2: Trial
          Knee Play 2
Act II: Scene 1: Dance 1 (Field with Spaceship)
          Scene 2: Night Train
          Knee Play 3
Act III: Scene 1: Trial/Prison
          Scene 2: Dance 2 (Field with Spaceship)
          Knee Play 4
Act IV: Scene 1: Building/Train
          Scene 2: Bed
          Scene 3: Spaceship
          Knee Play 5

1   Philip Glass, "Note on Einstein on the Beach," *Einstein on the Beach*, Tomato Records, TOM-4-2901 (1979).

One of the signal innovations of Glass's music for *Einstein* is that musical passages become a design element that can be reused from one knee play to another and one act to another.

I will begin, almost pro forma, by reviewing the recombinant elements that make up *Einstein*, since I'll be referring to them later. First of all are three recurring chord progressions, one with three chords, one with four, and one with five. (Music Example 4.1) (Glass's notes also refer to ideas of two chords and one chord, but these don't appear as frequently.) The famous five-chord progression modulates from F minor to E major, and is the basis of the Spaceship scene, appears in the Train and Building scenes, and is the basis of the internal knee plays. Glass refers to it in the original liner notes as "cadential," but the three-chord progression heard in the first and last knee plays seems cadential as well: a simple vi-V-I. The four-chord progression appears in the Trial and Bed scenes, always in the kind of slowly arpeggiated motion seen here. In addition, there are a few other features found from scene to scene. The upward A-minor triad with a variety of continuations serves as a prelude to the four-chord progression. A la-fa-la-si-do-si motto in A-flat appears as a kind of section marker in the Train and Night Train scenes, and the following figure of four modules appears in both those scenes and constitutes almost the entire notated material of the Building scene.

Many movements of *Einstein* seem to be written in a kind of stanzaic form, wherein a movement is divided into stanzas which are parallel in their function and similar (though varied) in their progress through the same harmonies and motifs. Sometimes the beginnings are marked by introductory motives which I will call incipits: such as the three perfect fourths in the saxophones at each new section of the Train scene, the two four-note patterns of Night Train, and the reduction of the Building scene to a 6/8 pattern (Music Example 4.2). Likewise, some of the stanzas end in signaling characteristic figures that I will call envois, after the medieval poetry term. These include a quick F-minor triad in the Train scene, the solo violin playing A minor scales in Trial 1, and, again, the la-fa-la-si-do-si motive in Night Train. Not all stanzas in the various scenes are marked by these devices, but in those that are the incipits and envois are quite clear in their framing intent.

There are moments in *Einstein* at which a more stereotypically linear minimalist logic prevails (Music Example 4.3). The most obvious is the bulk of the Bed scene, where the soprano sings over the four-chord progression. As this chart of the rhythms for each chord shows, the length of the rhythmic cycle expands in a fairly predictable manner with each iteration. The voice part (Music Example 4.4), however, is a more intuitive element, drawing lines that use only notes from the four triads. Out of 81 possibilities (not counting octave displacements), Glass chooses only seven of the possible such lines and repeats three of them, creating a mild climax by using sevenths in the 7th and 8th cycles.

Likewise, the violin part of the Trial 1 scene (Music Example 4.5) does, as Glass says, go through a process of expansion and subtraction, though not in a completely linear manner.

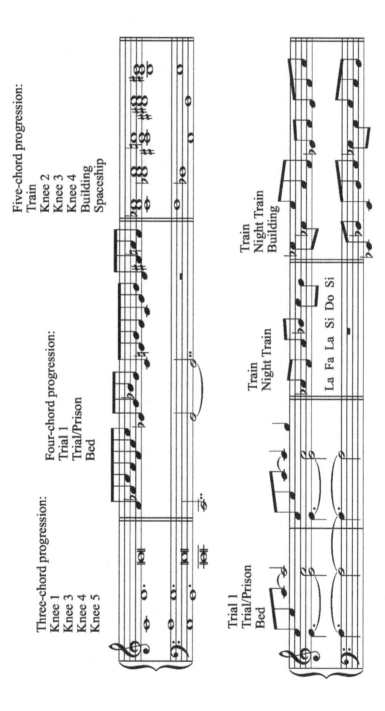

Music Example 4.1 Recurring elements in *Einstein on the Beach*

Incipits

Music Example 4.2 Incipits and Envois

From m. 35 on

f	Eb	C	D
4+3	4	4+3	4
4+3+2	4	4+3+2	4
4+3+2	4+3	4+3+2	4+3
4+3+2	4+3+2	4+3+2	4+3+2
4+3+3+4	4+3+2	4+3+3+4	4+3+2
4+3+3+4	4+3+2+2	4+3+3+4	4+3+2+2
4+3+3+3+4	4+3+2+2	4+3+3+3+4	4+3+2+2
4+3+3+3+4	4+3+3+4	4+3+3+3+4	4+3+3+4
4+3+3+3+3+4	4+3+3+4	4+3+3+3+3+4	4+3+3+4
4+3+3+3+3+2+2+4	4+3+3+4	4+3+3+3+3+2+2+4	4+3+3+4
4+3+3+3+3+2+2+2+4	4+3+3+4	4+3+3+3+3+2+2+2+4	4+3+3+4
4+3+3+3+3+2+2+2+4	4+3+3+2+4	4+3+3+3+3+2+2+2+4	4+3+3+2+4

Music Example 4.3 Additive process in *Einstein's* Bed scene

At the other extreme (Music Example 4.6) is the Building movement, in which only the two organs are notated, as the voices and other instruments drone and improvise. As notated, the piece is entirely in eighth-notes, much like several of Glass's minimalist works of the late 1960s (*Music in Similar Motion, Music in Fifths*), and in contrary motion (as in *Music in Contrary Motion*). The move from one pattern to another, however, is not at all predictable (Music Example 4.7). This chart shows all the pitches for the first 30 cycles, lined up vertically to show easily what notes are added or subtracted to get from one repetition to

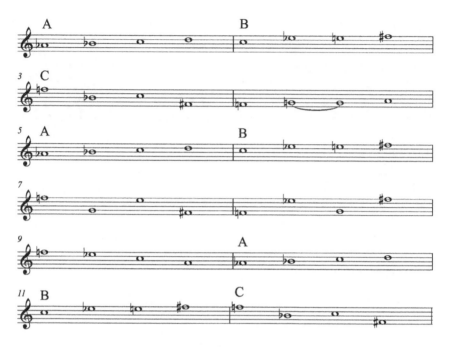

Music Example 4.4 Voice lines from the Bed scene from *Einstein on the Beach*

another (and with a lower-case "e" to denote the upper octave). What made this chart clear for me is that the movement is made up of only four modules whose changing combinations make up the form. (Music Example 4.8) Musical example 4.8 shows those four modules: the movement's seeming micro-complexity is due to the fact that module A is contained in module B, and likewise module C in D. The following chart shows the deployment of these four modules throughout the entire section (Music Example 4.9). At each step one can see a kind of additive or subtractive logic: the 3/8 modules start out with a 6/8 feel, and then the A module is added to give kind of a quarter-note bump to the repetition of BD, then another A is added, then steps 2 and 3 are added together, and so on. After expanding, the music strips back down to just B and D, after which module C starts to be added in. Towards the end the music begins to emphasize the ten-note pattern ABCD, and finally resolves to the opening BD with which it began.

The musical continuity here is not illogical, but neither is there any place where one could look at two or three successive phrases and guess (with any confidence of accuracy) what the next one will be. Glass's comment about "simple arithmetic progressions" notwithstanding, this is a very unpredictable sequence. And, it must be said, this is all background structure anyway, since in this scene the pentatonic drones and improvisations tend to override the subtlety of the organ patterns.

Violin Patterns in the Trial 1 scene

Music Example 4.5 Violin patterns in the Trial 1 scene

Music Example 4.6 Opening of the Building scene

```
                    EAF   EFA
  eA                eAF   EFA      eAF   EFA
  eA                eAeAF EFA      eAF   EFA
  eA                eAeAF EFA      eAF   EFAeAeAF   EFAeAFEFA
  eAF       EFA     eAeAF EFAeAeAeAF    EFAeAeAF   EFA
  eA                eAeAF EFA      eAF   EFAeAeAF   EFAeAFEFA
eAeAF       EFAeAeAeAF   EFA       eAF   EFAeAeA         eAFEFA
  eAF       EFAeAeAeAF   EFAeA     eAF   EFA   eAF   EFA
  eAF       EFAeA   eAF  EFAeA     eAF   EFA   eAF   EFA
eAeAF       EFAeA   eAF  EFA       eAF   EFA   eAF   EFA
eAeAF       EFAeA   eAF  EFA       eAF   EFA   eAF   EFAeAFEFAeAFEFA
eAeAF       EFA
  eAF       EFA
  eAFEF     EFA     eAF   EFA
eAeAFEF     EFA     eAF   EFA
eAeAeAFEF   EFA     eAF   EFA
eAeAeAFEF   EFAeA   eAF   EFA
eAeAeAF     EFAeA   eAFEFEFA
  eAeAFEF   EFA     eAFEFEFA
  eAFEF     EFA
  eAFEFEFEFA
  eAFEFEFEFA         eAF   EFA
  eAFEFEFEFA         eAFEFEFA
  eAFEFEFEFA         eAFEFEFA     eAF      EFA   eAFEFEFA
  eAFEFEFEFA         eAF   EFA    eAFEF    EFA   eAF   EFA
  eAF       EFA     eAFEFEFA
  eAF       EFAeA   eAF   EFA     eAF      EFA   eAFEFEFA
eAeAeAF     EFA     eAFEFEFA      eAF      EFA   eAFEFEFA
eAeAeAF     EFA     eAFEFEFA      eAFEFEF  AeAeAF   EFA
eAeAeAF     EFA     eAFEFEFA      eAFEFEFEFAeAeAF   EFA
```

Music Example 4.7 *Einstein on the Beach*: Building scene, RH organ 1, patterns 1–30

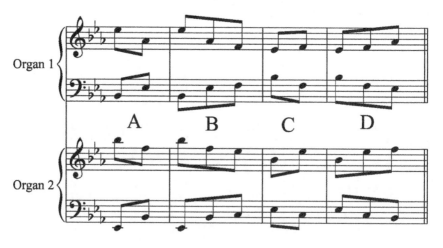

Music Example 4.8 Keyboard modules, Building scene from *Einstein on the Beach*

```
        B   D
       AB   D B D
      AAB   D B D
      AAB   D B DA B   D B D
        B  DAB DAAB   DAB D
      AAB   D B DA B   D B D
  AB DAAB   D B DAAB   D
   B DAAB  DAB D B   D
   B DA B  DAB D B   D
       AB  DAB D B   D B D
  AB DA B   D B D B   D B DBD
      A B   D
        B   D
       BC  D B D
      ABC  D B D
     AABC  D B D
     AABC  DAB D
     AAB   DABCD
      ABC  D BCD
       BC  D
       BCCD
       BCCD B D
       BCCD BCD
       BCCD BCD   B   D BCD
       BCCD B D   BC  D B D
              B D  BC  D
        B  DAB D   B   D BCD
      AAB   D BCD  B   D BCD
      AAB   D BCD  BC  DAB D
      AAB   D BCD  BCCDAB D
      AAB   DABCD  BCCDABCD
       AB   D BCD
      ABC  D B D
      ABC  DABCD  B   D B D
      ABC  DABCD  B   D B DBDBD
      ABC  D
        B   D
```

Music Example 4.9 Pattern of modules in the Building scene

The Train

The Train scene is made up of three recurring sections, structured in the form ABABCABC. The B sections, which seem to serve a connective function, are instrumental (without voices), using the four modules that we've just identified in the Building scene. The C sections are based on the five-chord cadential progression that is the basis of the Spaceship scene. The A sections are unique to this scene. The first two B sections are identical, the third one considerably expanded. The two C sections are identical except that the chorus is added in the second one; the rhythmic patterns here follow those at the beginning of the Spaceship scene. What I want to discuss as illustrative of Glass's approach to form in *Einstein*, though, are the three A sections.

The diagram in Example 4.10 outlines the three A sections in a kind of shorthand that isolates an abbreviated set of features (Music Example 4.10). A three-note drone ostinato in the saxophones runs throughout all the A sections, imposing an underlying 3/4 meter. The voices sing repeated patterns of various lengths, entirely in quarter-notes except for a recurring refrain which I will identify in a moment. When the number of quarter-notes in the voice pattern is not divisible by three, the voices and saxophones run through a brief out-of-phase pattern, and the number of their repetitions must be divisible by three to make the phrases come out evenly at the end of the measure.

The numbers on each left-hand column indicate the number of quarter-notes in each voice phrase. A number given as 4x3, 5x3, and so on, indicates that the phrase goes out of phase with the saxophone ostinato. A number given as 6+4+2 or 5+4+3+2+1 points to a subsidiary rhythm within the phrase suggesting an additive or subtractive rhythmic process; note that these occur only in the second A section. In each right-hand column are given the pitches in the solo soprano voice part, and since there are three flats in the key signature, A should be read as A-flat, B as B-flat, and so on. As earlier stated, all these melodic fragments are notated in quarter-notes except for a recurring refrain in 8th-notes on A♭FA♭B♭CB♭, sung on the solfege syllables la-fa-la-si-do-si, which recurs both here and in the Night Train scene as a kind of motto. One can see that here it appears twice at the beginning, and then at the end of each A section.

Other points that could be made here are even clearer in the next example (Music Example 4.11). This comparison of the three soprano parts (and the tenor is always either a perfect fourth or major third below, in parallel) shows that the soprano begins each section alternating between A♭ and B♭, gradually makes her way up to E♭ and then F, then descending back to B♭ before concluding with the la-fa-la-si-do-si motto. Notice, however, that the melodic and rhythmic character of the route is quite different in each A section. The first section reaches the high F relative quickly, the second takes a long time to get there, and the third stays on F and E♭ for a long time as a kind of climax. The second section, as we've noted, contains more patterns which contain an internal subtractive or additive process, and the third section contains the only additive process among phrases, and one additional subtractive process. At the end, each of them finally goes into

Einstein on the Beach Train scene A sections

A1 — mm. 1-17

3	rest
4x3	ABCB
3	AFABCB.♪
4x3,3	AFABCBFA, AFABCB.♪
4x3	ABCB
3	AFABCB.♪
4x3,3	AFABCBFA, AFABCB.♪
4x3	ABCB
4x3	ABCE
5x3	ABCEE
2x3	FE
4x3	FFEE
6	FFFEEE
5x3	FFEEB
4x3	FEEB
4x3	FEBE
3	FEB
2x3	EB
3	AFABCB.♪
4x3,3	AFABCBFA, AFABCB.♪

A2 — mm. 25-51

3	rest
4x3	ABAB
4x3	AABB
2x3,4x3	AB, AABB
6	AAABBB
6,4x3	AAABBB, AABB
6+4+2	AAABBBAABBAB
4+2	AABBAB
4x3	AABB
2x3	ABAB
5x3	ABABC
2+3+4	ABABCABCE
4x3	ABCE
5x3	ABCEE
5+4	ABCEEABCE
5+4+3+2+1	ABCEEABCEABCABA
2+3+4	ABABCABCE
2x3	FE
4x3	FFEE
6	FFFEEE
5x3	FFEEB
4x3	FEEB
4x3	FEBE
3	FEB
2x3	EB
3	AFABCB.♪
4x3,3	AFABCBFA, AFABCB.♪

A3 — mm. 60-89

3	rest
4+2	AABBAB
4x3	AABB
8x3	AABBCCBB
4x3	ABCB
4x3	ABCE
5x3	ABCEE
6	ABCEEE
5x3	FFEEB
10x3	FFEEBCCBEE
5x3	CCBEE
6	BBCEE
4x3	BCEC
4x3	ABCE
5x3	ABBCE
6	ABBCEE
6	FFFFFE
5x3	FFFFE
4x3	FFE
3	FFE
2x3	FE
4x3	FFEE
6	FFFEEE
5x3	FFEEB
4x3	FEEB
4x3	FEBE
3	FEB
2	EB
3	AFABCB.♪
4x3,3	AFABCBFA, AFABCB.♪

Music Example 4.10 *Einstein on the Beach* Train scene A sections

Music Example 4.11 Melodic line of the Train scene as observed in the soprano voice

a subtractive rhythmic process of 5-4-3-2 before lapsing into the la-fa-la-si-do-si motto. What is evident, then, is how many rhythmic and melodic options were open to Glass to get him from the A♭ up to the F and back to the closing refrain, and how carefully he recomposed this process for three parallel sections achieving the same function through different routes. This possibility of intuitively recomposing a section is far removed from the typical concept of early minimalism as being something logically predetermined. We're not just listening to an algorithmic or linear process here; we're listening to intuitively composed variations in a large-scale melody conceptualized as rhythm.

Dances 1 and 2

One of the most fascinating views of Glass's compositional process in *Einstein* is the subtle contrast between Dances 1 and 2. Many of the materials are identical from one dance to another, but the second is somewhat transformed in consequence of its use of the solo violin representing Einstein.

Both dances contain a trio of drone notes that sound throughout: the pitches A, D, and E (Music Example 4.12). These pitches are heard in the solo voices, the saxophones, and the left hand of Organ 1 in every measure. In addition, a fourth pitch, F, appears in the culminating repetitions of each large section.

These drone pitches are recontextualized by the changing harmonies around them. In Dance 1, the arpeggios in the organs and piccolo move among chords of F major, A major, B♭ major, G major, and C major, the constant D, E, and A being reinterpreted in each new harmony. (Actually, the way Glass describes it in the liner notes is as always returning to D, which is justifiable if you consider the F major as part of a D minor 7th chord; but which isn't the way I hear it.) The singers and saxophones use only the pitches D, E, F, and A, voiced as either quarter notes, dotted quarter notes, half notes, and at one arguably climactic point dotted half notes.

A listing of the chord progressions and the rhythms in each repetition throughout Dance 1 (Music Example 4.13) reveals a clear division into three parallel

Music Example 4.12 Figures and harmonies in Dance 1

Form of Dance 1

	Harmonic Scheme			Rhythmic Scheme		
Section: Patterns:	1ˢᵗ 1-17	2ⁿᵈ 18-33	3ʳᵈ 34-50	1ˢᵗ 1-17	2ⁿᵈ 18-33	3ʳᵈ 34-50
	F	AAAF	FF	2♩	4♩ 2♩ 2♩	6♩ 2♩.
	AF	AAAF	AF	4♩ 2♩	4♩ 2♩ 2♩ 4♩.	4♩. 2♩.
	AF	BbBbFAAF	AF	4♩ 4♩.	2♩ 4♩ 4♩. 4♩. 2♩ 2♩	4♩. 4♩.
	AAFF	BbFAF	AF	4♩ 2♩ 2♩4♩.	2♩ 4♩ 4♩. 4♩.	4♩. 2♩.
	BbF	BbFAF	BbBbFAAF	2♩ 2♩	4♩4♩ 4♩. 4♩.	4♩. 4♩. 2♩ 2♩ 2♩
	BbF	GF	GF	2♩ 4♩.	2♩ 4♩.	2♩ 4♩.
	BbBbF	GCF	GF	2♩ 4♩. 4♩.	2♩ 4♩. 4♩.	4♩. 4♩.
	BbF	CF	GCF	4♩. 4♩.	4♩. 4♩.	4♩. 2♩ 4♩.
	GF	FF	GCF	2♩ 4♩.	2♩ 4♩.	2♩ 4♩. 2♩
	GF	FF	GCF	4♩. 2♩	6♩ 4♩.	2♩ 4♩. 6♩
	GF	FF	GCF	4♩. 4♩.	6♩ 2♩	6♩ 6♩
	GF	F	GF	2♩ 4♩.	6♩	6♩ 6♩
	GF	GF*	GF*	2♩ 2♩.	12♩ (x2) 6♩ (x2)	12♩ 4♩.
	GF*	GF*	GF*	4♩(x2)6♩(x2)	12♩(x3) 6♩(x4) 12♩	6♩
	GF*	GCF*	GCF*	4♩(x3) 6♩(x4)	12♩(x2)12♩(x3)6♩(x2)	12♩ (4+3+2)♩ 6♩
	GCF*	GCFF*	GCFF*	4♩(4+3+2)♩ 12♩	12♩(x2)12♩(x3) 6♩ 2♩.	12♩ (4+3+2)♩ 4♩ 2♩.
	GCF*		GCFFAFAF*	4♩(4+3+2)♩2♩2♩.		12♩ (4+3+2)♩ 4♩ 2♩ 4♩. 2♩. 4♩. 4♩

* = DEFE pattern in voice

Music Example 4.13 Form of Dance 1

parts, though these are not marked by clear incipits and refrains as in the Train scene. Though there is no key signature, the general tonality of Dance 1 sounds to me to be in F major; the piece begins and ends on an F major chord (with an added sixth D), and the phrase rhythm frequently makes F major sound like a resolution, though it can also sound like a flatted-seventh adjunct to G major. Listing the harmonic progressions of each repetition, we see a clear parallelism among phrases 1 to 17, 18 to 33, and 34 to 50. That is, there are 50 phrases in the dance, divided into three stanzas with lengths 17 + 16 + 17. (By the way, the 2012 Nonesuch recording of Einstein, Nonesuch B000005J28, omits the second stanza.) As is clear from the diagram, each stanza starts by alternating F major and A major, adds in Bb major, and finally moves to an alternation of G and F, inserting between them a C major chord to make a kind of II-V-I cadence. Although this pattern is clear, there is some variety in the tonal emphasis: stanza 3 spends less time on Bb than stanzas 1 and 2 do, and stanza 2 has a long middle passage on F major lacking in stanzas 1 or 3.

Likewise, in an overview of the rhythms of each repeated phrase one can note rough parallels, but no clear isomorphism. In the first half of each stanza is one repeated pattern longer than the ones around it; in stanza 1 it's the fourth, in stanza 2 the third, and in stanza 3 the fifth. In stanza 1, half-notes appear in phrases 5 to 7, in stanza 2 in phrases 1 to 4, and stanza 3 contains no half-note rhythms, but offers dotted half-notes in phrase five.

The last four or five phrases of each stanza are rather climactic. While elsewhere the soprano and soprano saxophone use only the pitches D and E, in these final phrases they use a repeating DEFE, as marked in the diagram. Note that the rhythms here are entirely in quarter-notes, and that in stanzas 1 and 2 occurs a nine-note pattern of DEFE-DEF-DE, a kind of small 4+3+2 subtractive motif. (And by the way, we'll see Glass using this 4+3+2 pattern 15 years later in his Columbus opera *The Voyage*, and many of these other patterns as well.) These DEFE motives appear only over the harmonic progressions GF and GCF. All of these features point to an overall form divided into three parallel parts, but the musical continuity is so static, with its endlessly sustained A, D, and E, that the listener does not distinctly experience the piece as sectional, but as a smooth continuum with variations in the symmetry of the rhythm.

Turning to Dance 2 (Music Example 4.14), we find many of these same characteristics. Again the pitches D, E, and A are sustained throughout, the DEFE motive appears as a kind of relative intensification, and the rhythm moves among quarter-note, dotted-quarter, and half-note beats. But now the saxophones and piccolo are replaced by Einstein's violin, and the necessity of writing a playable if still extremely virtuosic part for that instrument seems to suggest quite a few alterations.

Most noticeably, the tonality of F that dominated Dance 1 is replaced with a feeling of A minor, or at least an A natural minor scale. The tonality of Bb no longer appears. For the first ten phrases the music merely alternates between an A natural minor scale and an A major triad. The DEFE motive appears only twice in the piece, about a third of the way through and for a long time at the very end.

Dance 2

1	a	2♩	
2	a	6♩	
3	aa	4♩ 6♩	
4	a	4♩	
5	aA	6♩ 4♩.	
6	aA	6♩ 4♩	
7	aA	4♩. 4♩	
8	aA	4♩. 4♩.	
9	aAaA	6♩ 4♩. 4♩. 4♩	
10	AA	4♩. 4♩	
11	GGGAA	4♩ 4♩ 4♩ 4♩. 4♩	DEFE
12	GGGAaA	4♩ 4♩ 4♩ 4♩. 4♩. 4♩	DEFE
13	GGCAaA	4♩ 4♩ (4+3+2)♩ 4♩ 4♩ 4♩.	DEFE
14	GGCaAaA	4♩ 4♩ (4+3+2)♩ 4♩. 4♩ 6♩ 4♩.	DEFE
15	a	6♩	
16	aa	6♩ 4♩.	
17	aaa	6♩ 4♩. 4♩	
18	aaaa	6♩ 4♩. 4♩ 2♩.	
19	aaaaa	6♩ 4♩. 4♩ 2♩. 2♩	
20	aaaaaa	6♩ 4♩. 4♩ 2♩. 2♩ 2♩	
21	aaaaa	4♩. 4♩ 2♩ 2♩ 2♩	
22	aaaa	4♩ 2♩. 2♩ 2♩	
23	aaa	2♩. 2♩ 2♩	
24	aa	2♩ 2♩	
25	a	2♩	
26	a	2♩	
27	a	2♩ 2♩	
28	GCa	2♩ 2♩ 2♩	
29	GCa	2♩. 2♩ 2♩.	
30	GCa	2♩ 2♩. 2♩	
31	GCa	2♩. 2♩ 2♩	
32	GCaa	2♩ 2♩. 2♩. 2♩	
33	Ca	2♩. 2♩	
34	GGGa	4♩ 4♩ 4♩ 2♩	DEFE
35	GGGaAaA	4♩ 4♩ 4♩ 2♩ 4♩. 2♩ 4♩	DEFE
36	GGCCCaAaA	4♩ 4♩ (4+3+2)♩ 2♩ 4♩. 2♩ 4♩	DEFE
37	GGCCCaAaAaAaA	4♩ 4♩ (4+3+2)♩ 2♩ 4♩. 2♩ 4♩ 6♩ 4♩. 2♩ 4♩	DEFE
38	GCaAaAaAaA	4♩ (4+3+2)♩ 2♩ 4♩. 2♩ 4♩ 6♩ 4♩. 4♩. 2♩ 4♩	DEFE
39	GCaAaAaaaAaA	4♩ (4+3+2)♩ 2♩ 4♩. 2♩ 4♩ 6♩ 4♩. 4♩ 2♩ 4♩. 2♩ 4♩	DEFE
40	GCaAaAaaaaaAaA	4♩ (4+3+2)♩ 2♩ 4♩. 2♩ 4♩ 6♩ 4♩. 4♩ 2♩. 2♩ 4♩. 2♩ 4♩	DEFE
41	GCaAaAaaaaaaAaA	4♩ (4+3+2)♩ 2♩ 4♩. 2♩ 4♩ 6♩ 4♩. 4♩ 2♩. 2♩ 2♩ 4♩. 2♩ 4♩	DEFE
42	GCaAaAaaaaaaAaA	4♩ (4+3+2)♩ 2♩ 4♩. 2♩ 4♩ 6♩ 4♩. 4♩ 2♩. 4♩ 2♩ 4♩. 2♩ 4♩	DEFE
43	GGCaAaAaaaaaAaA	4♩ 4♩. (4+3+2)♩ 2♩ 4♩. 2♩ 4♩ 6♩ 4♩. 4♩ 2♩. 4♩ 2♩ 4♩. 2♩ 4♩	DEFE
44	a	6♩	

Music Example 4.14 Form of Dance 2

Replacing the middle stanza is a long section (phrases 15 to 25) in which the violin articulates a strict process that is both additive and subtractive: it plays a scale starting on A and going up to G, then another phrase going up to F, then up to E, D, C, and B. After reaching maximum length it then begins subtracting the opening phrases one at a time, and I tried to spell out in the diagram the strict process of addition and subtraction. Later, starting in phrase 37, Glass reinserts this scalar process into larger phrases on the chords of G, C, and A, resulting in repetitive sections far longer than anything in Dance 1. At last the chorus and organ suddenly drop out, and the violin is left to play a solo transition to Knee Play 4.

Aside from the special case of sonata form, in which the composer rewrites the exposition as a recapitulation in order to transpose all themes into the tonic, this idea of using several *recomposings* of the same passage within one piece does not come up often in the history of music. The composer who wants to get from point A to point B typically figures out the best way to do so, and then proceeds to point C. To find three different and functionally interchangeable ways to get from point A to point B and then use all of them in the same piece, as Glass does here in the Train scene, is rather rare, I think. And one would have to go to the music of Erik Satie, such as the *Gymnopedies* or the *Pieces Froids*, to find a composer writing two large movements of a piece with such similar content as Glass does between these two dance movements. And yet the Dance 2 is quite different in feeling than Dance 1, with its focus on the violin soloist, its incessant running up and down the scale, its greater reliance on additive and subtractive process, and its lack of the comforting F major into which Dance 1 tended to resolve. All the usual jokes about minimalism aside, I find it remarkable that Glass could generate 45 minutes of his opera with so little material, shaping each internal stanza so intuitively, and differentiating the two dances into such different purposes and moods. It is a real piece of compositional virtuosity, and not at all the kind of predetermined logic that we tend to associate with early minimalism.

As my predecessor at the *Village Voice* Tom Johnson wrote in 1981 about Glass's *Music in Changing Parts*, "Yet as I listened once again to those additions and subtractions I realized that they are actually rather whimsical. Composers like Frederic Rzewski, Louis Andriessen, and William Hellermann have written such sequences with much greater rigor. By comparison, Glass is not a reductionist at all but a romantic."[2] *Romantic* is not the word I would have used – I would be loathe to think that the mere absence of a generating algorithm suffices as evidence of passion or individualism. (In fact, that Tom would use the word on such minor grounds in 1981 is indicative of the atmosphere I began this essay by describing.) But I do think that there is a kind of inherent mystery in Glass's circuitous, unpredictable paths through extremely circumscribed material, and that *Einstein on the Beach* would be less of a work than it is had he been more content with mere concept and less generous with his artistry.

---

2   Tom Johnson, "Minimalism on the Beach: Philip Glass," Village Voice, February 25–March 3, 1981; quoted in Johnson, *The Voice of New Music*, Paris, Editions 75, 249.

5 "Only pictures to hear"

Reading *Einstein on the Beach* through experimental theater

Pwyll ap Siôn

> To interpret a piece of music is [implicitly] to take the risk of noticing that there is an "I" involved in understanding, without whom the content of abstract forms would not be known.[1]

Introduction

When Philip Glass and Robert Wilson's *Einstein on the Beach* was first performed at the Avignon Festival in July 1976, it confounded audiences' understanding of opera, drama, and music theater. The sense of confusion that accompanied the work's initial reception was reflected in the kinds of questions directed at Glass and Wilson. Looking back many years later, Glass commented:

> We had everything [at the press conferences following the first performance]: "What the hell do you think you did?" "How dare you do this?" "What was that supposed to be?" ... The best questions were *both* inane and interesting. For example, the question "Is *Einstein* really an opera?" was both stupid and intriguing at the same time. Neither [Robert Wilson] nor I had any special preparation for those meetings. In the end, I don't think either of us really cared what people thought.[2]

Einstein has remained an elusive work not simply because it has eluded categorization. Its multi-layered and poly-textual design – a postmodern *bricolage* of music, movement, drama, and dance – frustrates one's attempts to impose a sense of order and unity. Visually and verbally, too, it's loaded with images and imagery. *Einstein* is ostensibly a plot without purpose – a drama without a distinctive pathway or direction.

Glass and Wilson have done much to advance such pluralistic readings of the opera. Glass once said: "It hardly mattered what you thought *Einstein on the*

---

1 Naomi Cumming, *The Sonic Self: Musical Subjectivity and Signification*, Bloomington and Indianapolis, Indiana University Press, 2001, 287.
2 Philip Glass, *Words Without Music*, London, Faber and Faber, 2015, 296–297.

Beach might 'mean' ... In the case of [*Einstein*] the story was supplied by the imaginations of the audience, and there was no way for us to predict ... what the story might be for any particular person."[3] Wilson also confirmed this view, claiming that the absence of any explicit narrative thread was there in order to free up rather than control or direct viewers' responses. Drawing on the idea of opera as a series of large, self-contained tableaux, Wilson pointed out that:

> You don't have to think about the story, because there isn't any. You don't have to listen to the words, because they don't mean anything. I'm not giving you puzzles to solve, only pictures to hear. You go to our opera like you go to a museum.[4]

From the very outset, then, *Einstein on the Beach*'s ability to wriggle free from the constraints of categorization and definition was predicated not simply on the work's built-in multiplicities but also on discourses about it presented by Glass and Wilson.

Thus, *Einstein*'s mosaic-like surface encourages the observer to piece together the opera in any way that makes sense to him or her; and this, in turn, places the opera in direct contradistinction to traditional operatic practice. We need not look for specific meanings because they're not there. Instead, we should give free rein to our imaginations and forget about plot, narrative, and all the dramaturgical conceits associated with traditional opera because they have been replaced in the opera with "pictures" and "music."

However, this new listening approach opens its own hermeneutic can of worms. Freed from the prison-house of meaning, where should the listener go? Towards the wide-open spaces of perceptual clarity or hide for cover in the thickets of ambiguous meanings? And without a map or compass to help navigate our way through the opera, there's a danger that we may end up being cast afloat on a sea of uncertain meanings. Despite ourselves – and Glass and Wilson's entreaties to exercise a complete free-play of the imagination when experiencing the opera – it is incumbent on us, as listening subjects, to feel a need to impose *some* shape and order to the work. Thus, any attempt to make sense of the inherent multiplicities belonging to *Einstein* inevitably encourages the listener to rationalize and regulate its meanings. While no fixed route is laid out in Glass and Wilson's opera, we are nevertheless provided with a set of coordinates: we are not traveling in complete darkness.

But what are these coordinates? In emphasizing *Einstein*'s novel qualities, there's a danger of ignoring aspects relating to explicit influence, which have clearly shaped the dramatic vision of both composer and director in various

---

3   Glass, quoted in K. Robert Schwarz, *Minimalists*, New York, Phaidon Press, 1996, 135.

4   Schwarz, *Minimalists*, 135. Jelena Novak has also described the opera's dramatic form in terms of a "dream-like tableaux"; see Novak, *Postopera: Reinventing the Voice-Body*, Farnham, Ashgate, 2015, 28.

ways. The following account tries to make sense of the opera according to a series of concepts and listening positions, which relate to Glass's own formative experiences and understanding of mid-century European theater. Terms such as estrangement, fragmentation, irony, and personalization are introduced and explained. These theatrical tropes inform Wilson's dramatic design, providing a series of perspectives in which to understand the opera's aesthetic and expressive language. Finally, an analysis of the function of the music's role in the five knee plays, which act as scaffolding structures across the opera's four acts, will serve to support this reading.

Subject positions and strategies of listening

If *Einstein on the Beach*'s meaning is not so much contained in "the work" but rather in the liminal space between the perceiver and that which is perceived, how can this be teased out in a reading of it? To what extent is it possible to situate a listening subject in *Einstein* that is engendered by both its musical and dramaturgical dimensions and conventions? How might one locate a subject position in the opera? What kinds of listening strategies can usefully be applied? How might such strategies shed further light on the meaning of Glass and Wilson's opera?

The "listening subject" forms the basis upon which subject positions are constructed in any given musical situation. Susanna Välimäki defines this as the point at which "the listener ... becomes subjected to the musical discourse."[5] Drawing on Naomi Cumming's work, Välimäki proposes that under such circumstances, "the listener is composed into the position of the ideal listener. She projects herself to subject positions offered by the musical text to make sense of it. Hence it is a matter of *identification*: music is experienced as sonic self."[6] As Välimäki points out, subject position presupposes the notion of *identification* established between the listener and the work (and, by extension, its composer), followed by a process of *transference*, where music "is experienced by the listening subject as a continuum of [the] self, a mirror or a screen of [the] self, a site of identity, a theater ... of mind." In establishing a relationship through the adoption of a specific subject position, music thus becomes a kind of "projection of the listener's psyche."[7]

Further distinctions have been applied in relation to subject position. Jacques Lacan and Émile Benveniste's writings adopt Ferdinand de Saussure's basic semiotic division of language and speech (*langue* and *parole*) to differentiate between the subject of uttering and the subject of the utterance. Kaja Silverman adds a third division – that of the spoken subject – which forms a connecting link between the *what* and *how* of communication: a site of negotiation and contestation where

5   Susanna Välimäki, *Subject Strategies in Music: A Psychoanalytic Approach to Musical Significa-tion*, Imatra, Semiotic Society of Finland, 2009, 133.
6   Ibid., 133.
7   Ibid., 134–135.

various meanings are located and understood. Välimäki calls this the *played subject*, which is "constantly reconstructed through the discourse and understood as an ideal subject position in the musical text," functioning as a site of "unsettled subjectivity unfolding at the border between the self and the other."[8]

While the notion of a subject position (or series of positions) can in practice be applied to any type of music, it seems particularly useful in approaching a work such as *Einstein*. Because of the absence of any clearly defined narrative content, the attention inevitably shifts towards the listener, much as it would towards the reader when encountering a Barthesian "writerly" text.[9] Studies such as postmodern rock parody in Frank Zappa or the use of satire in Pulp's pop songs about sex, subject position is gauged in terms of the semiotic efficacy of authorial intent.[10] A "literal" (i.e., non-parodic) reading of these songs would result in a complete reversal of the artists' intended meanings: a de- (or re-)positioning of the subject caused by misidentification.

Glass's music does not speak in inverted commas in the same way as Zappa or Blur's satirical songs, however.[11] One might more usefully position *Einstein* on firmer hermeneutic grounds by looking to existing scholarship on opera in general, including studies on minimalist opera. For example, in comparing Verdi's *Aïda* with Glass's third opera, *Akhnaten* (1984), John Richardson points out that one's subject position is likely to "fluctuate ... between [one] based on identification and one from the standpoint of which alienation is the more potent force."[12] Richardson does not propose an explicit methodology for identifying subject positions in *Akhnaten*, but he often encodes them in his readings of the opera's semiotic function and use of music-rhetorical devices. Thus, Amenhotep's role as narrator sees the pharaoh "invariably [speaking] from the subject position of a particular character" he inhabits, thus complexifying any straightforward association we may have with the conventional role of a narrator.[13]

Richardson's focus on a number of semiological "signposts" in *Akhnaten* – the relationship of particular keys and key centers within the work and to the operatic canon in general; number symbolism and triadic imagery; aquatic metaphors

---

8   Ibid., 136–137.
9   For a definition of "writerly" (and "readerly") texts, see Roland Barthes's *S/Z*, Oxford, Blackwell Publishing, 2000, 3–4.
10   See, for example, Eric F. Clarke, "Subject-Position and the Specification of Invariants in Music by Frank Zappa and P.J. Harvey," *Music Analysis*, vol. 18, no. 3 (1999), 347–374; Clare Dibben, "Pulp, Pornography and Spectatorship: Subject Matter and Subject Position in Pulp's *This Is Hardcore*," *Journal of the Royal Musical Association*, vol. 126 no. 1 (2001), 83–106.
11   Other than if we view his harmonic language *in toto* as functioning as a "commentary" on tonality, perhaps. John Richardson has suggested that "listening to Glass in relation to common practice tonality, either as commentary, prismatic distortion, or uncritical continuation, appears to have been a quite common strategy." Correspondence with the author, February 20, 2017.
12   John Richardson, *Singing Archaeology: Philip Glass's Akhnaten*, Hanover, CT, Wesleyan University Press, 1999, 194.
13   Ibid., 108. This leads Richardson to make the point that Carolyn Abbate's definition of the narrator in opera does not hold true.

and their intertextual references in Wagner and beyond; Akhnaten's androgynous sexual personae and the work's Oedipal and psychoanalytical subtext – all these are seen to provide the listener with a series of interpretative gateways into the opera's plot and meaning.[14] In Richardson's words, the opera is "pregnant with symbolic significance that encompasses much of the history of opera as a genre and perhaps a good deal more besides."[15]

Subject position in opera involves not just the presentation of a certain view-point but also a realization of who or what is being watched.[16] At the beginning of her book, *Unsung Voices*, Carolyn Abbate makes the point that female characters are often eliminated from operatic plots to satisfy the male gaze. However, even though they fall victim to the vagaries of a murderous plot or similar fate, these female voices nevertheless remain "unconquerable."[17] In *Einstein*, the operatic gaze is more difficult to determine. Jelena Novak points out that Einstein himself "appears only as a signifier – like a mute figure playing violin, not the character of [a] 'story,' as one might have expected [from] a conventional dramatic piece."[18] Cast in this unorthodox role, Einstein takes on a peculiarly diegetic character – we are made fully aware that he performs music on stage (the only character in the opera to do so), although it is unclear whether any of the other characters hear him play or recognize him as such.

However, in much the same way that we are made aware in the opera that Einstein is only a *representation* of his own character, Abbate also states that opera by its very nature is mimetic rather than diegetic: "Like any form of theater [or] temporal art, it traps the listener in present experience and the beat of passing time, from which he or she cannot escape."[19] Glass's looping patterns, circular progressions, and repetitive structures bring us ineluctably closer to the kind of "present experience" Abbate refers to, and it is these qualities that have drawn comparison with its non-narrative function. As one might expect from the title of her study, Abbate's critique projects different kinds of narrative forms on examples from the operatic canon. Referring to Anthony Newcomb, Abbate suggests adopting "strategies of listening." A composition usually forms part of a genre

14   Ibid., 99.
15   Ibid., 103. Even the image of the "gateway" is afforded metaphorical significance here, as articulating the liminal space between "relative and absolute planes of consciousness, between the living and dead, and perhaps also between the sexes ..." Ibid., 105. However, in comparison with *Akhnaten*, *Einstein* is more open-ended and therefore semiologically indeterminate. In fact, Richardson's argument revolves around the notion that Glass's style itself "[constitutes] a kind of all-encompassing prismatic surface wherein all the various threads and influences are perceived at a distance." Correspondence with the author, February 20, 2017.
16   A similar approach has been taken by David Schwarz in relation to the psychoanalytic gaze; see his *Listening Subjects: Music, Psychoanalysis, Culture*, Durham, Duke University Press, 1997.
17   Carolyn Abbate, *Unsung Voices: Opera and Musical Narrative in the Nineteenth Century*, Princeton, Princeton University Press, 1991, ix. She draws here on the work of philosopher and literary critic Catherine Clément.
18   Novak, *Postopera: Reinventing the Voice-Body*, 28.
19   Abbate, *Unsung Voices*, 53.

or musical "type," which can then provide the listener with a series of semiotic reference points. This enables the listener to then "compare what they are hearing to a collection of possible musical syntaxes or types."[20] A musical type "[invokes] history by calling upon established conventions or inherited past models," providing a perceptual window (or series of windows) onto the work.[21]

Reading through experimental theater

How might Abbate's "strategies of listening" – informed as they are by a set of "musical types" – help situate *Einstein on the Beach* in general? One obvious area to explore is Glass's and Wilson's interest in (and engagement with) experimental theater leading up to the period in which they started working on the opera. Both were involved in various ways with this tradition: Glass especially through his work with Mabou Mines, which he helped establish in the early 1970s, and Wilson through his work with the theater group the Byrd Hoffman School of Byrds. Indeed, it was through their shared interests in avant-garde theater and mutual enthusiasm for the work of artists such as Jerzy Grotowski's "Poor Theater" and the Living Theater that they were brought together in the first place. As Glass put it: "[Wilson] knew the artists that I knew, so we were clearly living in the same world and had been nourished by the same generation of people that had preceded us."[22]

Glass's experiences of working in theater during the late 1960s and then in the early 1970s as a core member of Mabou Mines provide useful contexts in which to establish a series of plausible listening strategies for *Einstein*. When asked in 1992 whether Eastern practices were largely responsible for his minimalist style, Glass instead chose to emphasize the importance of non-narrative theater:

> Nonnarrative [sic] theater and nonnarrative [sic] art is not based on theme and development but on a different structure … [these] writers took the subject out of the narrative. They broke the pattern of the reader identifying with the main character. Brecht does it with irony … Beckett does it through fragmentation, as in the theater piece *Play*. And Genet does it through transcendent vision.[23]

This passage is revealing in several ways. First, it connects the kind of non-narrative opera that Glass and Wilson established in *Einstein* with the kinds of non-narrative theater they would have been familiar with. Second, Glass points out that non-narrative theater broke away from "identifying with the main character."

---

20 Ibid., 47.
21 Ibid., 49.
22 Philip Glass, *Words Without Music*, 284.
23 Philip Glass, quoted in Richard Kostelanetz and Robert Flemming (eds.), *Writings on Glass: Essays, Interviews, Criticism*, Berkeley and Los Angeles, University of California Press, 1997, 320.

Finally, and crucially, Glass refers to three important characteristics of non-narrative theater, as found in the work of Bertolt Brecht, Samuel Beckett, and Jean Genet: irony, fragmentation, and transcendent vision. Tantalizingly, Glass stops short of drawing further parallels between his (and Wilson's) aesthetic and that of European experimental theater of the mid-twentieth-century.[24] Nevertheless, these concepts seem an obvious place to start exploring the meaning of the opera. What does Glass mean by irony, fragmentation, and transcendent vision? How do they relate to the theater of Brecht, Beckett, and Genet? And, perhaps more importantly, how do they come into play in *Einstein on the Beach*?

Bertolt Brecht: irony and estrangement

Bertolt Brecht's use of irony is linked with a distancing effect caused by (and to) the main characters in his plays that takes on the form of alienation and estrangement (or, in German, *Verfremdungseffekt*). The idea of using this process of defamiliarization came to Brecht after attending a performance in Moscow of traditional Chinese theater by the Beijing Opera in 1935, about which he wrote a year later in his essay "Alienation Effects in Chinese Acting." Brecht argued that the kind of emotional distance, brought about using irony, led to a truer and more nuanced understanding of the message behind his work. According to Fredric Jameson, irony is used as a rhetorical concept in Brecht.[25] This sets up a series of dichotomies and dualities, such as presence/absence, order/chaos, action/inaction, and speech/silence. As Jameson notes:

> [The] most obvious space of Brechtian freedom ... aims to project not only what will shortly have been done – that is to say, what is being done in front of us – but what might just as well not have been done, what might have been something else altogether, or simply have been omitted.[26]

Parallels can be drawn with *Einstein on the Beach*, which also defines itself through what it is *not* as much as through what it *is*. For example, Einstein himself appears not as a scientist but as a violinist, and the opera is defined not through arias and choruses but through movement, dance, image, and gesture.

Furthermore, Brecht's concept of estrangement – drawn from Eastern cultures that included Japanese theater and observing Chinese performers such as Mei Lanfang (1894–1961) spawned a kind of Brechtian "minimalism," which would have resonated with Glass's own aesthetic. Jameson refers to Brecht's "radical simplification of experience, a reduction of action and gesture alike to the very minimum." Like Brecht, Einstein's character is reduced to "[a] few sparse ...

---

24 In his autobiography, Glass does in fact elaborate further on the influence of Brecht, Beckett, and Genet; see *Words Without Music*, 104–105.
25 Fredric Jameson, *Brecht and Method*, London, Verso, 2000, 20.
26 Ibid., 58.

traits."[27] The importance of Brecht for Glass is demonstrated in his willingness to travel from Paris to Berlin in the mid-1960s (along with his wife at the time, JoAnne Akalaitis) to experience Brecht's plays performed in their original production under the direction of the playwright's widow, Helene Wiegel.[28]

Beckett and fragmentation

Of more direct impact on Glass was Samuel Beckett, with whom the composer worked in Paris on a production of *Play* in 1965, which was later turned into the film *Comédie* (1966). Glass's music for *Play* furnished his first String Quartet: one of his first truly minimalist works.[29] Beckett's fragmented, reduced style – "a cleaning of the decks" in Glass's expression – first inspired him to work with looping melodies over static harmonies.[30] Beckett's aesthetic of fragmentation combined with Glass's parallel musical processes produces what Takeshi Kawashima has described as a rejection of horology. Kawashima defines horology as "the unified temporary construction of fragmented moments."[31] Beckett eschews this notion of dramatic time. For Glass, the most revealing result of Beckett's anti-horological approach was that listeners would experience a moment of catharsis in the play in a different place each time.[32] Kawashima connects this notion with Beckett's concept of image, which "is more than a visual or optical conception; it is an epiphany of creative activity."[33] Glass's "Beckettian epiphany" is thus interlinked with his own psychological experience of image and time in the playwright's work. In Paul Frandsen's words, "Glass discovered that Beckett works in a way that incorporates the viewer into the work, thus providing the audience with an alternative option for interpreting or even contemplating the piece."[34]

Genet and transcendent vision

As much as the prospect of studying with Nadia Boulanger appealed to Glass, it was Jean Genet and Beckett's artistic presence in Paris that motivated the young composer to go there in the first place.[35] Glass attended the first performance of Genet's *Les Paravents* (*The Screens*), on April 16, 1966, witnessing the ensuing riot that took place outside the Théâtre de l'Odéon. Genet's transcendent vision can be understood as a form of "imaginative transformation" brought about

27   Ibid., 61.
28   See Glass, *Words Without Music*, 117–118.
29   Ibid., 202.
30   Ibid., 105.
31   Takeshi Kawashima, "Conjunction of the Essential and the Incidental: Fragmentation and Juxtaposition; or Samuel Beckett's Critical Writings in the 1930s," *Samuel Beckett Today*, Vol. 14 (2004), 477.
32   In Joseph Roddy's "Listening to Glass (1981)," in Kostelanetz (ed.) *Writings on Glass: Essays, Interviews, Criticism*, Berkeley and Los Angeles, University of California Press, 1997, 171.
33   Kawashima, "Conjunction of the Essential and the Incidental," 477.
34   See Paul John Frandsen's "Philip Glass's *Akhnaten* (1993)," in *Writings on Glass*, 214.
35   Glass, *Words Without Music*, 111.

through "an awareness of [one's] interchangeability with the rest of humanity."[36] This sense of interchangeability is communicated through Genet's use of ritual devices. David Bradby and Clare Finburgh propose that Genet's plays are "best described as ceremonies: ceremonies designed to exercise and transform."[37] These ritual and ceremonial elements result in a kind of "mystic transformation" played out in the presence of those "who believe in the efficacy of the transcendent power invoked."[38]

Immediate parallels can be drawn between the concepts of estrangement, fragmentation, and transcendent vision and the action that unfolds in *Einstein on the Beach*. Taking the character of Einstein as a preliminary example, the notion of breaking the pattern of "the reader identifying with the main character" is a Brechtian feature. Of course, we identify on a certain level with Einstein, but he is not portrayed as a person with feelings and emotions. The fact that nothing much "happens" to him (in terms of a quasi-biographical birth-to-death narrative) is a Beckettian trait. To paraphrase Novak, Einstein is not presented as a character might be in a story.

However, there's clearly a missing link in seeking to situate *Einstein on the Beach* in relation to European experimental theater. *Einstein* is no *Endgame*. The link lies with Mabou Mines. In her study of the New York experimental theater company, Iris Fischer begins by referring to three elements that particularly struck her when attending the premiere of the company's production of Henrik Ibsen's *A Doll House*. The three elements are emotional engagement, estrangement, and "personalisation."[39] Fischer relates these themes to specific moments in Ibsen's play, and although she does not expand in detail on their meanings and implications, we get a sense of what they mean in relation to Lee Breuer's innovative production.

The three terms appear at first glance to contradict each other. How can a listener became "estranged" from the action yet at the same time be "emotionally engaged" by it? Fischer argues that Breuer's production shows the audience "not just the melodrama" (emotional engagement), but also "ourselves looking at it and back to it" (personalization and estrangement). In Fischer's words: "While the estranging visual distortion of male and female relationships kept the audience off balance, the emotional texture given to Ibsen's words toyed with us, drawing us in and slapping us around."[40]

---

36   See David Bradby and Clare Finburgh, *Jean Genet*, London, Routledge, 2012, 28.
37   Ibid., 23.
38   Ibid., 41. Jean Genet was not the only writer to offer Glass a glimpse of transcendent vision. The novels of Hermann Hesse (1877–1962) – whose impact on Glass was "profound" – also explore transcendence, partly because of the Swiss author's interest in Eastern philosophies and religion; see Glass, *Words Without Music*, 105.
39   Iris Smith Fischer, *Mabou Mines: Making Avant-Garde Theater in the 1970s*, Ann Arbor, University of Michigan Press, 2012, 1.
40   Iris Smith Fischer, *Mabou Mines: Making Avant-Garde Theater in the 1970s*, 2.

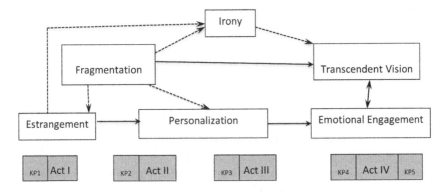

Figure 5.1 Dramatic outline in *Einstein on the Beach*.

In truth, Wilson is no closer to Ibsen then he is to Beckett, but the concepts which underpin Mabou Mines' aesthetic – as filtered through the European drama of Brecht, Beckett, and Genet – do provide a basis in which to set out an overarching dramatic design for the opera, as shown in Figure 5.1.

Figure 5.1 attempts to synthesize *Einstein on the Beach*, applying several key themes previously discussed, with each Act and knee play (KP) set out underneath. Fischer's threefold concept of estrangement, personalization, and emotional engagement is applied on an Act-by-Act level by charting a series of possible shifting positions experienced by the listening subject. Act 1's sense of estrangement and disconnection gives way in Acts II and III to different levels of personalization, which – by the end of Act IV – is transformed into emotional engagement, as shown in the connecting arrows. Estrangement is reinforced at the beginning of the opera by an emphasis on fragmentation. Fragmentation is also a recurring theme in Acts II, III, and IV: from the fragmentation of the individual to the fragmentation (and splitting) of the atom in Act IV, scene 3. In Act IV, emotional engagement – the way in which the audience is eventually "brought in" to the work – brings about two separate "visions," which, in the form of a Genetian collective realization or epiphany, attempts to "transcend" the moment. The first vision takes on a dystopian form in the Spaceship scene, followed in Knee Play 5 by an utopian alternative, which functions as a kind of epilogue.[41]

The following exegesis, set out in five steps or stages, attempts to provide a general overview of how these concepts might work.[42] On a basic level, the opera explores time, space, and energy – elements that connect both the music and action on stage while also acting as powerful metaphors for Einstein's own

---

41 The precise role of each knee play will be discussed in the final section of this chapter.

42 Two very useful personal accounts of the original *Einstein* production can be found by Robert T. Jones in Philip Glass, *Opera on the Beach*, 79–84; and David Cunningham's in Richard Kostelanetz and Robert Flemming (eds.), *Writings on Glass: Essays, Interviews, Criticism*, 152–166.

scientific discoveries.[43] While time, space, and energy function as foreground metaphors, of more obvious local significance is fragmentation, along with its antithesis: control and objectivity.[44]

Estrangement and fragmentation

Estrangement is brought about through the use of fragmentation during the opening Prologue/Knee Play 1 and "Train" scenes; but its opposite – order and stability – is also represented. The audience enters the auditorium in what Glass has termed the "'walk-in' prelude"[45] – *in medias res* – with the opera having already begun, albeit in a nascent state of formulating a beginning. Counting and random spoken images heard during the Prologue announce a "prelapsarian" or *noumenal* moment – a kind of time before the beginning of time.[46] This fragmentary narrative is underpinned by its opposite: a stable bass line on electric organ, which presents three pitches in the ordered relationship of 2:3:4. We are only made aware of the exact nature of these proportions when the choir counts them out in Knee Play 1. Like mathematical formulas, the music discloses a numerical order that lies hidden within a system.

Unity and randomness are thus placed in a contesting relationship.[47] The scene becomes increasingly fragmentary, mainly through the scraps of sentences provided by Christopher Knowles's text. However, this "stream of consciousness" idea is spoken in a very methodical, precise manner, with clear enunciation. Knowles's words are written in the present or future tense to underscore the opera's mimetic nature ("and these *are* the days my friends"; "*will* it get some wind for the sailboat" etc.).[48] As Abbate points out: "The time of telling is the time

---

43   In his 2015 biography, Glass recalls "with *Einstein*, the idea of an unstoppable energy was all there was" (Philip Glass, *Words Without Music*, 289). Further evidence can be found in Wilson's original drawing of the opera's title. Reproduced in K. Robert Schwartz's *Minimalists*, Wilson deliberately foregrounds the letter "E" in several places, setting it apart from the rest of Einstein's name, and draws attention to the scientist's famous equation E[nergy] = mc^2 (see K. Robert Schwartz, *Minimalists*, 131). On the nature of time and space in the opera, Wilson has said: "the images you see on stage are not decoration; they're architectural. At the very start, there is a vertical bar of light that appears three times. Then, in the second scene, you have a horizontal bar of light. Together, they represent the cross of time and space: time shown as a vertical beam, space as a horizontal line." (Robert Wilson, in "Robert Wilson and Philip Glass, 'How We Made: Philip Glass and Robert Wilson on *Einstein on the Beach*,'" www.theguardian.com/culture/2012/apr/23/how-we-made-einstein-on-the-beach), Accessed: February 1, 2016.

44   The latter can be found in Glass's music, which is rarely "fragmentary," but also in Wilson's mise-en-scènes, which vary between (in Bob Bernard's analysis) "landscapes," "portraits," and "still lifes" (see Bob Bernard, "Robert Wilson/Philip Glass Einstein on the Beach," in Bob Bernard's Corner, July 2013, www.operaleague.org/portals/0/bobbernardscorner/pdffiles/brainstorm.5.pdf), Accessed: February 1, 2016.

45   Glass, *Words Without Music*, 295.

46   For more on this, see Abbate, *Unsung Voices*, 49.

47   For more on contesting relationships in multimedia, see Nicholas Cook's *Analysing Musical Multimedia*, Oxford, Clarendon Press, 1998, 102–104.

48   My emphasis. See Philip Glass, *Opera on the Beach*, for a reproduction of the complete libretto (Glass, *Opera on the Beach*, 63–79).

being told about; there is no teller, only time itself."[49] There is no narrator as such in the opera either. The characters are mere vessels – Einstein included – through which time, and events taking place in time, pass. The choir stand in stylized randomized order, and one senses that there is an attempt here to rationalize the irrational: to bring order to chaos.

The Train scene that follows develops the notion of fragmentation by celebrating life's vibrant multiplicity. Music and dance coexist in synchronous motion but the scene also "glorifies" difference and fragmentation. Mathematical symbols are carved out of thin air in precise motions; a girl listens to the indeterminate sounds of the conch shell;[50] a dancer gradually moves diagonally across the stage with her hand extended upwards, holding a pipe – an Einsteinian gesture – while a train crosses the stage in slow motion in the background. At the same time, we are made to identify with the young Einstein, who appears with a bright cube in his hand (again a symbol of Euclidean order amongst the flux), throwing paper planes across the stage, possibly symbolizing the progress of science through empirical means. Through our introduction to the young Einstein, Act I, scene 1 also sets up a link between the audience and Einstein through the idea of the personalization of the individual. Likewise, Knowles's text makes the first explicit reference to love ("This love could be some one"), which anticipates the very final scene of the opera.

Estrangement and irony

Estrangement, personalization, and emotional engagement are presented at various points during the opera. For example, in Act III, scene 1 (Trial/Prison) collective estrangement and disconnection are projected through the scene's multimodal representation with its pop art-style texts and poly-textual communications about "prematurely air-conditioned supermarkets" and so on. Lucinda Childs's text – repeated like a tape loop – adds to the sense of detachment. Act IV, scene 1 (Building/Train) represents Einstein's own personal and individual estrangement, hidden away in his tower, as discussed further below.

Some of these states are placed in juxtaposition with irony, satire, parody, and so on. Irony is used in various places to deflect and defer one's sense of identification with a certain situation. This occurs for the first (and in many respects the most obvious) time in Act I, scene 2 (Trial). At this point, the opera's dramatic and musical presentation is coordinated towards regularity and uniformity: sound and movement (the gradual entrance of the judges and jury) are homogeneous, with every action directed towards a single aim or purpose. The procession, which moves almost in slow motion, eventually fills out the courtroom. It soon becomes clear that this is no ordinary courtroom scene, however. An old African-American man and young child preside as judges, each declaring solemnly: "This court of common pleas is now in session." But the scene's formalized pompousness gives

---

49 Ibid., 54.
50 Possibly a reference to John Cage's fascination with sounds generated by moving water around in large conch shells.

way to parody, humor, and ironic disruption when both judges pull faces at the audience, then followed by an extended speech in a mock-ironic fashion by the old judge, extolling the virtues of the equal rights movement and women's liberation (the so-called "all men are equal" speech). While the scene's sober formality is counterbalanced by humor, any sense of personal identification formed between the audience and the characters on stage is undercut by the judge's ambiguous ironic inflection.

The Night Train scene in Act II prompts emotional engagement from the viewer, but the ironic tone again drives a wedge between them. The "duet," which takes place against the backdrop of a lunar eclipse, anticipates the end of the opera with its musings on the synchronicity of love. Again, the personalization of both characters elicits emotional engagement from the viewer, but the scene takes a sudden turn when the woman "pulls a gun from her handbag and threatens her companion with it; he raises his hands; the train moves into the night."[51] What is the gun supposed to mean here? The heavily loaded symbolic image of the man with his hands sticking up suggests mock irony, which once again disrupts the viewer's emotional connection with the scene. Irony thus plays an important role.

Fragmentation and personalization
Fragmentation and personalization appear in the opera when the audience becomes increasingly aware of a sense of alienation between Einstein and the rest of the cast in the opera, or within members of the cast. In Act IV, scene 1 (Building/Train), Einstein appears inside a building while life carries on outside. It is probably the most obvious moment in the opera where a sense of distance and disassociation is created between Einstein and the rest of the world. The individual's sense of alienation is at its most poignant here.[52] The figures and tropes of culture and society emerge as stylized representations, with each character arriving on stage to strike a pose for the camera. The dichotomy between freedom and control is apparent, too. A lengthy saxophone improvisation – an atypical musical moment in the opera – suggests unrestrained freedom: fraternal individualism expressed within a collective musical context.[53] Einstein cuts an isolated figure in this scene.

The final section of Act I, scene 2 (Trial) combines fragmentation and personalization because Knowles's text is now read sequentially rather than randomly, as was the case in the Prologue. It is made to "make sense" in its "form" if not entirely in terms of "content"; in other words, it carries the *form* of meaning though not through its syntax. Another factor that suggests absence or fragmentation is

---

51 Jones, quoted in Glass, *Opera on the Beach*, 81. The scene is pure "pantomime" according to Jones. Richardson has suggested that "their manner of communication through stock expressions of romantic attachment is remarkably depersonalized." Correspondence with the author, February 20, 2017.

52 Brecht seems the obvious reference point here. See Glass's quote, above (footnote 38).

53 This was made particularly obvious during the 2012–14 tour, where saxophonist Andrew Sterman stood up in the pit and added several bebop-style jazz inflections.

the fingerless clock and the black disc that obscures it.[54] This can be read as representing the courtroom of Einstein's imagination. Twice the music fades out, leaving Einstein alone with his violin. This may be a reference to Einstein as a lonely figure, preoccupied with his own doubts, fears, and problems. The violin functions as Einstein's voice and thoughts during the opera, and therefore acts as a way of personalizing his character. Einstein's violin prompts us to become more emotionally engaged with his character.

Act IV, scene 2 (Bed) serves as a premonition of the Spaceship scene. It also includes an improvisational element, this time in the form of an organ cadenza. A horizontal beam of light rises slowly upwards, suggesting progress, prefiguring the spaceship's "ascent" in the next scene. Light normally signifies hope, but the music's function lies in a contesting relationship with the image here. The cadenza's music suggests sadness and longing, and the voice's haunting, floating lines offer some reflection on what Einstein may have discovered and its far-reaching implications. Einstein is absent from his seat during this scene, and the absence of a bass note in the last chord of the sequence heard in this section also suggests loss or deficit.

Personalization and emotional engagement

The two dance scenes featured in the opera bring about a synthesis of engagement and identification. Dance 1 represents the first moment in the opera where music and movement are indissolubly linked. The spins and turns, symmetries, patterns in circular motion, and "dervishlike spinning"[55] of Dance 1 in Act II, scene 1 gives way to the more nuanced, shadows-and-light choreography of Dance 2 in Act III, scene 2, whose folk-like Ceilidh seems to suggest a time before the advent of the technological age.[56] However, the symbol of the spaceship – which hovers above the dancers in both scenes – appears to lie in contrast to (or in a contesting relationship with) the choreographed movement. Thus, the transcendent vision expressed right at the end of the opera is left unresolved at this point; these two elements coexist without the synthesis provided at the end of the work.

The various levels of interaction in the opera can be summarized as follows: the interaction between people is at its peak during the Dance episodes, while the interaction between people and machines results in the greatest moments of

---

54   According to Jones, the black disc is "a visual reference to a confirmation of Einstein's theory of relativity which involved observing a solar eclipse and measuring the apparent displacement of light from stars visible next to the blanked-out sun" (quoted in Glass, *Opera on the Beach*, 80). The absence of fingers on the clock also signifies timelessness and the music's static nature also supports this idea.

55   Robert T. Jones, quoted in Glass, *Opera on the Beach*, 81.

56   Childs has described her choreography for *Interior Drama*, first performed only a year after *Einstein on the Beach* at the Brooklyn Academy of Music in November 1977, as "[bearing] a relationship to folk dance in its off-kilter rhythmic elements." See Suzanne Carbonneau, "An Art of Refusal: Lucinda Childs' Dances in Silence, 1973–78" http://danceworkbook.pcah.us/asteadypulse/dances/interior_drama.html, Accessed: November 21, 2016.

alienation. The most inhuman moment in the opera arrives in the Spaceship scene, however, where human beings are transformed into automatons and technology spins out of control.

Transcendent vision and emotional engagement

In the final reckoning, *Einstein on the Beach* presents the listener with two denouements: one is loaded with dystopian imagery while the other is utopian. The utopian resolution at the end of the opera occurs when audiences' emotional engagement with the opera is at its strongest. Act IV, scene 3 (Spaceship) presents us with the opera's apocalyptic climax, with scientific exploration ending in complete destruction. Emotional engagement is at its furthest remove at this point. Musicians become the operators of a sonic spaceship with Einstein as its conductor, and the scene becomes increasingly fraught with chaos and drama. Humans and machines interact in a nightmarish vision charged with chromatically saturated lines and layers. These automated machines eventually spiral out of control towards mutually assured destruction. The harrowing transcendent vision that remains with the audience signifies this terrible predicament; we are trapped but emotionally engaged by its grotesque implications.

The role of the knee plays

The role of the knee plays in *Einstein on the Beach*'s dramatic design serves to support the gradual progression in the opera from defamiliarization and estrangement via more direct identification and personalization and eventually to emotional engagement. Above and beyond bookending and connecting each act, the five knee plays fulfill an important function in the opera's dramatic design. Figure 5.2 provides a list of the main elements that comprise each knee play in terms of instrumentation, text, material, and "affect."

Note that a different set of variables is applied in each knee play, and various permutations utilized. In terms of instrumentation, other than electric organ, all other combinations are explored and we only hear all three (choir, organ, and solo violin) in the final knee play. Both numbers and solfege are used in Knee Plays 1, 3, and 5. Knee Play 2, for solo violin, uses neither, but instead juxtaposes a series of spoken texts written by Christopher Knowles, which again results in estrangement. Knee Play 1 uses the least amount of harmonic material, relying entirely on the vi-V-I figure, while Knee Play 4 uses the most: the scale pattern linked with the solo violin, the five-chord cadential sequence, and the "Trilogy" theme (thus called because of its use by Glass in his follow-up operas *Satyagraha* (1979) and *Akhnaten* (1983)), which – although bearing some similarity to the vi-V-I figure – is heard for the first time in this guise in Knee Play 3. Knee Play 5 is the only one which combines the vi-V-I figure with the "Trilogy" theme, thus making explicit what has been until that point a subliminal connection between both ideas. While none of the knee plays makes use of all elements, one can nevertheless identify a gradual accumulation of material from Knee Play 1, which uses five elements, to Knee Play 5, which uses 7.

	Instrumentation			Text			Material			Musical Affect
	SATB Chorus	Organ	Solo Violin	Numbers	Solfege	"vi-V-I" figure	Scale pattern	Cadential formula (f-D♭-A-B-E)	Trilogy theme	
Knee Play 1	✓	✓	✗	✓	✓	✓	✗	✗	✗	Estrangement
Knee Play 2	✗	✗	✓	✗	✗	✗	✓	✓	✗	Estrangement
Knee Play 3	✓	✗	✗	✓	✓	✗	✗	✓	✓	Estrangement leading to Personalization
Knee Play 4	✓	✗	✓	✗	✓	✗	✓	✓	✓	Personalization
Knee Play 5	✓	✓	✓	✓	✓	✓	✗	✗	✓	Emotional Engagement

Figure 5.2 Inventory of contents in Knee Plays I–V.

Of arguably more importance is the "affective" continuum provided by each knee play, taking the listener through a series of dramatic stages and emotional states. Read according to the subject positions set out in this chapter's interpretation of the opera,

Estrangement forms the key affective state in Knee Plays 1 and 2. The inclusion of Einstein's violin in Knee Play 2 brings about a further element of personalization, which is explored again in Knee Play 4 before finally giving way to emotional engagement in Knee Play 5.[57] The number systems (and later solmisation syllables) in Knee Plays 1 and 3 suggest the scientific process of converting codes into numbers and symbols. Knee Play 3 acts as a bridge, wherein alienation (chorus imitating theories and calculations) and personalization (the expressive "Trilogy" theme) overlap. Knee Play 4 hints further at the transcendent vision presented in Knee Play 5 in its extensive use of the "Trilogy" theme, probably the most consonant and lyrical of all the cadential patterns employed in the opera. Its melodic and harmonic movement around the Aeolian mode provides the theme with an almost folk-like quality, which again draws it closer to the personal (see Music Example 5.1). During these moments, the scene hints at the transcendent vision that arrives at the end, but the rest of Knee Play 4 juxtaposes these reflective moments with frantic and mechanical singing of solmisation syllables. A screen with many equations written on it also suggests "information overload." Knee Play 5 still uses numbers and codes, but science and art are now linked through the combination of number sequences and the use of the "Trilogy" theme.

What occurs in Knee Play 5 is an ending that seeks to resolve the horrors of the previous scene by presenting humanity's transcendent vision reified through

Music Example 5.1 The "Trilogy" theme as it first appears in Knee Play 3. *Einstein On The Beach* Words by Robert Wilson Music by Philip Glass © Copyright 1976 Dunvagen Music Publishers Incorporated. Chester Music Limited. All Rights Reserved. International Copyright Secured. Used by permission of Chester Music Limited.

---

57   Knee Play 2, a violin cadenza, foregrounds all the trappings of postmodern society: commercialism, advertising, soft lenses, selling, marketing, and mass production. Perhaps this was the kind of world Einstein eschewed.

the act of love. In Glass's words: "[Wilson] juxtaposed the most horrible thing you could think about, the annihilation that happens with a nuclear holocaust, with love – the cure, you could say, for the problems of humanity."[58] The opera begins with a combination of information overload and scientific objectivity but ends with a simple, direct, and unadorned expression of love.[59] What David Cunningham described as Act 4's "transmutation process" may therefore be explained in these more abstract terms, rather than through the visual symbolism of the train, the trial, and the field.[60]

Conclusion

In his article "The Return of the Aesthetic," Martin Scherzinger guards against the dangers implicit in any culture-centric study of a musical work to throw away the analytical baby with the bathwater. As Scherzinger puts it: "the social interpretation of music risks simply transposing those attributes formerly associated with musical form onto the world and then reading them as if they were a genuinely historical or sociological approach to the musical object."[61] Scherzinger guards against the dangers of using musical analysis simply to verify or support wider claims relating to a work's social and historical significance. Instead, he offers an alternative approach to, on the one hand, "an apolitical analytic practice," and on the other, "an anti-analytic political practice," which is designed to use structural and formal listening to open the doors of imaginative possibility.[62]

Taking its cue from Scherzinger's entreaty to "open the doors of imaginative possibility," the foregoing examination has attempted to devise a credible listening strategy for *Einstein* based on concepts drawn from European drama and on Glass and Wilson's backgrounds in experimental and avant-garde theater. In applying concepts such as estrangement, fragmentation, irony, and personalization to the opera, several layers of meaning have been revealed. The function of the knee plays across the opera's four acts provide interpretative openings to Glass and Wilson's opera. Irony remains an important (and largely neglected) element, while estrangement and fragmentation play important roles in Acts I and II, as seen in Knee Plays 1 and 2. Transcendent vision is reserved mainly for the last scene and final knee play, where it is juxtaposed in dramatic fashion. Thus, emotional engagement, estrangement, and personalization form subject positions that can be decoded in terms of one's individual perception, providing a series of

58 Philip Glass, *Words Without Music*, 286.

59 Although, in fact, Samuel M. Johnson's text says that "so profound was their love for each other, they needed no words to express it."

60 David Cunningham, quoted in Richard Kostelanetz and Robert Flemming (eds.), *Writings on Glass: Essays, Interviews, Criticism*, 152.

61 Martin Scherzinger, "The Return of the Aesthetic: Musical Formalism and Its Place in Political Critique," in Andrew Dell'Antonio (ed.), *Beyond Structural Listening? Postmodern Modes of Hearing* (California: University of California Press, 2004), 253.

62 Ibid., 253 and 272.

narrative strategies that enable us to get a clearer sense of what the opera might mean.

In his excellent overview of the opera, David Cunningham outlines the kind of "standard" subject positions assumed in this opera, which he sees as forming a process of "deduction and formulation." He explains: "the only way that the viewer can impose development on the work ... is to actually deduce and formulate on one's own behalf ... [because] *Einstein* functions partly on the basis that information is supplied, perception by its existence alters the information perceived – perception is a form of change."[63] My overview of the opera has attempted to demonstrate that what is represented in it and what one may think it represents – both musically and dramatically – can together form a kind of semantic window. Of course, there is always the danger that we might fall into the trap, as Abbate puts it, of "[creating] fictions about music to explain where no other form of explanation is possible, and ... look to literary categories [in order] to endorse them ..."[64] This seems preferable, however, to the many clichés to which Glass and Wilson's opera has fallen victim for many years, such as: "there is nothing to understand in *Einstein on the Beach*, nothing to 'get.'" Meaning is certainly not indelibly fixed in the opera, any more than it is in other examples of "postmodern" operas from around the same time (such as Robert Ashley's *Perfect Lives* and *Atalanta*), and may not even be immediately graspable, but it is clearly and cleverly shaped by what is seen on stage in Wilson's brilliant direction and through Glass's powerful and compelling music.

63   Ibid., 156.
64   Abbate, *Unsung Voices: Opera and Musical Narrative in the Nineteenth Century*, 46.

6 Creating beauty in chaos

Robert Wilson's visual authorship in *Einstein on the Beach*

Avra Sidiropoulou

For me it's all opera in the Latin sense of the word, in that it means work: and this means something I hear, it's something I see, it's something I smell. It includes architecture, painting, sculpture, lights. We are developing a theatrical language with the body that can parallel the language of literature.[1]

Go [to my performances] like you would go to a museum, like you would look at a painting. Appreciate the color of the apple, the line of the dress, the glow of the light [...] You don't have to think about the story, because there isn't any. You don't have to listen to words, because the words don't mean anything. You just enjoy the scenery, the architectural arrangements in time and space, the music, the feeling they all evoke. Listen to the pictures.[2]

Philip Glass's and Robert Wilson's opera in four acts, *Einstein on the Beach*,[3] which premiered at the Avignon Festival on July 25th, 1976, and has had several revivals since, is the apogee of "directors' theatre," raising important questions related to theater textuality and authorship. Besides being the director of the piece, Wilson assumes parenthood of the performance script – in so far as the visual dramaturgy goes –and establishes himself as the twentieth and twenty-first-century *auteur* par excellence. This chapter sheds light on Wilson's idiosyncratic stage *écriture* – the way the *mise-en-scène* shapes and defines storytelling – with particular respect to a formalist aesthetic that paradoxically resonates with humanist verve. At the same time, it addresses the ever-contested issue of artistic ownership, arguing that in *Einstein* the task of separating the text from its performance

1 Robert Wilson in conversation with Ariel Goldenberg, 1st May 1995 in Maria M. Delgado and Paul Heritage, eds, *In Contact With the Gods?: Directors Talk Theatre*, Manchester, Manchester University Press, 1996, 303.
2 Robert Wilson, quoted in Robert Brustein, "Introduction" in Shyer, Laurence, *Robert Wilson, and his Collaborators*, New York, Theatre Communications Group, 1990, xv.
3 The author of this chapter watched the opera at the De Nederlandse Opera/The Amsterdam Music Theatre in its most recent revival [January 2013]. For reasons of brevity, the opera will be hereafter referred to as *Einstein*.

is no less taxing than futile, because the staging of the opera is essentially a new visual text that will ultimately resist another director's attempt to place it in a different production context. My discussion of the opera examines the notion of authorship from the point of view of the director's creative agency; in so doing, it addresses the idea of Wilson's *mise-en-scène* as *text*: a text that stands side-by-side with the musical score and the libretto, insofar as the making of the opera goes; a sophisticated sensory composition which has its own autonomy and therefore is difficult to ignore in any future production of the opera by another director.

As its title suggests, the opera was inspired by the life and achievements of Albert Einstein,[4] building on collective perceptions of his theories and vision and fleshing out the myths that have been attributed to him. It is a visionary artist's treatment of a visionary scientist's life, a poetic rather than a biographical portrait of the subject. The *Einstein* libretto consists of writings by dancer-choreographer Lucinda Childs, African-American actor Samuel M. Johnson (who had performed the parts of the judge and the bus driver in the original *Einstein* production) and Christopher Knowles (an American poet and painter diagnosed with an autism spectrum disorder, and Wilson's long-time collaborator). The very beginning of Glass's and Wilson's collaboration on this nearly five-hour-long, no-intermission project testifies to its unique composition. The script was based on a sketchbook by Wilson, containing several visual themes and motifs. Interspersed with the writings of Knowles, Childs, and Johnson –largely based on improvisations – are numbers and *solfège* syllables (do, re, mi, and so on), recited by a chorus of singers, in the absence of a more conventional libretto, while two long dance sequences provide the opera's centerpieces. References to Einstein are only tangential; this is no dramatic biography of the scientist, but a quizzical, impressionistic evocation of Einstein-related themes and allusions. In fact, the figure of Einstein is more of a pretext; an opportunity for Wilson to further expand on his own original treatment of time and space.

As a philosophy and aesthetic movement, formalism has been associated with conceptual, stark, and often rigid artworks whose properties are removed from the gentle plasticity and transparent nature of more open and instinctual types of representation, where the energy falls on the intimate interaction of performer and spectator. What audiences sometimes miss is a sense of vulnerability – the tacit understanding between auditorium and stage that the frailties inherent in producing, directing, and acting are part of the performance's quality as a living entity, bearing an ephemeral allure. Despite the fact that it has often been described as a formalist work, Wilson occasionally likes to downplay the significance of form in his directing, claiming that it bores him, as it is "a means to get you somewhere.

---

4   The opera is the first of the Portrait Trilogy that Glass devised, with *Satyagraha* following *Einstein* in 1979, and *Akhnaten* coming in 1983. All three pieces were composed as "portraits" of famous historical figures, although the notion of a portrait opera series was not in Glass's mind when working on *Einstein*.

How you fill the form in is what counts."[5] A formal sensibility is nevertheless prevalent in all his oeuvre.[6] Yet, a keen perspective of generosity and sympathy also informs his performances. Alongside his exactitude with form, the unrelenting attention to detail and the sheer scope of his artistic ambition, one is also struck by his moving naiveté, the child-like tenacity of a dreamer who refuses to comply with the unequivocal mandates of realism and discursive logic, allowing instead his spectators' memory to relapse to hypnotic scenes from a cherished past and fast forward to stately visions of an imaginary future. Given the confounding mood of awe that spectators experience – largely owing to the suspension of plot, the exuberant spectacle, and the sleek design – the overall feeling remains that of a celebration of life. In *Einstein*, Wilson embarks on a meditative journey into the spectators' subconscious,[7] unearthing memories, fantasies, and deep-set anxieties and translating them into powerful stage metaphors that continue to dwell within us long after we leave the theater.

Complex dramaturgies

"When I make a play," confessed Wilson, "I start with a form, even before I know the subject matter. I start with a visual structure, and in the form I know the content. The form tells me what to do."[8] *Einstein*'s visual palette is apposite to Glass's music, exploding the concept of the opera to unimaginable extremes, with lightscapes and soundscapes that work alongside, counter to, or beneath the fragmentary verbal text. While the performance script may sometimes feel random and disconnected – an "essential" plot being replaced by a series of disjointed visual, verbal, and sonic references –the result is conspicuously articulate, if mostly inferential. Ostensibly heterogeneous materials blend and match to reveal a universe that has opened upto allegory. Notwithstanding the audience's disorientation, the mixture is fascinating, a mirroring of the human mind, where anything and everything is allowed to circulate freely. This is true of the work's composition, which, within Wilson's robust scenographic writing, builds narrative structure and holds together all the seemingly aleatory aspects of the basic – minimal, as well as non-linear – storytelling. The painterly perspective runs through most of the movement choices and the sensuous imagery – predominantly in hues of black, white, grey, and blue. Thus, while conventional, sequential narrative devices are abandoned, the visual introduction of mood and repetitive structures that accompany the stark imagistic storytelling render the opera non-narrative or in the very least, narratively

---

5   Quoted in Arthur Holmberg, *The Theatre of Robert Wilson*, Cambridge, Cambridge University Press, 1996, 122.

6   Lighting, for example, is for Wilson a rudiment of composition. In his own words, "I paint, I build, I compose with light. Light is a magic wand" (qtd Holmberg, *op. cit.*, 1996, 121).

7   In Lisa Hirsch's description, "both audience and performers are set adrift in Einstein, and it's incumbent on the audience to simply observe and absorb Einstein on a subconscious or subverbal level," See: Lisa Hirsch, "*Einstein* Casts its Spell," *San Francisco Classical Voice*, 26 Oct. 2012.

8   Quoted in Holmberg: *op. cit.*, 84.

experimental: A train arrives slugging on; A trial – presumably of landmark figure Patty Hearst – begins; A train pulls out of a station; The trial goes on, succeeded by a prison scene. A person is inside a building and a person is on a bed; A spaceship flashes its lights; And, finally, a bus appears. However simple the narrative line, consummate geometrical configurations and three-dimensional spatiality layer the performance event, especially in the two "field dances" choreographed by Childs. Objects and bodies are transubstantiated into still lives and portraits: As the audience arrives, two performers (Helga Davis and Kate Moran in the 2012 revival) sit calmly, reciting random numbers and nonsense text, while gradually more and more dancers fill up the pit next to the musicians, gesticulating in a stylized manner. The images are volatile and profuse throughout: Calculations are being scribbled on an invisible blackboard. A crowd of people stare up to the top of a tall industrial building, where a young man is placed, apparently engrossed in mathematical equations. Wilson's *mise-en-scène* is clearly informed by the principles of early twentieth-century experimentalist writer Gertrude Stein's landscape writing: by defining plays as *landscapes*, Stein communicated a desire to generate visual relationships in space through a play of words.[9]

Neither thematic, nor chronological,[10] but resolutely non-linear and repetitive, the organizational principles of the opera make up a complex dream structure: four acts, nine scenes, and five "knee-plays" (shorter entr'actes between major acts) are linked together by power of association mostly, digressing from a conventional path of storytelling. Setting up a succession of metaphors that carry through seamlessly into the performance, emphatically producing different modes of awareness of time, *Einstein* establishes a resonant poetry of dreams; each of the three motifs (train, trial, and field) is broken up into a set of images which, since homologous, may be reintegrated. The locus of this process of reintegration is the consciousness of the individual spectator. Structure is inborn, that is, emerges while the work is performed and the spectator spontaneously apprehends the relationships obtained among images. Thus, coherence is not a result of any logical sequence of images (the series train-trial-field repeated three times) as the program notes suggest, but resides in intuitively grasped similarities among images derived from a common motif.[11]

Einstein recalibrates the concept of "dramaturgy," iconicizing the stage to such degree that another term is required to capture this mode of creating, one from which the element of "drama" can be omitted quite unapologetically. Here, we are confronted with a different vocabulary altogether, a sensory stage pushed beyond

9   In 1922, in discussions of how and why she writes, Stein claimed that she used words to paint pictures and that she held the notion of writing plays as analogous to the practice of landscape painting, which actually absolved her of the conventions of linear storytelling. For more on Stein's *landscape plays* see: Elinor Fuchs and Una Chaudhuri, eds, *Land/Scape/Theatre*, Ann Arbor, University of Michigan Press, 2002.

10   Craig Owens, "Einstein on the Beach: The Primacy of Metaphor," The MIT Press, October, Vol. 4 (Autumn 1977), 24.

11   Ibid., 27.

its limits, an *ecriture corporelle* in Mallarme's description[12] and a powerful *poetry in space*, to take on Artaud's view of the ideal *mise-en-scène*. Framing is achieved by means of manipulating visual structures: mere choice of imagery does not necessarily yield a new form of text; instead, the audience's perception shifts thanks to the reordering and repositioning of the images. Concerned with "how the total stage picture looks at any given moment," Wilson is just as interested (if not more) in "the shape, proportion, and materials of furniture, the color, fabric, and design of costumes, placement and content of film, paths and gestures of performers, and lighting," as he is in the dialogue or the music.[13]

The strategy of building *Einstein* picture after picture dovetails with the practice of "bricolage,"[14] a mode of composition that brings together (heteroclite) materials from diverse sources. The amalgamation of styles –from surrealism and constructivism to symbolism and minimalism – forms a synthetic iconography defying characterization, wherein ambiguous textual fragments are foregrounded visually. Fundamentally, the compositional plasticity of the space generates a strong perceptual impact. Perspectives shift constantly (for example, at different points in performance we see the train from both back and front), resonating with echoes from Einstein's theory of relativity, since, "how you perceive is relative to where you are in space and time."[15] The largely black-and-white design borrows from Meyerhold's architectural arrangement of the stage on different levels of action, whereas the transforming spatial planes invite us to view the physical events from multiple angles. Thus, space is no longer limited to accommodating actors physically, but also forges dramaturgy. In effect, visual velocity makes up for narrative ellipsis.

The evocation of memory precipitates instinctual rather than cerebral processing. As it is, Wilson's theater "does not make history, only its poetic other side, memory. He lingers in myth, the space between literature and history."[16] Because it is impossible to access *Einstein* in its totality, aposiopesis and semicolons are popular punctuation marks in the syntax of performance. Spatial relationships configure the theater event in astonishing combinations, exploiting the depth, height, and length of the stage. In fact, as *New Yorker* critic Hilton Als pointed out, "seeing the show for the first time can feel a bit like space travel: the immediate atmosphere is so unfamiliar and discomfiting that you find it difficult to focus."[17] The concurrent sensory stimuli make it challenging to concentrate on

---

12 In Hans-Thies Lehmann, *Postdramatic Theatre*, New York, Routledge, 2006, 94.

13 Susan Letzler Cole, *Directors in Rehearsal: A Hidden World*, New York, Routledge, 1992, 160.

14 First introduced by Claude Lévi-Strauss in *The Savage Mind* (1962) in reference to the inherent patterns of mythological thought, the term has been thoroughly present in postmodern theory to suggest a process of intertextual exchange among seemingly unrelated compositional elements in writing. See: Claude Lévi-Strauss, *The Savage Mind*, Chicago, The University of Chicago Press, 1966.

15 Maria Shevtsova, *Robert Wilson*, London and New York, Routledge, 2007, 103.

16 Bonnie Marranca, "The Forest as Archive: Wilson and Interculturalism," *PAJ*, Vol. 11, No. 3/Vol. 12, No. 1 (1989), 36.

17 Als, Hilton, "Slow Man. Robert Wilson and his first masterpiece," The New Yorker. September 17, 2012. www.newyorker.com/arts/critics/atlarge/2012/09/17/120917crat_atlarge_als#ixzz2E1AiQzx9, Accessed: July 10, 2015.

one single element or area of the stage, and therefore, full-bodied perception is denied in favor of simultaneity and kaleidoscopic vision. Subjective and associational structure is then the responsibility of the spectator and a product of a mental operation of compiling the individual elements of the *mise-en-scène* and finding connections among them.[18] Being poetic, Wilson's work is metaphor-dependent, as becomes manifest in the symbolic function of set, costumes, and props. A diagram of the atomic bomb is perhaps the most obvious among these signs, but more enigmatic allusions are just as effective. For example, the glowing shell that one of the dancers brings close to her ear echoes, according to Wilson, Isaac Newton's conviction that one could hear the universe in a seashell. The impression of the lunar eclipse is just as alluring, as the moon passes through a cloud, only to emerge again. Sometimes the imagery is purely iconic, as in the large Einstein portrait displayed on the theater wall, the projected photograph of equations, or the young picture of the scientist pitted against a studio set of a beach. Similarly, the way actors are dressed in white shirt, baggy trousers, suspenders, and sneakers points straight to one of the physicist's best-known photographs. Directly associated with narrative focus, the recurrent symbolism channels the audience's attention by fine-tuning the aesthetic frame of the play. Many times, the performers move in a state of stylized frenzy, suggestive of the fluid complexities that govern the human mind, while the emblematic train brings to mind one of Einstein's most celebrated thought experiments, according to which, if a streetcar approached the speed of light, an observer looking back at a receding city clock tower would assume that the clock hands had stopped while his own watch continued ticking.

Being an author of images, rather than of words, Wilson creates "a gallery of melting pictures drawn by the grammar of dreams."[19] As form coincides with content, choreography turns into dramaturgy, and the structure of space is the plot.[20] Even in rehearsal, directing actors is done "visually." Wilson avoids words like "objective," "motivate," "justify," or "inner life." Favoring painterly over psychological terms, he asks, for example, actors to deliver one line with a very "hot texture," the next line with a "cold texture."[21] Acting is "presenting a character in time and space and textures."[22] Characteristically, Stefan Brecht, who used to work for Wilson as an actor, described the director's work as a process

---

18 Lehmann focuses on how Wilson's space –"divided 'into stripes' parallel to the apron of the stage" – allows for actions taking place in different depths of the stage to "either be synthesized by the spectator or be read as 'parallelograms.'" He refers to "the constructing imagination of the viewer," in so far as "whether s/he considers the different figures on stages as existing within a shared context at all, or only as synchronically presented." See: Hans-Thies Lehmann, *Postdramatic Theatre*, New York, Routledge, 2006, 79.

19 Ben Brantley, "Death, Destruction and Detroit III," New York Times, July 9, 1999.

20 Arthur Holmberg, *The Theatre of Robert Wilson*, Cambridge, Cambridge University Press, 1996, 85.

21 Susan Letzler Cole, *Directors in Rehearsal: A Hidden World*, New York, Routledge, 1992, 155.

22 Ibid., 158.

whereby "the mind is immersed in the body, at its service."[23] After all, acting is a matter of striking a balance between form and freedom, and for Wilson, interpretation is no longer grounded on psychology, but on movement and gestural pattern. In this process, character may also be *de-psychologized*, but remains no less compelling.[24]

Interpretation also extends to the perception of dramatic time. Within a non-linear chronoscopic sphere – elusive, intractable, and seductive – the narrative of Einstein's actual life span furnishes only a pseudo-historical structure. However, *Einstein* stands outside time: daydreaming conjures up the basic temporal metaphor for the play, reinforced by the hypnotic chanting of the 11-member chorus, who often sing nothing but the names of numbers ("1-2-3-4, 1-2-3-4, 1-2-3-4-1-2-3"). This renders the sense of time glacial – as spectators, we fall into a state of semi-slumber and dream Einstein's dreams. The hierarchy of temporal sequences – much like the hierarchizing of images – is arbitrary and still coherent, faithful to its own peculiar logic. Just as space is allegorical, time is no longer real but mythical – its function fluid and relative. Distorted through prolongation or emphatically extreme duration, it never ceases to readjust the spectator's perception. We agonize over the route of a large horizontal bar of light, which rises with excruciating slowness to a vertical position or over a clock cycling through 24 hours. Just as captivating are the strategies of hypnotic stasis, long pauses, silence, and slowness. The elongation of time admits the narrative to the expanse of myth,[25] magnifying the hallucinatory effect. The precise and mechanical dance movements, in sync with the repeated musical structures, are counterbalanced by a sense of the post-apocalyptic, conveyed in alternating metaphors of chaos and of tranquility, which encourage the audience to reflect deeply on the cycles of life and on their own mortality. Most theater deals with speeded-up time, but "I use the kind of natural time in which it takes the sun to set, a cloud to change, a day to dawn," Wilson once confessed.[26] Time's stillness, suspension, or grueling elongation – in some recorded cases of Wilson's productions, the action of crossing the width of the stage taking more than a half-hour to complete – turns theater into a landscape of the mind, where history and fact have frozen. The distension seems to effect spatial expansion; placed outside the regular coordinates of time or place, the human figure is reduced to infinitesimal points in the universe of the stage. After all, Wilson's theater is intuitive and his poetic impulses sit comfortably within a disciplined semiotic field. Slow motion encourages an immersive outlook: we absorb quietly *Einstein*'s cosmos, image after image, sound after sound.

23 Ibid.
24 Wilson's multisensory dramaturgy testifies to the idea that form can build its own emotional affect.
25 Avra Sidiropoulou, *Authoring Performance. The Director in Contemporary Theatre*, New York, Palgrave Macmillan, 2011, 115.
26 Quoted in Shomit Mitter, "Robert Wilson," in Mitter, Shomit and Shevtsova, Maria, eds, *Fifty Key Theatre Directors*, New York, Routledge, 2005, 188.

Rhythm and tempo are additional agents of dramaturgy. For one thing, visual and aural repetition is a supreme act of emphasis. Repetition of motifs (train, trial, field), of text, movement, and gesture, layers meaning, operating both as a framing strategy and a means of building ritualistic ambience. In two of the most memorable recitations that reverberate constantly ("this prematurely airconditioned supermarket" and "but I was reminded of the fact that I had been avoiding the beach") – the repeated words serving more as chants than as semantic units per se – add to the hypnotic effect. On the other hand, the additive choreographic pattern, following Glass's motivic music sharpens the dominant mood of urgency, as in the Spaceship scene, which builds into a musical, visual, and emotional crescendo. In general, each action's tempo – such as the uninterrupted typing, the choral singing, or the beating of the judge's desk with a hammer – is carefully regulated. The use of simultaneity[27] is also rampant, shaping time by means of compression; by setting one action, one body, or one space against another, Wilson simulates the effect of speed, radicalizing, coagulating, and elasticizing time at will.

Notwithstanding the precision and autonomy of Wilson's stage writing, the audience is free to choose out of a plethora of sensory quotations the connecting links that will ultimately yield meaning to the opera. Consequently, merely by choosing, spectators participate actively in the act of authoring the performance text. *Einstein*'s influx of impressions climaxes in a consummate experience, which ends in both post-apocalyptic overtones and a romanticizing final gesture, as the driver of a bus that slowly creeps into the scene, delivers the story of two lovers on a bench, ending on a mellow lullaby: "We have need of a soothing story to banish the disturbing thoughts of the day, to set at rest our troubled minds, and put at ease our ruffled spirits."[28]

Beauty in transcendence

Wilson's work has been described as a religious experience, "a spiritualized state of clairvoyance."[29] A meditation on life, *Einstein* escalates to a state of transcendence, to which Glass's highly repetitive music is integral. The sense of the sublime is imbued with ambiguity in imagery, characterization, and dramaturgical detail, inflicting a level of disorientation that gradually eases into a rite of initiation, a different understanding of theatrical time and space for the audience. Indeed, the opera seems radically inspired by Einstein's motto that the most beautiful

---

27 Apparently, as Holmberg argues, simultaneity gives Wilson the opportunity to create "a new aesthetic unity without denying the contradictions and chaos of experience," something that is achieved by "telescoping space and time," through a "kaleidoscope of clashing perspectives" (Arthur Holmberg, *The Theatre of Robert Wilson*, Cambridge, Cambridge University Press, 1996, 93).

28 *Einstein on the Beach*, Knee 5. TWO LOVERS, Text written by Mr. Samuel M. Johnson, Quoted from Einstein on the Beach libretto: http://culturebox.francetvinfo.fr/sites/default/files/assets/documents/eob_text_for_libretto.pdf

29 Bonnie Marranca, *The Theatre of Images*, Baltimore and London, PAJ Publications,1996, 39.

experience we can have is the mysterious; together, no doubt, with his conviction that imagination is more important than knowledge. On the level of subject matter, the pursuit of one's dream is an overriding theme; Einstein, who is portrayed sparsely, is nothing short of an emblematic figure, an ideal as well as a recurrent utopia, epitomizing the enlightened individual's capacity for greatness, beyond man-made boundaries. In the 2012 revival, in the orchestra pit, he is impersonated by a solo violinist (performed masterfully by Jennifer Koh), made to resemble the scientist through costume, makeup, and an unexpected sticking out of the tongue; a visual homage to Albert Einstein's famous photograph.

Made up of improvised fragments, the text is altogether associational: the numbers, *solfège* syllables, and deliberately nonsensical lines chanted out or recited in seemingly random fashion provide the backbone of a rudimentary storyline, their rhythm featuring a strong inner structure and logic. The cyclical motifs of Glass's music are well served by Wilson's contrapuntal direction, building a wide range of "mental environments."[30] Wilson's original approach to narrative structure is by and of itself attached to an understanding of performance more or less as a transcript of inscribed impressions, the purpose of which is to evoke states of creative unrest within the spectator. The non-linear dimension imparts the desire to see and to represent the world in terms of life cycles. The supremacy of pattern over fact advocates a humanistic outlook just as the distortion of time frames suggests that history is subjective and speculative. The construction of performance relies on a non-discursive awareness of the story. Visual, aural, and structural indices of dreams are everywhere: most characteristically, a huge bed dominates the court scene, in which, in the original version, lies one of the multiple Einstein personas, seemingly pondering on the ramifications of his inventions. Presumably, the bed is suggestive of Einstein's quality of a dreamer and a visionary, ultimately on trial for daring to engage in groundbreaking observations.

Much of the commentary emphasizes Wilson's ability to contrive striking painterly scenes. Notwithstanding *Einstein*'s epic imagination, as in Wilson's other productions, the images, elliptical and polished, ultimately ring a gentle, familiar tone, drawn as they are from the average spectator's arsenal of childhood memories that tap on the fantastical. Such chimerical arrangements include the arrival of the monumental locomotive (the advent of which signifies a historical moment, a step towards technological enhancement, and thus, cultural evolution), the gathering of a crowd around a brick building, the frenzied dancing, the mysterious bus and the climactic, perhaps most compelling scene of the play, in which the experience of being inside a spaceship is conjured up through powerful visual and aural indices. After the frenetic elevator sequence, where the young boy, accompanied by a clock, goes up and down in the glass cubicle, the stage is actually transformed to a three-stories high flame-orange structure, divided into small cabins, where only the shadows of the performers can be discerned.

---

30   Stefan Brecht, *The Theatre of Visions: Robert Wilson*, London, Methuen, 1994, 360.

Sublime lighting takes over, flashing brilliantly on and off, while roaring sounds and billowing smoke complete the post-apocalyptic landscape.[31] The spaceship, a legendary object, stands for the utopian desire to surpass our inborn limitations. Deeply allegorical, the compositional iconography of the piece is by no means accidental; both majestic and guileless, it is markedly synthetic, combining the ambition to create with our child-like veneration and awe in the face of human achievement.

The relentless pursuit of beauty is multifaceted: Wilson involves every aspect of the stage to create a sense of transformation; everyday objects or situations force us to seek connections among disconsonant elements. The "angled" visuality discourages the images from remaining internally static, despite their outward stillness. Each figure and object positioned on stage contains a secret (see, for example, the uncanny bewigged judges), a quality for instantaneous transformation. Birringer describes Wilson's seductive manipulation of our perception of what is real and what is "normal" as a process which "also depends on our willingness to be moved with a childlike sense of wonder, allowing the inexplicable and beautiful to take place before the critical mind questions the denials at work in the fetishism of images."[32] We are constantly struck by the juxtaposed pictorial allusions, which, notwithstanding the lack of an obvious referential center, finally manage to hold the narrative together. Fog covers the stage before the fairy-tale train enters the scene, a toy rocket flies over while a compass descends. The courtroom is divided into two to provide the set for both trial and prison scenes. In spite of the momentous scale and complexity of *Einstein*'s visuals, the dramaturgical, scenographic, and structural framework of the production is quite transparent, revolving around three very concrete and universally understood things:[33] a train, a trial, a field.

In fact, universals provide the emotional nucleus of the show: the cardboard train that moves slowly from right to left seems to have been taken straight out of a fairytale, an ordinary children's fixation. Generally, the impression of innocence is prevalent, nourished by eloquent "young" imagery, such as the sequence with the paper planes that the child throws repeatedly towards the smoke-filled stage, as he stands on a bridge over the railway tracks. Along the same lines, the powerful conceit of the young boy examining a luminous geometric shape foregrounds a communal feeling of childhood innocuousness; the boy could be a young version of Einstein or another prospective scientist to take on from where Einstein left.

31 Shevtsova's observation is apt: "you realise that what you are looking at resembles the control board of a spacecraft that you have seen in science fiction films or comics" (Maria Shevtsova, *Robert Wilson*, London and New York, Routledge, 2007, 111).

32 Johannes Birringer, "Postmodern Performance and Technology," *Performing Arts Journal*, Vol. 9. No. 2/3. 10th Anniversary Issues: The American Theatre Condition (1985), 83.

33 Susan Flakes, "Robert Wilson's 'Einstein on the Beach,'" *The Drama Review: TDR*, Vol. 20, No. 4. Theatrical Theory Issue (1976), 70.

Universal symbols such as clocks and compasses reinforce the impression of timelessness. To this end, everyday things are foregrounded to underline life's continual cycles and the comforting repetition of shared activity, as in, for example, the tableau of people sitting at their desks, polishing their nails or in the stylized depiction of a crowd eating packed lunches in unison. Wilson's humanistic perspective ultimately embraces the idea of a chorus consummating the classical ideal of *community*, even when it seems to undermine it. While individuality and "character" are often submerged in an endless, mechanical repetition of interchanged personas and actions (notably, there are more than one Einsteins), Wilson creates a sense of complicity that holds together what could certainly qualify as a posthuman world.

Equally fulfilling in an emotional sense is the "Night Train" scene, which follows Einstein and presumably his wife on a romantic trip; although the woman character suddenly pulls out a gun on her husband, her whole comportment indicates that this is "just a play in a continuing gender battle"[34] and therefore danger subsides before it actually sets in. In general, the opera plays at our secret fancies and customary fears: the nuclear apocalypse to which the title alludes – and more particularly the atomic bomb – is just one of the symbols at work in our unconscious mind. But even such ominous tokens are treated with a redeeming lightness. As John Rockwell relates: "There is a vision of the nuclear Armageddon, but also a sweetly sentimental faith in the power of love to overcome everything in the universe."[35] Essentially,

> The mystery of Robert Wilson's stage pictures and Philip Glass's music is in its guilelessness: the glassy chitchat, a bus driver's sappy love story, a judge's bad jokes, the music's endless major and minor triads, the blown-up photos of Albert Einstein, a children's-book illustration of a train in the countryside [...] Beneath the solemn ritual, 'Einstein' has a folksiness. Nothing is obscure even if little makes sense.[36]

Towards a humanistic formalism

In *Postdramatic Theatre*, Hans Thies Lehmann maintained that when the focus of a performance used to be to perceive the text in terms of a model of "suspenseful dramatic *action*," the constitutive elements of the *mise-en-scène*, namely, "the *theatrical* conditions of perception, such as the physical, visual, and aural life of the event"[37] became secondary. He pointed out that in many contemporary productions these formal aspects of the performance are essential, in fact, they are "precisely the

---

34   Anthony Tommasini, "Time Travel with Einstein: Glass's Opera Returns to the Stage," *New York Times*, September 16, 2012.

35   John Rockwell, "Einstein Returns Briefly," *New York Times*. December 17, 1984.

36   Holland 1992.

37   Hans-Thies Lehmann, *Postdramatic Theatre*, New York, Routledge, 2006, 34, emphasis in original.

point"[38] and certainly do not function as "merely subservient means for the illustration of an action laden with suspense" (2006, 35). Formalism's zealots argue for the usefulness of form as a "container in which the actor can find endless variations and interpretive freedom."[39] American director Anne Bogart observes that limitations invite the actor to meet them, disturb them, transcend them; she recognizes, however, that the shapes and forms that actors and directors seek in rehearsal should produce currents of "vital life-force, emotional vicissitudes and connection."[40] This claim goes hand-in-hand with Wilson's understanding of theater's function: "For me, the best way to [hold theater open as a forum] is [to do] something totally controlled and mechanical. And then there's freedom. Ideally, one would be a machine at work, one must become totally mechanical to become free."[41]

In recent theater practice, formalist criteria for directorial accomplishment have been granted vampiric properties, devouring those elements on stage that threaten their solidity. To a certain extent, the central issue in *auteur* theater needs to be redirected to how enterprising forms can generously accommodate the text's ardor as well as the actors' embodied emotion. Our attention never strays away from the bodies of either actors or musicians, engaged as we are in observing their struggle to keep up with the frenetic pacing of the music. In fact, the music's viscerality makes us aware of our own bodies as well as those of the performers. This thrilling co-existence – their bodies' potential for greatness in a way reflects our own desire to transcend our moral selves and achieve more lightness and indeed, more greatness. The complexity of *Einstein*'s "embodiedness," its embracing of the body's capacities and vulnerability –shared between the auditorium and the stage – further attests to its humanism.

That said, Wilson's work, for one thing, has been repeatedly criticized for being cold and stilted, devoid of meaning, for all its lavish spectacle.[42] Some *Einstein* reviews expressly document a part of the audience's alienation, which could be attributed to an overly formalist focus: As one reviewer put it, "Wilson transports us

---

38   Ibid.
39   Anne Bogart, *A Director Prepares. Seven Essays on Art and Theatre*, London and New York, Routledge, 2001, 46.
40   Ibid.
41   Quoted in Lehmann, *op. cit.*, 1985, 562.
42   The new revival performances of *Einstein* have not been spared disparaging criticism. See Andrew Clements' review in the *Guardian*: For all its historical importance, it seems rather old-fashioned now, and at times the experience was like watching the theatrical equivalent of a period performance, as if achieving the same results using today's technology would lose something essential. Many of the images in Wilson's tableaux would nowadays be conjured using video or computer-generated graphics rather than with smudgy slide projections, painted flats and cardboard cutouts; it would all seem slicker, less contrived.See: Clements, Andrew, "Einstein on the Beach," *The Guardian*, May 6, 2012. www.theguardian.com/music/2012/may/06/einstein-on-beach-glas s-review, Accessed: August 4, 2015. Much more vitriolic is *The Telegraph*'s Rupert Christiansen's utter condemnation of the production as "flatulently pretentious in its willful opacity and without aesthetic, intellectual or spiritual substance [as well as] asphyxiatingly tedious." See: Rupert Christiansen, "Einstein on the Beach," *The Telegraph*, May 7, 2012. www.telegraph.co.uk/cultu re/music/opera/9250317/Einstein-on-the-Beach-Barbican-review.html, Accessed: May 15, 2015.

from a train to a courtroom to a panoptic tower, offering us carefully curated images and characters but leaving them strangely unframed, unmoored from meaning."[43] Many directors' stance towards the (partial) inability of formalist performance to stir the spectator has been wavering and noncommittal. To his honor, while he has given true substance to the often contested as well as awkward labelling of a "formalist," as an unapologetic conceptualist Wilson has always treated his material intuitively. For sure, his work has been discussed in the broader context of non-realist theater, one which has renounced the understanding of character as a psychological entity. He follows a trajectory introduced by Bertolt Brecht's theory of the performer as eyewitness rather than an emotionally involved dramatic persona, leading on to Samuel Beckett's engagement with fragmented and often mechanistic bodies, and more recently to postdramatic notions of split/mediated/digitized identities. However, Wilson's manipulation of form is rarely separate from a perspective of sympathy or connection to the living; while he has often been accused of treating actors like pawns on the chessboard of a stage, the production process reveals a more generous attitude. Revisiting his production of *The Days Before* (1999), for example, he vindicates himself by arguing that the piece reminds him of his early work "where people could be themselves in the context of a situation and didn't have to assume a role." Reportedly, he has actually told his actors that the most touching thing about the piece are the moments when he could see who they are as individuals: "sometimes you're trying to act what's in your head, and then I don't believe you. But if you feel something, that's truth, it's your experience."[44] Wilson's "celebration of humanity"[45] may not be explicit, but it certainly feels genuine.

Despite the fact that *Einstein*'s critical reception has been nothing less than controversial, most scholars as well as reviewers have almost unanimously highlighted Wilson's imagistic acumen. The poet and literary critic David Shapiro praised Wilson's "quixotic scale,"[46] commenting also on the director's ability to "convert the opera into something as flat and usable as a map."[47] The Wagnerian notion of *Gesamtkunstwerk* –of a total work of art – seems central in Wilson's structuring of *Einstein*:

> Here opera draws attention to itself as a self-regulating whole, not by the usual thickening of language but by the deliquescence of so many seemingly central resources. While there is a little bit of the merely magical to Wilson, there is much of the necessary shamanism required to heal us in a restless universe agitated in its smallest parts.[48]

---

43 Coghlan 2012.
44 Quoted in Anne Midgette, "A Procession of Elusive Images by the Merlin of Surreal Form," *The New York Times*. July 04, 1999.
45 Ibid.
46 David Shapiro "Notes on Einstein on the Beach," in Gregory Battcock and Robert Nickas, eds, *The Art of performance: a critical anthology*, (1984), /ubueditions, 2010, 143.
47 Ibid.
48 Ibid., 145.

The humanistic significance of the piece, viewed mostly in terms of the audience's transcendental connection to the cosmos that surrounds us, is ubiquitous in the *Einstein* literature. See, for example, Brustein's ecstatic reaction to the production:

> It represents one of those rare moments in cultural history where the most gifted people at work in the performing arts combine their resources to wallop us into an oceanic perception of our relation to the cosmos. Few contemporary works have penetrated so deeply into the uncreated dream life of the race.[49]

Questions of authorship

Responding to theater's directional changes towards icono-centric dramaturgies, Wilson reveals that his responsibility as an artist "is to create, not to interpret." The fact that directors prepare a work for spectators and therefore should allow them "the freedom to make their own interpretations and draw their own conclusions"[50] sets out an understanding of the operation of "reading" and staging texts as an act of authorship rather than of reflection, illustration, and clarification. Directing is not just another *lecture* but essentially a new *écriture* based on the auteur's mental processing of intentions, perceptions, and stimuli. This practice falls right into the theory of *auteurism*, which espouses that directors are *authors* of the theater event when they leave upon it a distinctive imprint, expressing a sense of visual panache and a choice of subject matter constant across a body of work.[51]

In 1988, German opera director and painter Achim Freyer remounted *Einstein on the Beach* in an abstract style, adding textual fragments from early twentieth-century theorists (Antonin Artaud and Ludwig Wittgenstein, among others) at the Stuttgart State Opera. Freyer had staged the world premiere of Glass's *Akhnaten* in Stuttgart, Germany (1984), where he had also staged *Satyagraha* in 1981. His ambition was to mount the entire portrait opera trilogy, which included *Einstein*. He evidently saw it more as Glass's work than Wilson's. The production was generally considered a failure and many critics focused on the impossibility of removing *Einstein* from its original director-author context. Writing for the *New York Times*, Rockwell castigated Freyer's imposition of "his own personality" onto the "supposedly completed collaborative process": "*Einstein* dispenses altogether with the contributions of its co-creator, Robert Wilson, adding a 'text composition' by Mr. Freyer and Klaus-Peter Kehr, the Stuttgart dramaturge, as well as

---

49   Brustein, Robert, "Expanding Einstein's Universe," The *New Republic* 192, Issue 4 (1985), 23.
50   Robert Wilson and Umberto Eco, "Robert Wilson and Umberto Eco: A Conversation," *Performing Arts Journal* 15, no. 1 (January, 1993), 89–90.
51   Avra Sidiropoulou, *op. cit.*, 2.

a 'new scenic version.'"[52] Rockwell plainly attacked Freyer for having "jettisoned not only Mr. Wilson's stage pictures but also his entire scenario" and protested that his version of *Einstein* came as "a rude shock."[53] His critique was fierce and adamantly addressed the challenges involved in having another director (re)interpret *Einstein*:

> This is simply perverse. "Einstein" is a work intimately linked to Mr. Wilson's ideas and images. Even so, it might be exciting for another powerful theatrical personality to reinterpret Mr. Glass's music. But – to take the worst example – to see Mr. Wilson's extraordinary series of scenes he calls "The Building," "The Bed," and "Space Ship" reduced by Mr. Freyer to dim blips was very sad. This exercise is a denial – not only of Mr. Wilson, but also of Mr. Glass, the eager audience and Mr. Freyer's own finest instincts.[54]

Two years later, discussing Wilson's 1992 production *Danton's Death*, Rockwell once again puts the issue of authorship back on the table: "any Wilson production of a text by someone other than himself is still a Wilson work: not only does he direct, design and light the productions, he also reshapes the original text into something that counts as both his and the author's."[55] Modernist in its formal minimalism yet postmodern in its reliance on assemblage, intermediality, and pastiche, *Einstein on the Beach* is essentially a lustrous paradigm of a "director's text." In this sense, attempting to separate the writer-director of the piece from its "director proper" would be nothing less than impossible, since text in *Einstein* is an elusive as well as allusive network of sensory tropes, impossible to grasp and "compartmentalize" comfortably within a printable version of a script for production. In effect, *Einstein* is text and performance combined: staging elements such as scenography, lighting and sound forge dramaturgy, and reversely, any remaining fragments of drama are subsumed into the *mise-en-scène*. The very fact that Glass composed the opera as a response to Wilson's design sketches plainly confirms the function of Wilson's *mise-en-scène* – embedded as it is in the drawings – as a fundamental act of authorship.

Is there room for another director to create within the textual frame set by Wilson? Surely, one of the basic challenges to settle here would be the extent to which the "script *Einstein*" is distinct from its production. In that event, we need to determine whether it is still viable to use terms that apply to plays that feature a more conventional structure (namely, fully fleshed dramatic texts) as opposed to "texts as pretexts" that serve as blueprints for performance. To come back to the

---

52 John Rockwell, "Review/Music; 3 Philip Glass Operas Become a Sort of Modern 'Ring' Cycle," *New York Times*, June 25, 1990. www.nytimes.com/1990/06/25/arts/review-music-3-philip-glass-operas-become-a-sort-of-modern-ring-cycle.html, Accessed: April 17, 2017.

53 Ibid.

54 Ibid.

55 John Rockwell, "Robert Wilson Tackles the French Revolution," *New York Times*, November 3, 1992.

opera's genesis, it was Wilson's drawings that gave birth to *Einstein*, while everything else (music, words, choreography) was created around them. Describing the process of composing the opera, Philip Glass reminisces: "I put [Wilson's sketches] on the piano and composed each section like a portrait of the drawing before me. The score was begun in the spring of 1975 and completed by the following November, and those drawings were before me all the time."[56]

What would then be a good way of describing *Einstein*'s textuality? Should it be viewed as a narrative departure point for a long performance art piece? As argued profusely, for Wilson, the language of composition is not a matter of semantics, but a vocabulary of images, sounds, mental, and psychic impressions. He writes in pattern and motif rather than meaning and message, his lines – horizontal, vertical, and diagonal – and turns establishing a unique syntax of the stage. This brings us back to the ownership of images, and naturally, to the authorship of the visual text. Holmberg is right to point out that to appreciate Wilson's dramaturgy, one must learn to read images.[57] Because Wilson thinks "spatially," he fashions the rehearsal process accordingly: "Most directors would have been analyzing the text with you, discussing what it means [...] I don't work that way. I have no sense of direction until I have a sense of space."[58]

Is a different staging of *Einstein on the Beach* possible? Can a new *mise-en-scène* of *Einstein* outlive the opera's (visual) author?[59] These questions alone can potentially lead to a more profound investigation of the still unsettled – in matters of both practice and legislation – issue of authorship in the directing art: How is performance copyrighted? How does a director *text-protect* complex visual dramaturgies? Finally, what exactly constitutes *text* in the theater and who owns it? Interestingly, the opera's complex dramaturgy has not always been given the right constitutional attention. As Holmberg relates, three times the Library of Congress refused to copyright the visual portion of the work, saying that *Einstein on the Beach* was a suite of drawings, not theater.[60] In answering some of the above questions we might once again try to resolve within ourselves the unwarrantedly complicated duality of text and performance; to accept that, in at least some forms of theater practice, the work's content is not simply embedded in but coincides with its form; or, as Wilson himself put it in an interview, "the depth is on the surface."[61]

56   Quoted in Laurence Shyer, *Robert Wilson and His Collaborators*, New York, Theatre Communications Group, 1989, 220.

57   Homberg *op. cit.*, 77.

58   Ibid.

59   Corwin, Christopher, "Back to the Beach," 18 Sep. 2012. http://parterre.com/2012/09/18/back-to-the-beach-2/, Accessed: December 12, 2014.

60   Holmberg, *op. cit.*, 21.

61   Ibid., 121.

Knee chapter 3
Stay out of the way of Bob Wilson when he dances

Lucinda Childs interviewed by Jelena Novak[1]

How did it start for you with Einstein? *I understand you met Robert Wilson through a mutual friend, and then it evolved into collaboration?*

I was from the Judson group, a very experimental group connected with John Cage and Merce Cunningham and some friends of mine in the seventies told me about Robert Wilson. I knew him but I didn't know about his work. And the friend said *A Letter to Queen Victoria* is on Broadway, and I thought – well I must go to see this. I went to the production and I loved it. It is something that was in a way the opposite of my aesthetic. It was in the theater and normally we don't work in the theater, we work in alternative spaces. It had music, many things about it in some ways were very traditional but everything about it was completely contemporary. I happened to meet him a little bit later at some festival. He talked to me about *Einstein* and I said yes, of course I would like to be involved.

Did you have any audition?

No, he said, "let's get together, I will come by" – he knew that I was living in SoHo, and that I had my studio in SoHo – "and we can talk about it, and I will explain it to you further." And he did that, and then he said I needed to come on the day they are auditioning everyone for the opera, for the singers and the dancers and everything. So I came for that and I met Philip Glass and [he] asked me if I could sing. I was not a performer who could sing, but I did the spoken text.

It was quite a multi-tasking role you got.

Yes, in the end, I never really knew what he wanted me to do until we started doing it and I don't think he knew either. He just liked the idea of me performing in the piece. Bob is like that. He met me and he saw that I am someone he could

---

1   The interview took place at Centre National de la Danse in Paris on November 25, 2017. Some of the questions were inspired by *Einstein* - related research done by Robert Fink, Pieter T'Jonck, Leah Weinberg and Zeynep Bulut.

use, so I ended up being performer and choreographer. And I loved this, I loved working with the text. I worked with the text in the Judson group a lot, so this was not completely new to me, to combine the text with performing. Yvonne Rainer introduced me to this whole concept in a way.

Was it physically demanding?

I was on stage for three hours dancing and performing, and working with a [dancing] partner Sheryl Sutton in five knee plays. It was hard but it was wonderful.

Thinking about Einstein, *I immediately think of yours and Sheryl Sutton's voices, the voices that colored this piece a lot.*

We worked together very well as a team, because Sheryl is a musician, she is a singer and a choreographer, so we worked very closely with the comprehension and the sense of the music, this is how we connected with each other, and even though it might be a little bit different, a structured improvisation every night, we had this very strong connection how to work together.

Christopher Knowles also wrote spoken texts for Einstein *and it seems that he transcribed some parts of the text from the radio...*

I feel the Earth moves speech, the speech at the end of Act 3, is very much like that – "Steve O'Brian, 4.30 a.m." – That was very funny.

And Einstein *voices have this kind of "radio quality," the distance, the announcement quality...*

Not like telling a story, it is like a kind of reportage, exactly, and it has a different tone, and that's hard for an actress, but they did it very well in the revival.

The first choreographer of Einstein *was Andy de Groat. Do you recollect his choreography?*

Yes, I do, in fact he wanted me to be in the choreography and I said, "Andy I really have my own company and involvement with this production. I have to limit to just doing my own solo work." The reason why later, in the revival, they wanted me to work on the choreography, to replace him really, was that his connection to the music was more or less improvised and my relation to the music when I worked in the revival in 1984 was completely structured to the music in a very careful way and in a very precise way, so it is a huge difference with how we treated the music. And it just so happened that for the next production they preferred that I'd be involved also as choreographer.

One of the critics compared the choreographies, writing that Andy used some kind of an amateurish approach and that with Lucinda Childs we got "highly polished structured minimalism."

It is true that one of the things that people in some ways loved about Andy's is that they were not all dancers, they were not professionally trained dancers, in the way that my company is completely professionally trained. That brought a certain element to the piece that I think Wilson very much embraced at that time, in the seventies.

When you create the choreography, how exactly do you do your work? Do you experiment with your body movements, note them down, work with other people trying to put them in the space? How exactly does the process of creating the movement go for you?

I need the music, and when I have the music, my work is the sounding board coming from the music. At first it is a completely intuitive process of finding movement improvisation in my studio by myself, and then once I find the material
   that I feel is the right material, I start to structure it in terms of the music. Philip
   may be counting in six, and I may count in five, but after 30 counts we come
   out together and I like to play with this kind of dialogue between the music and
   the choreography. And then I bring in the dancers and I start to teach them
   the material, and start to structure the material, and then when I start to get
   clear how the relationship of the dancers in the space is, then I draw from an
   overhead point of view the storyboard of every ten second interval. So I have
   a record of what is happening in the space, of what is the relationship of the
   dancers to the music and to each other. It is quite a long process. At first it is
   very open and then it gets to be very precise. And I have these structures on
   paper, they are very helpful in terms of reconstructing.

You have them for Einstein*, if someone would like to restage your choreography?*

There is no movement material, they would need a video to see the actual movements. It is only the relationship in the space, like taking the melody out of the
   music. It is just the notes, just the steps in the space, the *trace dans l'espace.*

You were not happy with existing modes of notating the choreography?

The Labanotation is very complicated. I don't understand it. I don't know it. Maybe
   if I knew it, if I studied it, it would be different, but I look at it and it takes like
   three days to say hello in a way for me, like a ship putting flags up and down. I
   needed something that was shorthand, that I could use quickly. And this I can
   do pretty quickly although the drawings I make sometimes I end up making
   them nice, so it takes time to throw away an old copy and make it look better.

*You said you work in relation to the music, but it was not always like that. In your
   early pieces you worked a lot without music.*

This is true. The dancers have a very precise musical connection because they
   are counting this structure of what's happening with the choreography, but
   there was no actual music and this is how Cunningham worked actually with
   his dancers. Very often they didn't even hear the music of John Cage until
   performance and that music co-existed with the choreography. The choreography is held together by two-second intervals of counting. I thought it was
   very beautiful that the dancers could work like this, without attaching to some
   musical structure that they could follow.

*Today critics sometimes connect your work with Baroque. How would you com-
   ment on that?*

I work a lot with Baroque opera. It makes sense to me because I feel very comfortable with that music. I feel that I can fit into this. I worked a lot in opera,
   I did *Salome*, and *Don Carlos, Moses and Aaron*, but here in the territory
   of Baroque opera, I feel a certain connection to the music that relates more
   to the contemporary forms of Philip Glass. He would say the same. I mean
   especially [the] concept of Bach's harmony is something that he very much
   connects to.

How did you create the famous Three Diagonal Dance for Einstein?

The first rehearsals with Bob were improvised and he said that in the opening scene of Act 1, scene 1, with the train coming in, the train comes to three different points, and he would like to develop choreography on three different diagonals. Then we decided that the movement activity would be very simple – forwards and backwards in the space on the diagonal – and that in each instance the movement would become more and more complex. So I had wide open possibilities. And each day that we rehearsed that scene I would work on it, worked it out, and talked to Bob, so we decided to keep this and didn't keep that, back and forth, while I was working on it … He gave me a great deal of freedom to do more or less what I wanted.

The Judson group was also famous for adopting movements from everyday life in the choreography.

Stepping outside the traditional round of dance vocabulary was a very important element in terms of the philosophy of John Cage, and that was an extreme step that Cunningham did not take – so this Judson group wanted to go there, to involve the pedestrian movement and found movement. This idea of reaching outside of traditional vocabulary comes from Duchamp.

Like you did in Street Dance?

Yes, exactly.

The Three Diagonal Dance emanates hysterical, stiff, unpredictable movements… Where does this come from?

I worked a lot with six and seven because that would put me on and off of Philip's music in terms of stepping. I let the accent and changes of direction generate the upper body movement and I liked the idea that it would build as an accumulation and become almost out of control. This is a little bit experimenting with the idea of an explosion. It doesn't explode but it moves into a territory in which very simple movements begin to become confused. I did it in a way that becomes less and less predictable, as an equation to the concept of explosion.

The concept of explosion is significant in Einstein *because of the Spaceship scene, the implicit nuclear explosion that was on trial in a way.*

Of course.

You made the drawing that was used for the light bulb patterns in the Spaceship?

Bob asked me – since the third knee play is a little bit the introduction to the concept of the spaceship with the light bulbs – he asked me to design the pattern – the movement from the wrist, the movement from the elbow, and the movement from the full arm and this diagonal. Sheryl and I were doing these different patterns in the space along the light bulbs. So I just made this design for him and he liked it, and he decided to use the design for the spaceship.

The spaceship is all the light bulbs, a whole row of light bulbs, and it goes on and off, you can simplify the pattern or be more complex with it, and have the pattern on and off, there are many different versions, but it is based on the drawing from Knee Play 3 (see Figure 7 Knee).

In his Memoir, Glass explains how Einstein on the Beach *was named, he makes a clear connection to the post-apocalyptic novel by Nevil Shute,* On the Beach.

Figure 7. Knee – Lucinda Childs, Drawing from Knee Play 3 of *Einstein on the Beach*, used as a basic design for the Spaceship scene panels. Courtesy of Lucinda Childs.

Yes, and the film also, they were both thinking about it at the time. Many people never understood this title. Because the opera was called *Einstein on the Beach* they decided that I had to do a text about the beach, even though it didn't have to do with Nevil Shute, it had to do with what they wanted to have in the opera, some reference to the beach because of the title.

And that is how this famous "Supermarket" speech came into being. Recently I saw a video of your performance Carnation, *which looks like some kind of weird coronation with commonplace objects. I immediately associated it with the "Supermarket" speech.*

Commonplace objects – that is very much our territory in a way that we have adopted as performers in terms of the huge influence of Duchamp and John Cage.

Was it also some kind of critique of consumerist culture in general?

Well it was a little bit like a ceremony, but it's the opposite of ceremony because these objects don't belong together, and they are completely commonplace, and they are disposable in addition to being commonplace, so it is a deliberate conflict of ideas, almost like a royal ceremony with the crown, just playing around with this kind of idea.

The lines in the "Supermarket" speech – which became one of the most emblematic moments of Einstein *– connect to this way of thinking.*

The day that we worked on that scene also happened to be the day of the Patty Hearst trial. And there was a cover of her on the front page of the *New York Post* with handcuffs – a beautiful photo actually. Bob talked about it in that scene of the sequence at the end, where she transforms herself from debutant into a robber into a beauty queen, who becomes married to her bodyguard, this short sequence connects that a little bit to it also.

Einstein *deliberately brings in all kinds of associations with things that were happening around at the time.*

The whole Trial scene is a reference because that was happening to us at the time, something that Bob wanted to adapt into the opera which I thought was really interesting.

What was your impression when for the first time you watched the revival in 2012?

It was emotional to be on the outside looking in. There were all kinds of things that I never realized, the whole visual concept of Wilson's visions is not something you get from being on stage. So that was great that I had an opportunity to understand all of the different details of the decor, and how everything relates to Einstein in a wonderful way, very interesting.

I was struck by the similarity between the new young performers and the performers in the original production, like when a "retouched" version of a black and white film is done in color… Was it done on purpose?

Yes, of course. I admired the actress very much. Since she is not the dancer, and I was replaced also with a dancer, this was something that I felt – oh, they had to make this split – this made a difference, I would have preferred if it could have been the same person, as in the original, but that was not possible.

How do you see Einstein *today? Are you aware of the impact it made?*

I think we felt that with the revival especially with so many times in Paris – this opera had so many performances in Paris, more than anywhere else – and then of course in New York. This last revival does feel very different from how it was in the beginning. Some of the uptown people asked, Why don't you stay downtown? Over a period of 40 years things had changed radically in terms of the spectatorship of today.

There was Einstein *in 1976, and a collaboration on* Dance *with Glass in 1979, and in the meantime in 1984 you became the main choreographer of* Einstein. *I can see a lot from* Dance *in your choreography for the Field dances of* Einstein. *Could you comment on the relationship between the choreographies for* Dance *and* Einstein?

Philip is the first composer that I worked with and it is because of *Einstein* that we
decided to continue to work together on *Dance*, and I involved a company of
eight dancers at the time, and myself, and Sol LeWitt. And the idea for him
was not to make a traditional decor for me and my company, but to have the
decor be the dancers. That is why the film became so important a part of the
production. And I think that the movements of *Dance* started to move more
into a traditional territory because of the music and because of the demands
on the dancer, and because normally the silent pieces were much shorter,
ten minutes each one, and these were more like 20-minute sequences. And
it is very similar to the structure of Field Dances because I proposed that the
length of the Field Dances be in the vicinity of the same length as the sections
of *Dance*. The material is quite similar. But it is completely different in some
ways for me because it is all inspired by the music and the music for *Dance* is
very different from the music from *Einstein*.

It is interesting to see how Dance *in a way goes through* Einstein...

Philip and I had continued to work together. We did *Einstein* in 1976, and *Dance*
in 1979, and I did *Mad Rush* for the Paris Opera in 1981, so we had a kind
of ongoing relationship, and it was more or less logical that we would like to
continue to work together for the revival.

Will you collaborate soon again?

Philip has begun to compose the music for a collaboration that will actually be with
Robert Wilson. It is called *Distant Figure* and one part of that music was com-
missioned by Aarhus festival in Denmark, and I am just coming from Aarhus
where for the first time I heard one of the sections of music that he is writing. A
revival is one thing, but to create a new piece you need many, many sponsors,
and we are not yet at that point where we know how the piece will premiere,
but we are working on it. It will put Philip and myself and Bob together. I think
it will happen but it will not happen tomorrow; it takes time, it is a very ambitious project.

What were your impressions of Robert Wilson's own dance with the flashlights in
Einstein?

That was the best!

Did you help him with the choreography?

No, stay out of the way of Bob Wilson when he is dancing! It was really beautiful,
and fantastic, and that was how he was like in *Queen Victoria* too: bursts of
energy, nobody could do this, quite crazy and very beautiful. At the revival one
of my dancers did it. He had a lot of makeup but it was not as wild as Bob,
even though he tried.

Part 3

Beyond drama

Surfaces and agencies of performance

7 Heavenly bodies

The integral role of dance in *Einstein on the Beach*

Leah G. Weinberg

Introduction

Scholarship on *Einstein on the Beach* typically focuses on the artistic labor of the two men who conceived it: director and designer Robert Wilson and composer Philip Glass. As a glance at any of the opera's programs from its original and three revival productions reveals, however, Wilson and Glass were not the only creative minds behind the work. They recruited no less than eight company members to write and deliver the opera's speeches (Christopher Knowles, Samuel M. Johnson, Lucinda Childs), to engage in musical improvisation (Jon Gibson, Richard Landry, Richard E. Peck, Andrew Sterman), and to choreograph and perform four dances, two of which dominate entire scenes (Andrew de Groat, Lucinda Childs).[1] Opera is customarily a collaborative medium, but Wilson's and Glass's approach to developing the text with their performers in rehearsal sets *Einstein* apart from conventional works in the genre, allying it more closely with experimental performances the writer Richard Kostelanetz has described as a "theater of mixed means."[2] *Einstein*'s reputation as a groundbreaking work was, in fact, dependent on the grafting of this unusually open creative process onto opera, elevating the director to an equal position alongside the composer, and deliberately complicating traditional notions of operatic authorship.

Of the contributions that Glass and Wilson solicited from their company, the most visible and critically commented on were the dance sequences

---

1   These contributors included spoken text writers Christopher Knowles, Samuel M. Johnson, and Lucinda Childs, the Philip Glass Ensemble members Jon Gibson, Richard (Dickie) Landry, and Richard E. Peck (and Andrew Sterman in the 2012 production), who improvised during Act IV, scene 1A (Building), and the choreographers and dancers Andrew de Groat and Lucinda Childs.

2   Richard Kostelanetz, "A Theater of Performance, Not Literature," *Dialogue* 8, no. 2 (1975), 43. Kostelanetz writes, "In the past decade of American theater-going, my ... most satisfactory and memorable experiences have come in those activities often lumped under the term 'happenings,' which, since not all examples utilize chance developments, I prefer to call 'the theater of mixed means.' This new theatrical art is, in my judgment, the contemporary heir to the performance tradition of American theater, for not only is the author usually his own director and performer but various forms of communication are employed – sound, movement, film, sculpture, odor – to create a hybrid field of presentational activity."

choreographed and performed by their colleagues Andrew de Groat and Lucinda Childs. Certainly, the opera's 11 speeches and a woodwind improvisation in Act IV, scene 1A (Building) enlivened the rich semiotics of Wilson's surreal theater and Glass's mechanistic music. Dance, however, introduced a third distinct temporal art to the opera, honoring New York's radical dance scene while simultaneously inviting comparison between *Einstein* and Richard Wagner's Artwork of the Future (*Kunstwerk der Zukunft*). The nineteenth-century opera innovator had theorized his ideal total artwork as an integration of "the three primordial sisters" ("*die drei urgebornen Schwestern*") of dance, music, and poetry ("*Tanzkunst, Tonkunst und Dichtkunst*"), and its twentieth-century experimentalist pedigree notwithstanding, *Einstein* appeared to many critics to deliver on that promise.[3] Indeed, the year 1976 marked the centennial of Wagner's Ring Cycle, and celebratory productions of the tetralogy at opera houses worldwide – particularly director Patrice Chéreau's and conductor Pierre Boulez's infamous *Jahrhundertring* at the Bayreuth Festival – coincided with *Einstein*'s acclaimed summer and fall festival tour. This overlap primed theater critics to consider the downtown work as a postmodern heir to Wagner's interdisciplinary operatic ideal.[4]

In spite of dance's impact on *Einstein*'s early reception, however, it has been given short shrift in scholarship on the opera for a few reasons. From a practical standpoint, theater and music scholars tend to skirt in-depth considerations of *Einstein*'s dance because the topic, and its attendant historiography and terminology, does not fit comfortably within the boundaries of their own disciplines. Furthermore, because Glass and Wilson control the operatic text, writers frequently treat them as the work's *auteurs*, not unreasonably subsuming within their musico-dramatic vision the contributions of other company members. This approach is problematic, however, because artists living in New York's tight-knit downtown community were conceptually omnivorous, often exploiting the methods of one art by applying them to another, thus precluding an easy division of authorship by type of artistic contribution. As a case in point, the Judson Dance Workshop (1960–62) and the Judson Dance Theater (1962–64) that emerged from it formed the fountainhead of the postmodern dance scene, yet the workshop was led by the musician Robert Dunn at the behest of John Cage, and Dunn asked his students to study the compositional strategies of avant-garde composers from Cage to Karlheinz Stockhausen and Pierre Boulez. Moreover, the Judson dancers' iconoclastic interrogation of their medium in the 1960s led to performances

---

3   Richard Wagner, *Das Kunstwerk der Zukunft*, Wigand, Leipzig, 1850, 43.
4   A critic for *Le Monde* was the first to invoke Richard Wagner's theoretical ideas in discussing *Einstein*, a comparison that Italian, German, and American critics picked up in rapid succession. Writing under the pen name David Sargent in the *Village Voice*, the *New York Times* music critic John Rockwell was particularly forthright in his comparison: "Both Wilson and Glass work in a manner that can easily be called Wagnerian. Wagner, of course, was the most visionary reformer in the whole, 400-year history of opera." See, for example, A. R., "Trois temps dans l'espace du théâtre musical," *Le Monde,* August 5, 1976, 9; David Sargent [pen used by John Rockwell], "The Met Will Dance to a Mysterious Tune," *Village Voice*, November 22, 1976, 53, 55.

whose everyday motions, as well as elements like speech and use of props, deliberately effaced the lines between dance, theater, and performance art.[5] As a result, music and drama have always been part and parcel of downtown dance's identity. Unsurprisingly, then, the boundaries between *Einstein*'s drama, music, and dance – and accordingly, between Wilson's and Glass's creative input and that of their writers and choreographers – are ambiguous at many points throughout the opera.

The dances that dominate Act II, scene 1C and Act III, scene 2C (Field Dances) may seem unquestionably to be the province of their choreographers, but what of a solo dance (Childs's Dance on Three Diagonals) inserted in a Wilsonian tableau vivant containing other actors who move with expressive precision? And what of a scene-stealing sequence of spoken text and costume changes (Childs's "Supermarket" speech performance) that is not recognizable as dance at all, but that bears a striking resemblance to early conceptual performances of the Judson Dance Theater? Each of these instances blurs the lines between the arts and the disciplines by which historians categorize them: the scene-length dances employ the same mathematical patterns as Glass's music, while the dramatic solos fit seamlessly into Wilson's drama. All are byproducts of the composer's, director's, and choreographer's shared minimalist aesthetics and compositional strategies.[6] It follows that analysts have tended to treat *Einstein*'s speeches as part of the opera's peculiar libretto, and its dances as an extension of Wilson's unique brand of expressive movement. In this essay, however, I propose that by approaching *Einstein*'s dance much as scholars have approached its drama and music – that is, as a distinct art whose aesthetics and compositional strategies frequently overlap with those of its sister arts – we can better understand a vital but largely unexplored facet of the opera's dramaturgy. Simultaneously, we can retrieve two of *Einstein*'s less-discussed authors (de Groat and Childs) from the historical margins, connecting the opera to a vibrantly interdisciplinary downtown context sustained by conceptual and material exchange.

Both the dance itself and its context inform the story of *Einstein*. Textually, dance helps to structure the five-hour opera and bridges its music and drama, complementing visual aspects of Wilson's direction and design while using the body to explore the same repetitive compositional processes that drove Glass's score. Contextually, dance has also factored in the immediate and long-term critical reception of the opera as a pivotal ambassador to the conventional, or "uptown," art world. Specifically, critics at downtown publications like the *Soho Weekly*

---

5 Sally Banes, *Democracy's Body: Judson Dance Theater 1962–1964*, Ann Arbor, MI: UMI Research Press, 1983, xi, 1–7.

6 In his recent essay on minimalism in dance, film, and video, Dean Suzuki cites Andew de Groat's and Lucinda Childs's choreography as key examples of minimalism's incursion into modern dance practice, noting that "formal arrangement is laid bare" across *Einstein*'s design, music, and choreography, the dance "complement[ing] and bolster[ing]" the structure and aesthetic" that undergirds the opera. Dean Suzuki, "Minimalism in the Time-Based Arts: Dance, Film and Video," 109–128, *The Ashgate Research Companion to Minimalist and Postminimalist Music*, ed. Keith Potter, Kyle Gann, and Pwyll ap Siôn, Surrey, England, Ashgate, 2013, 114–115.

News, the *Village Voice*, and *Artforum* (as well as Glass and Wilson themselves) noted *Einstein*'s many gestures toward concurrent movements in the visual arts, architecture, film, and literature.[7] By foregrounding new modern dance practices alongside avant-garde theater and minimal music, Wilson, Glass, and their collaborators effectively managed to represent most segments of the downtown art community in a single work. In what follows, I examine both of these aspects of *Einstein*'s dance, beginning with its organizational role within the opera's structure of acts and scenes. From there, I shift to a discussion of the content of the dances in the four Glass/Wilson productions to date, with particular attention to how the replacement of de Groat's choreography with that of Childs affected the opera's aesthetics and raised questions about its collective authorship. Finally, I close by considering the relative durability of *Einstein*'s direction, choreography, and music in productions overseen by new directors.

Dance in the original production (1976)

Dance as structural pillars

During *Einstein*'s initial planning stages, Wilson and Glass incorporated dance into their project in two primary ways: as an opportunity for Wilson and the featured performer Lucinda Childs to perform solos; and as the central stage action of Act II, scene 1C and Act II, scene 2C, both subtitled "Field (Space Machine)." The Field Dances comprise only two of the opera's nine main scenes, but when viewed in combination with three prominent solos – Childs's "Dance on Three Diagonals" in Act I, scene 1A (Train), her "Supermarket" speech in Act III, scene 1B (Trial/Prison), and Wilson's "Flashlight" dance in Act IV, scene 3C (Spaceship) – the dances' function as organizational and dramatic pillars becomes readily apparent (Figure 7.1).

Because the common denominator linking drama, music, and dance is time, Wilson and Glass initially used that dimension to demarcate the structure of the work. They envisioned the five Knee Play interludes (K1–5) at 4, 4, 5, 4, and 4 minutes in length, and the main scenes (A1–3, B1–3, and C1–3) at 24, 23, 22, 23, 24, 22, 18, 16, and 17 minutes in length. Once Wilson and Glass had agreed on three central images (A: train, B: trial, C: field), they organized them according to a theme-and-variation structure (AB CA BC ABC).

As the bottom row of numbers in Figure 7.1 indicates, the scenes and interludes surrounding the Field Dances are of almost equal length. This balance,

7   See, for example, April Kingsley, "What You See Is What You See," *Soho Weekly News*, December 2, 1976, 15–16; David Sargent, "The Met Will Dance to a Mysterious Tune," *Village Voice*, November 22, 1976, 52–53; Barbara Baracks, *Artforum* (March 1977): 33; Philip Glass and Robert Wilson, interviews with Maxime de la Falaise, "Einstein at the Met (an operatic interview)," *Andy Warhol's Interview* 7, no. 2 (February 1977): 27–30; Robert Wilson and Philip Glass, interviews with Sylvère Lotringer, "Robert Wilson: Interview" and "Phil Glass: Interview," *Semiotexte* 3, no. 2 (1978): 20–27, 178–191.

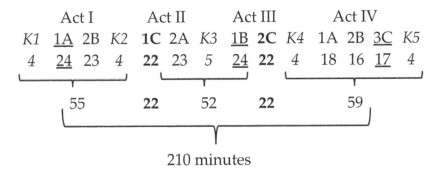

Figure 7.1 Early temporal structure (in minutes) of *Einstein*. The Field Dances are shown in bold, and the scenes that include the "Dance on Three Diagonals," "Supermarket" speech, and "Flashlight" dance are underlined.

Glass claimed in his first memoir, was intentional: "I always thought of the *Einstein* dance sections," he wrote, "as two pillars equidistant from the ends of the piece which provided the shocks that would drive it into the next section and give a dramatic balance to the whole," a function he emphasized by giving these scenes the same harmonic profile (D Minor).[8] Wilson added a visual dimension to this profile by staging the Field Dances in a painterly perspective distinct from the other scenes in the opera. As Wilson has explained in a number of interviews, he conceived the Knee Plays and Train and Trial scenes in the relatively intimate, static perspectives of the portrait and the still life. The Field Dances, however, he conceived as dynamic landscapes.[9] The sudden broadening of perspective they offer, enhanced by kinetic music and a whirlwind of bodily motion after nearly an hour of slow-paced tableaux, rendered each Field Dance a sort of dramatic "alarm clock" for spectators.

8   Philip Glass, *Music by Philip Glass*, ed. Robert T. Jones, New York, Harper & Row, 1987, 39. Furthermore, Keith Potter's neat diagram of *Einstein*'s tonal structure demonstrates that the opera's scenes mainly shift between C Major, its relative minor and modal variants on the A scale, and F Minor modulating to E Major. Within this scheme, the D-Minor Field Dances possess a distinctive harmonic flavor. Keith Potter, *Four Musical Minimalists: La Monte Young, Terry Riley, Steve Reich, Philip Glass*, Cambridge, Cambridge University Press, 2000, 328–329.

9   The most widely available such interview occurs as part of *Einstein on the Beach: The Changing Image of Opera*, directed by Mark Obenhaus (1987; Santa Monica, CA: Direct Cinema, 2007), DVD. Wilson explained, "I constructed the work in the three traditional ways of looking at painting, which are the three traditional ways of measuring space, and that is in portraits, still lifes, and landscapes. . . . The Knee Plays to me were portraits. They're the closest to the audience. And so we look at it in a different way. And then I thought of the trains and the trials and the building, those scenes, as still lifes. But the dance[s] I thought about differently. I thought about them as landscapes, as fields. And so the space is the biggest. And they break apart the space, so the energy is different, the perspective is different, and it happens twice." My transcription.

In addition to these ensemble dances, Wilson asked Childs to compose and perform two solos in *Einstein*. The first, a "Dance on Three Diagonals" that she developed through improvisation, was a scene-stealing study in the motion of walking forward and backward along three diagonal lines. The second solo, situated at the opera's midpoint, looks less like dance than performance art, but made extensive use of her Judson dance training in the mid-1960s. Finally, attentive to structural balance, the director himself took the stage in the last main scene of the last act to dance along the same diagonal trajectory as Childs had in the first scene. This time the dance took place against the backdrop of a spaceship rather than a train, and Wilson wielded two flashlights like luminous maracas. Like Childs's "Dance on Three Diagonals," Wilson's "Flashlight" dance also consisted of a gradual acceleration of corporeal energy that one *Soho Weekly News* critic aptly described as "his mad intelligence ... letting the havoc out of its cage."[10] Childs performed her two solos in both the original production of *Einstein* and in the 1984 and 1992 remounts, and she and Wilson carefully coached the dancer and actress who took over the solos in 2012. The Field Dances, on the other hand, underwent a more essential shift from one production to another, as Childs took over de Groat's role as choreographer. Both dancers lived and worked in the same art community, but de Groat's choreography stressed spinning, improvisation, and amateurism, while Childs's emphasized carefully graphed patterns, precision of execution, and a trained, athletic aesthetic.

Andrew de Groat's Field Dances (1976)

Like Wilson, who entered the theater following a formal education in art, architecture, and design, de Groat was a latecomer to his chosen field, beginning to dance shortly after meeting Wilson in 1967 while he was studying painting. "Bob was conducting a body movement workshop which I attended," he explained in an interview following *Einstein*'s 1976 tour. "I'm untrained in any formal sense, though I've choreographed pieces for as many as twenty dancers. Training for me is doing it."[11] Like Wilson, who also lacked formal dance training, he became enamored of the abstract choreography of George Balanchine, Jerome Robbins, and Merce Cunningham. As an amateur dancer, he also claimed to value an untrained aesthetic, telling one interviewer that "working exclusively with a trained company seems less interesting to me than working with untrained people," or a combination of the two.[12] Due in part to his own background, and in part to the financial necessity in 1975 of hiring performers capable of acting, singing, and dancing, de Groat worked with dancers whose abilities ranged widely. This restriction resulted in dances possessed of "a friendly, unassuming, *faux-naïf*

10   Marcia B. Siegel, "How to Build a Cloud," *Soho Weekly News*, December 2, 1976, 17.
11   Andrew de Groat, interview by Jeff Goldberg, "Robert Wilson and 'Einstein on the Beach,'" *New York Arts Journal* 2, no. 1 (Spring 1977): 18.
12   Ibid.

air," in the words of one critic, and of "an engagingly innocent awkwardness, as if humans were playing at being heavenly bodies," in the words of another.[13] In the opening to notes provided to *Einstein*'s early European presenters, de Groat described his choreography in the following way:

> The dances for Act II scene 1 and Act III scene 2 of *Einstein on the Beach* are based on combinations of four simple movements: jumping, walking forward and backward, a series of sixteen arm movements, and a twenty-two beat phrase of running and leaping with eight energy and spatial variations. These natural movements are performed at a fast, even pace to the simplest possible counts in interconnecting geometrical patterns. Dancers perform this simple vocabulary, variations of this vocabulary, and their own movements. All movements are danced in choreographed patterns and also in spontaneous, improvised patterns. All movements are structured for increasing and decreasing numbers of one, three, four, seven and eight dancers.[14]

Critics in 1976 commended the results. "Only Andrew de Groat's choreography," one French critic asserted, "introduces to the structures of vision and sound the breath of the body, the naturalness of racing and jumping, a certain harmonious improvisational quality," while another compared the innocent quality of de Groat's dances, based on everyday movements, with the intentionally pedestrian work of American modern dance pioneer Isadora Duncan.[15] Among American reviewers, the dance critic Anna Kisselgoff drew particular attention to the parallels between Glass's score and de Groat's "simple and restricted" movement vocabulary "whose repetitiveness also contains variation," concluding that the musical score "seemed almost to chant an aural echo of the dance, but actually created a highly theatrical resonance for it."[16] As de Groat confirmed in his notes, "the music and dance are separately but similarly constructed, and the dancers' moving and stillness are thought of as a kind of listening – to the music and to

---

13 John Howell, "Forum: What A Legend Becomes," *Artforum* (March 1985); Deborah Jowitt, "The Torsoi Tortoise Returns to the Finish Line," *Village Voice*, January 1, 1985.

14 Letter, Kathleen Norris to Paul Puaux, June 11, 1976, Folder 23: "Einstein on the Beach," 4-ACOL-1 709, Maison Jean Vilar, Avignon, France.

15 Jean-Jacques Lerrant, "La creation de 'Einstein on the beach': Cinq heures de fascination et de rêve au festival d'Avignon," *Le Progres*, July 27, 1976, 8. The original French reads: "Seule la chorégraphie d'Andrew de Groat introduit dans ses structures de l'image et du son le respiration du corps, le naturel de la course et du bond, un certain hasard d'improvisation harmonieuse." See also "'Einstein on the beach' au festival d'Avignon: Un opéra mathématique pour apprivoiser l'apocalypse," *Dauphiné* (July 27, 1976). The *Dauphiné* critic wrote, "Il multiplie les repères, pour trouver sous ces contraintes une autre liberté, une 'nature' innocente que laissant entrevoir, pendant deux séquences, des danses chorégraphiées par Andrew De Groat, qui se souvient d'Isadora Duncan."

16 Anna Kisselgoff, "Dance: Fascinating Work by Glass and deGroat," *New York Times*, May 27, 1976, 32.

each other."[17] A brief consideration of the interaction between music and choreography reveals the strong aesthetic synergy between them.

Musically, Dance 1 is a study in Glass's application of cyclic structure and additive process to both harmony and rhythm. On one hand, the music seems to rush forward, driven by rapid melodic parts (half note = 138 beats per minute) and slight alterations to a D Minor ninth chord that affect harmonic motion through a number of key areas: A Major, G Major, E Minor, and C Major. On the other hand, the music seems to stand still, repetition and a slow rate of non-functional harmonic change producing a sense of suspended animation. The music of Dance 2 is essentially a variation on Dance 1, with a few notable changes: texturally, scalar movement replaces arpeggios; instrumentally, solo violin replaces woodwinds; and developmentally, an absence of cyclic structure precludes the striking harmonic shifts of Dance 1.[18]

Responding to Glass's calculated deployment of the same few melodic, harmonic, and rhythmic materials, de Groat chose to work with a small number of everyday movements: walking (forward and backward), jogging loosely, leaping with one leg forward, and jumping (in place and to a crouching position), all with a number of predetermined arm movements (e.g., held at one's sides, lifted straight out to the sides). He then subjected them to analogous cyclical repetitions and additive development to produce a visual spectacle based on the constant assembly and dispersal of groups of dancers. The motif of the circle and its dynamic equivalent, spinning, were as central to de Groat's choreography in the 1970s as was the arpeggio to Glass's composition.[19] Lacking classical training, de Groat relied on the virtuosity of endurance rather than technical difficulty for dramatic effect. In fact, one of the most remarkable features of his first Field Dance is the dervish-like spinning of a single dancer. Her action required no special training to accomplish, but the uninterrupted performance of the single movement for up to ten minutes at a time rendered the ordinary act extraordinary. The minimalist roots of this approach are apparent in the choreographer's commentary: "The dances are an exploration of simple processes that provide maximum visual clarity and, simultaneously, allow maximum freedom to each individual dancer."[20] From the audience's perspective,

17 Letter, Kathleen Norris to Paul Puaux, June 11, 1976, Folder 23: "Einstein on the Beach," 4-ACOL-1 709, Maison Jean Vilar, Avignon, France.

18 For a concise and perceptive analysis of Glass's music for the two Field Dances, see Robert Haskins, "The Music of Philip Glass, 1965–1975: An Analysis of Two Selected Early Works and *Einstein on the Beach*," MA thesis, Peabody Conservatory of Music, Peabody Institute of The Johns Hopkins University, Baltimore, MD, 1992, 82–88, 95–97.

19 De Groat explained, "I have been working three years to define/refine my own dance – spinning. I find spinning as a dance form interesting because it is, or can be, continuous without stopping." Andy de Groat, "Rope Dance Translations," program for the 9th Festival of Arts, Shiraz and Persepolis, Iran (August 21–30, 1975), 1–2, Series 1, Box 225, Folder: "Book #21 June 1975– October 1975," Robert Wilson Papers, Rare Book and Manuscript Library, Columbia University, New York, NY.

20 Letter, Kathleen Norris to Paul Puaux, June 11, 1976, Folder 23: "Einstein on the Beach," 4-ACOL-1 709, Maison Jean Vilar, Avignon, France.

Dance 1 had two distinct components. The first was an ensemble section in which a varying number of dancers alternately walked, jogged, and leapt along circular paths, both clockwise and counterclockwise. The second was a contrasting section in which ensemble members, arrayed in offset rows on stage, stood still or jumped in place while one or a few others jogged and leapt between them. This section also introduced a degree of improvisation to the carefully patterned choreography. As de Groat explained in language reminiscent of Cage's instructions for chance compositions, a key compositional element used in both Field Dances was "the participation or stillness of the dancers, that is, their dancing or not dancing all or part of a given phrase based on prescribed cues involving the addition and subtraction of dancers, phrases, still intervals, and the dancers' own decisions."[21]

De Groat mirrored the additive development and cyclic processes of Glass's score for Dance 1 by using a small number of movements to generate subtly different patterns over the course of 17 minutes. He also did so by synchronizing certain motions with the additive process of Glass's score to make the musical structure more readily apparent. At one point, for example, the dancers gathered on stage, hopped in place nine times, then eight times, and so on down to one (and vice versa from one to nine), changing direction by ninety degrees with each shift in pattern to produce a simple but effective analogue to Glass's music. In Dance 2, de Groat offered another take on the circle motif, beginning by positioning his dancers in a formation like a spiral galaxy that rotated counterclockwise. Once again, the choreographer reflected Glass's additive and subtractive process, but offered a visual variation on Dance 1 by replacing jumping with walking: nine steps backward, eight steps forward, and so on down to one (and vice versa from one to nine).[22] In sum, then, Andrew de Groat's use of simple, repetitive movements based primarily on circles and spinning, and the endearingly playful aesthetic that resulted, reflected his late introduction to dance as well as a conceptual approach to that art that exalted commonplace movements over classical precision.

Lucinda Childs's Solos: "Dance on Three Diagonals" and "Supermarket" Speech (1976)

Einstein on the Beach marked a professional departure for Wilson, as he replaced the largely amateur casts of his earlier works with auditioned actors, dancers, and singers. One important exception was Lucinda Childs, who Wilson invited to join the company based solely on her reputation as a performer. "I'm again working with Sheryl [Sutton], and of course she's wonderful, but perhaps even more

---

21 Ibid.

22 Descriptions of Andrew de Groat's choreography for Dances 1 and 2 are based on archival audio-visual footage of the original production of *Einstein on the Beach*, including: *Einstein on the Beach: a new opera*, video recorded in rehearsal performance at the Video Exchange Theater, New York City, on March 3, 1976, NCOV 3006; and *Einstein on the Beach*, video recording, le XXXe festival d'Avignon, July 28, 1976, NCOV 3066 and 3067, Performing Arts Research Collections, Theater on Film and Tape Archive, New York Public Library, New York, NY.

exciting is Lucinda Childs – a dancer from the early 60's in New York," the direc-tor enthused in a letter to his friend Michel Guy, the French Minister of Culture and *Einstein*'s primary commissioner. "She just did a dance concert which is the most impressive concert I've seen in years."[23]

Childs attended Sarah Lawrence College in the late 1950s, studied with both Merce Cunningham and Robert Dunn, and thereafter began participating in the Judson Dance Theater (1962–1964). The aesthetic orientation of this founda-tional postmodern dance collective was, according to the dance scholar Sally Banes, "deliberately undefined, unrestricted," but Judson's heterogeneous prac-tices, encompassing both the freedom of open and improvisational work, and "a refined consciousness of the process of choreographic choice," were rooted in a few shared influences, attitudes, and working methods.[24] Key influences included the choreographers Merce Cunningham (especially his collaborations with John Cage), James Waring, and Ann Halprin, each of whom rejected the psychological connotations and hierarchy of authority that Judson participants negatively associ-ated with dominant modern dance choreographers like Martha Graham and José Limón. In reacting against established modern dance, downtown choreographers promoted a commitment to a democratic or collective creative process, reconsid-eration of the relationship between dance and music, and the stance that anything – including the work of visual artists, filmmakers, and musicians – might be identi-fied or approached as dance. The sculptor and conceptual artist Robert Morris, for instance, created task dances that used objects to focus the attention of both audi-ence and performer, while artists like David Gordon and Elaine Summers brought theatrical and multimedia perspectives to dance.[25] Although Robert Wilson did not participate in the Judson Dance Theater, his use of dance as a lens through which to create and understand theater ties his original dramas, of which *Einstein* is the most prominent, to the creative explorations of Childs and her colleagues in the early 1960s.

After taking a four-year hiatus from dance following her work with Judson, Childs formed her own company in 1973, establishing a reputation as an art direc-tor and choreographer as well as a performer, and shifting away from performance art toward "pure movement structures."[26] In *Reclining Rondo* (1975), for example, three performers repeated a series of 18 movements 12 times, changing direction each time to produce a slight alteration in the pattern. The result was a compel-ling visual analogue to the musical processes then being explored by minimalist

23   Letter, Robert Wilson to Michel Guy, February 11, 1976, "lettre manuscrite portant l'en-tête de Byrd Hoffman Foundation," 4-COL-70(226) (cote), Robert Wilson, 1972–1990, Département des Arts du spectacle, site Richelieu, Bibliotèque national de France, Paris, France. Wilson writes, "She just did a dance concert which is the most impressive concert of her own work I've seen in years," crossing out "of her own work" with black marker to intensify his praise.
24   Banes, *Democracy's Body*, xvii.
25   Ibid., xviii.
26   Ibid.

composers.[27] Wilson was sufficiently impressed with this first of Childs's mid-1970s "dances in silence" to ask her to join the *Einstein* cast as a featured actor, and to dance an extended solo of her own devising during the first main scene. During the rehearsal process, Wilson also asked her to compose a speech to deliver during Act III, scene 1B (Trial/Prison), ostensibly to remedy the absence of the titular beach elsewhere in the opera.[28] Although European critics by and large responded to the opera as a whole, Childs's solos made a strong impression on American critics familiar with radical dance currents in New York. "Among the amazing people involved," Alan Rich wrote in *New York Magazine* a week after *Einstein*'s second Metropolitan Opera House performance, "I bow with particular awe to a dancer named Lucinda Childs who, somewhere inside my head, is still dancing."[29] John Rockwell, writing under the pen name David Sargent in the *Village Voice*, likewise made a point of highlighting her performance and credentials lest they be overshadowed by the work of the opera's official choreographer. "De Groat is hardly the only dancer in *Einstein*," he explained. "Lucinda Childs has a solo career that goes back to the Judson Church days, and if any of the performers is the 'star' of the 26-member cast it is she."[30] His colleagues at the *Village Voice* agreed, awarding her an Obie in 1977 for her performance.[31]

Childs's "Dance on Three Diagonals" is the focal point of the action in Act I, scene 1A (Train). As the dance's pedestrian gestural vocabulary was not drawn from classical ballet technique, critics struggled to describe this performance, and a sampling of their accounts gives some sense of what early audiences experienced. To the uninitiated it appeared, as the English dance critic Dale Harris wrote, that "Lucinda Childs does nothing but march back and forth across the stage over and over again."[32] To those familiar with downtown dance, on the other hand, Childs's solo presented a dynamic process that one *Soho Weekly News* critic described as "a nonstop hesitating running back and forth on three succeeding paths, in which she seemed to be exhorting or haranguing a crowd and not

27 "Reclining Rondo (1975)," *A Steady Pulse: Restaging Lucinda Childs, 1963–78*, Pew Center for Arts & Heritage, Philadelphia, 2015, http://danceworkbook.pcah.us/asteadypulse/dances/reclining_rondo.html, Accessed: September 1, 2016.

28 Childs and Glass, interview by Mark Swed, "Philip Glass and Lucinda Childs Discuss *Einstein on the Beach*," and Robert Wilson, Philip Glass, and Lucinda Childs, interview with Matia Tarnopolsky, "Robert Wilson, Philip Glass and Lucinda Childs discuss Einstein on the Beach," Cal Performances, Zellerbach Playhouse, University of California, Berkeley, October 28, 2012, www.youtube.com/watch?v=k8iLOGPm7AY, Accessed: September 1, 2015.

29 Alan Rich, "From Byzantium to the Beach – The Lunatic Fringe of Opera," *New York Magazine*, December 6, 1976.

30 David Sargent, "Einstein on the Beach: The Met Will Dance to a Mysterious Tune," *Village Voice*, November 22, 1976, 53, 55.

31 Village Voice and American Theater Wing, "Obie Awards: 1970s," 2015, www.obieawards.com/events/1970s/year-77/, Accessed: September 1, 2015. Notably, Glass won an Obie Award for his operatic score, but the committee passed over Wilson in the categories of both direction and design.

32 Dale Harris, "Slow Mover," *The Observer*, August 1976. The same article was printed in *The Guardian*. Edmund White likewise recalls this particular dance, though he does not identify Childs by name. See Edmund White, "Einstein on the Beach," *Christopher Street*, January 1977, 53.

getting an answer, like a sideshow barker or someone demonstrating a potato peeler in a department store."[33] This description gestures toward the theatricality of Childs's performance, which develops gradually over the course of the long scene. Archival video shows Childs's walking motion, for instance, undergoing a measured transformation from a casual saunter through a loose swagger to a purposeful stride, and finally to frenzied pacing. During this process, Childs's upper body movement also escalates from the relaxed arm gestures of a musical conductor to jerky, tense arm and head motions that suggest a person on the verge of panic or madness.[34] Indeed, Childs has described the dance as "a kind of slow-motion explosion," using a cinematic analogy to describe a solo that, like Wilson's equally slow-motion tableaux vivant and Glass's minimalist score, stretches a small number of dynamic changes over an unusually long timeframe to alter spectators' perception of the temporal art on display.[35]

If the "Dance on Three Diagonals" reflected Childs's interest in the 1970s with the gradual development of "pure movement structures," the "Supermarket" speech sequence central to Act III, scene 2B (Trial/Prison) mined her familiarity with the process of combining gesture, dialogue, and objects in performance from her early work with the Judson Dance Theater. In her *Museum Piece* (1965), for instance, she had dropped colored circular mats onto the stage and used a mirror to navigate through them backwards while delivering an explanatory monologue that commented on her activity.[36] Similarly, for *Einstein* Wilson asked Childs to perform an original monologue while miming the then-current media spectacle of heiress Patty Hearst's trial (February 4–March 20, 1976). During the scene, Childs, outfitted in a white dress and playing the role of the Witness, lay on a bed in the center of the court, then gradually stood and moved to the half of the stage designed to look like a prison, miming the Hearst drama through a series of costume changes. Childs appeared first as a socialite, then as a bank robber, and finally as a prisoner, all the while intoning a brief, peculiar speech that is among the most memorable elements of the opera:

I was in this prematurely air-conditioned super market

and there were all these aisles

33   Marcia B. Siegel, "How to Build a Cloud," *Soho Weekly News*, December 2, 1976, 17.

34   To observe how Childs's dance evolved from rehearsal to performance, see: *Einstein on the Beach: a new opera*, video recorded in rehearsal performance at the Video Exchange Theater, New York City, on March 3, 1976, NCOV 3006; and *Einstein on the Beach*, video recording, le XXXe festival d'Avignon, July 28, 1976, NCOV 3066, Performing Arts Research Collections, Theater on Film and Tape Archive, New York Public Library, New York, NY.

35   Lucinda Childs, interview with Mark Obenhaus, January 28, 1985, 22–24, transcript, Box: "1984 Einstein on the Beach Material (Moldy)," Brooklyn Academy of Music Hamm Archives, Brooklyn, NY.

36   "Museum Piece (1965)," *A Steady Pulse: Restaging Lucinda Childs, 1963–78*, Pew Center for Arts & Heritage, Philadelphia, 2015, HYPERLINK "http://danceworkbook.pcah.us/asteadypulse/dances/museum_piece.html" http://danceworkbook.pcah.us/asteadypulse/dances/museum_piece.html, Accessed: September 1, 2016.

and there were all these bathing caps that you could buy

which had these kind of Fourth of July plumes on them

they were red and yellow and blue

I wasn't tempted to buy one

But I was reminded of the fact that I had been avoiding

the beach.[37]

Childs credits Wilson with the selection of this text, which he drew from a longer, improvised monologue that he asked her to generate relating to the beach.[38] Though this sequence blends seamlessly into Wilson's theater, resembling performance art more than dance, its roots in the collectively produced, often intermedial practices of the Judson Dance Theater serve as a reminder of the artistic and authorial fluidity that characterized the art scene in which *Einstein* participated and that it came to represent.

Choreography in the revival productions (1984, 1992, 2012–15)

Lucinda Childs's Field Dances

By 1984, de Groat no longer maintained a close working relationship with Wilson, and lived and worked primarily in Europe. As Childs had remained in New York, following up her performance in *Einstein* with individual collaborations with both Wilson (*I was sitting on my patio this guy appeared I thought I was hallucinating*; 1977) and Glass (*Dance*; 1979), she presented the obvious choice to replace de Groat for the Brooklyn Academy of Music remount.[39] Like the opera's first choreographer, Childs constructed her versions of the Field Dances by combining and recombining a small number of dance steps to form complex, continuously shifting patterns that parallel Glass's musical structures. However, her formal training, access to the dancers of her own company, and most importantly, her experience

37 Philip Glass, *Music by Philip Glass*, ed. Robert T. Jones, New York, Harper and Row, 1987, 74–75. Immediately preceding the text is the attribution, "Text written by Lucinda Childs; To be recited from lying on bed through exit, repeating as necessary.)"

38 James Dillon, "Lucinda Childs and Her World of Reason," *Nit & Wit*, November/December 1984, 17. See also Childs and Glass, interview by Mark Swed, "Philip Glass and Lucinda Childs Discuss *Einstein on the Beach*." My transcription. Responding to Swed's question, "Lucinda, had you written text before [*Einstein*]?" Childs answered, "Well, in the Judson Theater, we worked with dialogues and subject matter that, at moments, had something to do with what we were doing, but for the most part, didn't have something to do with what we were doing. And that was the nature of that kind of experience. And the supermarket speech was a request from Bob to come to the studio because he said, 'We need something about the beach.'"

39 *I was sitting on my patio this guy appeared I thought I was hallucinating* and *Dance* were, like *Einstein*, collaborative endeavors; the former included music by the composer Alan Lloyd, and the latter incorporated film by the visual artist Sol LeWitt.

collaborating with Glass on *Dance*, resulted in Field Dances that appeared more professional than their predecessors.

The *Artforum* critic John Howell pronounced Childs's dances "more complex, more inventive, and better performed" than those of de Groat, and Deborah Jowitt noted in the *Village Voice* that "Childs, a more accomplished choreographer now than De Groat was in 1976, has dehumanized and geometrized the dancing. ... Her dancers graph the cosmos that De Groat's dancers played in."[40] Indeed, de Groat's vocabulary can be described using everyday language, and his dancers' posture and execution evinced no formal training. Childs's choreography, on the other hand, was rooted in classical ballet technique: formal leg and arm positions, posture based on turned-out hips, and steps best described using ballet terminology (e.g., *chassé, coup de pied, grand jeté, arabesque, fouetté*). Childs deployed this technique, however, in decidedly non-classical ways, just as Glass inserted functional voice-leading and cadences in non-functional harmonic contexts. Similarly, although de Groat's dances visualized aspects of Glass's musical development, the precision with which Childs's compositional techniques mirrored those of Glass resulted in an aesthetically tighter music-dance pairing. In fact, in a 1985 interview for the documentary film *Einstein on the Beach: The Changing Image of Opera*, Childs even claimed that she and Glass were so aesthetically attuned to one another that they worried their contributions would not parallel, but rather double, one another.[41]

Glass and Childs both applied procedures based on addition, subtraction, and permutation to brief musical and gestural phrases, respectively, in order to create a sense of dynamism in the absence of linear narrative development. On a broader level, these procedures also echoed Wilson's structural design, which subjected three thematic images (train, trial, field) to a process of patterned variation over nine scenes divided into four acts (AB CA BC ABC). To prevent the sonic and visual components from becoming too closely aligned during the Field Dances, Childs approached Glass's music as "an opportunity to place a counterpoint against the structure, to create a structure of my own that didn't fit exactly with the structure that he had set up."[42] She produced this counterpoint by aligning units of dance with the large-scale harmonic cycles that Glass marks in his score using rehearsal numbers. Where Glass's score asked musicians to repeat a

40   John Howell, "Forum: What A Legend Becomes" *Artforum* (March 1985): 90, and Deborah Jowitt, "The Torsoi Tortoise Returns to the Finish Line," *Village Voice*, January 1, 1985.

41   "There are a lot of similarities [to my work] in the way he structures his thematic material," Childs explained. "The introduction of a new theme isn't just a step that has no transition. There's always a feeling of building up a phrase, and you never completely let go of where you're coming from." Lucinda Childs, interview with Mark Obenhaus, January 28, 1985, 7–9, transcript, Box: "1984 Einstein on the Beach Material (Moldy)," Brooklyn Academy of Music Hamm Archives, Brooklyn, NY. Childs addresses aesthetic aims in her choreography that correspond with Glass's aims in his music in James Dillon, "Lucinda Childs and Her World of Reason," *Nit & Wit*, November/December 1984, 17–18.

42   Lucinda Childs, interview with Mark Obenhaus, January 28, 1985, 7–9, transcript.

sequence of, say, two bars four times, however, Childs inserted directional variations to the dance pattern that matched Glass's sequence, so that each one of the four repetitions offered a slightly different visual presentation of the same material. In this way, Childs used dance to reinforce Glass's composition at the level of cyclical structure while creating tension between what is seen and what is heard at the bar-by-bar level.

At the opening of Dance 1, for instance, one dancer begins standing in the center of the stage (in a bent-legged *tendu en avant* position) facing upstage (Figure 7.2a). He pivots front-to-back three times to remain in place while two other dancers enter from opposite sides of the stage using the leaping traveling step *coupé-jeté en tournant*, moving parallel to one another until the three dancers form a diagonal line. All three dancers then perform the same brief sequence of steps in place: two *tours en seconde* that transition into an *arabesque croisé en tournant* (Figure 7.2b) The dancer at the center of the diagonal (who began on stage) completes this sequence facing in the opposite direction of the other two dancers so that he might exit stage left while they exit stage right, producing a visual ABA pattern. This directional variation signals the first phrase in a minimalist dance process that correlates with the harmonic cycle of Rehearsal 2 (Rehearsal 1 functions as an extended upbeat). Glass's score directs the musicians to repeat the same two bars three more times before moving on to Rehearsal 3, and Childs mirrors this structure by having an additional three sets of three dancers enter (Figure 7.2c), perform the *tours en seconde–arabesque* sequence, and exit. By changing the directions from which the three dancers enter and exit each time, however, Childs adds a layer of permutation that is not present in Glass's cyclical structure, varying visually what repeats sonically.

Just as Glass used a limited number of pitches and rhythmic figures throughout Dances 1 and 2, varying them over time at the note-by-note level, so Childs constructed her dances using a restricted collection of steps.[43] Likewise, just as Glass exploited subtle permutations of duration and pitch to produce metrically irregular and harmonically shifting cycles, so Childs produced a tapestry of human bodies that reflected this music by exploiting spatial and corporeal permutations: ensemble size, orientation of dancers' steps (inward/*en dedans* or outward/*en dehors*), direction of dancers' entries and exits (upstage/downstage right/left),

---

43 Childs introduces several other steps, and they serve precisely the same purpose in her choreography that non-chord pitches like C-sharp and B-flat serve in Glass's score: they facilitate a repetitive, cyclical structure whose dynamism comes from a gradual accumulation and/or permutation of steps or notes. For example, a two-step sequence (*développé en avant* followed by a 180° directional change to a *croisé arabesque*) presents a variation on the primary sequence of turns in second and arabesque positions, and this new sequence coincides with a harmonic shift in Glass's music away from D Minor. Similarly, Childs gradually introduces the traveling, spinning step *chassé en tournant* as a variant on the more forward-moving *coupé-jeté en tournant*, enabling tighter circular motion on stage that calls to mind the orbit of planets around a star, or electrons around a nucleus.

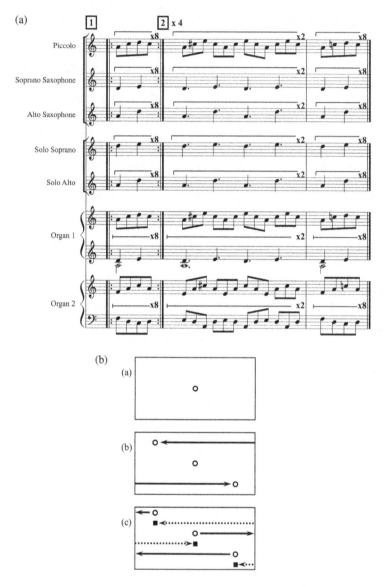

Figure 7.2 Einstein on the Beach, Words & Music by Philip Glass & Robert Wilson, Dance 1, page 64, rehearsal 1–2; (a) Childs, first figure, corresponding with Glass, rehearsal 1; (b) Childs, second figure (first of four trio ensembles), corresponding with Glass, rehearsal 2, bar 1; (c) Childs, third figure (first trio ○ exits as second trio ■ enters) with Glass, rehearsal 2, bar 2. The (b) and (c) dance/music pattern repeats twice more before the arrival of rehearsal 3 prompts Childs to begin a new dance segment. (Score courtesy of the composer and Dunvagen Music Publishers Incorporated. Copyright © 1976 by Dunvagen Music Publishers Incorporated, all rights reserved.)

and dancers' locations on stage and the shapes they outline when traveling (e.g., circles, diagonals).

It would be disingenuous to claim that de Groat's and Childs's choreographic approaches are entirely unrelated. Both choreographers used minimalist processes to bring dance and music into aesthetic conversation with one another. Likewise, both dancers emphasized geometric patterns that echoed the illustrative props and scenic design with which Wilson constructed an impressionistic portrait of Albert Einstein. Few spectators, however, would confuse de Groat's work with that of Childs. John Howell phrased it best when he wrote that "Childs's dancers graph[ed] the cosmos that De Groat's dancers played in."[44] That is to say, her choreography replaced de Groat's deliberately naive, semi-improvisational, pedestrian minimalism with a highly polished minimalism whose reductive, repetitive design belied its elegant classical underpinnings.

Childs as a member of the creative team

Childs's choreography has remained a fixed element of *Einstein* over the course of three revival productions, and its attendant impact on authorship and billing has not gone unnoticed by the opera's composer and director, nor by its presenters. Although Childs has adopted an exceptionally modest attitude toward her claim on the opera, even refraining from performing the Field Dances with her company outside revival productions of the opera, her long association with the work as both a performer and choreographer invites consideration of her evolving role in the company, and the ways in which it challenges our assumptions about creative authority and control in music theater. In fact, six months before the first remount at the Brooklyn Academy of Music in December 1984, internal correspondence at BAM related that the Lucinda Childs Dance Company wanted "to be mentioned whenever the Philip Glass Ensemble is mentioned" in order to benefit from the same publicity, and to alert the public to the fact that Childs had replaced de Groat as *Einstein*'s choreographer.[45]

Later that summer, the program too became a site of negotiation. The production's general manager Michael O'Rand suggested in a letter to Wilson that Childs's choreography be billed at 55% the size of the opera's title, compared with Childs's and Sutton's featured performances (50%) and Glass's and Wilson's contributions (75%). "I feel that in this version," O'Rand explained diplomatically, "the relationship of Lucinda's choreography credit to yourself and Phil is reduced sufficiently by limiting 'Choreography by' above and in a smaller type size than Lucinda's name so that, in comparison to the 60% version, it clearly indicates

44 John Howell, "Forum: What A Legend Becomes," *Artforum* (March 1985): 90.

45 Internal correspondence, E. J. to J. V. M., June 21, 1984, Box: "1984 Next Wave Festival: Einstein on the Beach, Desert Music by Performance," Folder: "Einstein PROD. NOTES," Brooklyn Academy of Music Hamm Archives, Brooklyn, NY. The subject of billing arises again in another internal memorandum dated June 19, 1984.

that Lucinda is not a co-creator of the opera with you and Phil."[46] Though exacting attention to billing is hardly remarkable in the theater world, this particular example of backstage bargaining suggests that even though Glass and Wilson had signed a legal contract ensuring their joint control over the opera's future productions and recordings five years earlier, authorship of the collaborative work continued to be subject to discursive negotiation among the original creative team. The director and composer ultimately billed Childs's choreography at 60%, a decision that turned out to be prescient, for by the time of *Einstein*'s third revival in 2012, presenters had begun to refer to Childs as an original member of the creative team.

There are several reasons why the authorial gap between Childs and Glass and Wilson gradually narrowed over succeeding revival productions. First, as Childs became established as a major downtown choreographer of her generation, critics and presenters increasingly treated her as a respected cultural figure in her own right. Also, because all three artists were over 70 at the time of the 2012 revival tour, they elected to remain offstage, a decision that set them apart from their company and placed them in roughly equal positions of authority over the performers they directed.[47] Finally, between 1976 and 2012, all of the original *Einstein* company members with the exception of Glass, Wilson, Childs, and three members of the Philip Glass Ensemble (Jon Gibson, Michael Riesman, and Kurt Munkacsi) had either passed away or moved on in their careers. This gradual exodus left the composer, director, and choreographer as the three most prominent remainders of the original creative team. In the process of promoting the third revival tour, presenters thus frequently arranged opportunities for interviewers and critics to invite the artists to speak about the work, granting Childs a degree of authority over *Einstein*'s history and aesthetics along with Glass and Wilson. Childs's participation in such events was, however, carefully managed.

During a public interview with Glass and Wilson at the University of Michigan's Ann Arbor campus in January 2012, for example, the moderator Anne Bogart invited Childs onstage halfway through the event, a pre-planned gesture that was designed to appear spontaneous.[48] Like Childs's billing in the 1984 program, this choreographed performance of authorship simultaneously affirmed her status as a crucial contributor to the opera while reminding those in attendance

46 Letter, Michael O'Rand to Robert Wilson, August 27, 1984, Box: "1984 Next Wave Festival: Einstein on the Beach, Desert Music by Performance," Folder: "Einstein PROD. NOTES," Brooklyn Academy of Music Hamm Archives, Brooklyn, NY.

47 During the 2012 production, Ty Boomershine performed Wilson's wild "Flashlight" dance; Mick Rossi took over Glass's second keyboard part alongside Michael Riesman; and the Lucinda Childs Dance Company member Caitlin Scranton performed Childs's "Dance on Three Diagonals," while the actress Kate Moran performed her "Supermarket" speech.

48 Philip Glass and Robert Wilson, interview by Anne Bogart, "The Power of 2," Penny W. Stamps Distinguished Speaker Series, University of Michigan Penny W. Stamps School of Art and Design (January 15, 2012), Ann Arbor, Michigan, HYPERLINK "http://playgallery.org/video/the_power_of_2/" http://playgallery.org/video/the_power_of_2/, Accessed: April 5, 2014.

that the director and composer were the opera's official (and legal) authors. As if to drive home that point, when Cal Performances arranged a similar interview on the University of California, Berkeley campus in October 2012, the organization mirrored the subtle social engineering of the Michigan event. A third empty chair on stage, awaiting Childs's arrival partway through the interview, eloquently spoke to the unsettled nature of her authorial relationship to *Einstein*.[49] Publicly, these presenters honored Glass, Wilson, and Childs as equally longtime participants, but at the same time they adopted a deliberately ambivalent position toward Childs's claim on the work, and by extension, toward dance's relative importance in relationship to the opera's drama and music.

Because neither de Groat nor Childs participated in the initial conception of *Einstein*, and because both choreographers were invited contributors who received similar treatment regarding directorial authority and billing, it is unlikely that gender has played a significant role in the director's and composer's management of Childs's authorial status. In fact, given the sturdiness of the glass ceiling that continues to confront many aspiring female ballet and contemporary dance choreographers, downtown dance in the 1960s and 1970s was remarkably equitable with respect to gender.[50] Nonetheless, Wilson's and Glass's intentions aside, the secondary authorial status of a female choreographer within an intensively collaborative theater work does invite gender critique. Due to the complicated social, legal, and financial history of *Einstein* and the even more complex historical associations of ballet and modern dance with gender and sexuality, such a critique is beyond the scope of this essay.[51] The fact that the aforementioned interviews took

49 Robert Wilson, Philip Glass, and Lucinda Childs, interview with Matia Tarnopolsky, "Robert Wilson, Philip Glass and Lucinda Childs discuss *Einstein on the Beach*," Cal Performances, Zellerbach Playhouse, University of California, Berkeley, October 28, 2012, www.youtube.com/watch?v=k8iLOGPm7AY, Accessed: September 1, 2015.

50 See, for instance, Luke Jennings, "Sexism in Dance: Where Are All the Female Choreographers?" *The Guardian*, April 28, 2013, www.theguardian.com/stage/2013/apr/28/women-choreographers-glass-ceiling, Accessed: March 2, 2017. In contrast, when asked if sexual discrimination had been a factor in the downtown art world of the 1960s–1970s, the composer Laurie Anderson replied, "In the art world men and women dressed the same, they looked the same and it felt equal. That was what attracted me to it more than anything." The curator and arts administrator Alanna Heiss suggested, "Perhaps the lack of discrimination was because of the dancers. They had developed that unisex look with their drawstring pants," to which Anderson added, "Yes, the dancers and their costumes were revolutionary," and dancer Trisha Brown explained, "My costume choices were based on wanting neutrality and . . . by not having money." "'All Work, All Play,' in conversation with Laurie Anderson, Trisha Brown, Jane Crawford, RoseLee Goldberg, Alanna Heiss, and Lydia Yee at The Clocktower Gallery, New York, September 27, 2010," Barbican Centre [Catalogue]. *Laurie Anderson, Trisha Brown, Gordon Matta-Clark: Pioneers of the Downtown Scene, New York, 1970s*, London, Prestel Publishing Ltd., 2011, 74–75.

51 See, for example, Judith Lynne Hanna, *Dance, Sex and Gender: Signs of Identity, Dominance, Defiance, and Desire* (Chicago: University of Chicago Press, 1988); Helen Thomas, ed., *Dance, Gender and Culture* (Hampshire, UK: MacMillan Press, Ltd., 1993); Kim Grover-Haskin, ed., *Dance and Gender* (The Netherlands: Harwood Academic Publishers, 1998); and Wendy Oliver and Doug Risner, eds., *Dance and Gender: an Evidence-Based Approach*, Gainesville, University Press of Florida, 2017.

place on university campuses, however, offers a sobering reminder that although historians endeavor to treat archival evidence impartially, we are not always far removed from the reception that produces that evidence, reception that may be reproducing systemic social inequities. Indeed, it is no accident that this essay on *Einstein*'s dance and its choreographers should appear in the wake of a revival tour that featured such promotional interviews, inviting Childs in from the margins of *Einstein*'s public reception, and accordingly, its academic reception.

Over the course of the *Einstein*'s production history, de Groat and Childs have contributed vital structural and aesthetic labor to an opera that has come to be seen as one of the most representative works of New York's vibrant downtown performing arts scene in the 1970s. As a performer and writer, and later the choreographer of the two scene-length Field Dances, Childs is more strongly associated with *Einstein* than any other member of its four companies. Although her authorial rank remains unsettled, the evolution of her creative and directorial roles offers unique insight into the tight-knit art community from which she, de Groat, Glass, Wilson, and many of their performers hailed. Furthermore, by treating *Einstein*'s dance sequences not just as elements of Wilson's stage design, but rather as distinct artistic contributions that interact with and build aesthetic bridges between the drama and music, we deepen our understanding of *Einstein* as both an avant-garde opera and a downtown "theater of mixed means" par excellence.

Dance in other productions

Although the four major productions of *Einstein* overseen by Glass and Wilson have enjoyed the lion's share of critical and academic attention, a parallel production history has existed since 1988, when the German director Achim Freyer presented Glass's operatic "Portrait Trilogy" – *Einstein on the Beach* (1976), *Satyagraha* (1979), and *Akhnaten* (1983) – in Stuttgart. This production, establishing *Einstein* as the first installment in an operatic cycle, has since become the most common way to present the opera without the creative involvement of Wilson, Glass, and Childs.[52] Productions lacking the star power that Wilson, Glass, and Childs brought to the 1984, 1992, and 2012–15 remounts have understandably had smaller critical impacts outside their immediate geographical contexts, as *Einstein*'s symbolic capital derives as much from the presence and directorial oversight of its creators as from physical manifestations of the opera (e.g., the musical score and text). The marketability and institutional practicality of presenting *Einstein* alongside Glass's more conventional portrait operas has nevertheless

---

52   The critic and musicologist K. Robert Schwarz explained, "The idea was to bring together all three operas, in three new productions by Freyer, as a sort of Glassian 'Ring' cycle." According to Schwarz, the October 1988 performances of *Einstein*, with Glass's music and Freyer's direction, were popular at the box office. K. Robert Schwarz, *Minimalists*, London: Phaidon Press, Ltd., 1996/R2008, 145. Other directors who have taken on *Einstein* include Berthold Schneider (State Bank of the GDR, 2001; Berlin Parochialkirche, 2005), Leigh Warren (State Opera of South Australia, 2014), and Kay Voges (Opernhaus Dortmund, 2017).

led to new versions of the experimental work, and has also had important implications for the fate of Wilson's and Childs's contributions. Namely, although much of *Einstein*'s subversive appeal derived from its collaborative creative model, the fixed quality of the opera's direction and choreography has provided a challenge to directors staging novel versions in the context of conventional opera seasons. New productions have therefore retained only Glass's music and, in most cases, the text by Christopher Knowles, Samuel M. Johnson, and Lucinda Childs.[53]

The opportunity to produce a fresh take on a landmark work, rather than simply a reproduction of a museum piece, is just one reason for the conventionalization of new productions of *Einstein*. A second reason involves technology and genre expectations. To explain, Wilson produced illustrative sketches of his *Einstein* staging (what he calls a "visual book"), and both de Groat and Childs created choreographic "scores" as learning aids for their dancers, yet in the world of opera, audio recordings remain the dominant form of documentation and reproduction. In 1976, VHS technology had not yet reached the United States, while records were easily produced and disseminated. The release of a four-LP set of *Einstein*'s music in 1979 (Tomato, TOM-4-2901, 1979) thus set a precedent for reception that has treated *Einstein*'s music as the primary operatic text, and staging and choreography as secondary (and thus replaceable) elements.[54]

New productions of *Einstein* may not include either de Groat's or Childs's original choreography, but dance has nonetheless remained an important artistic resource for new creative teams. The opera's distinctive blend of minimalist and surrealist impulses precludes conventional plot development, necessitating a heavy reliance on imagery and expressive movement to sustain the drama. Faced with Glass's minimalist score, a "libretto" composed of numbers and solfège syllables, and a handful of speeches that have little to do with one another or the life and work of the opera's titular scientist, some directors have chosen to foreground dance, essentially combining direction and choreography. The choreographer Leigh Warren, for instance, reinterpreted Glass's entire Portrait Trilogy through dance at the State Opera of South Australia in 2014, an approach one local critic described as "dopera," or dance opera.[55] Warren dealt with *Einstein*, according to

53 The directors Achim Freyer (1988), Berthold Schneider and Veronika Witte (2001, 2005), and Kay Voges (2017) removed and/or replaced some or all of Knowles's, Johnson's, and Childs's texts in the pursuit of their own creative visions for the opera. For a detailed account of versions of *Einstein* produced by artistic teams other than Glass and Wilson, refer to Chapter 10 of this volume.

54 Philip Glass and Robert Wilson, *Einstein on the Beach*, The Philip Glass Ensemble, The Tomato Music Company, Ltd. TOM-4-2901, 1979, stereo LP. Later audio recordings of the opera's music and spoken text include: Philip Glass and Robert Wilson, *Einstein on the Beach*, The Philip Glass Ensemble, CBS Masterworks M4K 38875, 1985, CD; Philip Glass and Robert Wilson, *Einstein on the Beach*: highlights, The Philip Glass Ensemble, Orange Mountain Music 0083, 1984, CD; Philip Glass and Robert Wilson, *Einstein on the Beach*, The Philip Glass Ensemble, Elektra Nonesuch 79323-2, 1993, CD.

55 Emily Morris, "Opera Review: Philip Glass Trilogy: Einstein on the beach," *Glam Adelaide*, August 11, 2014, www.glamadelaide.com.au/main/opera-review-einstein-on-the-beach.

the company's seasonal brochure, by treating "dancers, singers and musicians as equally matched pillars of the performance," and, like Childs, molding the dance to mirror Glass's musical structure. In essence, by focusing his production on movement, sound, and light, Warren took the three elements that comprised the Field Dance scenes and expanded them to encompass the entire opera.[56] "Its stark choreographic saturation wipes out much of the bold, exaggerated theatricalism of Robert Wilson's original staging," Ben Brooker wrote for the online arts periodical *Daily Review*. "Beyond a number of mysterious floating objects such as a black slab and a series of neon tubes, there is little in the way of stage decoration. This is Glass as filtered through Grotowskian poor theatre."[57]

As *Einstein* has provided stage directors with an opportunity to feature dance more prominently in the opera house, the reverse has also taken place as Glass's score has entered the dance repertory. In 2006, for instance, the choreographer and New York City Ballet soloist Benjamin Millepied created the ballet *Amoveo* at the Paris Opera Ballet using music from the fourth Knee Play interlude and the scenes associated with the "trial" image (Act I, scene 2B; Act III, scene 1B; Act IV, scene 2B). "For me, music is inexhaustible source of inspiration," Millepied claimed in his notes on the ballet. "It was in rediscovering Philip Glass's and Bob Wilson's *Einstein on the Beach* that ideas came to me. I was seized by the force emanating from this opera, and seduced by the strange, double dimension that runs from end to end." Although *Amoveo* was not based on the original three themes of the opera, Millepied continued, "[Glass's] artistic world, like that of Bob Wilson, was very present in my imagination."[58] In summary, then, performances of *Einstein* outside the original and three revival productions have retained only Glass's music, leaving the opera's visual elements to the creative agency of new directors. As Millepied's commentary indicates, Wilson's unique dramaturgy continues to influence many such performances, but no matter how far directors and choreographers may venture stylistically from the *Einstein* of Wilson, Glass, de Groat, and Childs, expressive movement remains a critical ingredient in the work's success.

56   State Opera South Australia 2014 Season Brochure, HYPERLINK "https://issuu.com/stateoperas a/docs/sosa_2014" https://issuu.com/stateoperasa/docs/sosa_2014, Accessed: September 1, 2016.

57   Ben Brooker, "Review: Philip Glass Trilogy (Her Majesty's Theatre, Adelaide)," *Daily Review*, 2016, http://dailyreview.com.au/philip-glass-trilogy-her-majestys-theatre-adelaide/10100,   Accessed: January 30, 2016. For more detailed descriptions of this particular production, see: Anne-Marie Peard, "State Opera of SA: Einstein on the Beach," *AussieTheatre.com*, August 14, 2014, http:// aussietheatre.com.au/reviews/state-opera-sa-einstein-beach, Accessed: August 26, 2016; Graham Strahle, "Making the Glass Shine Like New," *The Australian*, August 11, 2014, arts section, 12.

58   Program notes on *Amoveo*, *Réliques*, and *Genus*, Catalogue of the Opéra National de Paris: Opéra National de Paris, Ballet de l'Opéra: Millepied/Paul/McGregor, Palais Garnier, 7, 10–11, 13–15, 19–22 November 2009, VMC 14792 (199), Département de Musique, Bibliotèque nationale de France, Paris, France. The original French reads: "La musique est pour moi une source d'inspiration intarissable. C'est en redécouvrant *Einstein on the Beach* de Philip Glass et Bob Wilson que les idées me sont venues. J'ai été saisi par la force qui se dégageait de cet opéra et séduit par l'étrange et double dimension qui le traverse de part en part. . . . Son univers artistique, comme celui de Bob Wilson, sont très présents dans mon imaginaire."

Conclusions

Einstein on the Beach's dance has long lingered on the margins of the opera's reception, and the foregoing essay offers a historical intervention on two fronts. Analytically, focusing attention on Andrew de Groat's and Lucinda Childs's contributions to *Einstein*, and the reception those contributions have elicited, unveils dance's structural and aesthetic significance to a work that scholars have discussed primarily with respect to theater and/or music. Historically, Glass's and Wilson's prominent inclusion of dance in *Einstein* also evinces the opera's deep roots in the interdisciplinary 1970s lower Manhattan art community. By approaching dance as a distinct art whose integration with *Einstein*'s drama and music largely conceals its unique artistic contributions, we appreciably enrich our understanding of the opera's debt to the postmodern dance experiments of the Judson Dance Theater.[59] We also more fully reveal *Einstein*'s cultural significance as a "downtown" ambassador to conventional "uptown" operatic institutions, one perfectly calibrated to appeal to critics familiar with Wagner's *Gesamtkunstwerk* ideal, as well as those conversant in the "theater of mixed means." Even in the context of new productions, dance has remained a vital component in *Einstein*'s success, offering directors a flexible dramatic tool with which to assert their creative autonomy in the absence of a traditional plot or libretto. With that utility in mind, Childs's remarkable choreography may eventually pass out of *Einstein*'s performance practice as de Groat's did in 1984, but expressive movement has always lain at the heart of the opera's dramaturgy, and there can be little doubt that it will remain so in the future.

---

59 In fact, responding to *Einstein*'s return to the Brooklyn Academy of Music during its 2012–15 international tour, one *New York Times* dance critic opened his review thus: "Although 'Einstein on the Beach' . . . is labeled 'an opera in four acts,' the tag that Mr. Wilson gave to some of his earlier theatrical works might also serve: 'dance play.'" Brian Seibert, "An Opera's Real Story is its Choreography," *New York Times*, September 18, 2012: C3.

8   Anonymous voice, sound, indifference

Zeynep Bulut

Einstein on the Beach features musicians, dancers, actors, and a choir that sings numbers and solfège syllables. At the core of melodic and harmonic variations, actors' reading, a choir's singing, and individuated sounds aligned with the movements of dancers and staging, there is an obsessive act of counting. The obsessive counting exhausts both the act of counting and the accountability of language. In effect, one could consider this state a spectacle of speech, or what I here call "foreground speech." In this chapter, I will discuss how foreground speech generates anonymous voice and an affective sense of indifference. I propose that two aspects constitute this foreground: (1) actors' simultaneous readings mingling with the choir's obsessively sung numbers and letters, and (2) voices distributed to various bodies of sound, image, and movement. Foreground speech leads to the loss of sensible order in the opera. I argue that such loss evokes a sense of indifference, a sense, which emerges not as a case of apathy or numbness but as attunement to the precariousness in language, be it verbal, musical, and visual. As such, the opera mobilizes Einstein as a contested body, as anonymous voice before and beyond any given name. I suggest that anonymous voice can offer new insights into notions of agency and passivity, and encourage consideration of a shared voice that may speak without an object of intention. I will investigate the emergence of anonymous voice in the opera in four sections: (1) physicality of language in minimalist music, (2) a history of obsession, (3) indifference arguments in philosophy, and (4) imagination of the beach as it relates to Christopher Knowles's poetry and condition of autism.[1]

Physicality of language

By physicality of language, I refer to non-semantic vocalism, which heightens the spatial distribution of sound, voice, and speech patterns in the physical environment. We can find this vocalism in minimalism, in line with the use of the

---

1   This chapter was largely developed during the last year of my postdoctoral fellowship at the ICI Berlin Institute for Cultural Inquiry. My sincere thanks to my colleagues and fellow researchers at the ICI Berlin for their contributions to the conceptual thread of this chapter, in particular, to David Kishik and Daniel Colucciello Barber, with whom I had the opportunity to discuss *Einstein on the Beach*.

non-linguistic voice[2] in the twentieth- and twenty-first-century European avant-garde and American experimental music.[3]

Repetition is often thought to be at the heart of minimalism.[4] For instance, composer Wim Mertens considers the non-dialectical and non-representational potency, intensity, and rapture of repetition on the one hand, and the infantile and regressive aspect of repetition on the other. In *Repeating Ourselves: Culture of Repetition, American Minimal Music as Cultural Practice*, musicologist Robert Fink provides a critical account of this consideration.[5] Drawing on Gilles Deleuze and Felix Guattari's *Anti-Oedipus* and Jean Francois Lyotard's *Libidinal Economy*,[6] Fink

2   Various scholars in musicology, literature, performance studies, media and communication studies, psychoanalysis, political science, and philosophy have discussed the nonlinguistic voice (Anhalt, Kramer, Weiss, Connor, Dolar, Cavarero, Ihde, Sterne, Chion, and LaBelle). More recent writings include literary scholar and theorist Steven Connor's *Beyond Words*, and writer, artist, and theorist Brandon LaBelle's *Lexicon of the Mouth*, which discuss the dynamic and contingent relation of pre- and paralinguistic vocalizations to physical and cultural surroundings; musicologist, singer, and voice teacher Nina Sun Eidsheim's *Sensing Sound*, which underlines the multisensory and material foundations of singing and voice, drawing on 20th century opera examples; writer, composer, and sound artist Miriama Young's *Singing the Body Electric: The Human Voice and Sound Technology*, which addresses the non-linguistic voice at the heart of the mediation and embodiment of sound technology; the volume *On Voice*, edited by Walter Benhart and Lawrence Kramer, which reflects on the tensions between the operatic voice, narrative, and the capacity of the voice to deviate from narrative; and the colloquy, *Why Voice Now?* convened by musicologist Martha Feldman with contributions by musicologists Martha Feldman, Emily Wilbourne, Steven Ring, Brian Kane, and James Q Davies, which engages with the nonlinguistic, sonic, and physical aspects of the voice while responding to the question of "why voice now." Steven Connor, *Beyond Words: Sobs, Hums, Stutters, and Other Vocalizations*. London, Reaktion Books, 2014; Brandon LaBelle, *Lexicon of Mouth: Poetics and Politics of Voice and the Oral Imaginary*, London, New York, Bloomsbury, 2014; Nina Sun Eidsheim, *Sensing Sound: Singing and Listening as Vibrational Practice*, Durham, Duke University Press, 2015; Miriama Young, *Singing the Body Electric: The Human Voice and Sound Technology*, Farnham, New York, Ashgate, 2015; Walter Benhart and Lawrence Kramer (Eds.), *On Voice*, Amsterdam, New York, Rodopi, 2014; *Why Voice Now?* Convened by Martha Feldman, *Journal of the American Musicological Society*, Vol. 68, Number 3, pp. 653–685.
3   One can find uses and implications of the nonlinguistic voice in a wide spectrum of examples, some of which includes early Futurist and Dadaist sound poetry such as F. Marinetti's *Zang Tumb Tumb* (1912–1914) and Kurt Schwitters' *Ursonata* (1922–1932) lettrism, 60s tape music and electronically manipulated voices, such as Steve Reich's *Come Out* (1966), Alvin Lucier's *I am sitting in a room* (1970) and Luciano Berio's *Visage* (1961), Trevor Wishart's extended techniques and Phil Minton's extended vocalism, Stockhausen's use of atomic units of language and nonverbal vocalizations in *Microphonie II* (1965) and *Momente* (1962–69), Pauline Oliveros's *Sound Patterns* (1961), and performance pieces such as Cathy Berberian's *Stripsody* (1966), Fluxus performances, John Cage's *Song Books* (1970), and more recently, Pamela Z's *Bone Music* (1992), and Juliana Snapper's underwater singing and opera project, *Five Fathoms* (2008).
4   Wim Mertens, *American Minimal Music*, Trans. J. Hautekiet, London, Kahn and Averill, 1983.
5   Robert Fink, *Repeating Ourselves: American Minimal Music as Cultural Practice*, Berkeley, CA, University of California Press, 2005.
6   See Gilles Deleuze and Félix Guattari, 1972, *Anti-Oedipus: Capitalism and Schizophrenia*, Trans. Robert Hurley, Mark Seem, and Helen R. Lane, London and New York, Continuum, 2004, and Jean Francois Lyotard, *Libidinal Economy*, Trans. Iain Hamilton Grant, Bloomington, IN, Indiana University Press, 1993.

discusses minimalist music as a sonic constituent and manifestation of a "repeating self" that is informed by consumer culture and its desires.[7] As he writes, "what we think of as 'minimal music' can be interpreted as both the sonic analogue and, at times, a sonorous constituent of a characteristic repetitive experience of self in mass-media consumer society."[8] Fink draws attention to a parallel history, which engages both in "the rupture and the rapture"[9] of repetition, that is the 70s disco culture. He indicates disco as a way to "uncover in detail the libidinal realities of the rhythmic repetition and process it shares so obviously with minimalism."[10] Let us now look at the idea of "libidinal reality" closely.

Lyotard argues that desire is a libidinal pleasure produced by the surplus and alienation of the capitalist economic system. The critique of this economy, however, also becomes a generative form of desire and libidinal pleasure, as he posits. *Anti-Oedipus* is not invested in such libidinal economy. Contrary to the discourse of psychoanalysis and its logic of regression, Deleuze and Guattari argue for "desiring machines"[11] as a constructive force and relational component for weaving social texture. Imagine foreground speech as the relational production of social fabric, and minimalist music in the wake of foreground speech. What musical, sonic, and performative aspects suggest minimalist music as a case of foreground speech?

In their Introduction to *The Ashgate Research Companion to Minimalist and Postminimalist Music*, the composers, music theorists, and musicologists Kyle Gann, Keith Potter, and Ap Siôn convey some of the defining characteristics of minimalist music as the use of "minimum material, a single idea, a single chord, a single tone, repeating melodic and rhythmic phrases and gradual change and extension."[12] In his article, "Minimal Music," Michael Nyman employed the term "minimalism" in a similar way.[13] However, as Gann, Potter, and Ap Siôn note,

---

7   Fink, *Repeating Ourselves: Culture of Repetition, American Minimal Music as Cultural Practice*, 3–4.
8   Ibid.
9   The idea of rupture and rapture of repetition can also be found in Tim Lawrence's well-noted book on disco culture, *Loves Saves the Day: A History of American Dance Music, 1970–1979*, Durham, Duke University Press, 2004.
10 Ibid., 31.
11 With this concept, Deleuze and Guattari substitute the Freudian narrative of "primary scene" with the idea of "impersonal machines at work in a factory." As Guattari notes, the idea of machine is useful for understanding how "desire begins production at a stage at which there is as yet no question of a structure." Anti-Oedipus depicts the "organ-machine" as such: "An organ machine is connected to a source-machine which emits a flow; the breast is a machine that produces milk, and the mouth is a machine connected to it." David Macey, The Penguin Dictionary of Critical Theory, London, New York, Penguin Books, 2000, 96.
12 Kyle Gann, Keith Potter, and Pwyll ap Siôn, "Introduction: experimental, minimalist, postminimalist? Origins, Definitions, Communities," *The Ashgate Research Companion to Minimalist and Postminimalist Music*, Eds. Kyle Gann, Keith Potter, and Pwyll ap Siôn, London, Ashgate, 2013, 3.
13 Ibid., 2. See also Michael Nyman, "Minimal Music", The Spectator, October 11, 1968.

these characteristics would not suffice to understand, for instance, drone music.[14] Take Pauline Oliveros's *Horse sings from cloud* (1982), which engages with one single sustained tone. Sustaining the tone, one hears the force and movement of sound, its varied colors, shape, and contours, as well as the harmonics or unfolding of one tone into many. There are no constant or percussive repeating patterns, melodic or harmonic variations that mark the duration. However, in effect, sustained tone gives way to the recognition of duration.

Endurance – the physicality of duration – and resistance to finitude can be considered common themes among various "minimalist" compositions. With its long, almost never-ending loops and episodes, *Einstein*, in particular, draws attention to endurance, to resistance against finitude, which I will later elaborate on in the context of obsession. The point here, however, is that there is no single characteristic or list of criteria which could define minimalism. Gann, Potter, and Ap Siôn reiterate this point, while recapturing what we often notice in this music: "harmonic stasis, repetition, drones, gradual process (additive process, phase shifting, permutational process), steady beat, static instrumentation, metamusic (overtone phenomena), pure tuning, audible structure (easily audible structure, which is on the surface. The singers' counting of beats in Einstein was iconic.)"[15]

I consider these compositional and auditory techniques worth noting for reflecting on the texture of vocalizations. In the context of *Einstein*, as mentioned above, the choir's counting of beats and numbers, along with its singing of solfège syllables generate a literal voice. By literal voice, I simply want to underline how the choir sings what it is meant to sing, without necessarily representing anything other than itself. With her notion of postopera, cultural theorist Jelena Novak makes a similar point. Novak considers *Einstein* a "paradigmatic example" of "postopera," a term which she coins to contest the current condition and stakes of opera, manifesting its transition from modernism to postmodernism.[16] The idea of postopera is informed by Lehmann's concept of post-dramatic theater. "Just as 'post-dramatic theatre is beyond drama,' so is postopera: drama represented by the text of the libretto is not given a primary position," writes Novak.[17] Novak's point sheds light also on the sense of literal voice in *Einstein*. In addition to the choir's singing of numbers and syllables, the way sounds in *Einstein* are employed is not necessarily driven by the semantic content of a text. Take the train scene. Novak exemplifies how Glass, does not attempt to mimic or imply the sound of the train. Instead, he "represents the very procedure

14 Ibid., 3.
15 Ibid., 4, 5, 6.
16 Jelena Novak. "From Minimalist Music to Postopera: repetition, representation, and (post)modernity in the operas of Philip Glass and Louis Andriessen," *The Ashgate Research Companion to Minimalist and Postminimalist Music*, Eds. Kyle Gann, Keith Potter, and Pwyll ap Siôn, London, Ashgate, 2013, 135–36. Also see Jelena Novak, *Postopera: Reinventing the Voice-Body*, London, Routledge, 2015.
17 Ibid., 134, 135.

of representation," Novak argues.[18] Without referencing what we consider train sound or employing it directly, Glass's composition encourages us to be engaged in the very process of weaving sounds together and articulating a non-linguistic voice.

Actors' simultaneous reading of different texts in different pitch ranges, tempos and dynamics, vocal treatment of words as extended and distorted, and the choir's singing of numbers and syllables generate the non-linguistic voice of *Einstein*. Almost juxtaposed to the choir's knee-plays, which function as intermezzos between the acts, and Einstein's violin playing, we hear the recited poems and spoken texts written by Lucinda Childs, Samuel M. Johnson, and Christopher Knowles. Consider Knee Play 2 and the Trial/Prison scene from Act 3. In Knee Play 2, actors' simultaneous readings are joined by violin ostinatos and variations. In the Trial/Prison scene, the choir sings numbers with a moderate tempo in a legible way. The downstage dancers gesture typing, while the choir gives a timeline to the scene. Yet the timeline is not consistently proceeding or receding. It goes back and forth. It occasionally pauses. In the meantime, we hear Lucinda Child's poem *Prematurely air-conditioned supermarket*, followed by Christopher Knowles's poem *Mr. Bojangles and I feel the earth move*. I will come back to these poems in the section on the beach. Here I wish to draw attention to how, with this mingling, the scene resists any sense of offering a self-contained or complete language. The mingling of sounds rather facilitates hearing speech as sonorities, coming from a variety of bodies acting in syncopation, in a zone of resonance where fragments of voices overlap, are superimposed, compete with one another but remain distinct. This texture blurs the position of an identifiable voice. The bodies of voices are varied and contested in the staging of sounds. None of these aspects is perfectly central or cohesively accompanies another. They rather come to the foreground together.

Further to this point, note the additive, subtractive, and cyclical operation of the choir. Take Knee Play 3. Here the choir sings the numbers with considerable speed. We lose track of whether what is sung is a letter or a number. As the choir responds to the spoken texts, it rhythmically punctuates or extends and expands the texts. We can hear the voices as units added to or subtracted from one another. One might also argue that the choir functions as the connective tissue between the movements of the dancers and the mise-en-scène, and between the spoken text and other instrumentation in the piece. Also consider the Spaceship scene from Act 4. In this scene, musicians, dancers, and the choir are placed in the space machine, as part of geometrical shapes such as circles, which also resemble word-like images or letters. With this staging, voices appear as distributed figures. These examples, I suggest, reinforce a sense of foreground speech, where sonic, musical, visual, and performative aspects complement one another and come to surface together. In what follows, I will explain how counting becomes a dynamic of weaving together this foreground speech.

18   Ibid., 136–137.

Obsession, counting, indifference

I want to discuss the act of counting in relation to a historical account of obsession, which, I suggest, leads us to a narrative of indifference. The history of obsession and its transition to indifference is not far-fetched as means of accounting for the actions of actors in *Einstein* or its aesthetics. The narrative of indifference that I wish to explore here is not a case of apathy, but rather a case of neutrality that can result from hypersensitivity or excessive sense. I draw from arguments about indifference in ancient philosophy, the conception of indifference in ethics, and Barthes's notion of neutrality, because they provide the necessary insights to explore how we progress from "passion" to "neutrality." In particular, I will focus on the work of physical language in this transition.

Obsession

Literary and disability studies scholar Lennard J. Davis examines the historical origins and cultural evolution of obsession. As he explains, obsession in Latin – "obsession" and "possessio," has to do with the "battle metaphor" of "demonic possession."[19] However, obsession and possession were differentiated based on the "victim's awareness of the devil."[20] That is, obsession is understood as something over which we have partial control. Davis unfolds the "secularization" of obsession as such:

> First, demonology had to be disconnected from physical maladies. Second, mental states had to be separated from physical states. Third, the nervous system had to be discovered. And fourth, a notion of partial insanity had to be developed that would allow for one to be "crazy" while at the same time being aware of being "crazy."[21]

What Davis reminds us in this process is the transformation of madness from a "totalizing state" to a "partial state," what he calls, "democratization of madness."[22] The "democratization of madness" is related to the historical moment of the eighteenth century, people's rebellion against aristocracy and the heightened sense of altruism. The enlightenment conceptions of sympathy and resonance are important manifestations of this historical moment, as cultural historian and ethnomusicologist Veit Erlmann argues. Erlmann's well-known book *Reason and Resonance* underlines the eighteenth-century physician Claude Nicolas Le Cat's non-mechanical notion of "sympathetic resonance."[23]

---

19   Lennard J. Davis, *Obsession: A History*, Chicago, University of Chicago Press, 2008, 31.
20   Ibid.
21   Ibid., 32.
22   Ibid., 41, 47.
23   Veit Erlmann, *Reason and Resonance: A History of Modern Aurality*, New York, Zone Books, 2010.

Le Cat's notion of resonance suggests an organicist attitude towards auditory perception.[24] Two terms are central to his theory: gradation and progression, associated with the "imperceptible, insensible, innumerable... endlessly progressing..."[25] In conjunction with this theory, the idea of functional progression in arts and science manifests itself in the form of "social harmony and ethics."[26] The newly emerging noisy city, polluted environment and plague heighten sensory perception on the one hand, and crystallize "the vibrating air" as "the spherical joint for resonance, sympathy and happiness" on the other, as Erlmann explains.[27]

The eighteenth-century conception of resonance indeed resonates with Davis's account of obsession; in particular, with the way he introduces the role of obsession in transitioning "absolute madness" to "partial madness."[28] In the eighteenth century, categories of madness – such as vapor, melancholia, hypochondria, and spleen – were considered to emerge from the "populous and unhealthy town"; however, associated with the "material and cultural wealth and abundance" of England, they were called "English diseases."[29] Referring to physician George Cheyne and his notion of the "English malady," Davis notes that the "sufferers" of these diseases were "made up the cream of society" and often celebrated as superior minds, the ones, in Cheyne's words, "whose faculties are the brightest and most spiritual, whose genius is most keen and penetrating, and particularly where there is the most delicate sensation and taste both of pleasure and pain."[30] "English diseases" were treated as "disposition or temperament" rather than "a disease of rationality or will."[31] Obsession, on the other hand, was partial madness. Termed by French physician Philippe Pinel, partial madness indicates "monomania"; that is "only a single idea or a faculty of the mind is affected."[32] This diagnosis, as Davis explains, blurs the boundary between the "normal" and the "pathological." Monomania, later obsession, was becoming ordinary for many. The gradual transformation of obsession into passion, scientific discovery and pursuit, measurement, categorization and expertise makes obsession and compulsions "move to the fore, to signify a very human essence, and ... a characteristic of genius, good birth, good character... [the] good citizen and consumer"[33] in the nineteenth and twentieth centuries.

Explaining this transformation, Davis turns to literature such as Mary Shelly's well-known novel and character Frankenstein, Balzac's conception of idée fixe

24   Ibid., 114.
25   Ibid.,120–22.
26   Ibid., 124–125.
27   Ibid., 127, 130, 131.
28   Davis, *A History: Obsession*, 50, 53.
29   Ibid., 39–40.
30   Ibid., 40.
31   Ibid., 41.
32   Ibid., 67.
33   Ibid., 51.

and Zola's realism, and to the foundations of eugenics and psychoanalysis. Take the character Frankenstein, a young science student. Unlike a Renaissance man who is interested in a variety of topics, Frankenstein is obsessed with mastering a single conception. Frankenstein directly echoes the juxtaposition between the liberal arts and science in the novel, as Davis reminds us: "you go as far as others have gone before you, and there is nothing more to know; but in a scientific pursuit there is continual food for discovery and wonder."[34] Similarly, Balzac's and later Berlioz's notions of *idée fixe* are inflected with such wonder, employing the recurrence of one single theme, idea, or character as pursuit.

Counting

In *Einstein*, the figure of Einstein is not musically employed as an idée fixe. Instead, there is the obsessive act of counting. The historical transformation of obsession from monomania to scientific wonder informs and is informed by the activity of counting and the use of numbers as a discourse of accountability. Literary scholar Steven Connor considers the "horror of numbers" to be the "imaginative numerosity" of literature, arts, and humanities.[35] The invention of number, as well as the numbers' invention of time, as Connor notes, is associated with the narrative of efficiency, "the economical use of time, space and resources."[36]

Allow me to underline the connection between the narrative of efficiency and the foundation of modern acoustics and sound. I draw attention to this connection for two reasons. First, the foundations of modern sound are useful and suggestive for observing the recurring question of to what extent and in what forms the production and distribution of sound can be measured and controlled. Second, the quest for the measurement of sound informs the obsessive act of counting in *Einstein*. That is, sound becomes the embodiment of both efficiency and redundancy. Historian Emily Thompson highlights the question of efficiency versus redundancy, examining the invention of modern sound as "signal-like clear" in the architectural design of Boston Symphony Hall at the beginning of the twentieth century.[37] The pragmatic approach of the late eighteenth century, especially explorations on the relation between the physical properties of materials and the motion of sound waves, constitute the foundations of "modern physicalism" and acoustics, as music theorist Benjamin Steege posits.[38] Such physicalism contributes to the visualization, objectification, and standardization of sound. The

34   Ibid., 74–75.
35   Steven Connor, *The Horror of Number: Can Humans Learn to Count?* The Alexander Lecture, University College, University of Toronto, October 1, 2014, http://stevenconnor.com/wp-content/uploads/2014/10/Horror-of-Number.pdf
36   Ibid., 3.
37   Emily Thompson, *The Soundscape of Modernity: Architectural Acoustics and the Culture of Listening in America, 1900–1933*, Cambridge, MIT Press, 2004, 4, 5.
38   Benjamin Steege, "Acoustics," *Keywords in Sound*, Eds. David Novak and Matt Sakakeeny, Durham, Duke University Press, 2015, 24–26.

founder of psychophysics, Gustav Fechner, however, shows us the double end of physicalism.

Fechner tests the correlation between stimulus and sensation by measuring the sensitivity of skin. In this he follows Ernst Chladni's vibrating plates, and Ernst Heinrich Weber's experiments with the eardrum and touch sensation. Historian Alexandra Hui, in her recent book, *The Psychophysical Ear: Musical Experiments, Experimental Sounds*, explains how "musical knowledge" holds the key to making such "scientific knowledge."[39] Hui's work on Gustav Fechner discusses the psychophysical experience as an "aesthetic one," which was essentially informed by the musical hub of Leibniz in the nineteenth century. In particular, Fechner's severe blindness, from which he recovered in his later life, led him to consider psychophysical experience in terms of "all inclusive consciousness."[40] Fechner's theory of "all inclusive consciousness," or psychophysical monism, challenges any form of dualism such as matter and mind, God, and the universe. It thus suggests the unity of life and death, as well as belief in the afterlife or "beyond life."[41] The afterlife becomes the supernatural companion to life. Consider this unity in terms of obsession. The psychophysical experience – intensity, unknown spatial magnitude, as Fechner puts it – demonstrates the unity of life and death, yet also the impossibility of grasping this unity as one, while resisting finitude. This approach also points towards continuity between excessive measurement and the impossibility of measurement, between the narrative of efficiency and redundancy.

I argue that the work and play of counting in *Einstein* highlights this continuity between efficiency and redundancy. The counting here can be understood as a case through which we embrace the imaginative redundancy and the uncertain knowledge of sound, as well as the obsession of making sound indexical, reliable, and visible. The counting marks yet also interrupts the simultaneous readings of actors. In line with the fragmented and non-linear worlds of the texts, the sung numbers contribute to a loss of track. Recall the Trial/Prison scene. Following the melodic and harmonic sequences, counting brings the poems to the foreground, gives form to the spatial spread, punctuation marks, and multiple temporalities of sound, the voice, and speech. The choir indeed resists the idea of pursuit by means of creating musical and theatrical forms of loss and redundancy. It presents the process of weaving together a foreground that is outside of any given time and space. I propose that this process can be considered a pivot point from obsession to indifference.

Indifference

Philosopher Stephen Makin draws on indifference arguments in the presocratic atomism of Democritus and Leucippus. He underlines two criteria associated

39   Alexandra Hui, *The Psychophysical Ear: Musical Experiments, Experimental Sounds, 1840–1910*, Cambridge, MIT Press, 2012, xx.
40   Ibid., 8, 9, 10.
41   Ibid., 12–13.

with indifference arguments: The Principle of Sufficient Reason, which he draws from Leibniz, and rational belief.[42] One example of the indifference argument is as follows: "at the appropriate position in a magnetic field the charged particle has no more reason to move in one direction than in any other, and so since it cannot move in all directions at once it will not move."[43] In this argument, one could see the symmetry between all positions and no position, and the implication of rational belief. Makin discusses the structure of these arguments, that is they almost always include "no more...than..." or "not...rather than..."[44] He particularly situates this structure within the philosophy of presocratic atomism, and argues that the Zenonian arguments of plurality might lead to Democritus' atomism, which addresses the "number, shape, size, motion and variety" of atoms.[45]

The fifth-century Greek philosopher Zeno speculated about the impossibility of motion, and the Zeno of Citium was the founder of Stoicism. Consider the association of Stoicism with endurance. Stoicism implies a state of indifference towards material changes in nature and hence acknowledges difference. Indeed, despite its speculative and universalistic claims, Western metaphysics seems to understand indifference as differentiation. In the *Logic of Sense*, Deleuze discusses the implications of Stoicism as differentiation. As he argues, the Stoic practice brings "everything to surface" while allowing "effects" – be they causal, sonorous, optical, linguistic, etc. – to "manifest themselves" as they "act."[46] As the excessive sense "climbs to surface,"[47] it becomes "impassive," synonymous with nonsense. The extended length and the expansive spectrum of sonorous, visual, and theatrical effects in *Einstein* generate a case of *in*difference as Deleuze indicates. The texture of vocalism, weaving together the effects, leads to symmetry between all and none, between equally possible directions of movement and the impossibility of motion, between excessive sense and nonsense. The point of departure both for Stoics and for presocratic atomists is the acknowledgment of possibility. The question, then, is how these possibilities result in impossibility. Here the obsessive pursuit or empirical skepticism of the scientist is missing. Given the symmetry between all and none, we would also be left with questions of intention, responsibility, and accountability, as well as questions of choice, action, and consequence. Yet there seems to be common ground between the obsessive pursuit of the scientist and the indifference of the Stoics: differentiation, and constant scrutiny over the limits of justification and knowledge.

42 Ibid., 2.
43 Ibid., 6-7.
44 Ibid., 8-9.
45 Ibid., 9.
46 Gilles Deleuze, *The Logic of Sense*, Trans. Mark Lester and Charles Stivale, London, Athlone Press, 1990, 7.
47 Ibid.

Indifferent love

A few years ago a friend of mine told me that *Einstein* was indeed a love story. First I did not understand what he meant by that. Considering the ending of the opera, which uses Samuel M. Johnson's poem, *Lovers on a Park Bench*, his comment later made sense; but still I was left intrigued. In the above section, I attempted to argue for the transition between obsession and indifference as differentiation. Indifferent love seems to crystallize the ethical value of differentiation, as well as the value of not knowing.

There are different ways of giving and receiving love that we learn and perform. Love is not reduced to the context of romantic love or to the formation of a couple, family, or kinship, which often forces us to merge into "one." We could also look at love as a force of the collective, as a form of friendship and solidarity, as shared, partial, and *in*different. Although *Lovers on a Park Bench* depicts a couple, I suggest looking at the following section in the poem, in the light of *in*different love:

> And what sort of story shall we hear? ... It will be a familiar story, a story that is so very, very old, and yet it is so new. It is the old, old story of love.
>
> ...
>
> "How much do you love me, John?" she asked.
>
> He answered: "How much do I love you? Count the stars in the sky. Measure the waters of the oceans with a teaspoon. Number the grains of sand on the seashore. Impossible, you say. Yes and it is just as impossible for me to say how much I love you. My love for you is higher than the heavens, deeper than Hades, and broader than the earth. It has no limits, no bounds. Everything must have an ending except my love for you."[48]

Johnson's poem remarkably captures the movement from obsession to indifference in *Einstein*. The love described is impossible to count, impossible to measure. It resists against finitude, against bounds. Yet the love also desires to be present, to be tangible in the present. The symmetry between possibility and impossibility, redundancy and loss of sense, perfect sense and nonsense, all and none is at play in the lovers' union. There is the will to merge into one; yet there is also the impossible, perhaps the partial awareness of the impossibility of becoming one. Hence the question: "How much do you love me?" This is "a familiar story of love," a story "that is so very, very old, and yet it is so new." What makes the story new? Is the story new because of the differences of two lovers, albeit the desire to pursue the one as impossible?

---

48 My transcription of Samuel M. Johnson's *Lovers on a Bench*, See *Einstein on the Beach* manuscript, courtesy of Columbia University Rare Book and Manuscript Library.

Philosopher Charles E. Scott discusses the ethical value of indifference as plurality.[49] One of his cases is indifferent love, which he draws from Friedrich Schelling's conception of love and potency. We consider love as associated with passion, rather than indifference. As Scott argues, for Schelling, "indifference and love find their numbing coherence in their differentiation."[50] Looking at Schelling, Scott shows how love could be a neutral state, one that is associated with dispossession.[51] Because of its indifference, the soul is always at work, as Scott posits.[52] Schelling's potencies – first "withdrawal," then the potency which is "self-communicating" and "a force" outside of the first two – lead to indifference as a "disinterested force" that gives way to unexpected and unknown affairs.[53] Such indifference allows differentiation to happen. The unity can only be achieved with the "will" that does not "will" anything in particular. This idea is further discussed in Roland Barthes's lectures on the neutral.

The Neutral follows Barthes's book *How to Live Together*.[54] The time of the lectures coincides with the death of Barthes's mother and thus with his withdrawal and exploration of being in the present. In his preface to the *Neutral*, Thomas Clerc captures the question that Barthes asks: "... who speaks the Neutral and how the Neutral speaks..."[55] These questions significantly contribute to the discussion on the affective state of indifference, and the production of anonymous voice in *Einstein*. Barthes draws attention to the neutral as it relates to "paradigm," "choice," and "conflict."[56] He situates his thoughts within the field of ethics, "the discourse of the good choice or of the 'non choice,' or of the 'lateral choice,'" which he sees in practice, in everyday life.[57]

The discourse of indifferent love is embedded in this practice. The *in*difference of love encourages a space where definitive identities are under scrutiny not by means of dogma or moral skepticism but by means of a welcome uncertainty. In other words, indifferent love does not doubt, yet does not attempt to know or accomplish anything in particular either. The ethical value of indifferent love is then a capacity to observe the ways in which we respond to the matters that surround and happen to one another, without being dictated by or limited to discursive presuppositions or ends. I would like now to introduce the beach.

49   Charles. E. Scott, *Living with Indifference*, Bloomington, IN, Indiana University Press, 2007.
50   Ibid.,106.
51   Ibid., 108–109.
52   Ibid., 110.
53   Ibid., 111.
54   Roland Barthes, *The Neutral: Lecture Course at the College de France (1977–1978)*, Trans. Rosalind Krauss and Denis Hollier, Text established, annotated, and presented by Thomas Clerc under the direction of Eric Marty, New York, Columbia University Press, 2007, xxv.
55   Ibid., xxiii.
56   Ibid., 8.
57   Ibid.

The beach

The beach is a transitional space, where land meets sea. There are beach cultures, constituted by certain climates, people, regulations, rituals, and festivities. However, we do tend to associate the idea of beach with freedom and play, a place where we are allowed to lie down and do nothing. Historically, this has not always been the case. In *The Lure of the Sea: The Discovery of the Seaside 1750–1840*, cultural historian Alan Corbin introduces different narratives and implications of the seashore.[58] Corbin begins with the interpretations of the sea implied in the book of Genesis, the Psalms, and the book of Job. The story of the Great Flood and Creation understands the sea as an "unfinished and unconquerable element, undifferentiated primordial substance, on which form had to be imposed," indicating "disorder" before civilization.[59] The "abyss" of the Flood versus the man-made nature of Creation, Corbin argues, led to the consideration of the ocean as punishment and curse, as well as a monstrous "liquid mass" and infinite appearance, which later fed into controversial narratives of the Garden of Eden, theories of the earth and geology, the notion of the immersive sublime in the nineteenth-century romanticism, and the association between oceanic feeling and return to womb.

The cycle of life and death, of abyss and creation are indeed implied in the conception of the beach from antiquity to today. Historian John Gillis, in *The Human Shore: Seacoasts in History*, discusses the invention of seacoasts and beach in the age of colonialism and empire.[60] Take sixteenth and seventeenth-century European colonial history. Here the sea represented and facilitated discovery and conquest of unmarked territories, as well as geographical expansion and economic growth. However, as Gillis posits, the Bible provided the "foundational" narrative for "both history and geography" of the West until the eighteenth century.[61] The sea was "an alien environment"[62] for Westerners, perhaps evincing the need both for wonder and exploration and for escape and protection. With the Industrial Revolution and urbanization, the seaside and beach were invented. In the eighteenth century, as Corbin explains, the British coast became a bourgeois escape from city life and its madness and illnesses. Sea bathing, getting fresh air, and being out in nature were highly popular among the aristocracy. What was once a curse was now a recipe for health, physical exercise, psychological recovery, and well being.[63]

---

58   Alain Corbin, *The Lure of the Sea: Discovery of the Seaside 1750–1840*, Trans. Jocelyn Phelps, London, Penguin Books, 1995. Also see Daniela Blei. "Inventing the Beach: The Unnatural History of a Natural Place," June 23, 2016, www.smithsonianmag.com/history/inventing-beach-unn atural-history-natural-place-180959538/, Accessed: September 28, 2016.

59   Corbin, *The Lure of the Sea*, 1, 2.

60   John R. Gillis, *The Human Shore: Seacoasts in History*, Chicago, University of Chicago Press, 2012.

61   Ibid., 13.

62   Ibid., 7.

63   See Daniela Blei, "Inventing the Beach: The Unnatural History of a Natural Place," June 23, 2016, www.smithsonianmag.com/history/inventing-beach-unnatural-history-natural-place-180959 538/, Accessed: September 28, 2016.

But what was the seaside? The seaside was a human invention, the product of nineteenth-century coastlines, which were "first imagined, then discovered, named and ultimately, surveyed and settled."[64] The settlement of coastlines was due to "the nation-building efforts of a newly independent territorial state" deriving from "a new capitalism that was less based on trade than on agrarian and industrial production."[65] Coastlines were thus a project of domestication of the sea, of mapping and "drawing the line."[66] However, as Gillis, and anthropologist Tim Ingold remind us, there are no straight lines in nature. Seaside, coastlines, are indeed "fractal and broken" and fictions, "a virtual icon of modernity."[67] This history holds the key to a more contemporary conception of the beach as a space of emancipation from work, as well as from worries about the self and everyday life. The nineteenth-century seaside promoted the notion of vacation not simply as a recipe for health, but also as "pleasure" and "recreation."[68] The seaside offered immersion in nature as a key to self-wonder and self-transformation, on the one hand, and drew a territory in which emptiness referred to a space available for building villas, hotels, and resorts, on the other. In the midst of these two states, beach became a spectacle of the middle class. Perhaps for this reason, "emptiness" and "artificial desertification" has always been the "appeal" of the beach, as Gillis suggests.[69] Gillis points out a resemblance between different beaches and their lack of "locality" that we see from the nineteenth century to today. He uses sociologist Marc Augé's term "non-place" to qualify this situation:

> The beach is what Marc Augé defines as nonplace, something to pass through, not to dwell in…The beach suggests beginnings and endings but offers no narrative, for the beach has no history and beachgoers have no connection with earlier *Homo littoralis*. Instead it presents itself as a point of eternal return that promises never to change – a place where nothing ever happens… Its true relation to nature and history must always be concealed, for it functions in modern culture as a primary place of getting away, of oblivion and forgetting.[70]

As Gillis explains above, "nothing really happens" on the beach. Baring the cultural history of beach in mind, one could imagine this emptiness as a spectrum

---

64 Ibid. 99, 101, 104.
65 Ibid.
66 104.
67 Ibid.,104. Also see Tim Ingold. *Lines: A Brief History*, London, New York, Routledge, 2007, 152.
68 Ibid. 150-152. Also see Daniela Blei, "Inventing the Beach: The Unnatural History of a Natural Place," June 23, 2016, www.smithsonianmag.com/history/inventing-beach-unnatural-history-natural-place-180959538/, Accessed: September 28, 2016.
69 Gillis, *The Human Shore*, 150.
70 Ibid., 150–151. Also see Marc Augé. *Non-Places: Introduction to an Anthropology of Supermodernity*, Trans. John Howe, New York, Verso Books, 1995.

of nonsense that departs from excessive sense, be it excessive fear, danger, need, joy, or pleasure. The symmetry between excessive sense and nonsense suggests the beach as a place of *in*difference.

Consider this idea in *Einstein*. In the context of both Wilson's staging and Knowles's autism, the conception of the beach heightens a similar symmetry between excessive sense and nonsense, a state of *in*difference informed by spatial thinking and the sensory aspects of language. Apart from the title, the main reference to the beach appears in the Trial/Prison scene, in Lucinda Childs's text, *Prematurely Air-Conditioned Supermarket*. Lying on bed, one of the witnesses recites the poem with a moderate tempo and a steady voice:

> I was in this prematurely air-conditioned super market
>
> And there were all these aisles
>
> and there were all these bathing caps that you could buy
>
> which had these kind of Fourth of July plumes on them
>
> they were red and yellow and blue
>
> I wasn't tempted to buy one
>
> but I was reminded of the fact that I had been avoiding
>
> the beach.[71]

Repeating the poem in a gradually quickening tempo, the witness animates the recitation. What makes this recitation all the more striking is what follows in the scene: Knowles's poems, *Mr. Bojangles* and *I feel the earth move*, recited by the lawyer and the witness. The titles of the poems are from two well-known songs, country music artist Jerry Jeff Walker's *Mr. Bojangles*, and singer and songwriter Carole King's *I feel the earth move*. In part, Knowles refers to the original lyrics of both songs. To address the concept of the beach, I will look here at *I feel the earth move*:

> I feel the earth move... I feel the tumbling down the tumbling down...
> There was a judge who like puts in a court. And the judge have like in what able jail what it could be a spanking. Or a smack. Or a swat. Or a hit.
>
> This could be where of judges and courts and jails. And who was it.
>
> This will be doing the facts of David Cassidy of where in this case of feelings.
>
> That could make you happy. That could make you sad. That could make you mad. That could make you jealous. So do you know a jail is. A judge

---

71 My transcription of Lucinda Childs's *Prematurely air-conditioned supermarket.*

and a court could. So this could be like in these green Christmas trees and Santa Claus has about red. And now the Einstein trail is like the Einstein on the beach. So if you know the faffffffff facts. So this could be into Lucy or kite. You raced all the way up. This was a race. So now the eight types will be into the pink rink and this way could be so very magic.

…

Jay Reynolds from midnight to 6 AM.

Harry Harrison from 6 AM to 10 AM.

Ron Lundy from 10 AM to 2 PM.

Dan Ingram from 2 PM to 6 PM.

George Michael from 6 PM to 10 PM.

Chuck Leonard from 10 PM to midnight.

Johnny Donovan from 10 PM to 3 AM.

Steve O'Brion from 2 PM to 6 AM.

Johnny Donovan from 6 PM to 10 PM.

Chuck Leonard from 3 AM to 5 AM.

Johnny Donovan from 6 PM to 10 PM.[72]

…

Wilson's staging of *Einstein* and language in the opera was inspired by Christopher Knowles's imagination. Wilson had a mild speech impediment, worked with a movement therapist for his condition, and later worked as a therapist himself as well. His experience of movement therapy, along with his training in architecture, informs his interest in the breakdown of language, narrative, and voice. Literary critic and cultural theorist Sylvère Lotringer, in his interview with Wilson, asks why Wilson is not interested in a theater "based upon language."[73] Wilson responds to this question explaining his background in painting and architecture and his architectural use of words. "For instance, when Lucinda speaks in *Einstein on the Beach*, what matters is the sound of her voice, the patterns of her voice…" he says.[74] Antonin Artaud's physical theater, Gertrude Stein's poetry, and John Cage's conception of music undoubtedly influenced Wilson's use of language, in particular *Einstein*'s deconstructed language and non-linear and fragmented

72 My transcription of Christopher Knowles's *I feel the earth move*. See *Einstein on the Beach* manuscript, courtesy of Columbia University Rare Book and Manuscript Library.

73 Sylvère Lotringer, "Interview with Robert Wilson," *Schizo-Culture*. 2-Vol, Semiotext(e), Eds. Sylvère Lotringer and David Morris, Cambridge, MA, MIT Press, 2014, 20.

74 Ibid., 20–21.

narrative. As dramaturg Arthur Holmberg posits, with this use of language, "Wilson foregrounds spatial and temporal, not narrative, structure."[75] Similarly, "people are not characters, but performers engaged in physical activities."[76] Neither activities nor speech patterns resolve into a totality of language. As such, Wilson's aesthetics goes beyond representation and signification. Wilson explains his aesthetics, referring to his staging in the opera, *A Letter to Queen Victoria*:

> I wanted to put together these different rhythms, different ways of speaking in order to create a vocal effect. I wasn't primarily concerned with the content. At the same time, it is there... I consider what I am doing as a kind of visual music.[77]

I wish to underline "vocal effect" here. How do the sounds of voice and different ways of speaking create a "vocal effect"? And how does this effect become content, become literal? These questions seem to be vital in Knowles's perception of language and writing, related to his autism. Medical discourses often classify autism spectrum disorders based on "the delay in language development, excess of stimulation and excitement, perceptual load, lack of attention, eye contact, and emotional expression, disengagement from social interaction, and repetitive behavior."[78] I do not intend to discuss Knowles's autism as such or as a metaphor in *Einstein*'s staging of language. Likewise, I do not wish to suggest Knowles's perception of language as an advantage or disadvantage when creating *Einstein*'s staging. Given Wilson's aesthetics and personal history, I rather intend to highlight Knowles and Wilson's collaboration as an exploration in and out of verbal language attending to different conditions of imagination. This exploration is not invested in generating a particular meaning. It rather points towards the spatial thinking and sensory aspects of language.

Spatial thinking is a physically and conceptually significant register to look at the interrelations between Knowles's conception of the beach and fragmentation, repetition and expression, and surface and depth. One could understand Knowles's spatial thinking within language, but also before and beyond the semantic order of words. Knowles tackles the rhythmic and sonic patterns, the shape and visual forming of words. In this activity of fragmentation, he brings together seemingly

75 Arthur Holmberg, *The Theatre of Robert Wilson*, Cambridge, Cambridge University Press, 2005, 11.

76 Ibid., 14.

77 Lotringer, "Interview with Robert Wilson," 20–21.

78 See Stephanie Blenner, Arathi Reddy, and Marilyn Augustyn, "Diagnosis and management of autism in childhood," BMJ: British Medical Journal, Vol. 343, No. 7829 (October 29, 2011), pp. 894-899; Anna Remington, John Swettenham, Ruth Campbell and Mike Coleman, "Selective Attention and Perceptual Load in Autism Spectrum Disorder," Psychological Science, Vol. 20, No. 11 (November 2009), pp. 1388-1393. See also Adam Ockelford. *Music, Language and Autism: Exceptional Strategies for Exceptional Minds*, London, Jessica Kingsley Publishers, 2013, and Steve Silberman, *Neurotribes: The Legacy of Autism and the Future of Neurodiversity*, London, Avery-Penguin, 2015.

irrelevant words – as well as images and sounds –and draws attention to the concrete process of (de)forming sense. The idea of background and foreground disappears in such imagination and experience. That is, all patterns interact with one another on the surface and there is no necessary divide between surface and depth. Surface is, in itself, depth,[79] one that can be imagined as horizon, as the beach perhaps. The fact that the words – and their pairing – do not necessarily suggest symbolic content underlines the forming of a literal voice, of the physicality of language. Performance studies scholar Telory D. Arendell and philosopher Erin Manning's accounts of autism reinforce my point.[80]

Arendell provides a critical reading of Wilson and Knowles's collaboration in terms of disability studies. Questioning the ways in which Wilson appropriates Knowles's imagination for his staging, she argues that Wilson draws a fine line between representing difference and representing cognitive disability. In this discussion, Arendell refers to writer, artist, and activist Amanda Baggs, who introduces herself as someone with multiple disabilities, one of which is autism. Baggs considers herself part of the "developmental disability self-advocacy community," which is based not on "diagnosis" but on a "history of shared experiences."[81] Using a communication device for most of her adult life, Baggs was regarded as "nonspeaking":

> I grew up sometimes able to speak and sometimes not, and with a complicated relationship to speech and receptive language. I slowly lost both speech-in-general and speech-as-communication starting in adolescence and continuing into early adulthood. I use both typing and picture symbols depending on what I need at the time. I communicate best outside of language altogether, but they haven't made tools to interpret that. I am sometimes a good writer, but language is extremely tiring for me… My biggest hobby is crocheting. I do it all the time, day and night. It gives me something to do with my hands. And I need things to do with my hands. I need things that are concrete, things outside the world of words…[82]

Baggs needs to touch things with hands and move through a physical environment. This is her way of being. Similar to Knowles's poetry, she attends to the patterns of rhythm and sound, shape and texture of words. One could associate these qualities with aspects of spatial thinking. One of Baggs's writings, "Being

---

79 Holmberg quotes Robert Wilson's personal interview (March, 1993): "The depth is on the surface." Holmberg, *The Theatre of Robert Wilson*, 121.

80 See Telory D. Arendell, "Thinking Spatially, Speaking Visually: Robert Wilson and Christopher Knowles," *International Journal of Music and Performing Arts*, Vol. 3, No.1, June 2015; Erin Manning, *Always More Than One: Individuation's Dance*, Durham, Duke University Press, 2013.

81 See Amanda Baggs's website: https://ballastexistenz.wordpress.com/about-2/, Accessed: December 28, 2015.

82 Ibid.

a spatial thinker," explains spatial thinking as a way of "organizing things" and "thinking outside of language."[83]

In My Language, Baggs's most well-known video, exemplifies this thinking. In the first part of the video, Baggs uses her hands to sense the environment. She dances to the room that she is in with her hands, and touches various objects. In the second part, using a voice synthesizer, she translates her acts and talks about her capacity to interact with her physical environment, albeit the bias against autism, that is autistic people are not able to socially relate to others. Philosopher Erin Manning also draws attention to *In My Language*. Looking at Baggs's account of sensory experience, Manning posits that autistic people do not lose the quality of "intensive relationality."[84] Manning explains this notion drawing on psychiatrist Daniel Stern's notion of relational self and reference to "cross-sensory modality." For Stern, there is no "presupposed" or "contained" self which interacts with its environment out of necessity, but there are "several senses of self" which "lead toward the creation of a multiplicity of strata, each of them differently expressive under variable conditions."[85] Cross-modal correspondences refer to the experience of a multi-sensory matrix, that is the occurrence of hearing in seeing, of seeing in touching, etc. Cross-sensory modality, as Manning posits, emphasizes the experience itself. It underlines differentiation, instead of difference, and the process of forming instead of a given form.

This modality can be observed in the weaving of surface, experience and expression both in Knowles's imagination of the beach and poetry, and in Wilson's staging. Recall the vocal effects in *Einstein*: The side-by-side recitation of the texts, the spatial distribution and layering of the choir's singing, the fragmented appearances of voices aligned with the movements of the dancers. Also consider the "surface" of Knowles's writing in *I feel the earth move*, in particular the last section, which is a list of names and numbers that repeat and are similarly situated. The proper name of the voice gets lost in *I feel the earth move*. Likewise, the proper name of Einstein gets lost in the opera. What happens when the proper name of a voice gets lost?

"The voice, which is embodied in the plurality of voices, always puts forward first of all the *who* of saying" writes philosopher Adriana Cavarero.[86] Cavarero asks what constitutes the speaking person and his or her uniqueness. This may be the embodied presence of the word and the act of speaking rather than the presumed logos and discourse of a linguistic order and its communicative content,

83 Amanda Baggs, "Being a Spatial Thinker (one kind of autistic thought)" and *In My Language*. Arendell, "Thinking Spatially, Speaking Visually," 20. See Bagg's video, *In My Language*, www. youtube.com/watch?v=JnylM1hl2jc, Accessed: February 1, 2016.

84 Erin Manning, *Always More Than One: Individuation's Dance*, 8.

85 Here Manning also draws attention to other psychoanalysts, such as Bick and Ogden. She argues that, in both cases, self is bounded, "rests in a containment of skin" and she questions "the containment of skin" in the beginning of her chapter. Ibid., 3, 4.

86 Adriana Cavarero. *For More Than One Voice: Toward a Philosophy of Vocal Expression*, Trans. Paul A. Kottman, Stanford, Stanford University Press, 2005, 30.

as she argues. Looking at the "vocal effects" in *Einstein*, I want to contest the "who of saying." The plurality of voices in *Einstein* stays with us not in the form of a name or a word, but as foreground speech woven together by sound, image, and movement. Foreground speech, as I have argued in this chapter, encourages embracing the non-dualist modes of being, as well as undoing the dualist divide between "agency and passivity."[87] With this speech, *Einstein* puts us both at work and at rest. It exhausts us with its length, obsessive counting, imaginative redundancy, and uncertain knowledge of sound, fragmented narratives and multiple temporalities on the one hand, and it makes us rest on its "beach" on the other. The beach of *Einstein* decentralizes speech as fragments of sound, movement, and image, which resonate with one another in difference, which resists the duality between "agency and passivity." The beach makes us endure feelings of excessive sense and nonsense side by side, recognizing the nonsense as sense, and rendering the loss of a track, the precariousness of language tolerable. In so doing, we generate anonymous voice; a voice that is neither fully countable nor fully accountable, a voice that is *in*different.

---

87 I take my cue from literary scholar Eve Kosofsky Sedgwick. Sedgwick pronounces texture a way of undoing the dualist understanding separating "agency and passivity." Eve Kosofsky Sedgwick, *Touching Feeling: Affect, Pedagogy, Performativity*, Durham, Duke University Press, 2003.

Knee chapter 4
Artists recall and respond

Under the influence – Philip Glass

Suzanne Vega
(Performing songwriter and musician based in New York City)

I became aware of Philip Glass's music as a teenager studying modern dance in
New York City in the 1970s. Many choreographers used Steve Reich's music
to dance to. I enjoyed Steve Reich's music, but once I discovered Philip Glass
I felt his work had more emotional content for me personally, and this made
me want to explore it further.

I understood the concept of minimalism, and knew both composers to be part of that
scene. Take a musical idea, usually a small one, and repeat it, sometimes with minute variations. I began practicing Nichiren Buddhism at the age of 16 and learned
to chant the very simple mantra that is central to the practice, which I do to this day.
When I hear Philip Glass's music I feel a deep sense of spirituality, and familiarity,
and the similarity in approach to my own religious practice may be why.

My roots are in folk music. I learned to play by teaching myself Woody Guthrie
songs I found on a collection of albums in a thrift store. In folk music, you
have a few chords that make up a verse – you repeat those chords – then you
play a chorus, repeat that in between your verses. Small modules, repeated.
Simple ideas, usually.

I wrote "Cracking" at the age of 20 and that was my first attempt at a minimalistic
folk song. I didn't even want a melody, just a few repeating chords that deepened as you got to know this person (herself a kind of "narrator") and a flat
statement of what she was experiencing – a kind of "breakdown." Yes, I had
to explain it to more than one person. I included this song on the first demo
tapes that went out and A&M Records turned it down several times saying I
had "no sense of melody."

I met Philip Glass after I got my record deal in 1984 at the age of 24, through Nancy
Jeffries, the A&R person who eventually did sign me to A&M Records. Her
husband is Kurt Munkacsi, the engineer and sound designer with the Philip
Glass Ensemble. Philip was collecting lyrics for his *Songs from Liquid Days*

album – he had lyrics by David Byrne, Paul Simon, and Laurie Anderson and was looking for someone relatively unknown to fill out the fourth place.

He invited me to his townhouse in New York City one afternoon. I felt nervous standing on the stoop with my sheaf of unused lyrics. I was eating an ice cream cone as I rang the bell. Phil answered the door himself, and gave me a long stare. "If I had known you would be hungry, I would have prepared you lunch," he said.

"No, no problem!" I said. After this auspicious beginning, as I recall, we got right to work. I was pleased that he liked my piece called "Feather & Bone," a song that I had sung to small audiences, but as it was never well received, I felt it was destined to stay private. He said it was "erotic" but decided against it, as it was too similar to the Mishima soundtrack that he had just finished. He chose "Freezing" and "Lightning" which were, as he put it, "both static songs which take place in an apocalyptic setting." He felt they were a good balance to each other. I was so happy and never forgot it.

I saw *Einstein on the Beach* in 1984, at the BAM revival. I was there for the opening night as I recall, sitting with Nancy Jeffries. The show is so long – four and a half hours – that people in the audience brought food to join in with the cast on stage. When they opened their meals, so did we. We brought sushi. Before the show even began, I saw a young man a few rows ahead of mine, with his head thrown back, fast asleep. "That's Philip's son," Nancy whispered to me. The event was thrilling and the air crackled with anticipation and humor. I bought a poster of the event, which stayed on the wall of my boyfriend's apartment right up until the day I left, and it was the backdrop of our lives there.

Two years later I endured a stormy breakup with that boyfriend, and moved into my own studio apartment. I became obsessed with Philip Glass's *Mishima* album, as it was so passionate and sorrowful. I slept on the floor on a futon and spent many hours alone, dancing to the soundtrack. It seemed to express perfectly what I felt in that moment, a sense of anguish. I feel Philip Glass's influence in the song "Solitude Standing" itself, in the minor key and the circular repetitions. Later I asked if he had been feeling anything intensely while he wrote the soundtrack. No, he said, not particularly – he wrote it the same way he wrote all his music.

At some point in my mid-twenties, I dreamed of him, possibly more than once. Under his watchful eye, in the dreams I found I could do things as a dancer that were incredibly difficult in real life – I could turn *en pointe* slowly and perfectly, sailing around the circumference of a circle, balanced and yet constantly moving. I have never forgotten these dreams and the sense of being lifted up into a kind of difficult perfection while under his influence.

Philip invited me to the first Tibet House Benefit in New York in 1988, an event with Philip, Richard Gere, Spalding Gray, Laurie Anderson, and myself. Unfortunately this led to an argument with my stepfather who said I should not have supported an alternate type of Buddhism to the one I practice. It caused a deep rift, and I told Philip I probably shouldn't do another one to keep the peace in the family. As a consequence I was invited one more time and when

I refused, I understandably was never asked to do another one. My stepfather passed away more than ten years ago. I had intended to support the concert as a cultural event, not as a religious one. I regret this now and feel I should have accepted Philip's invitation. I love the pictures from this event in particular – the mood was festive and the company very stimulating.

The idea in giving Philip the lyrics for *Songs from Liquid Days* was that eventually he would repay me by doing a string arrangement of one of my songs. This came to pass on the *Days of Open Hand* album, from 1990, on my song "50-50 Chance," a song about an attempted suicide by a young woman. Phil faxed me the arrangement and it got stuck in the transmission, causing the musical staff lines to bend, twist, and melt down the page like lines of taffy. I still have it in a scrapbook as a piece of art.

"The melody stands for the girl herself, and the eighth notes are the machines keeping her alive," he informed me briskly. I thought it was a strangely literal way of writing music but then, he thought singer/songwriters had odd ways of writing too. "Do you know that Paul Simon once wrote a song about a photograph and it was a real photograph from his life?" he asked me.

He is generous to other young developing artists, such as I was. Many Sundays he hosted brunches at his townhouse celebrating younger composers like Nico Muhly, whom he still promotes. His work ethic is formidable. Once he came to a Christmas party I threw in a huge loft downtown in the early 90s. He came at 6pm – sat with me, ate his dinner, and left before any of the other guests arrived, saying it was perfect, and he had to get up early to compose! I admire his adherence to his schedule. Composing in the morning, every morning, then business in the afternoon, and family events and friends at night.

I remembered the episode where the *New York Times* in a review of *Ahknaten* said, "Mr. Glass's works… stand to music as the sentence "See Spot run" stands to literature." I asked him – did negative criticism ever bother him? "Oh yes," he said. "Once I was so bothered by a critic that I couldn't work for a whole hour." I have remembered this line often, humorously.

In 1994 Philip asked me to sing the final song of a film called *Jenipapo* by Monique Gardenberg. The lyrics were a poem by Antonio Cicero, the Brazilian poet and writer. My daughter Ruby had just been born, and I felt physically altered. My ribcage had been opened by about two inches all around from the pregnancy. Philip was in a good mood in the studio. "Suzanne! You have three good notes, and you'll be pleased to know that I put all three of them in this song for you." I was pleased, actually, and I felt this song marked a fuller, richer kind of singing for me.

Around this time he asked if I would interview him for NPR. I asked him how he chose his characters to put in his operas? Einstein, Martin Luther King, Gandhi. "Oh, that's easy," he said. "It's their ideologies."

This was in the mid-90s – Madeleine Albright had yet to be named Secretary of State, which was a turning point for women in roles of leadership in the US. I began to wish we had more works of theater that featured women and their ideologies. I suppose there are always Joan of Arc, and the poetry of Emily

Dickenson, but when I wrote a play about the life and work of the author Carson McCullers I made sure to feature her ideology of agape love – brotherly love, love of humanity. So Philip has influenced my work in many ways.

I consider him a friend and an early influence. Being around him is always challenging and entertaining, as his mind is intense and his humor unexpected. I love his social awareness and his expansive nature – for example, he told me once that he tours often because he is from Baltimore, and no one ever came there on tour. He cares about art and wants to make sure it is available to those who might not otherwise be exposed to it. I haven't seen him much since his biography *Words without Music* came out, but I think it is an excellent mirror of how his mind works and a beautiful telling of his life. I really recommend it.

He was very kind one day in giving my daughter's friend Avery an interview at a sound check for "Philip Glass and Friends at the City Winery." I was one of the friends that day, and we sat and listened as he told Avery about his journey to India and how it affected his spirituality and his music.

One of the most recent times I saw him, I accompanied him to a benefit out in Brooklyn. He was performing a bit of *Einstein on the Beach* and asked me to read the part of the Narrator in the knee play at the very end, the same part I will be playing with the Belgian contemporary orchestra The Ictus Ensemble this fall and next year. They approached me, saying they wanted someone who was a musician for the part, not an actress. I don't expect to be singing, but I am sure I will be playful in the approach. I haven't mentioned this to Philip yet, as I haven't seen him recently! Philip was and remains a treasured part of my life.

Suzanne Vega
October 2018
New York City

Two Finnish composers reminisce

Juhani Nuorvala
(Composer and composition lecturer, Sibelius Academy, University of the Arts, Helsinki)

I hold in my hands the 1979 issue of *Stereo Review*, vol. 43, no. 3. After all these years, I still have it. On page 100 is Eric Salzman's review of the Tomato recording of *Einstein on the Beach*. This two-column article had an overwhelming effect on my life and musical worldview; this effect continues still to this day. Leafing through the yellowing pages, I revisit advertisements for macho men's whisky, cigarette ads, pictures of enormous cassette decks, and a story about a revolutionary recording technique titled *The Dawn of the Digital*. But the text on page 100 describes a work of art that has managed to retain its freshness and radical aura of novelty decade after decade.

The article is an ecstatic account – the word "magic[al]" appears five times – of this strange music, in which small, simple patterns are repeated and gradually varied for the length of four complete LP records. Back then, in my late teens,

I had already listened to contemporary concert music for some years; I was planning to start professional studies in music and had begun composing. In high school, which I was just about to finish, I'd written essays about Berg and Stockhausen. I was aware that there was such a thing as repetitive music, but only from having read about it in some books and having caught a glimpse of Steve Reich's ensemble in an episode of Yehudi Menuhin's TV series. But when I received the album that I'd ordered after reading Salzman's review and put *Einstein* on the record player, what I heard shocked me. It was as if this music was from another planet! It insistently repeated the simplest elements of tonal music: arpeggios and scales. It was comprised almost exclusively of materials deemed obsolete! Everything about it was wrong! And it was seductive, hypnotic, exciting, and moving. It filled the room as a bubbling fabric and billowed into the space as a lush wall of sound, simultaneously hectic and in suspended animation. I immersed myself in the changes in the repeated patterns; I dwelled in the layers and listened to the relations within the superposed modules. The sudden changes of texture and harmony at the start of new sections felt earth-shattering.

That LP box of mine soon passed from curious composer to composer. Magnus Lindberg reported having listened the whole of it three times in a row. There was a seminar at the Sibelius Academy where students listened to the LPs. I finally got the worn and tattered box back from professor Einojuhani Rautavaara, who later went on to quote the sleeve notes in his own essay on opera. (At the composers' seminar, he'd mused that in this music one hears *Zeitgeist.*) Even so, Finnish composers remained mostly immune to the temptations of minimalism. For me, it became a lasting partner.

I am in the process of writing a piano piece for pianist Nicolas Horvath's *Hommage à Glass* project. It's going to be a little fantasy meditation on the Spaceship chords in *Einstein*, that five-chord progression about which the composer has said that there's something strange, because it never fails to lift the audience to its feet.[1]

I was a tad disappointed when professor John Richardson confirmed from Mr. Glass that the minor major-seventh chord (FAbCE) in both organ parts, rehearsal no. 64/66, full score, p. 213, is a misprint. As Kyle Gann and I noted, this chord would have cleverly combined E, the resolution of the leading tone, to the F minor tonic chord; this would have been, to my knowledge, the first instance, after Glass's student works, of his use of bitonality, a phenomenon that would become important in his later works.[2] Admittedly, that misprinted chord would have sounded somewhat peculiar, but I think I'll put it in my own piece, anyway.

1   Cagne, Cole & Caras, Tracy, *Soundpieces*. USA, The Scarecrow Press, 1982, 226.
2   Kyle Gann, "Prepping *Einstein* for the Dissection Table," www.artsjournal.com/postclassi c/2008/03/prepping_einstein_for_the_diss.html, Accessed: June 8, 2016.

The magic of the *Spaceship* finale is, no doubt, created by its hyperactive avalanche of *tutti* sound, as well as the constant changes in rhythm, but the chords themselves are important, too. The composer's own analysis of the chord progression in the sleeve notes, while technically correct, has never really satisfied me. I don't hear the A major chord as a major chord on the lowered fourth degree in F minor, as he suggests. Rather, this is a magic trick made possible by the division of the octave into 12 equal steps: the roots of the first three chords form an augmented triad, a symmetrical structure that Glass would explore further in works to come. Even though discovering Indian music proved a pivotal source of inspiration for both Glass and his West Coast colleagues, La Monte Young and Terry Riley, unlike them, he has never shown much interest in tuning systems other than that of our standard equal temperament. The kind of progression-by-major-thirds of the Spaceship chords wouldn't even be possible in other tuning systems; in fact, it's based on 12 equal divisions. These kinds of chord progressions and modulations, foreign to diatonic logic, became common in the nineteenth century, the time when 12-tone equal temperament became established. They are typical of Schubert, one of Mr. Glass's favorite composers. For the Romantics, they evoke "the strange, magical and inscrutable," as Richard Cohn, a specialist on the subject, writes in his *Audacious Euphony*.[3] Perhaps it is no coincidence that a chord progression based on the augmented triad represents a spaceship – science fiction – in *Einstein on the Beach*, as it would again two decades later in the opera *The Voyage*.

I haven't yet decided what I'll call my piano piece. I'm tempted to steal a title from a chapter in Cohn's book, *Hexatonic Trance*, but perhaps I should, equally truthfully, title it *The Five Chords That Changed My Life*.

Petri Kuljuntausta
(Composer, sound artist, writer, and musicologist based in Helsinki)

When the *North Star* album was released in 1977, I borrowed it from a friend. Philip Glass was then an unknown name to me and I didn't know what to expect, but as the album was released by Virgin, a well-known British progressive music label, I was curious to hear it. I listened to the album twice and copied it to a C-cassette for further listening. From that moment on I was fascinated by the music of Philip Glass and I bought almost all of his albums that were released over the next 15 years.

In the mid-1970s I discovered the music of Tangerine Dream, Mike Oldfield, David Bedford, Klaus Schulze, Peter Michael Hamel, Ash Ra Tempel, Tonto's Expanding Head Band, and other synthesizer and progressive albums produced by labels such as Virgin and Charisma. I was also fascinated by the piano improvisations of Keith Jarrett and the music of other artists on the ECM label. This was an important time in my musical development. I was like a

3   Cohn, Richard, *Audacious Euphony*, Oxford, Oxford University Press, 2012, x.

music magnet; when visiting local record shops weekly, my record collection expanded with each visit by several new albums. I was eager to learn from different musical styles and the cultures of which they were a part.

To my innocent ears, Glass's music was in much the same category as synthesizer music based on repetitive sequencer patterns. But the music of Glass was also different from what had come before: it was strictly composed from start to finish, and it was fast and virtuosic. Most of the other music I listened to at the time was based on improvisation and more or less open structures. I didn't know then that Glass's background was in the classical tradition. I learned that a little later, when I began studying the Western classical music tradition. *Victor's Lament* and *Ik-ook* from *North Star* were the pieces that affected me most profoundly. These are solo pieces where Glass himself overdubbed all the keyboard parts when recording.

I played guitar and developed my improvisational skills, and played in a band. But when I realized that it was possible to compose using multitrack technology, I bought a reel-to-reel tape machine and started to experiment with different instruments, acoustic and electronic, composing works for the multitrack recorder. I remember locking myself in my home studio every weekend after school, and spending hour after hour composing and recording. The instruments I used were acoustic and electric guitars, piano, flute, bells, rattles, and percussions – later synthesizers. I can't say how much Glass influenced me or could this be heard in my early recordings for the late-1970s and early 1980s, but it certainly affected my approach to composition.

When I first heard *Einstein on the Beach*, I remember thinking this is the same Glass that I already knew, but there was something new about this music too. I recall that I had problems with the work, such as how to explain the vocal parts in the opening section: the recitation of numbers. I was familiar with the South-Indian konnakol style. I heard it live for the first time in 1978 in a concert by One Truth Band, a jazz band in which the guitarist John McLaughlin and the Indian violin player L. Shankar collaborated. The group performed konnakol vocal improvisation as an encore. Konnakol is the art of performing percussion syllables vocally. But the vocalizations in *Einstein* were different. The recitation of numbers here sounded strange. Just numbers without meaning, and no story to tell? And why Einstein, on the beach? What does it all mean? I started to understand what *conceptual art* means. I liked mathematics, numbers, and counting in school, but I didn't know then how important a role numbers would play in my later life. The theory of music analysis I formulated in my master's thesis in musicology was built around the logic of change (as theorized by the philosopher Georg Henrik von Wright). I like to organize pieces of information and make chronological lists. I perceived some strange connection between these ideas and the numerical basis of Glass's work.

The rhythmical world and the changing meters of *Einstein* were another aspect that caught my attention immediately. I was familiar with unusual time signatures; it is second nature to me to count different time signatures in my head, especially those based on the number seven, despite the fact that I rarely compose rhythmical music these days. Since I was a teenager, I have admired John McLaughlin's compositional style where East meets West in his use of unusual meters, like 5, 7, 11, 15, and 20. But in jazz music, the repetitive structure provides the foundation for improvisation and the meter does not typically change during performances.

In *Einstein*, you cannot count the meter as it is constantly changing. There is no fixed time signature, no regular metrical repetition in this music. Since I couldn't follow the music and count the meter, this was initially a huge problem to my counting mind. Finally I understood that there is no sense in counting the meter; just forget it and let the flow of the music carry you away.

Einstein is very close to me in many ways. It is metrically complex and linear; I like good bass lines, ostinatos and contrapuntal layers (over harmonic approaches). The music is rhythmic and the sound of the Ensemble is fresh, sparkling. The string section is at the hub of much Western classical music, but here the strings do not dominate, nor do they create heavy textures – the music is cheery. It is fast, percussive and tonal, which is untypical of contemporary Western music and of Glass's generation of composers.

Glassworks, *The Photographer*, *Koyaanisqatsi*... I collected albums and studied them. I also discovered the music of Steve Reich (his releases on ECM Records) and Terry Riley. *Coming Together* (1971) by Frederic Rzewski was also an important work to me. In 1985, I performed *Clapping Music* with friends.

I understood that it was the objective nature of Glass's music that fascinated me. It wasn't so much a question of self-expression in the composition work, as would have been the case in romanticism and later movements, but the creation of rhythmical pitch systems that gave direction to an unfolding process. That was my interpretation.

While studying music, composing multitrack works, and playing jazz gigs in the 1990s, I began to study Glass's music more intensively from a new standpoint. Around this time, I was looking for a new direction in my own music. I was searching for objectivity in the music. I thought the musical materials should initiate the process, and my intentions should only support the process.

I composed minimal music for my group, the Petri Kuljuntausta Ensemble. The group consisted of a string quartet, winds, guitar, piano and synthesizers, double bass, and two percussion players. I was deeply influenced by *Akhnaten* (1983) during those years. I had a chance to study the score of the opera, and many other scores by Glass, with the help of my good friend, professor John Richardson. One of the works that I composed for my group was a string quartet entitled *Chain* (1994), in the time signature 7/8. This is perhaps one of three compositions of mine that were unquestionably influenced by Glass. I additionally made an alternative version based on the first part of the work. This is an arrangement for string quartet and drum machine. The drum machine plays a drum'n'bass beat that the quartet was synced to. In fact, the musical style drum'n'bass would become established only later; the style was then called "jungle." *Enigma* (1994), a composition in several parts, was another work I composed for the Ensemble. The opening part is for solo piano, and here too Glass's influence is clear. The full ensemble elaborates on this same music in the parts that follow and some overdubbing was needed to play additional lines.

In 1996, I started to combine the techniques from this work with Reichian phase-shifting techniques and devised a new compositional strategy to take this to a new level. First I made a program for a sampler, and later I adapted this for computer, and since then I have composed phase-shifting process pieces regularly. Some of these works can be heard on my *Momentum* (2003) album. A few of these early works are still unreleased, including *I Wouldn't Do Nothing but Hurt Myself* (1998), which is based on spoken passages from the film *Thin Blue Line* (directed by Errol Morris, with music by Philip Glass). The latest work, entitled *1918* (2013) from the *Emergence* (2013) album is based on multi-layered phase-shifting sounds. The phase-shifting process in this work is played out on different layers and using different sound samples.

Around the mid-1990s, I moved to the field of Sound Art and Electronic Music and left my groups, both jazz and minimalist, behind me. However, despite the change in musical materials and instruments, I compose electronic works that could be connected to the term minimalism. I can't say if minimalism is any more the best possible term for what I do, but basically I am keen to explore the basic ingredients of music. As a sound artist, I have often reduced sound materials to their most fundamental level. Many of my recent sound installations are based on a single sound frequency, its repetition and intervening silences.

My early experiences of *Einstein* and other works by Glass influenced my development as a composer, sound artist, and musician profoundly. Looking back from the standpoint of the present day, I can easily draw a line back to those years when I heard this music for the first time. Decades has passed, but *Einstein* still sounds like stunning, timeless music!

May 3, 2016
Helsinki

Rehearsing *Einstein on the Beach*: Philip Glass and Robert Wilson[4]

Tom Johnson
(composer and writer on music based in Paris)

There hasn't been much in the papers about Robert Wilson since *A Letter for Queen Victoria* and *The Dollar Value of Man* last season, but his Spring Street

---

4   This text was previously published in Tom Johnson's book *The Voice of New Music: New York City 1972–1982, A collection of articles originally published in the Village Voice.* A digital edition of this book is available at: http://tvonm.editions75.com/index.html#toc. Below is a direct link to the article (dated January 26, 1976), which is reprinted in this book courtesy of the author: http://tvonm.editions75.com/index.html#tochttp://tvonm.editions75.com/articles/1976/rehearsing-einstein-on-the-beach-philip-glass-and-robert-wilson.html, Accessed: January 2, 2019.

studio is as busy as ever. From ten in the morning until seven at night every day, a company of 26 has been preparing a new work, tentatively called *Einstein on the Beach*. The first performances of the work, in Germany and France, will not begin until August, so it is far too early to say anything final about what it will be like. But since theater is a new genre for Philip Glass, who has already spent about a year composing the music for *Einstein*, it seemed worthwhile to drop by one afternoon and find out what is going on.

Glass's approach in the new piece turns out to be a fairly predictable outgrowth of the work he has been doing during the past few years with amplified winds and organs, and his regular ensemble will be carrying much of the show. In fact, the piece which the group premiered last spring, under the title *Another Look at Harmony*, is included in this score. But in addition there will be sections for solo violin, others with vocal solos, and others featuring a 12-voice chorus. The five hours of music will be divided into a number of shorter segments, generally alternating between large ensemble pieces and smaller groups. Much of the music will be carried by the chorus, which will apparently be onstage playing roles most of the time.

The vocal lines in Glass's choral music employ the same kind of rhythmic modules as his instrumental parts. The little melodies repeat over and over, shifting to slightly new patterns maybe once every 10 to 30 seconds. The only lyrics are "do re mi" and "one two three," which are used simply to articulate the melodies. Most of the time the music is diatonic, though there are a few chromatic passages.

It's hard work for 12 singers to keep together on such fast rhythms, but judging from what I heard, and considering that they have several months of rehearsal time left, they just might be as crisp and unified as Glass's regular ensemble by the time the production begins its European run in August. The curious thing about this chorus, however, is that Glass has selected thin, relatively untrained voices for his group, despite the plans to perform in a large hall without choral amplification. The singers were barely holding their own against the loud electric organ Glass was playing at the rehearsal, and knowing the kind of high volumes he normally uses in concerts, I couldn't imagine how he was going to achieve a balance in this piece.

Glass says that he is interested in the natural resonance of the voice, and wants to avoid soloistic qualities, since he rarely writes solos. He went on to explain that trained voices, working with supported tone and nominal vibrato, never blend very well. I asked him if he had heard any groups like the Robert Shaw Chorale or the Gregg Smith Singers lately, and he said he hadn't. In any case, the composer was quite confident about his group, and assured me that they would be producing two or three times their present volume by the time the show opens.

Glass's way of working with Wilson appears to involve the same kind of give and take which one normally finds in collaborations where both artists respect each other, and neither is determined to dominate. But it was curious to learn how they got started when they first began working together about a year ago. Glass told me that Wilson did a lot of preliminary sketches of what he expected various scenes to look like, and that Glass began working out musical ideas based largely on these visualizations.

I was not surprised to learn this, because it had always seemed to me that Wilson is basically a visual artist, and that his feelings for the exact placement of people and objects on the stage, his color sense, and his sets are the most fundamental aspects of his work. His scenes always become animated paintings for me, and I have the feeling that if we ever have any really useful criticism of Wilson's work, it is going to come from an art critic, or at least someone who really understands surrealism, Hopper, O'Keefe, and so on.

Meanwhile, back at the rehearsal, the group was completing a short physical warm-up, and Glass was asking me if I would like to sing along on a section they were about to rehearse. I jumped at the chance. I'd been hearing Glass's pieces for some time and had often wondered what it would be like to try to read one of his parts. It is obvious just from listening to the long repetitions and quick pattern shifts that there has to be a lot of counting involved. But what kind of counting? Is it tricky, difficult counting that requires heavy concentration? Is it dull drudgerous counting that bores the hell out of you? Is it the kind of counting that can alter your consciousness, as in so many yoga and Zen exercises?

It's really none of the above, though it's a little like each. Let's say we're working on pattern number 65, and our part is something like "fa si la si." And let's say that there is a little "4" off to the right side, meaning that after we've sung "fa si la si" four times we've completed one sequence. And let's say that there is another "4" above the music, meaning that we have to sing four sequences before going on to pattern 66.

If you followed that, you're probably thinking, as I did, "Glass, can't you multiply? Why didn't you just say to do it sixteen times instead of going through all this four-times-four stuff?" And if you are pretty headstrong about your opinion, as I was, you would decide to do it your own way, and the downbeat would come, and everyone would start charging through their quick little patterns, and everything would be fine until you discovered that you weren't sure whether you were on the twelfth repetition or the fourteenth. And meanwhile the music would be going by so fast that every time you tried to figure it out you would just become more confused.

I decided I'd better try it Glass's way, the 1976/how-to-perform-john-cage time around, and for some reason it was a lot easier. It still took a lot of concentration, but somehow the challenge seemed fun, a little like keeping track of how many times the runners have gone around the track, or something like that. It felt good as the sequences went by, feeling the fours within the fours, or the twos within the eights, or whatever, and getting ready for the 1976/how-to-perform-john-cage shift. And sometimes I could make it through three or four patterns without losing count.

The problem is that a single segment might involve 10 or 20 patterns, and there are an awful lot of choral segments in *Einstein on the Beach*, all of which Glass expects the singers to memorize. But of course, every time I started thinking about something like that, I lost the count again.

I enjoyed the challenge of the whole thing, and I guess I was doing all right, because during the 1976/how-to-perform-john-cage break, Glass offered me a job. I figured he was kidding, but by the time he'd mentioned it three times, complimenting my sight-reading and complaining that they really did need another good musician on the tenor line, I decided I really ought to consider the prospects.

The rehearsal atmosphere seemed quite pleasant, the money would be adequate, and the months in Europe wouldn't be hard to take. But then I started thinking about how I'd have to do the four sequences of the three-note pattern four times and the eight sequences of the four-note pattern two times, and about how it would all have to be memorized, and I realized that I'd probably never be able to muster up the kind of dedication the task would require.

Two steps forwards but three steps back, and then one step forwards again – Peter Greenaway interviewed by John Richardson[5])

I want to start by asking you to talk about your longstanding interest in the composer Philip Glass and musical minimalism

I'm about to make a new opera with him, on Hieronymus Bosch.

Really? And one of your Four Composers *films was about him. You've collaborated a great deal with minimalist composers and I'd be interested to learn more from your perspective. We're currently editing a book on* Einstein on the Beach *and I was wondering if you have any views on that opera and any influence it might have had on you. It seems that there's a strong affinity.*

Bob Wilson asked me to make the definitive film of *Einstein on the Beach* way back, about 15 years ago, but we could never raise the money. My access to all these people was of course through Michael Nyman. Michael Nyman and I met when he was a music student and I was still at art school. We met through a third person, I think, and we decided to see what indeed we could do. I had a great interest in minimal music, I'd mainly heard Steve Reich rather than Philip Glass. I suppose the first *Einstein on the Beach* parts I heard were the 1-2, 1-2, 1-2-3-3-4-4, which of course I was deeply intrigued by, because it's obviously extraordinary music from which to edit and structure. It's a gift for film editors. I was a film editor at that time. So that's how it began.

Then Michael Nyman and I, we planned a whole series of cartoons, which the world has never seen. I still have the drawings. I think Michael might still have the music. And then he made a band called The Campiello Band, which used to play at the National Theatre, which is right next door to the National Film Theatre, beneath Waterloo Bridge in London. And we decided, I suppose

5   Interview conducted on August 14th 2014 in Turku

our first big collaboration was on *The Draftsman's Contract*. And then I think Michael was the pianist for the Steve Reich band. They traveled around Europe doing concerts. Then he created his own Michael Nyman Band, and then I think we did five feature films. We did a lot of other stuff as well. I think the last thing we would have done would have been *Prospero's Books*. And then we parted terms and I've certainly worked with a lot of other composers. I've worked with Glen Branca and Wim Mertens. I was always fascinated by minimalist music of the second generation and third generation. Now I'm working with Giovanni Sollima …, who has just written the music – we're just going to do a remake of Visconti's *Death in Venice* [*Food of Love*], and he's already written all the music, and we're going into production probably next spring. So a whole series of post-minimalist, first generation, second generation, third generation, fourth generation, I suppose we're almost into fifth generation minimalists now. Not that the original minimalists want to be called that anymore. It's highly sensitive subject matter. I suppose it's a bit like impressionism. There were very few painters prepared to be called impressionists. And I suppose minimalism was originally given as a sort of insult, a derogatory statement, like so many statements in art. Baroque was an insult, Rococo was an insult. All created by musicologists like you. Like minimalism.

Michael Nyman actually claims to be responsible for that one!

Well, it's a whole area of debate and apocrypha.

But, of course, you share many of the priorities of the minimalists. You spoke today about an interest in non-narrativity, in awareness of the present moment. Philip Glass spoke about similar things when I met him in Amsterdam recently. About attention and being present in the moment. There are also questions about frame of reference, which is important to your work. Einstein on the Beach *was intended to be an open-ended piece of work.*

Well, I enjoyed it because it was basically non-narrative. At last. I basically think opera is quite stupid, as I've suggested. Its slavery to narrative is a terrible, terrible penance that really holds you down and traps you. I think Messiaen said there were really only five good operas, even though there must have been several million written since, what, the 1450s?

How do you feel about working with a preexisting composition?

Sometimes that's happened, but what I like to do and what we did with Michael, often we'd say we need 17 pieces of music, and it's entirely up to you what you do, but you must give me absolute freedom to use them as I see fit. But I don't want anyone illustrating my themes because they always get them wrong, and the dream goes wrong and they become illustrative, and illustrative music, I really hate. But then often all sorts of interesting things happen. There's always a nice sense of irony about Michael's music and I was always interested in that. Music seldom is ironic but he had a great ability to be able to do that. So he would write an extraordinarily fast and furious positive piece and I would use it on a deep melancholy phenomenon, so we could play opposites in counterpoint, you know *the mood*, as it were – where the appearance of the imagery counterpointed the use of the music. There was a lot of that going on, and it gave us a certain nice sort of sharp edge sometimes, because I think that musically the best collaboration we ever did was on the *A Draftsman's Contract*.

I agree. So what would you say the music brings to imagery. I have my own theory about this and listening to your talk there are some similarities between our thinking. It maybe has to do with the aestheticization of images, distance from the narrative and a kind of sensory heightenedness.

Yes, and the excitement, though I think opera is really incredibly stupid. It has an ability to associate notions of high drama and melodrama in a way that probably nothing else can do. Which I think is one of the reasons why it's so intimately associated with misogyny as well. Sadly.

In traditional opera that's certainly true. I wanted to talk about frames as well. You mentioned Derrida in your talk and the big thing for Derrida was the idea that the frame doesn't only define what's inside the frame, it also …

Indicates what's outside the frame. Yes, that interests me.

And, of course, you're one of the pioneers in that respect, your use of multiple frames, embedded frames. But still there aren't many people working in that way. The music video director Chris Milk is one: he works with new technologies and video art, installation art, that sort of thing. But surprisingly few people are working in that way.

[These days] we have a whole series of new tools and actually very few people are using them. It feels like someone ignoring the saxophone when it was invented, for example. Which seems to be very curious to me, but cinema, as I suggested, is very old fashioned and jealous of what it feels its position is, and it's very slow to change, and always believes that by sort of fiddling with I suppose the externals, like the rattle and excitement of 3D – and once I've punched you three times on the nose, the whole thing is over.

It becomes gimmicky.

It doesn't do anything to the syntax and synopsis and grammar and vocabulary of cinema whatsoever.

But we're living in an age of multiple screens, we have smart phones, tablets, computer screens.

But who is actually using them? Why does the devil have all the best tools? It really is rather curious.

The technology is there but its use is mostly unreflective. Or is there a new, reflexive digital revolution happening somewhere?

Well I think the first cinematic masterpiece is Eisenstein's *Strike*. He was 26 years old when he made it and it's an extraordinary film for a very young man. Cinema began in 1895, so let's think – it was made in about 1924, so it takes nearly 30 years to make the first cinematic masterpiece. So that suggests it takes about 30 years for our sensibilities about a new medium to mature. I believe the digital revolution in visual terms began in 1983, and '83 to 2014 [the year of the interview], that's longer than 30 years, but we're still waiting in a sense for the particular Eisenstein of our times to come together. I very arrogantly made a huge project called the *Tulse Luper Suitcases*, which I thought was the ideal phenomenon for the information age, but it was very expensive to make and I was going to make 92 episodes based on the atomic number of uranium, though we ran out of money and ended up making 14. But we were going to make a library of books, we made a play, we made an opera, which turned up in Frankfurt, we made an internet game. I certainly wanted it associated with all the new formats. And I'm a VJ. We presented it around the world as a VJ show, so I wasn't just interested in the classic forms, I wanted it to be relevant to what the internet generation is interested in. It still goes on, I still love VJing. But it's an extraordinary privilege, I do operas, stage plays, make all different types of cinema, webmaster. But it's still good to look over your shoulder at old art forms like opera and see if you can still breathe some life into them, but certainly to also deeply engage in what is new.

Your work is known for referencing the past, the Renaissance, the Baroque, bring-ing all of that into the present day. What do you think we can learn from those styles? Obviously, there are formal things, but is there more than that?

Nothing is complete, nothing is finished, of course, there's always something more to say. (...) Two things are really interesting: periods of lack of cultural con-fidence, like mannerism, for example, is really fascinating. So the periods of cultural confidence like Michelangelo, Raphael, and Leonardo da Vinci, they are so goddam confident that there's no way in. I think Michelangelo is dif-ferent because that's the beginnings of mannerism, but the other two seem to lock us out because they're so perfect. They've said everything. But of the triumvirate, if you pick out Michelangelo and follow that, there's a huge amount to still be considered and discussed. And I suppose the other period would be Rococo, again, which is often trivialized and not considered impor-tant. So there's that period between the *Ancien Régime* and romanticism, to which England has a lot to offer. I mean people like William Blake are not realized for how incredible they were. People go for Hogarth, who was a bril-liant illustrator, but they forget about Blake. I suppose in some ways we're in a period of mannerism again, associated with the coming Baroque, although some people think it's already gone. But for Michelangelo, Raphael, and da Vinci, you could say Stravinsky, Corbusier, and Picasso. They seem to have done everything in a holistic way. They set off so many new heirs and possi-bilities that there's an awful lot to reconsider. It seems to me that history's one long continuum. When we talk about the past, that's not quite the right way to talk about it, especially in terms of really, really first-rate art – it's always, always, always present tense. For me, I've only just rediscovered the most banal of composers, who is Vivaldi. I think Vivaldi is absolutely extraordinary! And incredibly prolific. We're remaking *Death [in Venice]* [here Greenaway accidentally refers to his own *Death in the Seine*], and I'm replacing Visconti's Mahler with Vivaldi – of course, because he's an ideal venetian composer, and I think some of those bassoon concertos are astronomically amazing. But, of course, Vivaldi's played in airports like … muzak, so you pick up a phone for an insurance office, and there it is again.

The Four Seasons *has in some ways been his worst enemy.*

They've somehow made him totally banal because he's somehow been overused for the wrong reasons.

There's a line from surrealism to your work that is often neglected. Fredric Jameson called postmodernism surrealism without the unconscious, although I'm not sure that's entirely true. Certainly, this could be said of Glass and Einstein on the Beach. *In your films, too, the plot lines are not naturalistic but manneristic, there's an interest in collage aesthetics, attention to the sensory, a style that is texturally rich and evocative. For me there are clear affinities.*

I've been mostly interested lately in Eisenstein, Vertov, Pudovkin, and all those people. That's a whole area that needs to be re-examined, and is being re-examined. There's a brand-new generation of Russians now who are beginning to dig deeper and deeper, and that's really fascinating.

When you watch the Russian formalists now it does seem surprisingly relevant. I can see the continuity. The interest in rhythmic editing, the musicality of editing, also seems very today.

People are starting to realize now how brilliant Eisenstein was as an editor, and all of the films that he wasn't allowed to edit, don't have that brilliant touch that he had, his sense of organization, even tying up with the notion of structure, structuralism, and so on. It really is interesting to have taken two steps forwards but three steps back, and then take one step forward again. There's an awful lot to be reconsidered – it's really very exciting.

Part 4

Operatic machines and their ghosts

9　Leaving and re-entering

Punctuating *Einstein on the Beach*

Sander van Maas

Artists like Duchamp were so prescient here – the idea that the piece of work is not finished until the audience comes to it and adds their own interpretation, and what the piece of art is about is the grey space in the middle. That grey space in the middle is what the 21st century is going to be all about.

– David Bowie[1]

Wandering

With regard to performances of *Einstein on the Beach*, Philip Glass and Robert Wilson expressed that they would like audiences to walk in and out of the venue at liberty. The original program note reads, "As *Einstein on the Beach* is performed without intermission, the audience is invited to leave and re-enter the auditorium quietly as desired."[2] A review of the 2017 production of the work directed by Kay Voges in Dortmund shows how this invitation is often understood in purely practical terms, as an invitation "to leave the auditorium during the performance at liberty, in order to drink something or to go to the bathroom."[3] As an intervention in conventional opera performance practice, however, the invitation should be understood for its artistic value. Although large-scale works commonly have intermissions for practical or economic reasons, often external to the work, intermissions also fulfill a function related to its internal layout and structure. Intermissions belong to the dramaturgy of the performed work, which they follow,

1　David Bowie, quoted from a BBC Newsnight interview with Jeremy Paxman in December 1999. Online at: https://www.theguardian.com/technology/2016/jan/11/david-bowie-bowienet-isp-internet, Accessed: March 20, 2018.

2　*Einstein on the Beach: An Opera in Four Acts*, program notes, online at www.laopera.org/documentslao/press/1314/lao.einstein-iw-f-web.pdf, Accessed: November 18, 2016. "Einstein broke all the rules of opera. It was in four interconnected acts and five hours long, with no intermissions (the audience was invited to wander in and out at liberty during performances)." Tim Page, from liner notes to *Einstein on the Beach*, CD, 1993, Nonesuch 79323-2.

3　Honke Rambow, "Premiere in Dortmund: Einstein on the Beach von Philip Glass," blogpost, 24 April 2017, online at https://www.ruhrbarone.de/premiere-in-dortmund-einstein-on-the-beach-von-philip-glass/141771, Accessed: March 20, 2018.

shape, or express. As such, they represent a collective and synchronized form of *(inter-)punctuation*, to which devices such as applause, claque, vocal response and walk-outs, also belong.[4] The decision of the makers of *Einstein* not to have any intermissions – or, viewed from a different perspective, to de-collectivize and de-synchronize the concept of intermission – is significant in that it raises questions about the work's implied regime of spectating, both in light of Glass's and Wilson's previous attempts to create different settings for the experience of art, and in light of the conventional opera venues the work was intended for. As I intend to show in this essay, the invitation suggests how *Einstein on the Beach* navigates the "grey space in the middle" (Bowie), between stage and audience, by carving out a new and still to-be-explored space for spectatorship and listenership.

The creative context *Einstein on the Beach* was conceived in – notably in the experimental performance art community of The Kitchen in New York, which brought together makers from theater, dance, music, visual arts, poetry, and per-formance – was rich in ideas about the relation between art and life.[5] Some of these ideas involved a rethinking of the "proportion" between the scale or duration of an art work and its experience, experimenting with unusually long durations.[6] Wilson's breakthrough work, *Deafman Glance* from 1970, for instance, lasted about seven hours, including intermissions.[7] It was based on his chance encounter with a deaf boy, who became his adopted child and performed many times, star-ring as himself, in this theater work. After *Deafman Glance*, in 1972, Wilson cre-ated a work for the Sixth Shiraz-Persepolis Arts Festival in Persia involving some 700 people from local communities and lasting seven days uninterrupted (entitled *KA MOUNTAIN AND GUARDenia TERRACE: a story about a family and some*

---

4   See in particular the conceptual exploration of punctuation practices by Peter Szendy, *À coups de points: La ponctuation comme expérience*, Paris, Minuit, 2013.

5   On the downtown experimental performance scene at The Kitchen, which included the artists and initiatives Lucinda Childs, Robert Rauschenberg, The Living Theater, Richard Foreman's Ontological Hysterical Theater, Trisha Brown, Meredith Monk, The Open Theater, Philip Glass, and John Cage, among others, see Sally Banes, *Subversive Expectations: Performance Art and Paratheater in New York, 1976–85*, Ann Arbor, The University of Michigan Press, 1998.

6   In music, experiments with long duration had already started in the late 19th century with Satie's *Vexations* (1893), which was rediscovered and performed by John Cage and others in 1963, taking 18 hours and 40 minutes. Experiments with long duration can also be found with other compos-ers, notably with Morton Feldman, whose six-hour String Quartet No. 2 (1983) remains the long-est in the genre to date. Cage's longest piece by far is the organ work *Organ²/ASLSP*, currently performed in a church space in Halberstadt (Germany) and requiring some 639 years for the per-formance in its entirety. See Alexander Rehding's discussion of works whose performance dura-tion exceeds the life expectancy of human listeners, in "The Discovery of Slowness in Music," in Sander van Maas, ed., *Thresholds of Listening: Sound, Technics, Space*, New York, Fordham University Press, 2015, 206–225.

7   A shorter, three to three and a half hour version was performed at the Brooklyn Academy of Music in 1971 and went on tour in Europe. According to a *New York Times* reviewer, this version had no intermissions. Review online at www.nytimes.com/1971/03/07/archives/stage-deafman-glanc e-robert-wilsons-story-of-a-black-youth-is.html, Accessed: March 20, 2018.

people changing).[8] Wilson described the work as "a kind of frame or window to the world where ordinary and extraordinary events could be seen together."[9] Around the same time, Philip Glass started to experiment with long performances, inspired by the all-night *kathakali* music theater he visited in Southern India in 1973. "If you had to take a nap, you would go into the bushes and sleep for a few hours. When you came back, the performance would still be going on."[10] Glass's ensuing three-hour-long *Music in Twelve Parts* (1971–1974), however, is articulated by a number of formal intermissions.

At first sight, the general approach in *Einstein on the Beach* is in line with these earlier theatrical and musical experiments. Excerpts from the news at the time of its creation, such as the Patty Hearst kidnapping and bank robbery case, play a major role, as do the typewritten texts and visual art objects made by the autistic youth, Christopher Knowles – again the contribution of a non-professional artist, lifted, as it were, from Wilson's personal life and integrated in his theater work.[11] *Einstein* too is a long work, taking some four and a half hours to perform, and begins in a "rolling" form before the audience starts to flock into the venue. It has no intermissions. Considering that its makers explicitly referred to the work as an opera, the frame of reference for its performance would fall into the conventional culture of opera houses and opera festivals. Wagner's Bayreuth, for instance, would occur as a model for long opera; Grand Opera for flocking audiences and *flânerie*; and opera *tout court* for grand gesture. Yet, *Einstein* is markedly different, and would hardly fit the genre requirements of opera, despite the claim of its makers. Being closer in many respects to the (para-)theater of the earlier Wilson, evoking the experience of cinema and installation art in its use of discontinuous shots and scenes, and – for the style of its amplification – resembling a rock concert or festival (Woodstock and Isle of Wight having redefined the rock festival only five years previously) rather than an opera, the work would seem in the proper position to open a space for alternative modes of attending.

The fact that Wilson and Glass wanted *Einstein* to be performed in formal, overdetermined performing arts venues such as the 1824 Opéra Grand in Avignon (world premiere) or the Metropolitan Opera in New York (United States premiere) creates a context in which their invitation acquires a different meaning than it would in places less burdened with history, ideology, and convention. Wilson was aware of this when he mixed variously priced seats at the 1976 Met performances,

8   Arthur Holmberg, *The Theater of Robert Wilson*, Cambridge, Cambridge University Press, 1996, 117–118.

9   www.robertwilson.com/ka-mountain-and-guardenia-terrace/, Accessed: March 20, 2018.

10   Philip Glass, *Words without Music: A Memoir*, New York, W.W. Norton, 2015, 186. Glass returned to the topic of sleeping during performances in a 2012 interview devoted to the *Einstein* re-stagings. "Philip Glass: Have a Sleep During Einstein on the Beach." Online at www.bbc.com/news/entertainment-arts-17958400, Accessed: March 20, 2018.

11   Wilson's interest in the social-therapeutic dimensions of art had also led to the creation of the experimental performance company, the Byrd Hoffman School of Byrds, which doubled as a commune.

putting the two-dollar next to the two-thousand-dollar ticket owner.[12] The choice of venue, then, rather than reflecting mere practical concerns, seemed to be part of what *Einstein* intended to accomplish as a work of art. The audience side of the divide between stage and audience was included in the conception of the work, albeit in a different way than the audience had been *in-dwelling* the Shiraz festival piece or than it would *attend* a regular opera house performance – even a very long one. The "invitation" extended by Wilson and Glass to wander around during the performance of *Einstein* – if read against the performance situation as a whole – provides a key to what the work *is* as well as what it *does*.

One way to study what *Einstein on the Beach* is and does, is by looking into theories that account for the relation between performances and audiences as integral "systems."[13] In cinema, the theory of the *dispositif* or apparatus has covered some of this ground since the 1970s and has made somewhat of a comeback more recently in relation to the early theatrical "cinema of attractions."[14] The concept of the apparatus or *dispositif* has been variously theorized, one relevant meaning for the discussion of contemporary opera being close to that of its earliest proponent, Jean-Louis Baudry, who in the early 1970s defined the *dispositif* as a material-technical apparatus producing conditions (such as a particular form of address) that predetermine the subjective position of the spectator.[15] Baudry's contribution has been to shift the discussion of cinema from a focus on the screened film to the analysis of the viewing situation as a whole, allowing apparatus theorists and film music scholars to account for the ways in which cinema – as a technological installation and a philosophical machine – sutures the viewer-listener into a technologically mediated fabric of synchronizations, identifications, subjectivations, presence effects, modes of address, and discursive or institutional (power) relations.[16]

This is not to argue for a return to the Marxist and Freudian analysis that apparatus theory helped perform, but for a revaluation of certain concerns and concepts that shaped this theory in the first place: absorption, interpellation, address, performance, framing, resistance, affordance, and what I shall later call dorsality. The first of these, absorption, is of special importance both to Wilson's aesthetics

12   Wilson interview, online at www.thefader.com/2012/05/01/theory-of-relativity-director-robert-wilson-on-einstein-on-the-beach, Accessed: March 20, 2018.

13   On the influence on *Einstein* of cinematic techniques such as storyboards, see Susan Broadhurst, *Liminal Acts: A Critical Overview of Contemporary Performance and Theory*, New York-London, Cassell, 1999, 84. The storyboard stills used in the conception phase of the work have been published in Robert Wilson and Philip Glass, *Einstein on the Beach*, Paris, Éditions Dilecta, 2012.

14   An excellent discussion of *dispositif* theory, including its extension to television and video, can be found in Joachim Paech, "Überlegungen zum Dispositiv als Theorie medialer Topik," in *Medienwissenschaft*, nr. 4, 1997, 400–420. Frank Kessler, "The Cinema of Attractions as Dispositif," in Wanda Strauven, ed., *The Cinema of Attractions Reloaded*, Amsterdam, Amsterdam University Press, 2006, 57–70.

15   Paech, "Überlegungen zum Dispositiv," 400–405.

16   David Neumeyer, ed., *The Oxford Handbook of Film Music Studies*, Oxford, Oxford University Press, 2014, 395 ff.

generally, whose characters on stage often seem absorbed in their own worlds for hours, and to the basic division between stage and audience that informs the *dispositif*. Watching *Einstein* is often like viewing and listening into a world absorbed in its own processes, on the one hand oblivious of the spectator while, on the other hand, as I shall discuss, seemingly attempting to acknowledge their presence. As Michael Fried has argued for the historical development of painting, Tom Gunning for the early cinema, and Stefan Castelvecchi for the historical experience of opera, the logic of absorption has remained a central technique for promoting (emotional) engagement, stillness, and a sense of illusion in audiences across the arts.[17]

Einstein is no exception to this larger historical trend, which bears a relation to the history of media including television and video, but its insistence, through the extension of an explicit invitation, on mobility in its audience, indicates a complex ambition to break away from the normative aspects of the system.[18] By creating a discontinuous experience of the work – now sitting down and watching and listening, now turning one's back and only listening, now hearing it all from a distance in the aisles of the performance venue, now missing entire sections altogether or falling asleep – one will have had the impression of taking part in an event that, despite presenting itself as a show before an audience, contains a strategic negation of audience that powerfully affects the experience of the work – as I shall argue, in a most affirmative and "therapeutic" manner.

Overhearing totalities

The poetics of *Einstein* suggest the importance of the production of, and reference to, singular totalities. On several levels it relies on a reduction of complexity to *single* ideas, of ambiguous representations to *fixed* signifiers, of multiplicities of perspective to *single* viewpoints. These undialectical entities account for the strong visual and aural imprint the opera makes on its spectator. Examples of this formal reduction abound. Thematically, the opera is focused on "Einstein" as a mass media presence rather than the historical person of Albert Einstein. Einstein-the-opera-theme is a figure whose identity is constructed from popular images and

---

17 Michael Fried, *Art and Objecthood: Essays and Reviews*, Chicago, The University of Chicago Press, 1998. Tom Gunning, "The Cinema of Attraction: Early Film, its Spectator and the Avant-Garde," in *Wide Angle* 8 (3–4), 1986, 63–70. Stefano Castelvecchi, "From 'Nina' to 'Nina': Psychodrama, Absorption and Sentiment in the 1780s," in *Cambridge Opera Journal*, Vol. 8, No. 2 (July, 1996), 91–112.

18 As Robert Ashley, whose innovations of the opera genre will continue to inform its relation to other media, writes about his operas, "I put my pieces in television format because I believe it is really the only possibility for music. [...] The form [of stage opera] is related to the architecture. La Scala's architecture doesn't mean anything to us. We don't go there. We stay home and watch television." Robert Ashley, quoted in Kyle Gann, *Robert Ashley*, Urbana, etc., University of Illinois Press, 2012, 2. See also Bianca Michaels, "Opera for the Media Age: Composer Robert Ashley on Television Opera," in *The Opera Quarterly*, Volume 22, Number 3–4, Summer-Autumn 2006, 534–537.

ideas that have filtered into western cultural memory. Einstein does not appear in the opera as a protagonist-subject (or persona) in its own right, but as a finite set of iconic attributes and narrative clichés attached to a name (strategically employed as a signifier), and carefully distributed over the time and space of the four acts. The opera neither has the ambition to tell its audience anything new about Einstein, nor to dramatize biographical material in order to facilitate a new understanding of the historical figure of Albert Einstein. Rather, it operates as a mirror for what we already know, or could have known, about Einstein, the "genius" and "phenomenon," on the basis of cultural memory. The experience of the set of attributes presented to the audience is one of recognition, repetition, the reaffirmation of sharply delineated markers that have become attached to a signifier and set of items (icons, clichés, images, and so on) named Einstein. Because of this insistence on the repetition of the items contained in this relatively closed set, the experience of the opera's theme ("Einstein") is to some extent substituted for the experience of the set as such. Embodying, as it does, a totality, the set is one answer the opera provides to the meaning of the individual items contained in the set.

The tendency toward totalities also shapes what any individual spectator, acting as member of another set, named "audience," may feel to be the immediate object of listening and watching the opera. Several critics, including Guy Scarpetta, have emphasized their impression of the opera as a "free-floating" experience, hinting at the continuity of its "atomic" process and work's own space-time in which one is required to submerge oneself, or pointing to the non-narrative form that provides listeners few fixed points for their orientation while experiencing the work.[19] Such comments hint at what Freud might have called an "oceanic" feeling, that is, a general sense of the limitlessness and comprehensiveness of the given (the world, being) in its totality. In *Einstein*, the totality is an effect of the repetition of, or insistence on, elements that do not appear to develop in a way that invites the spectator to *follow* its process, to *identify* with a (finite) perspective within that process. The gaze, if we may use this term here, remains external. The development of elements is replaced with logical variations (e.g., based on subtraction or addition of counts) that leave the identity of a given element intact. Through its variation we observe and hear the same gesture. Watching *Einstein*, one soon realizes there is much to be seen and heard, but there is little opportunity to develop one's *finite perspective* on the totality of the to-be-seen and to-be-heard. The work is not about generating perspectives, that is to say, it does not encourage *interpretation*. It is about gaining access to the virtual point of view (or point of audition) from which one can oversee (*surveiller*) and overhear (*surécouter*) the *totality* of each tableau (I will return to this below).

These totalities emerge most clearly in the transitions between acts and scenes, when the stage blackens out while the music continues. Wilson has emphasized his wish to separate entire sensory fields in order to be able to shift their roles

19   Guy Scarpetta, "The American Body: Notes on the New Experimental Theater," in Patrick ffrench [sic] and Roland-François Lack, eds., *The Tel Quel Reader*, New York-London, Routledge, 1998, 229.

around: "In many of my pieces what you see and what you hear do not go together. [...] What I am trying to do is give individual lives to both sound and picture."[20] According to media theorist Friedrich Kittler, the combining of sound and image in such a way that they remain independent as sensory fields has only been possible since the proto-media-technology in Richard Wagner. In his music dramas, Kittler argues, for the first time in history the conditions were met for separating sound from vision by hiding the orchestra in a "mystical abyss" and by making images appear as mirages that seemed to float independently across a blackened-out stage (Wilson's technique of floating a beam of light in the dark is close to this *Gesamtkunst* imaginary). Furthermore, Wagner's dramas contain several instances of characters who remain essentially invisible, like inhabitants of what Nietzsche called the "total world of hearing" (*volkommene Hörwelt*).[21] As Kittler writes,

> Only when the total world of hearing is created with media-technical precision can it be coupled with a "world of seeing" and enter the technical era. A space of sound that, thanks to its feedbacks, no longer needs the old-fashioned visibility of actor's bodies enables parallel connections with the new (i.e., technical) visibility of film. Already when the *Ring* premiered in 1876, the Bayreuth *Festspielhaus* employed a *laterna magica* to create the hallucination of the nine Valkyries riding on horseback – that is, born aloft on orchestral sounds. Finally, in 1890 – five years before the feature film was introduced – Wagner's son-in-law suggested a "night-dark" room, in whose "background" moving "pictures" would "fly by" to the sound of his father-in-law's "sunken orchestra" and put all spectators into a state of "ecstasy."[22]

Recombining the "total world of hearing" with the world of seeing, Wilson revisits Wagner's dream of unheard music-theatrical technics. For the spectator the separation and recombination thus achieved is close to the magic performed by the psyche in the act of dreaming. According to Roland Barthes, in his theory of listening, it was psychoanalysis which first recognized not only the separation of the sensory fields but also their modern displacement and substitution.

> In dreams, the sense of hearing is never solicited. The dream is a strictly visual phenomenon, and it is by the sense of sight that what is addressed to the ear will be perceived: a matter, one might say, of *acoustic images*.[23]

20 Quoted in Susan Broadhurst, *Liminal Acts: A Critical Overview of Contemporary Performance and Theory*, New York-London, Cassell, 1999, 89.

21 For his comments on "the relation between the total world of hearing and the entire world of seeing" (*das Verhältnis der volkommen Hörwelt zu der gesamten Schauwelt*), see Friedrich Nietzsche, "Richard Wagner in Bayreuth," in *Richard Wagner in Bayreuth/Der Fall Wagner/ Nietzsche contra Wagner*, Stuttgart, Reclam, 1986, 30.

22 Kittler, "World-Breath," 134.

23 Roland Barthes, "Listening," in *The Responsibility of Forms: Critical Essays on Music, Art, and Representation*, trans. Richard Howard, New York, Hill and Wang, 1985, 257. My emphasis.

Wilson touches on this logic of displacement when he advises the spectator to follow the world of hearing as it expresses itself in pure image. "Just enjoy the scenery, the architectural arrangements in time and space, the music, the feelings they all evoke! *Listen to the pictures.*"[24]

When we see the stage picture, this seems to imply, we may in fact be *hearing* – consciously or unconsciously. With the exception of those rare moments when the strict sensory-field order is interrupted by expressive interventions or events (such as, visually, when near the end of the diagonal walk scene the dancer breaks into excited gesticulation; or, sonically, at the first appearance of the space ship when "would it get some wind for the sailboat" breaks into near-cacophony) the order of intact totalities is kept firmly in place. Regardless of the way we are attuned to totalities of hearing and of looking, these totalities can only be perceived from points-of-view *beyond* the finite views of individuals. The girl, in the opening scene, with the conch shell, who would most explicitly seem to be enacting hearing totality from a position *within* the opera (Wilson intended her pose as a reference to Newton's remark that one can hear the universe – that is, totality – in a sea shell) appears not to hear, but to *depict* an iconic gesture of hearing, thus performing no finite, perspectival rupture with the surface of the stage picture as a totality, to which Wilson invites us to listen (Figure 9.1). In addition, it may be claimed that, in *Einstein*, the "total world of hearing," though appearing to be populated by hearing individuals, *as such* is not heard at all – rather, it is evoked as something to be *seen*. In "Train," for example, the silent scream of the male actor evokes the aurality of silent-film images, or – more iconic – of Edvard Munch's *The Scream*.

In *Einstein*, listening, then, could only take the form of *overhearing* – of *surécoute*, as Peter Szendy argues.[25] Overhearing as a mode of listening, it should be remembered, was practiced by the gods when they listened in on the world and its inhabitants – to the aural in its totality – and this is what spectator-listeners in *Einstein*'s auditorium are required to mimic: to overhear the stage pictures and their sound world from a standpoint exterior to that totality (akin to Fried's notion of absorption). The score of the opera encodes this type of aurality. An example of the larger works that musical minimalism was producing in the mid-1970s, *Einstein on the Beach* highlights the diversity of musical techniques available to Glass at that time. He elaborated on these techniques – cyclical structure and

Whether dreams, as Barthes and his co-author claim, actually exclude the (un-displaced) experience of sound remains controversial. More important in the present discussion is the general notion of separation and substitutability of sensory fields implicit in this claim.

24 Wilson, quoted in Mladen Ovadija, *Dramaturgy of Sound in the Avant-garde and Postdramatic Theatre*, Montreal, etc., McGill-Queens University Press, 2013, 13 (my emphasis). Other examples include the experience of four to seven hours of silence in Wilson's *Deafman Glance* (1970/1971), and, more anecdotally, his preference for watching television with the sound turned off. See Hilton Als, "Slow Man: Robert Wilson and his First Masterpiece," in *The New Yorker*, September 17, 2012.

25 Peter Szendy, *Sur écoute: Esthétique de l'espionnage*, Paris, Minuit, 2007, 52–53.

Figure 9.1 Girl listening to conch shell. Video still from *Einstein on the Beach*, dir. Don Kent (2014).

additive process – in his brief essay of 1978 on the opera.[26] Detailing the thematic and material connections between the acts and scenes, Glass emphasizes the importance of the general time frame (template) and large-scale harmonic structure. Even though we learn that the structure is based on a five-chord "cadence," a key point is that this cadence works as a generic framework, "a formula that invites repetition," as Glass comments, meaning repetitions on the surface level of the music.

What strikes here is the precedence of the general and the generic over the particular and singular, which is also reflected in the treatment of time as objective rather than as lived experience. If time is a key factor for any experience of harmony as "structural" (as Glass writes, *Einstein* is part of his project to take "another look" at *structural* harmony), the "take" on time this work foregrounds on both levels – time frame and harmonic structure – starts out as Aristotelean.[27] In *Einstein*, time is typically homogeneous and linear (the counting out loud and the solmization explicating its discrete process), perceived as, though, from outside of time, from a distance, creating a sense of infinity in the act of spectating-listening. Nothing in the work, however, validates a further account of the work's experience in terms of pure transcendence: the outside-time effect remains an immanent aspect of the overseeing and the overhearing of the music – *sub specie*

26 Philip Glass, "Notes: Einstein on the Beach," in *Performing Arts Journal*, Vol. 2, No. 3, Winter, 1978, 63–70.
27 Paul Ricoeur, *Time and Narrative*, Vol. 1, trans. Kathleen McLaughlin and David Pellauer, Chicago, The University of Chicago Press, 1990.

aeternitatis, as Michael Fried writes in his analysis of aesthetic absorption – as it restlessly attempts to overcome its finite horizon, and its dependence on the general and the generic, through constant variation and recombination.[28]

Punctuating smiles and guns

Even though the totalities in *Einstein* set the stage for its unfolding as an experience in time, the wholes discussed above do not simply subsume their parts. As we will see, they remain dissociated both from one another (sound, image) and from the individual parts that comprise the work. The sense of dream and alienation critics associate with *Einstein* also pervades the closed-yet-dissociated world(s) that comprise the work as structure. How, then, would the work allow itself to be navigated by its wandering audiences? What does it provide in terms of anchor points for spectators in their engagement with its elusive frameworks? In order to zoom in on the various layers and dimensions that articulate and provide access to *Einstein*, its interaction with media – television and cinema, in particular – will be instructive.

The performance at the Théâtre Musical de Paris-Châtelet on January 7, 2014, was broadcast on French television and international subscription channels.[29] Don Kent, who is known as a director of television movies and several operas, oversaw the production, which presents the first official full-length registration of the work. Whether Wilson and Glass had a say in the way the opera was filmed is not clear. The result is no less interesting, however, for what it reveals with regard to the function of details, framing, and aesthetic distance. Intended for live television broadcasting, archiving and digital replay, the recording was shot using contemporary television norms. Filming mainly uses static shots: a wide shot for the full stage picture, long shots for individual actors, and close-ups. Whereas the first two match the camera position with the viewpoint of individual spectators, who, depending on their seated or wandering position, will blend full stage views with a focus on individual actors and events on stage, the close-ups stand out by introducing a new level of information. Through the television images one gets to

---

28   The film *Koyaanisqatsi* (1982, dir. Godfrey Reggio, music by Philip Glass) is one more example of the world viewed *sub specie aesternitatis* (under the aspect of eternity; *with* space and time rather than *in* space and time) or, using Michael Fried's terminology, seen under the aesthetic regime of "absorption." Michael Fried, *Why Photography Matters as Art as Never Before*, New Haven, Yale University Press, 2008, 328–330. If the stage picture in *Einstein* ventures to encode the total world of hearing, the music goes toward creating an invisible supplement to the visual rhythms present in the stage picture. Again, however, there is no-one present in the work to see this music (and the work as apparatus or *dispositif* may tend to exclude this function altogether). The most explicit instantiations of seeing in *Einstein* are depictions of iconic representations of seeing, such as the upward gaze toward the stars (or it is the future coming?), beholding the totality of the visual field with eyes that seem to mirror its gaze.

29   A co-production of the Théâtre Musical de Paris-Châtelet, Telmondis Productions, and Mezzo TV with participation of France Télévisions and the Centre national de la cinématographie et de l'image animée. This filming was broadcast live by Culturebox, the digital channel of France Télévisions and Mezzo TV.

see an unsettling amount of detail in isolation from the full stage picture, which is not available at mid- or long-range seating positions. These details – such as the makeup on faces designed to enhance mid- to long-range effectiveness within the auditorium, the obvious trembling of the actor's bodies during their static poses – somehow show more of the production of the illusion than *Einstein* seems to have been designed for.[30] As Kittler writes, the close-up as a media-technical intervention, through selection and cut-out, in the distribution of attention separates spectators from "the spell of the medium" – in this case the spell of theater, to which the close-up as a cinematic technique has had to remain alien.[31] This separation suggests that, for spectators, it is essential to keep a distance that will allow attention to focus on long-shot scale events, to remain open to the totality of the stage picture. *Einstein* appears to exclude both isolated, self-reifying details and modes of perception that mimic the selective attention and affect (Deleuze: close-up as *affection-image*) produced by the television camera close-ups.[32]

According to theorist Hans-Thies Lehmann, the poetics of Wilson's theater revolves around the concept of framing. As he explains,

> The theatre of Robert Wilson is exemplary for the effects of the stage as tableau. It has justly been compared to the tradition of the *tableau vivant*. In painting the frame is part of the tableau. Wilson's theatre is a primary example for the use of frames. A bit like in baroque art, everything begins and ends here – with framings. Framing effects are produced, for example, by special lighting surrounding the bodies, by geometrical fields of light defining their places on the floor, by the *sculptural precision* of the gestures and the heightened concentration of the actors that have a "ceremonial" and thus again framing effect.[33]

Rather than isolating objects or characters, as Don Kent's cameras do, Wilson's frames tend to remain frames referring to other frames. In *Einstein*, the concept of the frame clarifies the disturbing power of the detail: the work is constructed, one might say, to foreground the middle-ground, mediating structures rather than singular close-upped details and their affecting power.

The role of these mediating structures recalls Adorno's analysis of popular music as based on a separation of the whole and its most individual parts or

---

30 Metaphorically, Glass and Wilson have referred to the knee plays as close-ups. Holmberg, *The Theater of Robert Wilson*, 12. The intelligibility of the knee plays' intricate uttering of solmization names and numbers requires a "close-up" aural interfacing which, in *Einstein*, is secured by the omnipresence of on-person microphones.

31 Friedrich Kittler, *Gramophone, Film, Typewriter,* trans. Geoffrey Winthrop-Young and Michael Wutz, Stanford, Stanford University Press, 1999, 162.

32 Gilles Deleuze, *Cinema 1: The Movement Image*, trans. Hugh Tomlinson and Barbara Habberjam, London – New York, Continuum, 1986, 87ff.

33 Hans-Thies Lehmann, *Postdramatic Theatre*, trans. Karen Jürs-Munby, New York-London, Routledge, 2006, 151.

"details." The products of popular music are structured in such a way, Adorno claims, that "the whole is pre-given and pre-accepted, even before the actual experience of the music starts," while the details, understood as those features that make a song recognizable, lack a singular relationship both to other details and to the whole.[34] Details in this sense are only capable of playing a role if their position endows them with situational meaning.

> Details which occupy musically strategic positions in the framework – the beginning of the chorus or its reentrance after the bridge – have a better chance for recognition and favorable reception than details not so situated, for instance, middle bars of the bridge.[35]

The emerging middle ground of popular music, then, is structured by standardized ("frozen," as Adorno writes), formatted and formulaic musical entities (hooks, choruses, bridges) that secure the relation with a listenership focused on a vague remembrance of what, in the repertoire, has been heard before.

The details in the work hold something in common with the type of detail Adorno described in the popular music of the early twentieth century (the general reliance in *Einstein* on modern history, the sense of pastness created by costumes and scene decoration techniques, in particular from the 1930s and 1940s, seems to support this connection). Indeed, in *Einstein* details are often used as devices for the framing elements in time or in space. One powerful device is making eye contact with the audience, as is the case with the man with the red jacket in Scene 1, who has his back toward the audience before he starts his routine. Eye contact is again used by the last person to exit the stage at the end of "Building" and by the stenographers to frame their cycle of work and distraction. Another example is hand gestures, such as the final open hand gesture of the bus driver after speaking the last word of his monologue which ends the opera as a whole (while repeating the repetitive hand gesture made by the attorney in Trial). As framing devices the details are often connected with speed: their appearance and disappearance is irruptive, contrasting them with the general slowness like a blinking sign. Their moments and mode of appearance turn them into signposts that not only articulate the strict coherence of *Einstein* as a diagrammatically organized whole – formally indicating the frames of parts and wholes – but they also play a key role in organizing the dramaturgy of watching and listening as the performance unfolds.

In introductory talks for the restaging tour of 2012–2014, Wilson framed *Einstein* as a critique of contemporary theater, which according to him, has absorbed a negative influence from television.

---

34 Theodor W. Adorno, *Essays on Music*, with introduction, commentary, and notes by Richard Leppert, trans. by Susan H. Gillespie, et al., Berkeley, University of California Press, 2002, 439. Cf. Adorno in ibid., 293: "The liquidation of the individual is the real signature of the new musical situation."

35 Adorno, *Essays on Music*, 439.

If you go to the theater tonight, if you go to Broadway, it's every 20 seconds, 10 seconds, no more than 30 [seconds] you have to react, it's always "do you understand? do you get it?" (...) and after a while you don't understand anything. So in this work it's okay to get lost. [...] Doing it now, almost 40 years later, [I was curious to know] what a public that is now used to television and the way theater is directed and even written, how they would enter a piece like this where you are not given something specific to which you have to react every 10, 30, 5 seconds. The whole evening is something you can freely associate with and you can continue thinking well after you leave the theater.[36]

Wilson's dismissal of densely rhythmic content that solicits a response from the audience might seem remarkable given the presence of similar devices in his opera. Even though the signposts do not seem to have a definite content to which one might react, their function being more ceremonial, the fact is that over the course of its unfolding *Einstein* provides a dense and almost continuous series of focal points that hold and feed back and forward the spectator's attention. Beyond the framing devices, examples include the carefully distributed high-frequency movements such as the shaking head of the person reading a book in Trial and Building, the finger-play with pencils by the choir and the judges in Trial, and most dramatically the static appearance of an enigmatic silhouette seen through the ruptured backdrop at the transition from Prison to Dance 2.

This perceptual strategy for guiding attention over time – a navigational tool reminiscent of Wagner's *Leitmotifs* without their deep symbolism – provides a context for spectators to leave (physically or mentally) without the risk of not being able to come back and reconnect with the work. This is not to say that *Einstein* does not require the presence of listeners-spectators, that everything in it has somehow been pre-arranged, pre-listened, even pre-felt by the opera as an apparatus. On the contrary, the signposts are structured in ways that complicate their very operation as feed-backs and feed-forwards. Personal note-taking at one of the Amsterdam performances of January 2013 may illustrate this point. In the Trial scene, both female stenographers, who are seated perpendicular to the central axis of the performance venue, turn toward the audience – and smile. As I noted, with regard to one of these moments,

Again she slowly turned her head to face the audience and she suddenly smiled. It looked like a grimace, a faked smile. But one could not be sure. The way she made the smile disappear and morph into a neutral expression, made me feel as though, by withdrawing her smile, she was trying to tell us something or teach us a lesson. It was as if she wanted to say: this bright

36 Robert Wilson, Philip Glass, and Lucinda Childs discussing *Einstein on the Beach* on October 28, 2012 at Zellerbach Playhouse, Berkeley, California. On YouTube, www.youtube.com/watch?v=k8iLOGPm7AY, Accessed: November 18, 2016.

face, large eyes and white teeth – this is the screen. Follow the movement of my face as it slowly turns back and disappears, as if nothing ever made itself manifest. Had she really been looking into the audience, through the fourth wall, or had she been grimacing, like an automaton? Was hers a statement about naturalist or formalist acting, about intention, idolatry, scopic desire?

Instantiating the concept of a framing device for the spectator, the smile may also illustrate how, in *Einstein*, the frames and signposts also contribute to the emergence of points of intense ambivalence and uncertainty. Throughout the work, there is a tension between the many things that it *shows*, and a certain reluctance to *say*, or to *tell about*, let alone explain, the things it shows. If Craig Owens has claimed that Wilson's images are resistant to interpretation because they are "immediate, presentational," this claim may be qualified by hinting at the mechanisms *Einstein* puts into operation to unhinge the spectator's sense of (self-)presence, to mobilize the devious aspects of presentational immediacy, and to point up the darkness that lies beyond and behind the show as it presents itself before its audience.[37]

Puncturing spectators

Philip Glass claimed that *to be meaningful* is more important as a notion for understanding what *Einstein* attempts to *do* than the question of what the opera means.[38] The emergence of sense requires a structure of response allowing spectators to *return* – to feed back – the im-pression, the im-pact, of the icons, types, formulas, indeed the punching and puncturing devices the opera exposes them to.[39] As discussed above, despite its reference to Albert Einstein, and despite Glass's portrayal of the opera as belonging to a series of three "portrait operas" (with *Satyagraha* [1979], on Gandhi, and *Akhnaten* [1983]), *Einstein* does both more and less than drawing a portrait as an image of the soul, as the classical portraiture would require it to. On the level of the *studium* (Barthes), elements from the popular image of Einstein – most of which are familiar or retraceable to the finite set of Einsteinalia – are mobilized and held within the work's strict diagrammatic framework. However, they hardly create a discernable portrait at all, if portraiture in the classical sense aspires to create an image of the soul.[40] Rather than creating a likeness of the biographical subject of Einstein, through its rhythmic processes

---

37　Craig Owens, "*Einstein on the Beach*: The Primacy of Metaphor," in *October*, Vol. 4, Autumn, 1977, 24.

38　Quoted in Susan Broadhurst, *Liminal Acts: A Critical Overview of Contemporary Performance and Theory*, New York-London, Cassell, 1999, 82.

39　In addition to the analysis of punctuation proposed by Szendy, this aspect would merit a reading against Philippe Lacoue-Labarthe's theory of typology and syncope in *Typography: Mimesis, Philosophy, Politics*, Stanford, Stanford University Press, 1998.

40　For *Einstein*'s diagram as created by Lucinda Childs, see: http://lucindachilds.com/gallery/Lucinda-Childs/lucindachilds3, Accessed: November 18, 2016.

it creates an "Einstein" of its own. It is through these processes, I should like to point out in closing, that we gain access to the opera's singular *punctum*.[41]

From the point of view of the spectator, the partial objects holding the attention appeal – due, in particular, to their irruptive appearance – to a type of response that belongs to the *alert*. For the sense of hearing, Barthes developed this domain as the "indexical" form of listening practiced by most living beings as a mode of vigilance.[42] The spectator's ear is alerted, for example, by a sudden cry in the background while a sleepy lady recollects her experience in a prematurely air-conditioned supermarket, the disturbing cries of the female jury member, or, for that matter, visually-aurally (in a mode of anticipation) by the shock appearance of a machine gun pointed at the audience near the end of Trial 2. Apart from these indexical surface effects, and the dominant modes of surveillant perception (overhearing and overseeing), the opera appeals to a third mode, again identified by Barthes in his essay on listening published in the same year as *Einstein on the Beach*. He refers to this alternative mode as panic listening (*écoute panique*): "there is a disintegration of the Law that prescribes direct, unique listening" in the intentional and disciplined sense.[43] In this mode, listening has lost connection with "determined, classified" signs to decipher; it can no longer be construed as vigilance, nor as act of reading with the ear. In the absence of the orientation and sheltering theory, Barthes writes, listening becomes a means of "trapping signifiers" that would allow the unknown territory on the other side of language, to the point where listening is displaced, becoming concerned with images rather than sounds. Exposed to the uncertainties caused by the lack of readable signs and point of aural orientation, this third kind of listening resonates with such concepts as Luigi Nono's "tragedy of listening" and the general search for the thresholds of the listening in musical and sonic modernism.[44]

Einstein on the Beach not only plays on the displacement aspect identified by Barthes as an important feature of modern listening, and playing out on the level of totalities (vision, hearing). It also appeals to a sense of uncertainty, insecurity, and even terror lurking in the background and echoing Nietzsche claim,

---

41 As an irreducible expression of personal singularity through the photographic image, the concept of the *punctum* has already been brought to bear on Wilson by Barthes in 1976, the year when *Einstein* was created. He confessed to be "held" by the image of Wilson in Robert Mapplethorpe's double portrait of him and Philip Glass, unable, as he writes, to determine precisely which element of Wilson's image captivated him. Roland Barthes, *Camera Lucida: Reflections on Photography*, trans. Richard Howard, New York, Hill and Wang, 1981, 54.

42 Barthes, "Listening," 247.

43 Barthes, "Listening," 258.

44 As Raymond Fearn explains, Luigi Nono's take on modern listening in his opera *Prometeo: Tragedia dell'ascolto* (1984), "*Prometeo* is a work in which the listener is invited to explore the aural landscapes of which the work is made up, and to find a relationship to the mythical elements with which both its text and its music are profoundly imbued, but he is not given any kind of 'route-map' in advance of these explorations." Raymond Fearn, *Italian Opera Since 1945*, New York-Abingdon, Routledge, 1997, 189.

in *Daybreak* (section 250) that the ear is the "organ of fear."[45] These elements pervade the work on multiple levels. To the "smiling" stenographer, for instance, who disrupts coherence and meaning by triggering a host of conflicting readings of a single social signifier, may be added the frequent repetitions of phrases (e.g., by the judges) which empty them out of meaning; hyperbolic gestures and props, such as the oversized handgun in Train, which self-ironizes the scene into a parody; the self-assured diagonal walking, which is cut short and made to retrace its steps; and the sugar-sweet love story, which is cast in vaguely pompous, ill-fitting, and subverting language. Added to this is the constant, erratic variation of pattern, tempo, and duration in Glass's music (with the inclusion of acoustic images), and the separation of musical "data streams," which creates a conflict between modes of overhearing, and modes of alerted and panic listening.[46] The ensuing sense of imminent threat and chaos caused by these elements is intensified by the thematic of the opera: its references to nuclear destruction, to quantum-physical realities that determine human experience yet defy control; its presentation of friendly but ultimately isolated human individuals; the motif of organized crime and the suggestion of murder, and so on. The grand theme that suggests itself for *Einstein* through all this is loneliness, as it is above all expressed by the lone spaceship in space; by a humanity attempting to understand the cosmos and to defy its own tragic destiny; by the lone world of autism; and by the interaction with an audience that, through the opera's hybrid mode of address, is partially absent, or totally negated.

Ultimately, however, the theme of loneliness and its (re-)enactment through the work's *dispositif* and regime of spectating create a space for compassion, affect, and melancholy. They harbor the punctum of *Einstein*. For Barthes, in his analysis of photography, the punctum on the level of *intensity* (rather than of form, as is the case with details) creates a medium for the interiorization of finitude, both as a spectator and as a biographical subject. The punctum wounds and exposes, but it also helps in coming to terms with finitude – in other words, it may be thought of as being therapeutic in a Wittgensteinian sense. Under the general law introduced by Wilson and Glass, the spectators of *Einstein* may produce a different type of response to the affective impact of the punctum. Rather than implicitly insisting that spectators remain immobilized in their seats and deal with the experience in a socially and bodily restrained and interiorized manner, the opera's makers explicitly encourage spectators to mobilize themselves.

By presenting this code as integral to their work, they make a radical departure from similar forms of audience mobility in other institutional contexts, or for that matter in similar contexts in previous centuries. In the eighteenth century,

---

45 On the concepts of the safe, secure, whole and intact in relation to musical modernism, see also Sander van Maas, "The Curvatures of Salvation: Messiaen, Stockhausen, and Adams," in Robert Sholl and Sander van Maas, eds., *Contemporary Music and Spirituality*, London-New York, Routledge, 2016, 258–274.

46 Paul Théberge, Kyle Devine, Tom Everrett, eds., *Living in Stereo: Histories and Cultures of Multichannel* Sound, New York, Bloomsbury, 2015.

for example, as a function of social stratification, a night out included various levels of migration, not only in and out of the main performance venue but also among venues.[47] As William Weber notes about the conventions in London in the first decades of the eighteenth century,

> It was conventional [for members of the *beau monde*] to visit several such places in an evening; a regular theater-goer might take in an act at Covent Garden but hear the part of a concert where a musician he or she admired was performing, and also stop by a coffee shop to chat with a political colleague. Attendance at a theater was presumed to be a social act; to go was by definition to mingle with the assembled company as much as to see a production.[48]

This mode of attending and non-attending, however, remains different from the one installed in *Einstein* performances, in that it is based on a generic form of social-cultural behavior which to some extent remains independent of the works programmed.[49] Wilson's and Glass's pre-meditated audience mobility, by contrast, is different: as a built-in device, it functions as an *expressive instrument played by Einstein on the Beach's audience*.

If theories of the *dispositif* provide an answer to the question of how the film viewing situation as an ideological-technological environment produces the viewing subject, the performance venue may be identified as an analogous form in the domain of music theater. *Einstein* was created for venues that would be large enough to accommodate its sets, and that would arrange for the audience to be seated in a frontal position with regard to these sets, facing the visual spectacle and its amplified sound projection, and exposing it to the interpellation inscribed in this situation. *Einstein* acts upon this frontality by introducing (at least) a second interpellation, hinting that spectators should sensibilize themselves to whatever lies *behind* them, by calling out to them, before anything appears to have happened, to stand up and "quietly" respond to the "invitation" to turn one's *back* at the performers and wander into the relative darkness of the venue behind one "as desired." By including the *dorsal* space of the audience in the interpellative

---

47 William Weber, "Did People Listen in the 18th Century?" in *Early Music*, Vol. 25, No. 4, 25th Anniversary Issue; Listening Practice, Nov., 1997, 682.

48 In more recent times, walking out of a performance has remained an option available to individual spectators at any time. Due to its over-coding as a sign of protest against the performance or as rude behavior toward other spectators, however, the experience and meaning of this act is very different. As it would be perceived as another (and even worse) disturbance, returning to one's seat during the same performance is often discouraged by attendants.

49 Modes of attending were becoming more stationary in the course of the century. As Stefano Castelvecchi argues in reference to Michael Fried's thesis on the rise of the concept of absorption, opera in the late eighteenth century responded to the new interest among performing art audiences in the experience of absorption ("the separation between stage and audience – the importance of absorption in the actor, of involvement and illusion in the spectator") by adapting the stage play of opera performances. Stefano Castelvecchi, "From 'Nina' to 'Nina': Psychodrama, Absorption and Sentiment in the 1780s," in *Cambridge Opera Journal*, Vol. 8, No. 2 (July, 1996), 97–98.

structure of the *Einstein* experience, the makers would seem to expand their claim on the audience to envelope the totality of their situation (both art and life, inside and outside the venue) and their expressive options.[50] The strict distinction between being present, attending, and paying attention, on one hand, and being absent, falling asleep, wandering off, or for that matter leaving the venue in a gesture of protest, is suspended. This, however, would only seem to intensify the pressure on spectators in search for adequate modes of response, for responsiveness, and for the human responsibility the opera ultimately appears to call for, to the point of inspiring restlessness, undecidability, perhaps a vague sense of panic. But it also opens a space for affirmation and punctuation.

Mobilizing as it does the finitude of spectators as it manifests itself through their hunger, thirst, and fatigue, as well as through their desire, *Einstein*'s work-specific code creates a visual and social pattern in the venue that is each time unique. The view from the stage will resemble a punched card: rows of seats filled and seats empty in a constantly shifting pattern. This (dorsal) play of presence and absence enacts in a realistic manner the finitude of the audience by visualizing the rhythm of its attendance, its movement of withdrawal and return, of ebb and flow, perhaps like a different sort of *Einstein*, on the beach of its internal shoreline. Internal, for this play is integral to the work: the expressive apparatus thus created responds to the fixed dramaturgy of attention-holding devices on stage by creating patterns of resonance and dead spots (that is, empty seats) that interrupt the synchronizing effect the devices would normally have on the audience.[51] Within the framework of an opera that not only controls the rules on stage but also in the seating area, that is, that controls the *totality* of the situation, the gesture of desynchronization is a powerful one. On the one hand, it may be regarded as a continuation of the structures seen and heard on stage, each of which follows its own speed, rhythm, and course. An audience walking in and out, and following their proper (micro-)rhythm and speed, seems fitting for a work in which all elements move in their own stream of space-time. On the other hand, *Einstein*'s code allows the audience to *perform* its own finitude by creating a punctum of their own – an inter-punctuative *counter-punctum* – that, beyond its interest as a source of information for audience studies, may be perceived by spectators as a co-creative, affirmative, indeed "therapeutic" act: a coming to terms with finitude through the polyrhythm of leavings and re-enterings of the auditorium.

50   On the concept of dorsality in listening, see David Wills, "Positive Feedback: Listening behind Hearing," in van Maas, *Thresholds of Listening*, 74.

51   On the production of audience through (hyper-)synchronization in cultural-industrial, mass-mediatized culture, see Bernard Stiegler, *Technics and Time, 2: Disorientation*, trans. Stephen Barker, Stanford, Stanford University Press, 2008.

10 Historia Einsteinalium

From the beach to the church, via theater and "state bank"

Jelena Novak

Writing about his early operas, Philip Glass tells us about the first ever staging of his "portrait" opera Trilogy at the Stuttgart Opera, directed by Achim Freyer.[1] It seems that there were no major problems with the staging of *Satyagraha* and *Akhnaten*. *Einstein on the Beach*, however, was due to be staged for the first time without the involvement of its co-creator Robert Wilson, and that raised interesting, important, and difficult questions for both Wilson and Glass. It turned out to be a huge challenge – aesthetic, artistic, and even legal.[2] *Einstein* brought into sharp focus the enhanced status of the opera director, who becomes in effect the co-creator of the piece. As a result, Wilson's imagery is firmly interlaced with Glass's music, and the structure of the piece relies both on its musical and its visual elements.[3] Over a long performance history, spanning more than 40 years, *Einstein* has been staged by artists other than Wilson on only four occasions. In this chapter, I focus on those stagings.

In relation to *Einstein*, Glass's instincts had been that "in the long run, fresh interpretations can only strengthen a work."[4] Despite the fact that the authors were in basic agreement on this point, major questions were raised:

---

1   In Stuttgart, Freyer staged *Satyagraha* (1980) in 1981, the world première of *Akhnaten* (1984), a commission from Stuttgart Opera, in 1984, and *Einstein on the Beach* (1976) in 1988. Stuttgart opera went on to perform the entire Trilogy in 1990.

2   For more about the issues between Glass and Wilson in relation to *Einstein*, see Leah Weinberg, "Opera behind the Myth: An Archival Examination of Einstein on the Beach," PhD thesis, 2016, available online: https://deepblue.lib.umich.edu/handle/2027.42/120839, Accessed: May 2, 2017.

3   The "libretto" that Glass had when he started composing the music was the notebook with Wilson's storyboard images, and with no words at all. See this visual 'libretto' in Appendix 1.

4   Speaking about the different versions of the staging of his opera *Satyagraha*, Glass notes: "I feel that only through reinterpretation of the standard repertory does a true understanding of a work emerge. Given this point of view, there is no final version of a work. Nor do the original authors necessarily have the final, or even the best, interpretations. Only through many productions of a work – *King Lear*, for example – can one begin to glimpse the real dimensions of the piece. I'm absolutely convinced of the validity of this point of view, though I know from personal experience that it can lead to very difficult experiences for the authors, should they allow this view to prevail." See: Philip Glass, *Music by Philip Glass*, New York, Harper and Row Publishers, 1987, 110.

Exactly *how* such a work as *Einstein on the Beach* could be reinterpreted, though, was not at all clear. The fundamental problem lay in Wilson's unique approach to theater. He had combined the elements of story, libretto, design and direction into something very new. A Bob Wilson "libretto," for example, might have no words at all, only pictures. Therefore, to redesign a work (or redirect it, for that matter) could mean to change its basic vocabulary. And in that case, what would be left of the original idea?

This question prompted yet another, one with which Wilson, as well as many others working in the "new theater," were concerned: How would it be possible for these works, which, from their very inception, were so strongly linked with design and directorial concepts, to survive their creators?[5]

Aside from the integral role of Wilson's directorial concept in *Einstein*, the opera also draws into itself something of the true spirit of performance art. Thus, in the last series of performances in which Glass, Wilson, and Lucinda Childs were not on the stage (2012–15), there was an inherent tendency for the new protagonists to model themselves on the original production characters, rather as remakes of movies which can resemble black and white originals.[6] It is as though the original visual quality of *Einstein* is determined to remain a constant and constituent part of the piece.

While Stuttgart Opera was still at the planning stages of the first production of the Trilogy, Glass and Wilson agreed upon a strategy for further performances of *Einstein*. They wanted first to remount the original production as a revival and then to proceed to a full documentation of that production. They felt that the 1976 production had not been adequately documented primarily due to the lack of finances available at the time. Although some video recordings of the 1976 production do exist, and today can be found in New York Public library,[7] the authors considered that, due mainly to poor lighting, the recordings are "inadequate for even basic reference purposes."[8] The idea was to make a video of the performance to the highest professional standards at the revival. That would have ensured the preservation of Wilson's original concept. The score, however, was not an issue, since it "was committed to paper years before and was unlikely to change further."[9]

The intention gradually crystallized that in the final instance two versions of the piece would be available for future stagings.

The first would be an "original version" that would have to be based on the video tape and would be obliged to faithfully reproduce the lights, images and movements. We would also allow another version to be done. This need not

5   Philip Glass, *op. cit.*, 141–142.
6   For example Kate Moran and Helga Davis resembled Lucinda Childs and Sheryl Sutton.
7   See: https://catalog.nypl.org/, Accessed: June 5, 2017.
8   Philip Glass, *op. cit.*, 142.
9   Ibid., 142.

follow the original design concepts but would still adhere to the structure of the work as it appears in the music and with the prescribed divisions into acts and scenes. It would, further, follow the general outline of the original sequence of Train, Trial, and Dance sections. This approach provides both a reference point to the original version and a departure point for new interpretations.[10]

Before the staging of *Einstein* in Stuttgart in 1988 by Freyer, an opportunity to document the piece had already arisen, with the first *Einstein* revival produced in Brooklyn Academy of Music in 1984, and with a film duly made: *Einstein on the Beach: The Changing Image of Opera*.[11] It combined interviews with the authors and the performers introducing the production with footage of the performance itself. This film, as a documentation artifact, was an important step towards the avowed aim of documenting the piece and making two versions available for the production.

After the whole Trilogy had been put together in Stuttgart in 1990, another set of performances directed by Wilson took place in 1992 at Princeton University and in a subsequent world tour. However, more than 20 years passed since the commercially available DVD recording of the entire performance of *Einstein* (directed by Wilson) became available.[12] It was only made after the 2012–15 world tour of *Einstein*. That DVD set seemingly brought the attempt to provide video documentation of the piece to the end, at least as far as Philip Glass and Robert Wilson were concerned.[13]

After Freyer's staging of *Einstein*, it took more than 20 years for another artistic team to get involved with the adventure of staging it differently. Berthold Schneider and Veronika Witte presented *Einstein* as an opera installation that crossed over to the field of visual arts to a very large extent. The installation took place in the former building of the Staatsbank of the German Democratic Republic (GDR) in Berlin in 2001, appropriately enough since the building was at the time a kind of artistic laboratory named "Staatsbankberlin" and performance space whose artistic director was Schneider himself. After this intriguing staging in the building of the Staatsbank, Schneider and Witte repeated the performance in 2005 using the same concept, but in a different space, since the Staatsbank had by then been transformed into a luxurious hotel. The new space that accommodated the piece was the building of the Parochialkirche in Berlin. Another staging took place almost a decade later, when a quite different production of the entire

10 Ibid., 142–143.

11 *Einstein on the Beach: The Changing Image of Opera*, directed by Mark Obenhaus, 1985. Produced by the Brooklyn Academy of Music.

12 *Einstein on the Beach* DVD, Opus Arte, 2016.

13 As no one from the original team of authors (Glass, Wilson, and Childs) performed in *Einstein* during the 2012–15 tour, this recording was unfortunately too late to capture the members of the authors' team on stage. So some emblematic moments of the piece, such as the "Three diagonals dance" performed by Childs and Wilson's own dance with the flashlights in the Spaceship scene, are only available in the videos in NY public library, which have restricted availability. There are, however, few clips in *"Einstein on the Beach:* The Changing Image of Opera" documentary.

"portrait" opera Trilogy was given in 2014 by the State Opera of South Australia, directed by Leigh Warren and with a set designed by Mary Moore. Himself a choreographer and dancer, Warren based the staging of *Einstein* on movement and in effect made a "dance opera" of it. The most recent restaging was by director Kay Voges, who brought *Einstein* to the Dortmund Opera in 2017. Voges created a futuristic allegory inspired by the Theatre of the Absurd.[14]

This chapter sheds light on the above-mentioned and little-known "beyond Wilson" stagings of *Einstein*. The cases differ considerably. Freyer and Warren place *Einstein* within the scope of the "portrait" opera Trilogy, while Schneider and Witte and Voges set it apart as a unique piece. I am interested in how these different directorial perspectives illuminate the original *Wilson-Glass* concept and give it new meanings, especially in those cases where the authors draw it beyond the conventional opera genre by way of installation and dance.

It is not my primary intention to compare Wilson's and others' interpretations; more so because some of the directors claimed that they had not even seen Wilson's *Einstein* in live performance before they decided to stage it. However, some spontaneous comparisons emerged uninvited. That being the case, I focused on the end of *Einstein* as a point of reference, paying special attention to the Spaceship scene as a kind of climactic finale of *Einstein*. The Aria that precedes the Spaceship and Knee Play 5, which comes after it and ends the piece, together reveal interesting perspectives on enduring problems of humanity and how they might be represented onstage.

Achim Freyer and surreal two-dimensionality

Commenting on the staging of the Trilogy in Stuttgart in 1990, critic John Rockwell compared it to "some kind of modern Ring cycle."[15] Although *Satyagraha* and

14   I saw *Einstein on the Beach* directed by Kay Voges in Theater Dortmund: Opernhaus on June 4, 2017, and afterwards obtained the video recording from the staff of Theater Dortmund: Opernhaus for research purposes. While in Dortmund I also interviewed Voges; Concerning Leigh Warren's staging, the director himself provided the video recording for me to use for work on this chapter. Mary Moore and the State Opera South Australia provided further useful materials. I met Berthold Schneider in Wuppertal, where he is currently an intendant of the Opernhouse Wuppertal. In interview he explained his concept of staging *Einsten* as an installation. I also learnt a good deal from photos, press reviews, and other documents concerning the production that Schneider and Veronika Witte generously shared with me. There were some video fragments too. Concerning Freyer's staging at Oper Stuttgart, I received the video recording of the performance, and although it is very dark it still offers some insight into how the performance looked. The Archive of the Akademie der Künste in Berlin helped me tremendously by providing several other documents relevant for Freyer's production, including an interview with him and negatives of some photos. For Freyer's, Warren's, and Voges's versions, I also received the program booklets from the opera houses. I am extremely grateful to all authors, their assistants, photographers, together with these institutions and their staff, for help, permissions, and support while I pursued this "Einstein hunt." Thank you also to Tanja Tomić Ćurić and Emilija Nikolić who provided help with German translation.

15   John Rockwell, "Philip Glass Operas Become A Sort of Modern 'Ring' Cycle," See: www.nytime s.com/1990/06/25/arts/review-music-3-philip-glass-operas-become-a-sort-of-modern-ring-cycl e.html?pagewanted=all, Accessed: July 4, 2017.

Akhnaten were received warmly, *Einstein* was greeted with less enthusiasm. Rockwell praises Freyer for the staging of *Satyagraha* and *Akhnaten*, but he considers the staging of *Einstein* a complete failure:

> Mr. Freyer begins and ends with a striking image, which he calls a "Surreal dinner party," like Alice at the Mad Hatter's, with Surrealist monster-characters chatting away, their dialogue a jumbled collage of fragments from the likes of Salvador Dali, Max Ernst, Ludwig Wittgenstein and Antonin Artaud.
>
> In between – for more than four hours, with one intermission – Mr. Freyer unfolds an utterly dehumanized series of geometric, numerical and Surrealist symbols animated two-dimensionally behind a gigantic black and white grid. Even when dancers are visible, they are masked and padded, strutting and posing in a way that denies their individuality. Toward the end, things get dimmer and more fragmented, a grim working out of a dubious concept.[16]

This review, aside from expressing Rockwell's view of the staging, also has considerable descriptive value. If we compare this and other descriptions with the recording from the archives of Stuttgart Opera, photographs, and interviews and reviews from the archive of Akademie der Künste in Berlin, and the program booklet of the performance, we can reconstruct to some extent what the staging looked like. Asked about his relationship to Wilson's staging, Freyer confirms that he liked it very much, but that his own staging was entirely independent of Wilson's, and was not influenced by it.[17] The outcome of Freyer's conception looks different from that of Glass and Wilson, but the critique of the destructive powers of humanity does remain as a common denominator.

I understand Rockwell's uneasiness when he tried to direct his Wilson-influenced gaze towards quite different imagery, but I do not share his disappointment. However, I felt some uneasiness myself when I first saw *Einstein* "after Wilson," and I find that unease intriguing. It is similar to the disquiet experienced by art critics upon seeing Marina Abramović's early performance art pieces reenacted by young artists in the Abramović MoMa retrospective in 2010.[18] The immediacy, intimacy, and exclusivity of performance art pieces are jeopardized in their reenactment. Through its performativity, conceptual nature, duration, and

16   Ibid.
17   Vielleicht doch eine Frage zum Stück: Sie haben die Musik von Philip Glass und einen scenischen Ablauf von Robert Wilson vorgefunden. Wie sind Sie damit umgegangen?Wilsons Ablauf habe ich gar nicht benutzt, von Anfang an nicht, Das kann ich ja nicht. Das sind ganz subjektive, individuelle Bildfolgen gewesen – wunderschön, sehr beeindruckend. Das gehört allein Wilson. Das muß er machen. Ich bin ja nicht sein Assistent. (Freyer interview by Wolfgang Veit, 20 October 1988 at the occasion of the premiere of *Einstein on the Beach* at Wurttemberg Statsoper, p. 12. Material available at the archive of Akademie der Künste in Berlin.)
18   See, for example: Diana Taylor. "Saving the "Live"? Re-performance and Intangible Cultural Heritage," *Etudes Anglaises*, 2016/2 (Vol. 69), p. 149–161.

a visual quality emanating from the world of visual culture rather than opera, *Einstein* shares a good deal with performance art. And the unease of seeing repeat performances of art pieces, especially if they are reenacted differently, is because reenactment and repetition are in contradiction with some of the basic postulates of performance art.

In the case of *Einstein*, an additional cause of disquiet is the memory of Wilson's staging, at least for those who witnessed it, since their gaze will remain shaped by, if not seduced by, Wilson's very particular imagery, strongly inter-linked with Glass's music. Moreover, the fact that for more than a decade the piece was known only in Wilson's direction added to the exclusivity and authority of Wilson's conception. This remained the case even after Freyer's staging, since that was not known well enough to "compete" with Wilson's. The same goes for the other three directors' stagings of *Einstein*.

It was not just the imagery that was changed (in comparison to Wilson) in Freyer's staging. The spoken texts were changed, as was the language (it was performed in German), and the dance sequences were different too. The music remained the same. The program booklet published those fragments of texts that were used to replace the spoken texts that Glass and Wilson featured in the orig-inal version. Instead of Christopher Knowles's, Lucinda Childs's, and Samuel Johnson's words, fragments of texts by Albert Einstein himself, Leonardo da Vinci, Pablo Picasso, Ludwig Wittgenstein, Francis Picabia, Bertrand Russell, Antonin Artaud, and Wsewolod Meyerhold were used as spoken texts. To hear, for example, "Die Geometrie des Gesichtsraums ist die Grammatik der Aussagen über die Gegenstände im Gesichtsfeld"[19] by Ludwig Wittgenstein is to witness a different *Einstein* from the one in which radiophonic emblematic voices and texts in English, recited by Lucinda Childs and Sheryl Sutton, mesmerize the audience. For someone like myself, encountering *Einstein on the Beach* for the first time by way of the audio recording, hearing different texts in a different language changed the experience significantly.

There is one aspect of Freyer's staging that I find tantalizing, as it strongly connects to Glass and Wilson's idea of building a crescendo in the last act, which would lead to the imaginary (nuclear) blast at the end (linked also with Einstein's legacy). In one of the interviews about the production, as well as in the pro-gram booklet, Freyer talks about the fantasy of the end of the world.[20] He asserts that in all the mannerist, non-classical epochs, including the one he himself is

---

19 *Einstein on the Beach*, program booklet, Oper Stuttgart, 1988.
20 "In allen manieristischen Epochen, und wir leben ja in einer, ist das Grundthema immer die Weltzerstörung gewesen. Und genauso die Auflösung des Körpers, wenn Sie El Greco sehen, diese unheimlich in die länge gezogenen, zerdehnten Körper, die mit lauter valeurs noch weiter aufgelöst werden noct weiter aufgelöst werden.Immer wieder haben diese nicht-klassischen Perioden ihre existenzielle Vernichtung im Auge und Leben warnend gleichzeitig aber auch genießend mit diesem prozeß. Wir sind ja die Zerstörer der Welt, auch wenn wir sagen, wir wol-len sie erhalten. Wir alle sind schuld an dieser Zerstörung, in jedem Augenblick." (Wolfgang Veit, Freyer interview, p. 8).

living in, apocalyptic themes are common. However, his point of view is that "we" are destroyers of our own world, even when we act to save it. The music of the Spaceship scene, in which the cadential-like formula is constantly reworked towards the climax, obviously intrigued Freyer, since in the synopsis of the fourth act the blast is mentioned, as is the beauty of the explosion.[21]

Certain apocalyptic references in *Einstein on the Beach* chime with Nevil Shute's novel "On the Beach" (1957), a connection that has eluded most commentators.[22] This novel tells a post-apocalyptic story following nuclear conflict, with life on Earth effectively destroyed by inhabitants of the Northern hemisphere.[23] In the novel, and in the films based on it, a tiny population is left alive in Australia, the remotest of the continents.[24] The post-nuclear war drama is related to the clouds of highly contaminated radioactive matter that make slow but steady progress towards Australia, threatening to make it a dead place too. Like Lars for Trier's movie *Melancholia* (2011), the main protagonists battle to come to terms with their own ends in particular and unique ways. I have no evidence that Freyer

---

21 Die Druckwelle der Explosion hat ihre unbarmherzige Schonheit und Größe. Die Atomisierung aller Elemente wird im vierten Akt zu einer sich verselbstädingenden unaufhaltsamen Gewalt. Die Einsamkeit der Dinge des neutralizierten Ego ist nicht meht tatsächlich; ist ein Vorgedachtes, Gedankliches, Die Elemente Zeit, Raum und Figur in ihren relativen Größen sind Dartsteller geworden. Der Blick zurück in die Zukunft findet noch immer und wieder am Tische statt – oder ist er das alte Bild einer Erinnerung? "The pressure wave of the explosion has its merciless beauty and size. The atomization of all elements is becoming independent and it turns into an unstoppable violence in act four. The loneliness of the things is no longer reality; it is a premeditated, notionally, the elements of time, space and figure in their relative sizes are turned into actors. The view back to the future keeps on happening on the table – or is it the old pictures of the memory?" (translated from German by Emilija Nikolić).See: *Einstein on the Beach*, program booklet, Oper Stuttgart, s.p.)

22 Nevil Shute, *On the Beach*, New York, William Morrow and Company, 1957.

23 In his *Music by Philip Glass*, Glass gave little credit to Shute's novel as a pre-text for *Einstein*: "Let me make a probably-not-very-important disclaimer. I had not read Nevil Shute's 1956 postnuclear, end-of-the-world novel, *On the Beach*. Neither, I believe, had Bob. Further, neither of us had seen the film. That doesn't mean that the title isn't connected to ours; it just means that any connection is an indirect one."(Glass, *Music by Philip Glass*, 29–30.). Looking back from today's perspective, the reference to Shute's novel becomes kind of obvious, and Glass himself underlines it in his recent *Memoir*: "The original title, which I have on the cover of a book of drawings that Bob gave me, was *Einstein on the Beach on Wall Street*. Somewhere along the way the "on Wall Street" was dropped, but neither Bob nor I remember when. "On the Beach" referred to the Nevil Shute novel from the 1950s, which takes place in Australia, when the world has experienced a World War III nuclear apocalypse. In the penultimate scene of *Einstein on the Beach*, there is a spaceship and a huge explosion that Bob wanted, and I wrote a piece of music to go with it. We were aiming for a big finale that was apocalyptic, which, by the way, is followed immediately by a love story written by Mr. Samuel Johnson, the actor who played a judge and also the bus driver at the end. Bob juxtaposed the most horrible thing you could think about, the annihilation that happens with a nuclear holocaust, with love – the cure, you could say, for the problems of humanity. (Philip Glass, *Words Without Music: A Memoir*, London and New York, Liveright, W.W. Norton and Company, 2015, 286).

24 One feature film was based on this novel in 1959: *On the Beach* by Stanley Kramer. And in 2000 a television film on the same novel was directed by Russell Mulcahy.

was aware of this specific reference to Shute's novel, but at the very least he was deeply engaged with notions of the apocalypse.

In Wilson's vision of the Spaceship scene in *Einstein*, performers and musicians are placed within a light-structured geometrical "machine" representing the Spaceship.[25] Whirling cadential formulae are the building blocks of the music, constantly increasing the tension *en route* to the "big bang," after which the last knee play takes place. This anti-climactic episode exists also in Shute's novel and in the films based on it, with several featured couples desperately waiting for the end to arrive, speaking of their love as the only bright thing that keeps them alive. Indeed, the Spaceship scene becomes not only the climax of the piece, but also the vanishing point on the horizon, into which all the lines of fragmented narrative finally dissolve.

In Freyer's staging, the *Aria* that precedes the Spaceship scene is performed in almost complete darkness, with the singer hardly visible as a pale light spot against the black background. In the Spaceship scene itself the performers of the ensemble are also in darkness, but the music creates the illusion that we reach the climax and final blast towards the end of Act IV. When the Spaceship scene is over, the ticking of a clock is heard in silence and darkness, suggesting, one might imagine, that the amount of time left is now severely limited. In the final knee play that serves as an anticlimax to the Spaceship scene, the group of characters is gathered at the long table again (Figure 10.1), speaking in German, while the choir sings their 1-2-3-4, 2-3-4-5-6, 1-2-3-4-5-6-7-8 incantation. Several characters speak (more than two, as was the case in Wilson/Glass version). As the final words are spoken after the music stops playing, the tick-tock of the clock draws the piece to a close.

Berthold Schneider and Veronika Witte: installing the operatic

Enacting a radically different vision of *Einstein*, Schneider and Witte staged it as an opera installation. Like Freyer, they included the original musical score, but excluded any trace of Wilson's staging, Lucinda Childs's choreography, and Christopher Knowles's and Childs's texts. The only spoken text that remained was the one by Samuel M. Johnson, about the two lovers, in the last knee play. With Veronika Witte responsible for the space-concept presentation, Ari Benjamin Meyers as musical director, and Tino Sehgal as choreographer, Schneider had a team ready to share the adventure of restaging *Einstein* as a complex installation on different floors in the huge historical building. By inviting visual artists and scientists to create the work within the performance space, Schneider and Witte "inhabited" *Einstein* with various artworks pertaining mostly to the extended field of visual culture.[26] Most of the installations were interactive so members of the audience were invited to participate.

---

25   See the image on the cover of this book.
26   Participating artists in the 2001 installation at Staatsbankberlin were Barbara Hindahl, Fred Rubin, Ilya Rabinovich, fettFilm, Sven Sahle/Hans Diebner, Anke Westermann, and Veronika Witte.

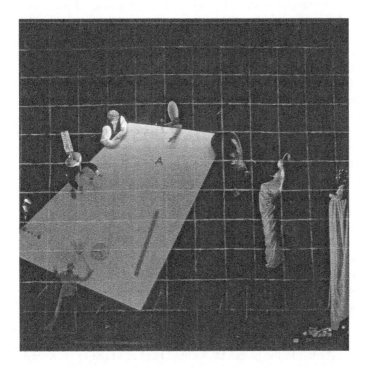

Figure 10.1 Einstein on the Beach by Philip Glass and Robert Wilson, directed by Achim
Freyer, photo © Matthias Horn

Schneider pointed to several factors in the cultural scene and in his own
artistic personality that encouraged him to present *Einstein* in this special
way. He noticed that the Berlin club scene had started to change at the turn of
the millennium, with an old-style discotheque replaced by clubs with several
floors. He saw this as an important development. "There was something in the
air for me there," he remarked, and went on to note that music was also being
perceived differently. "Endless concerts started to take place as popular music
was drifting away from the idea of the song, and that matched what *Einstein*
does."[27]

In 2000 Schneider became the artistic director of an arts venue Staatsbankberlin
within the former Staatsbank building that at the time had become an especially alluring space for those interested in broadening the boundaries of the performing arts

In the 2005 installation, Raimund Binder, Hans Diebner/Sven Sahle, Barbara Hindahl, Reiner
Maria Matysik, Fernando Niño-Sanchez, Daniela Risch, Frauke Wilken, Veronika Witte, Ari Benjamin Meyers, Jo siska, Raöf Hartmann, and Constanze Fischbeck participated.

27   All Schneider quotes are from Berthold Schneider in conversation with Jelena Novak, Wuppertal
Opera House, October 8, 2016 (unpublished manuscript).

and interdisciplinary crossover. It consisted of several different levels with numerous separate rooms, including a "main room" and a space in the cellar that used to be a vault. Although *Einstein* in the Staatsbankberlin was a site-specific performance, Schneider denies that the financial context inspired the staging. It was rather the structure of the space, and the possibility of using several spaces at once (10 to 15 of them, according to Schneider) that was important to his and Witte's concept.

Another circumstance that strongly influenced the way *Einstein* was installed is that it "hit" Schneider right at the end of his anti-Wagnerian phase and offered him a freedom he was unable to find in Wagner's musical theater:

> In this kind of performance you can still stay an intact human being which I didn't feel during Wagner performances. I felt strongly that Wagner's music theater is highly manipulated and that it tries to control my emotions, and tries to control what I see and think. And I found all works of Bob Wilson, especially this one, as extremely supportive: as a human being you stay intact. You are invited to a tremendous artistic experience without giving up your identity. Coming from a German background, that of the Regietheater, where everything was explained to you, meaning for me dramatic change, dramatic freedom, which opened before my eyes and I thought it is so rewarding. So it was immensely attractive for me to approach this piece, to see that it can say very strong things without being patronizing, and without putting the listener into the position of recipient, but rather opening things up. That was also why I found truth in the pieces by Samuel Becket which I was always tremendously fond of.[28]

Indeed, as an opera that extends "beyond drama," is fragmented, which is susceptible to multiple interpretations and open to different meanings, *Einstein* opposes Wagner's ideal of *Gesamtkunstwerk* while at the same time flirting with it.

The installation in Staatsbankberlin functioned in this way: a day would start with the opening of the Staatsbankberlin spaces to the audience. The installations by various artists were permanently there, so the space already functioned as a kind of exhibition space. Then, at some point that was not previously announced, the *Einstein* music would start: "We used the lounge aspect of the music by actually putting the lounge there. The music was really soft. People were chatting. It was like you were going to the club, and the music is Philip Glass. (…) The music was audible wherever you were."[29]

For the first three hours of the performance it did not matter to the spectator which of the Staatsbankberlin's rooms s/he was in. The music of *Einstein* was performed as in the score, with no interventions. The music ensemble was mostly situated in "the main room" and singers performed throughout the building. A visual transcription of the opera score visualized on 15 monitors allowed Schneider to direct the

---

28   Ibid.
29   Ibid.

singers in the whole building and the singers to follow the conductor everywhere. The sound of the performance was transmitted in real time, with loudspeakers carrying it to dozens of different rooms, corridors, and staircases where the artists' installations were placed. The spectators could walk freely between performance spaces. This obviously makes reference to the original production by Wilson/Glass, where audience members were allowed to enter or exit the space as they chose. Veronika Witte emphasizes that the space concept changed the Wagnerian "totalperspektive" in multi-perspectives for each visitor, as the hierarchy of the central perspective was deconstructed.[30] The staging encouraged audience members to move around, as it was not possible to see several things at the same time. Some of the singers were video recorded while singing, with their image transmitted in real time to screens in other performance rooms, effectively creating further video installations. "We wanted people to move around … They were on the grass, lying on air mattresses, watching the video from the VJ, and that had the same value as watching the art show, or watching the singers performing. There was no bias. It was completely leveled out."[31] "There were only a few chairs, no fixed seats. When a singer needed a seat for his/her performance, s/he had to ask the spectator to stand up or to improvise… All the floors were prepared that you could sit or lie on them," Witte remembers.[32] After three hours, somewhere before the Spaceship scene, the performance itself became more theatrical, so it was more important for spectators to gather in the vicinity of the performers. "The exhibition" at that point would be closed, and all the members of the audience would be invited to the main room, "where something would happen that was clearly performative."[33]

This gathering of the audience for a "performative event" was also a feature of the second version of this staging in the Parochialkirche in Berlin in 2005. The concept remained the same, but the result was quite different, since the two venues were completely unlike one another, and a quite different set of artists and scientists had been invited to create the work for the opera installation. In the 2001 staging, Witte and Schneider had a huge building with three floors and partly curated the exhibition themselves, while in the 2005 staging they used the church with one large space (ca. 700 square meters) and invited a curator to enlarge the team. Some artists from the 2001 production were again involved and produced new installations. Only the installation ISF done by Witte herself for the 2001 staging stayed the same in the Parochialkirche production since it is totally woven into the performance. At the point when the audience was supposed to gather in one space, the huge inflatable partitions that previously divided the church were deflated (Figures 10.2 and 10.3), so that the whole church became a single space "with one singer

30   Veronika Witte quoted from the email correspondence in March 2018.
31   Schneider, Ibid.
32   Veronika Witte, Ibid.
33   Schneider, Ibid. Witte clarifies this position of the spectator even more: "But if the spectator wanted to be somewhere else in the 'exhibition' or would refuse to be part of the 'climax,' s/he could also stay in the 'club-installation,' listen to it as 'live background' music or stay in the basement in an installation, which allowed him/her to be alone with the live music." Witte, Ibid.

Figure 10.2 Einstein on the Beach by Philip Glass and Robert Wilson staged by Berthold
Schneider and Veronika Witte, 2005, Parochialkirche in Berlin, Photo ©
Veronika Witte

going/beamed up to the dome, carrying the DNA of other singers."[34] Obviously
this staging removed *Einstein* from its generic context, arguably revealing that it
owes a lot more to traditions of visual culture than one might originally suppose.

While Freyer paid special attention to the mannerist obsession with apocalypse, it was the "survival fantasy" that informed Schneider and Witte's vision
of *Einstein*. Schneider puts it like this: "How can a community survive when the
whole planet is in danger?" It was at that time often supposed that mankind would
end up in space, and this is reflected in *Einstein*'s spaceship "finale":

> The 20th century was the century where there was this option of destroy-
> ing the whole planet. And there was the necessity to be able to find a new
> planet to be able to survive as a species. That was the background for us in
> this piece. And with this background the piece goes with the very popular
> imagery and fantasy of the 'sixties and 'seventies – we go to the space ship,
> together with enough people to have chromosomes on board, and we go to a

34   Witte, Ibid.

Figure 10.3 Einstein on the Beach by Philip Glass and Robert Wilson staged by Berthold
Schneider and Veronika Witte, 2005, Parochialkirche in Berlin, Photo ©
Veronika Witte

planet that hopefully is inhabitable so that the species of humans might survive. That is the basis of the apotheosis of the end of piece – the spaceship.[35]

Schneider and Witte wanted to show that this fantasy was no longer valid. Their
staging emphasized that science had shifted its focus from space to the cells of
human body, to DNA. "We were no longer thinking about the whole species, we
were thinking what does it mean for me… which option will medicine be able
to offer?," claims Schneider. So they insisted that the public view of the piece in
1976 embodied a quite different perception from the private view they opted for.

The "survival fantasy" interpreted by Schneider and Witte zoomed in on the
human body and its identity by using various technological "fissures" as spaces
for voyeurism, spaces where the individual might rethink her or his own sense of
performance and of identity. "The human will be the new battlefield for manipulated DNA instead of escaping in the spaceship," explains Witte.[36] They wanted to

35   Schneider, Ibid.
36   Witte, Ibid.

look at science from the "outside," as a kind of critique, rather as one might have looked at *Einstein*'s discoveries from the standpoint of its potential contribution to nuclear eradication.

What they did in redirecting the gaze to the human body, in interrogating its identity, and in shifting the focus from public to private, from macro- to micro-cosmos, was to put together a questionnaire that members of the audience were supposed to complete. This questionnaire done by Witte herself was actually part of the installation and audible in the performance. Audience members, as well as some of the performers, entered a kind of booth, where they responded (in writing) to questions about their own identity. They would be requested, for example, to choose the three parts of their body that they liked the most, and then a new kind of organism would be suggested inspired by those body parts. The idea was actually to question one's own identity. And exactly at that point a different kind of emotional climax was supposed to occur. Schneider talked about the urge that exists in *Einstein* to say something very emotional. "This urge we intensified as Bob Wilson did himself. It was overwhelming in a Wagnerian sense."[37]

Leigh Warren and *Einstein* as dance

Choreographer Leigh Warren and set and costume designer Mary Moore staged *Einstein* together with *Satyagraha* and *Akhnaten* at the State Opera of South Australia in 2014.[38] This production presents *Einstein* as a dance. Dancers are present in all the scenes, and with reference to the "extreme physicality of the performance" the authors decided to break up *Einstein*'s emblematic four-and-a-half-hour continuity. They introduced two shorter intervals (between parts 1 and 2, and parts 3 and 4), and a further "dinner break" between parts 2 and 3. For *Einstein* devotees it must have been quite an unusual experience to have these breaks between the acts, as the option to freely enter and exit the performance had become one of *Einstein*'s most characteristic features. However, for newcomers this move ensured a more conventional way into this radical piece. Warren and Moore believed that by having the breaks, the audience would be more focused on each one of the parts of *Einstein*. Probably this intervention in the very structure and time frame of the piece was the most radical departure Warren and Moore made from the original Wilson/Glass concept.

In some other ways, the performance stayed quite faithful to the original *Einstein*. For example, spoken texts by Knowles, Childs, and Johnson were used as in the original production. Also, the score was not subject to any changes. One of the reasons that in its performance history *Einstein* was most often done in

---

37   Schneider, Ibid.

38   Each of the operas had three performances: *Akhnaten* on August 5, 12, and 19; *Einstein* on August 7, 14, and 21; and *Satyagraha* on August 9, 16, and 23, so the order of the performances did not follow the chronology of operas' composition. The musical director was Timothy Sexton. The lighting designer was Geoff Cobham.

opera houses is that it needed an orchestral pit to place the musicians. In the State Opera of South Australia production, the musicians together with the conductor were placed on the stage where they took a central position, and where they stayed during the entire performance. Mary Moore explains how they came upon the idea of putting the ensemble on the stage. For her, part of the challenge of designing *Einstein* was to create abstract spaces that might function as visual metaphors for Albert Einstein's theoretical physics:

> In the first half of the opera, the space is dominated by the weight of Mass: oppressive yet still floating. In the second part, the geometric space is intended to create a sense of infinity to embrace multiple expressions of Light, from the modern light bulb to the aurora borealis. Linking both parts is Time, which is why the controller of artistic time, the conductor, is placed so prominently within the performing space.[39]

This decision brought the Warren performance of *Einstein* close to a semi-staged, or concert version. It helped to destroy familiar operatic illusions by exposing the ensemble and trying to make it visually relevant. The "spontaneous" corporeality of the ensemble was thus confronted by the "composed" and choreographed corporeality of the dancers, creating an unexpected dynamic on the stage. Figure 10.4 shows the stage, with the prominent diagonal giving the set an unusual dynamic, while at the same time providing "shelter" for the members of the choir who stand, like some kind of "talking heads," behind the diagonal line.

Warren admits that the inspiration for his conception of the work was Einstein's equation $e=mc^2$. In the first and second parts of the piece he was preoccupied with questions of mass and energy, while in parts 3 and 4 he was more interested in speed, light, and classical numbers.[40] In the Spaceship scene in particular it is possible to see this engagement with speed and light very clearly. The scene is inhabited by two dancers sitting and dancing on the bench. They are in the dark, with the only light coming from the light bulbs below. Their movements suggest some kind of courtship. Meanwhile, as the dancers, male and female, are engaged in their erotically charged dance, a singer – a "talking head" – sings the Aria from the diagonal "shelter." Another pair of male dancers join them, bringing their own bench, and with similar, erotically charged choreography. As the third bench appears the mirror seems to reflect light on to a place near the singer, illuminating the solo female dancer. The Spaceship music then starts. The three benches remain on stage, the light brightens, and the choir members take their place behind the diagonal. The increased intensity that is symptomatic of this scene in general

---

39 Mary Moore in Philip Glass Trilogy program booklet (compiled by Lara Francis and edited by Debra Pahl), August 5–23, 2014, Her Majesty's Theatre, State Opera South Australia, 7.

40 The director Leigh Warren in: Philip Glass Trilogy program booklet (compiled by Lara Francis and edited by Debra Pahl), August 5–23, 2014, Her Majesty's Theatre, State Opera South Australia, 6.

Figure 10.4 Philip Glass and Robert Wilson, *Einstein on the Beach*, directed by Leigh Warren, Photo © Mary Moore

does not lead here to some kind of "big bang," but rather to more and more energetic choreography. The straight couple is in focus, and their relationship evolves in more complex ways. As the gay couple enters, the straight couple leaves the stage. Symmetry is often an important element of this choreography.

The lovers on the bench embrace each other, and Knee Play 5 follows. A female dancer, looking self-sufficient, dances while the choir counts. An older man in a shirt comes in, sits on the bench, and starts to deliver the last speech. At the end, she puts her arm on his shoulder, and the lights go down.

Kay Voges and the futuristic absurd

Voges staged *Einstein* without having previously seen Wilson's staging of the piece. He had been listening to Glass's score and, as he said himself, he was a bit disappointed when he finally had a chance to see the DVD. In his own words, he felt that Wilson's language in *Einstein* was very far removed from his own language.[41] What Voges imagined while listening to the score did not correspond to Wilson's idea of the piece. Still, some of the original concept of the piece

41 Kay Voges in conversation with Jelena Novak, Theater Dortmund: Opernhaus, June 4, 2017 (unpublished manuscript).

remained. It was performed by Dortmund opera in 2017 without intermission, with the audience entering and exiting the hall *a piacere*. The overall duration was somewhat shorter than in the original production (around three and a half hours), and Voges explained that this was due to the omission of the Trial scene, as well as to a curtailment of the repetitions that had originally served to allow more time for changing the set. Voges's staging did not require complicated changes as the set relied more on the video projections.

This director was much inspired by Samuel Beckett's plays. Indeed he arrived at the music of Glass by way of Beckett. Thus Voges incorporated Lucky's monologue from Beckett's *Waiting for Godot* into *Einstein*. The rest of the spoken texts were employed as in the original production. Moreover, since the concept of synesthesia was important in Voges's staging, he included a text following synesthetic principles written by a schizophrenic person. One significant difference in Voges's staging when compared to the original production is that there was no choreographer and no choreographed dances.

A favored Voges postulate, drawn from the words of André Breton, is that although we live in an age of logic, our experience has many limitations, and that in order to see the bigger picture we need to liberate ourselves from logic. As Voges sees it, Albert Einstein had grasped this bigger picture, and it is in this achievement, according to Voges, that the political dimension of *Einstein* is to be found. If we want to change the world we need to start to think in a different way, Voges claims. So what he tried to do in his staging of *Einstein* was to make a dream within a dream within a dream…

One of the most impressive scenes in Voges's production is the Aria that precedes the Spaceship. The intense absurdity of the diva character in *Einstein* is here underlined. Wilson and Glass had considered the fact that in opera an aria, or group of arias, is invariably heard. In *Einstein* the "aria" preceding the Spaceship scene is anything but conventional. It has no text at all, apart from the names of the syllables (La-Si-Do-Re, for example). The soprano is alone on stage and the singing part is melancholic, slow, and repetitive, continuously repeating the ascending motive. In Kay Voges's interpretation the singer appears as a creature from some other planet. From her physique she rather resembles the diva in Luc Besson's film *The Fifth Element* (1997), a similarly anthropomorphic creature who is made to appear "beyond human." Her "hairstyle" contributes a lot to this impression, as it looks as though she has her brain in her hair, outside her skull (Figure 10.5).

She is on stage, accompanied by a large video projection of her singing head on the curtain behind her. Wearing an elegant red dress, and with this peculiar hairstyle and stiff posture, she exhibits attributes typical of a "diva." But this diva figure, together with the musical material she brings, is clearly intended as a critique of the institution of the diva. She is an empty signifier, a diva who is at the same time an anti-diva, indicating that Voges understood well the game that Glass and Wilson were playing. Staging the diva as an otherworldly creature makes for a fitting introduction to the Spaceship scene that follows immediately after.

Figure 10.5 Philip Glass and Robert Wilson, *Einstein on the Beach*, directed by Kay Voges, Photo © Thomas M. Jauk

In it video projections with dynamic concentric cycles (a voyage through a galaxy?) are displayed on the luminous curtain. A funny red anthropomorphic creature appears on stage. S/he has long hair, bumps on the limbs, a furry abdomen, hysterical movements, and appears to be dancing. This creature looks like a representation of some kind of alien. The "diva" again passes across the stage, and waves to the audience in a posture that is similar to a Hollywood star on the red carpet, or to some kind of dignitary, or royal figure. Beside her, a huge ape puppet waves to the audience as though calling them onto the stage. It leaves, as it had arrived, in a wheelchair. Suddenly, a host of "aliens" similar to the red bumpy one invade the theater, making the audience uncomfortable by passing between them and squeezing through the rows between the chairs. Finally all these figures/creatures return to the stage, with plastic toy guns pointed towards the audience, and with dynamic concentric circles (the voyage through the galaxy) projected onto the luminous curtain behind them. They really do resemble muppets, pointing their guns as the music takes us towards the big bang. A strong light is pointed towards the audience, and indeed it produces a kind of shock impact, a luminous but silent climax.

After that shock, in Knee Play 5, two cyborg-like women dressed in white appear onstage, with the ensemble also onstage behind them. The names of the numbers are projected onto the back wall, giving the impression of some kind of counting machine (possibly with a distant reference to Stanley Kubrick's *2001: A*

Space Odyssey (1968)). Einstein plays the violin, the ape takes off his ape mask, and the ape actor gives the final monologue (written by Samuel M. Johnson), in German. When all the masks are removed, love remains, perhaps the real point. It is the Einstein character himself playing a melancholic violin solo that ends the piece.

*****

Three particular moments from my personal history with *Einstein on the Beach* seem relevant to any possibilities for taking the piece beyond Wilson's staging. I have already mentioned the first: the fact that my first ever contact with this piece was via an audio recording. It was back in 1998 during my studies in Belgrade. I listened to the music many times, and while contemplating its sounding world I was eager to see any photo I could find of its visual world. The impossibility of seeing the piece live or on video at that time stimulated my imagination. Every photo from *Einstein* was primarily an incentive to imagine the rest.

A second moment occurred at the beginning of the new millennium, when the group of artists and theorists to which I then belonged decided to dedicate the second issue of the *Walking Theory Journal* to *Einstein on the Beach* and its impact.[42] I wrote a text for the issue on *Einstein* and architecture, provoked by *Einstein* visuals that I still did not know very well. I was looking at *Einstein* as a kind of building, a spatio-temporal architectural experience, and I asked an architect to make a drawing of *Einstein* as though it were a building (Figure 10.6). I provided some measurements and other relevant information for the architectural drawing, which was really a simulation of a building in which every level represented a section of *Einstein*.

This drawing helped me understand how *Einstein* unfolded in space. For me it was a kind of imaginary visual synopsis of the piece, a hypothetical visual reconstruction.

After finally seeing *Einstein* live in January 2013 in De Nationale Opera in Amsterdam, I learnt that excerpts of the music were used for a fashion show featuring the spring/summer 2013 collection of Louis Vuitton, designed by Marc Jacobs. I never did see the whole show, but only excerpts of the video on YouTube.[43] The collection was obviously inspired by the geometry of minimalism in the visual arts, and the choreography of its cyborg-like models evoked *Einstein*. It all resembled some kind of Space Odyssey. *Einstein* in (or even as?) a fashion show: I was skeptical, but it turned out to be intriguing.

Starting with the black and white photos of the original production I went on to commission the architectural drawing of "Einstein as building," then saw it live under Wilson's direction, and finally saw the video excerpts of the fashion

---

42   TkH 2: *Beyond Einstein on the Beach*, See the entire journal issue online at: www.tkh-generator. net/portfolio/tkh-2-beyond-einstein-on-the-beach/, Accessed: December 12, 2017.
43   Louis Vuitton, Spring/Summer 2013, Full Fashion Show (excerpts),www.youtube.com/watch?v= CsuorSZEURs, Accessed: May 2, 2017.

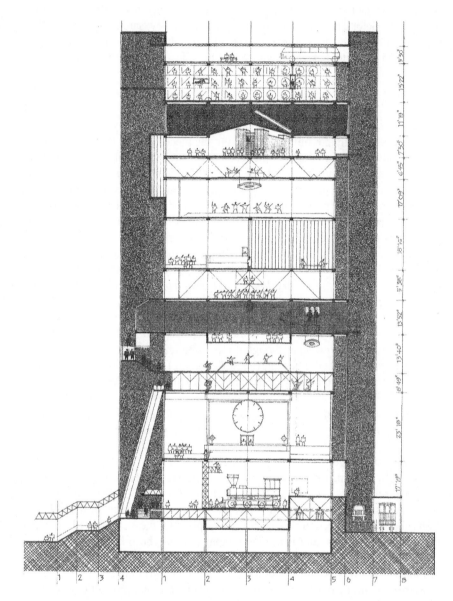

Figure 10.6 Mirjana Novak, drawing of imaginary building in cross-section inspired by
Einstein on the Beach © Mirjana Novak

show using excerpts of its music. That was my history with the piece before I saw
versions by other directors. In all these circumstances, *Einstein* worked surprisingly well. And it was only after all this "Einsteinalia" that I got to know the four
cases of "beyond Wilson" staging that I have discussed in this text. I realized that
Einstein as an installation in the "Staatsbankberlin" was somewhat similar to what

I had imagined when trying to contemplate the piece as a building. Both bank and church were occupied by *Einstein* as though by a kind of alien that adapted surprisingly well to these unfamiliar surroundings. It actually felt quite cozy there.

There was a similar transplantation at the fashion show. I watched the models descending the escalators accompanied by the music from *Einstein* and Samuel M. Johnson's speech "Two Lovers." And quite suddenly the models already belonged to *Einstein*. They seemed to find their "natural" origin there. Likewise with the dancers in Leigh Warren's staging, which presented *Einstein* as an extensive dance piece and with a quite different dance from the one by Lucinda Childs. Even here the dancers were engulfed by the music and by the structure of *Einstein*, and were easily accommodated. Indeed, I observed this in every case where *Einstein* changed its medium (installation, fashion show, dance) and its performance strategy. The transition to something new, extending beyond original borders, was accomplished rather easily, as though the piece itself actually demanded this kind of border crossing. Even the anecdote about staging *Einstein* with toddlers somehow seems almost feasible.[44] It is as though this piece's radical spirit both seeks and enables ever more radical transformations, even today when it is more than 40 years old. And when it stays in the proscenium theater, as in Freyer's and Voges's stagings, the piece itself seems to set up more resistance.

In all these stagings, the Spaceship Scene might be considered a kind of "clue." How the director positions him/herself towards this scene tells us a lot about how he understands *Einstein*. For Freyer, the scene was a polygon by means of which he sought to evaluate the highest reaches of humanity; for Schneider and Witte it was an obsolete fantasy; for Warren little was left of the spaceship fantasy, since he focused on the micro-universe existing between the particular dancing characters. Against the background of these different conceptions, Voges's Spaceship scene appears as a kind of puppet caricature of such "serious" apocalyptic subjects. Each of these spaceships has its own trajectory. But what they all have in common is that in discovering new galaxies for *Einstein* they give it new meanings, inspiring for all future stagings.

---

44 *Baby Einstein on the Beach*, advertising video of Brooklyn Academy of Music, April 1, 2013 www.youtube.com/watch?v=ipMkm1_5jf8, Accessed: May 2, 2017.

Knee chapter 5
Critical excavations

How democratic baroque came about in *dance* and *Einstein on the Beach*

Pieter T'Jonck
(Architect and Art critic)

From 1963 until 1968, Lucinda Childs was a member of the Judson Group. This loose assembly of artists came into being in the slipstream of a "composition class" Robert Dunn organized at the request of Merce Cunningham in the Cunningham Studios. Dunn was highly influenced by the ideas of John Cage, but no one could have foreseen where this would all lead. By questioning rigorously every possible dogma, every routine, every aesthetic, or other judgment, the possibility was created to use everyday movement without any stylistic intervention as the basic material for a dance performance, or to integrate film, theater, or any other possible medium into such a performance. The boundaries between different artistic disciplines waned away almost as fast as they did already half a century ago in the Fine Arts under the influence of the Dadaists. You could call this movement for that reason neo-Dadaism in dance. Among the members of the group, there were indeed not only choreographers and dancers such as Steve Paxton, Trisha Brown, Yvonne Rainer, Deborah Hay, and Simone Forti but also visual artists such as Robert Morris and Robert Rauschenberg. However legendary this group may have become afterward, it did not last very long. After the first success in 1963, the different members were always more involved with the development of their personal careers.

Lucinda Childs entered the New York art world through her participation in the Judson Group, but she was also one of the first to quit definitively in 1968. For the next five years, she studied dance and ballet, and taught and wrote down her reflections on her earlier work. She concentrated especially, as Sally Banes noted, on "problems of cognition and perception."[1] In 1973 she came to the stage again and founded her own company. At once, it is obvious that something funda-mental has changed. In her former solos, she often resorted to everyday objects

---

1 Sally Banes, *Terpsichore in Sneakers*, Boston, Houghton Mifflin Company, 1980, 136.

which she used in a slightly absurd way. A work such as *Street Dance* (1964) incorporated chance events from the street. Quite often, she made ample use of her (comic) talent as an actress. Witnesses of the period sometimes compare her deadpan expression to that of Buster Keaton.[2] From 1973 on, however, her work focused on pure movement. Her other artistic talents were put to use elsewhere, such as in the long and intense collaboration she had with Robert Wilson, as well in theater projects like full-scale operas, including *Einstein on the Beach*. That in itself was enough for a claim to eternal fame. Through these projects, she also got to know Wilson's friend and composer Philip Glass and eventually also the visual artist Sol LeWitt.

Actually, Robert Wilson may have been attracted by her gift as an actor, because when he first approached her to collaborate on *Einstein on the Beach*, he wanted her to play the role of Einstein.[3] But eventually they abandoned that plan. Instead, they worked together closely on the development of the very detailed movements the performers made throughout the piece. As Childs recalls in an interview,[4] it was often Wilson who prompted some ideas through structured improvisations, but it was probably Childs who developed the minute and highly detailed and complex variations of the movement material that they discovered.

This certainly goes for the five so-called "knee plays," which separate the four acts. They were already part and parcel of the piece from the 1976 production on. They basically have the same structure: two women, Childs herself and Sheryl Sutton, dressed like Einstein usually was, in a white shirt and grey baggy pants; they are seated on or lie on Spartan stools and tables made of steel tubes, designed by Wilson. In a deadpan way, they execute quirky movements, moving about their fingers, arms, feet, or their whole bodies as if they were signposts. The rather simple nature of the movements belies the extreme concentration required to execute these movements in exact rhythm, which makes them look slightly absurd or enigmatic. These movements are not unlike the movements of slapstick actors – which was precisely the kind of acting Wilson was looking for. The complexity of these knee plays is even heightened at those moments when Childs and Sutton also recite texts in a toneless voice, as if you would hear an answering machine repeating the same messages over and over again, without ever making full sense of what you hear. Childs was also prominently present in a few solos, such as scene Ia (The Train), when she moves up and down the stage frantically on the tips of her toes while swinging around her arms and torso. She even contributed a small part of the text (i.e., as the "witness" talking about the "prematurely air-conditioned supermarket" in scene I of act III.[5]

2   See for instance Banes, Op. Cit., chapter about Childs.
3   Childs refers to this in an interview: "Einstein on the Beach: A discussion with composer Philip Glass and choreographer Lucinda Childs" moderated by Mark Swed, April 29, 2011, Zellerbach Hall, UC Berkeley. See: https://www.youtube.com/watch?v=e8Cx7XOYj_w, Accessed: March 8, 2017.
4   Ibid.
5   Childs gives an account of the way this text came about in the same interview: Ibid.

However important her contribution was in determining the quality of timing and expression of the actors in *Einstein on the Beach*, she did not choreograph the two dances of the original production. Andrew DeGroat was mentioned as choreographer in the original 1976 version. It was only for the 1984 revival of the piece that her two choreographies, Field One and Field Two, were included instead of the original ones, as Robert Wilson wanted something more demanding and ambitious. In that way, Childs came to be responsible in the 1984 version for two of the three "visual planes" or "formats" of the play and was involved in all of them. Wilson uses the terms "visual planes" or "formats" to describe the different ways in which the work has an effect on the spectator, or the different perspectives that are adopted in it.[6] He makes use of painterly terms such as portrait, still life, and landscape to describe these "visual planes." The knee plays in his view are similar to the portrait, as there is a strong intimacy between the audience and the performers. The dances however take a very broad view. It seems as if the dancers are far in the distance. Thus, the dance can be compared to a landscape, in which the spectator has the feeling of watching a distant visual field. Most other scenes then should be compared to still lives in the way they combine heterogenous objects and actions into one image.

But in 1976, Childs did not choreograph the opera in its entirety, and was working mainly at the time without sound or music. *Einstein on the Beach* was her first encounter with highly complex musical structures. As she mentions in an interview together with Philip Glass, she was fascinated by the strict separation Merce Cunningham maintained in his choreographies between the dance score and the musical score, which the dancers might not even hear before the premiere of a new work. For that reason, her research between 1968 and 1973 focused on dancing in silence.[7] This might have inspired the creation in 1979 of *Dance*, one of her most important works, for which Philip Glass wrote the score. This work evidently laid the groundwork for the 1984 choreographies, Field One and Field Two, in *Einstein on the Beach*.

As a choreographer, she indeed worked without any recourse to a musical score for a long time. Between 1973 and 1979, she devised works that comprised nothing but movement. No music or scenography was used. It is precisely this extreme limitation that allowed her to draw attention to the fact that even the simplest of movements or movement schemes opened up the possibility for an endless number of combinations, which in turn, offered an endless number of different perspectives on that same material. Very often her movements were based on direct observation of human behavior, and not on some "dance vocabulary" or even a "dance language" such as ballet. In that sense, she was still the heir of

6   Wilson gives an account of this in the BAM movie *Einstein on the Beach: the changing image of opera*, 1985, New York, NY, USA, https://www.youtube.com/watch?v=j1P xYB0wqSE, accessed: March 8, 2017.
7   *Einstein on the Beach,* A discussion with composer Philip Glass and Choreographer Lucinda Childs moderated by Mark Swed, Ibid.

Cage and the Judson Group. Childs herself indicates for instance that the move-ment material of *Dance* was based on the image of a person who is going in one direction, suddenly changes his mind and turns back.[8] This material contains very typical actions: slight hesitations, slow pivotal movements, a tiny capsizing of the body. She omits from that material every trace of intentionality, however. She reads and presents it as a series of empty signs, pure differences that may show a resemblance to the original movement in the effort they require, but do not convey the same meaning, nor ask for interpretation.

A series of empty signs such as this one can, for that reason, be endlessly split up and reconfigured. Sally Banes again provides an excellent summary of this:

> But in the dances of the 1970s it is the very structure of the dance that sup-plies divergent points of view. Phrases and fields of movement are stated, bro-ken down, and reconstructed. Paradoxically, what seems to be an undeviating reductionist strategy proliferates minute variations on already basic themes. In a given dance, although a single movement phrase appears to be repeated over and over, with close viewing the spectator can see that within the strict limits of the phrase, small insertions are made, changes of direction alter the paths of one or a pair of dancers, the phrase reverses or inverts.[9]

This explanation is at the same time an accurate description of what happens in *Dance*, Childs's 1979 masterpiece. But there is also an important difference. *Dance* is not just the culmination of the movement research Childs conducted between 1973 and 1978. For the first time, she also made use of classical aspects of choreography such as music and scenography. What is more, she chose to col-laborate with leading figures working in other fields: Philip Glass as composer, Sol LeWitt as scenographer, Beverly Emmons as lighting director.

Dance consists of three parts. The first is for four male-female couples and the second is a solo Childs originally performed herself, while in the third part the same cast as in the first is onstage again. In part 1, the dancers move again and again with wide sideway jumps along the stage. The number of couples that performs this action simultaneously or in opposite directions is varied all the time. Sometimes, the dancers seem to capsize when taking off, or it looks as if their jump is stuttering for a split second, as if they would want to stretch their jump for an extra count. Very regularly, the ongoing movement is interrupted also for a pivotal movement with small jumps on the spot. But, overall, the dance mate-rial remains almost identical to itself for the full twenty minutes of this part. It is however never shown twice in exactly the same order, with the same variations, rotational direction, or speed. This is dizzying, because one's expectations are constantly betrayed every time one thinks one understands how the system works.

8　Personal recollection of an interview after the Brussels performance of 'Dance', Kaaitheater, Brussels, 2012-Oct. 12.
9　Banes, Op. Cit., 136.

It is an exceptional visual paradox: extreme simplicity and strict conformance to a system that still achieves constant surprise.

The combination with the musical score of Philip Glass enhances this experience further. The dance follows the rhythm and composition of the music closely, which was written before the choreography. Usually, this mirroring between dance and music results in a transparent, predictable dance form. This is not always the case here because the music as well as the dance only seemingly repeat the same motives. Very soon it appears that only a relentless bass tone is more or less constant. On top of that, all kinds of secondary motives and variations appear in capriciously changing orchestrations and accelerations. Here, as well, it appears as if constantly changing variations and perspectives are pouring out of the same "monad" or basic cell of a simple musical phrase. Music and dance reinforce each other's action.

This also goes for the solo. It is built on a straight line from the back to the front of the stage and on a second circular movement. Again, the movements consist of rotations, slight jumps and large strides executed in imperturbable order, but they are still unpredictable through slight variations. The visual paradox might be even greater here, because there is only one dancer at work (there has been an alternative version in which two dancers execute it as perfect mirrors of one another). Because of that, the brain has a hard time to accept the sheer impossibility of pinning down the exact algorithm of these variations, despite the simplicity of the movements.

The third part probably is the most spectacular. In its spatial configuration, it unmistakably brings to mind *Quad* (first presented as a Television play in 1981, a text edition followed only in 1984[10]) by Samuel Beckett. In the same way, dancers walk from one corner of the stage to the middle diagonally, to choose a different direction, whether or not with an elegant turn around this center point. However, in Beckett's piece, dating from 1981, thus two years later, the feeling you have is that the performers are trapped in a treadmill. Six steps along the border of a square, four on a diagonal towards the middle, making a small circle and stepping to the next corner. In Childs's work, the spatial configuration is larger, and the dancers do not in the least look like small mice or formless shapes. While jumping, hopping, and turning around, they seem to defy fate every time they all but collide into each other in the middle of the stage. Imperturbably they go on and on, like wheels in a gigantic clockwork, a kaleidoscope of variations on a theme.

Dance is a solemn, almost exalted work. The arms of the dancers reinforce this impression in the three parts subtly. They let them hover at chest height in front of their torsos or lift them in an elegant way, as if the dance was no effort at all to them. These arms do not define the dance; that task is left to the legs and feet, but they function as flywheels or stabilizers that keep the clockwork on its due course flawlessly. This is the exact principle of Baroque ballet. The movements are fast and light, but they don't aspire to the extreme virtuosity of romantic ballet. This

10 *The Complete Dramatic Works of Samuel Beckett*, London, Faber & Faber, 2006.

is not a dream reality. The movements stay close to ordinary ones, but they are transcended in order to lift the mundane to a different plane of reality, to a glorious, solemn realm of pure grace. They glorify the world without altering it. Virtuosity is of a different nature here than in romantic ballet: it is about the concentration required not to lose track of the endless number of combinations. This in a way dehumanizes the dancers: they coincide completely with the positions they have in the clockwork machine. There is no time or space to show any inner feeling, to "act out," personify, or inhabit a character, which are key principles when performing in the Romantic ballet tradition.

Loftiness and intensity without meaning: the essence of Baroque dance. Of course, Becketts *Quad* is just as baroque, but it shows the suffocating flip side of the splendid image: how "I" is completely annihilated in the clockwork of the performance. Sally Banes perceived this tendency already in 1980[11] when she claimed that Childs's work was "almost Baroque" in its sense for variations on minimal themes. But that something of a "slip of the tongue," because elsewhere she readily agrees to the prevailing interpretation of that period. Critics used to compare Childs's formal research in the work of minimalist visual artists such as Elsworth Kelly or Frank Stella. Their rigid, explicitly non-figurative paintings drew attention to the painterly reality of the canvass in and of itself and its effect on the beholder. Indeed, one can say that Childs's dance has the same neutrality and flatness. There is nothing to be seen "behind" the movement. Still, the analogy does not really suffice. Kelly and Stella used their neutral, flat compositions to settle their score with the myth that the painterly gesture would testify to, or the evidence of an original genius or inspiration. (Robert Rauschenberg stressed this point even more strongly in his *Twin Pieces* (1957), *Factum I* and *Factum II*. Both of these works show the same "spontaneous" brush strokes, exposing the stereotypical nature of seemingly spontaneous painterly expression.)

It is not that Childs is claiming that she made extraordinary discoveries in movement material. But it is a completely different matter to trace a line on a canvas in an imperturbable and well-considered way than to execute an extremely demanding number of tiny variations on one movement on the spot without any outward sign of effort or affection. That calls for a very different type of discipline and concentration, because there is no way back, no improvement is possible. Every error is fatal without any recourse. The performance of the dance in itself mobilizes the attention of the spectator, precisely because of its seeming effortlessness. In exactly the same way, Glass's music draws attention to its performance because of the concentration and discipline required to keep track of its progression. Indeed, music is a much better point of comparison than painting to identify what is at stake here. Childs's work offers maximum intensity with minimal content in a brilliant compositional form. Exactly what Baroque theatricality always was about.[12]

11   Banes, Op.Cit., 144.
12   This notion of the baroque theatricality essentially draws on 'Rome/Over theatraliteit', Bart Verschaffel, Vlees en Beton 16, Ghent, 1990.

That is not all, however. *Dance* is more impressive than any other work of Childs's, even more than *Available Light* (1983), and that is certainly not only because John Adams, and not Philip Glass, wrote the score of that piece. It lies, I suppose, in the contribution of the visual artist Sol LeWitt. At first sight, the formal starting points of his work are closely related to those of Childs and Glass (or even Stella or Kelly for that matter). In many of his works, he had no part in the actual execution, but simply defined a strict set of rules on how to combine elementary components such as a line of a certain length and color into a composition. In that way it was possible that some of his works were completely remade for an exhibition in Leuven in 2012, despite the fact that LeWitt died in 2007. It sufficed that a team of young painters applied a set of pictorial elements on a wall in the way he prescribed. That is enough to give the work a tangible, and sometimes truly dazzling, shape in any specific location. It speaks for itself that this art does not try to reveal any emotion or feeling of its author. One may conjecture about what it does to a person to draw straight lines of a certain length for days on end, but that does not in any way detract from what the resulting image in itself shows or tells. The extreme reduction and concentration of means of this work lead to an image that would otherwise never have become apparent. In that respect, at least, it is obvious why LeWitt and Childs can be considered kindred spirits: both of them rely on minimal movements or lines and a strict set of rules to provoke a specific perceptual experience.

Despite this analogy, it is obvious that LeWitt had little to contribute to a choreography with such a "procedural" drawing. Unlike the music, which functions almost in unison with the dance, as a kind of mirror-image, a work of LeWitt could never be actually executed in the course of a stage performance. There would be no other option than to show the final result, an image that can only be perceived as a kind of backdrop, not as a partner in the choreography. That is why LeWitt refused to make this kind of contribution. Instead of inventing a backdrop or scenery, though, he came up with the idea of using movement in itself as a form of scenography, in which way the scenography would become an extra dancer. This idea took the form of a 35 mm black-and-white movie that was projected over the dance on invisible gauze screens. The real point of the film, however, is that it is made of images of the very dance that is at the same time performed live on stage. For someone who sees the work these days, that is an interesting experience, because you see at once that the dancers Childs works with nowadays have a more relaxed attitude towards the solemn poses than the original dancers. In my opinion, however, the main issue in LeWitt's film is not the discrepancy between the live movements and those on the screen, but the radically different effect of film images and live images.

Even if it may seem as if the film is pure registration of the dance, it actually modifies the original work in an incisive way. For one thing, the dance was done on a floor that was marked by a conspicuous grid of squares. Such a gridded floor pattern is lacking in the live performance. The grid, however, enabled LeWitt to enhance the perspectival effects of the performance. In so doing, he revealed its Baroque character even more. Baroque theater is indeed all about putting things into perspective.[13] Paradoxically, however, it seems as if LeWitt does this mainly to undermine the power of these baroque effects, by making very specific choices for his point of view or the composition of the image. Sometimes his shots are taken from a point very high above the stage, a point of view that is inaccessible to a spectator. At other times, he films at very short range, an equally impossible point of view for the spectator. When images such as those are projected onto the gauze screen, this produces odd effects. The close-ups for instance superimpose larger than life images of the dancers on the relatively tiny actual dancers. This provokes the illusion that the film image is slowed down. LeWitt reinforces this experience by inserting still images now and then. When the same scene is shot by two cameras, LeWitt presents both points of view as a split screen. A film image with a high point of view can be projected over the full proscenium screen, but every once in a while LeWitt also decides to use a vertical split screen, with a semi-close-up on the lower part and an aerial shot on the upper. Finally, he also makes use, a few times, of the technique of an image within an image, combining a close-up and a view of the entire stage. The most conspicuous feature, however, is that sometimes there is only film, no dance and vice versa. This is an apparent demonstration of the fact that the film and the live performance each have their own temporal logic, even though they show – when running simultaneously – the same movements.

This operation considerably heightens the complexity of Childs's already very intricate figures. Curiously enough, it even strengthens the puppet-like impression the dancers make, as if they were only extremely complex mechanisms, because the film projection makes one extremely aware of the presence of the gauze screen in front of the stage, and as such of the fact that the dancers are "locked up in an observation space," a "box." This very image of a panoptical box is typical of Baroque theater. But at the same time, the film projection contradicts the sensation of a panopticon because a filmic image is, unlike a theatrical image, largely indifferent to the position of the spectator as it is a flat surface, and it can therefore be watched almost as well from any angle. Movies are indeed a far more "democratic" medium than theater. This paradox reaches its high point in vertical split screens, but implicitly it is always present. There is even more to it than this: the dance appears on the screen in an unprecedented way: the close-ups allow for a degree of detail that was unthinkable before. This, by the way, was the reason Lewitt insisted on using the 35 mm format. Finally, the film reduces to a large degree the authority, the compelling force of the extremely exacting choreography because it disengages the images from the factual performance to reintegrate them into the editing of the film, which follows a wholly different logic of image and time composition and rhythm. Editing indeed is a filmic game that mobilizes the attention of the spectator in a totally different way than theater does.

This extraordinary combination of live dance and film turns *Dance* into something of an oxymoron. It forges into one work two distinct ways of watching and composing in such a way that they enhance and annihilate each other at once. The

---

13 Verschaffel, Op. Cit.

other choreographic works of Lucinda Childs in this period of her career might give one the impression that she is always hitting on the same nail, that she goes on developing the same principle over and over again. That is not the case in *Dance*. *Dance* is democratic Baroque. That was never done before or after this single work.

But inasmuch as *Dance* reveals the Baroque nature of the work of Childs as a choreographer, it is also very telling about the nature of *Einstein on the Beach* as an opera. The Field Dances, which were not choreographed by Childs in the 1976 production, but only in 1984, are "cut from the same block" as the choreography of *Dance* in their dazzling combination of movements that in itself seem simple and vaguely familiar. They are, however, integrated in the threefold perspective – portrait (the Knee Plays), still life (images such as the train) and landscape (the Field Dances) – that Wilson envisioned. Childs's seminal contribution to the 1976 production for the Knee Plays and some of the "still life" images was complemented here with this third perspective from far away. This evidences the tremendous impact sheer compositional work has in the way a spectator can apprehend the work. It is Wilson's composition that wrests a meaning, however "open" it may be, out of the combination of in their own right nonsensical texts, images, sounds, and movements; which are all strictly separate, not "logically" connected elements. In this way, the work is a veiled tribute to the compositional technique of Merce Cunningham, who abided by the strict principle of juxtaposing music, dance, lighting, and scenography. Wilson, however, also leaned on popular imagery, such as, of course, images of Alfred Einstein himself, and the more intricate and rhythmically conscious interweaving of these elements to form the overall dreamlike structure that makes the work so extremely compelling to watch. Especially where dancing is concerned, the alternation of different perspectives on movement as an expressive element is, in a sense, akin to the way LeWitt changed how one could understand the meaning of the choreography in *Dance*. Which is as groundbreaking as *Dance* itself was.

Einstein in the press

Frits van der Waa
(Music journalist at *de Volkskrant*, Amsterdam)

Over the past four decades a large number of articles and essays have been written about *Einstein on the Beach*, especially in 1976, when the opera was first performed, and again in 2012–15, during the opera's extensive international tour. This article presents an impression of this material, which is by no means exhaustive.[14] For one thing, articles from all those years ago are not easily accessible. Especially in the Netherlands, getting hold of older newspaper articles proved to be a bit of a problem, so my account of *Einstein*'s Dutch reception is not as complete as it should be.[15]

14 This text is based on an address given on January 6, 2013, during the *Einstein on the Beach: Opera after Drama* symposium, University of Amsterdam.
15 I am very grateful to Thom Donovan, Bob Wilson's archivist, who sent me a considerable amount of mainly English-language articles.

Because I was first and foremost interested in *Einstein*'s critical reception, I put aside a lot of material, such as the many interviews with Robert Wilson, Philip Glass, or both. Interesting as they may be, they usually contain similar information. Many reviews or previews were merely descriptive, and the shorter newspaper reviews usually contain very few critical insights, so this selection can be regarded as the tip, or tips, of the iceberg(s).

It should come as no surprise that most reviews – from the seventies, but also the more recent ones – were positive in tone, sometimes even ecstatic in their praise of performances. Nevertheless there are also pronounced differences, and sometimes critics are completely in opposition to one another. There's no accounting for taste, but this undoubtedly also has to do with the backgrounds of critics in different artistic fields and intellectual disciplines; musical, theatrical, and choreographic elements all play more or less equal parts in *Einstein*.

Something that is highlighted in many articles is the remarkable way in which Wilson's theatrical approach affects experiences of time and duration. Writing about the Rotterdam performance of October 22, 1976, the Dutch theater critic Nic Brink described this in *De Groene Amsterdammer*:

> Despite the fact that there is no explicable action, one's attention is constantly captured. Despite the fact that things develop at a provocatively slow pace, one doesn't get bored in the least. It is as if Wilson magically converts the hall into an iron lung, where all vital functions assume a much slower pace. Awareness of time and velocity disappears.[16]

Brink is one of the few theater critics who shows a keen sense and understanding of music, although he pretends to know little about it. Recalling his fascination when he first heard *Six Pianos* by Steve Reich, he comments: "Suddenly I realised that certain, melodyless music by older composers gives me the same sense of euphoria." By way of example, he refers to the first prelude of Bach's *Well-Tempered Clavier*, which in essence is nothing more than a series of arpeggiated chords: "The difference is that minimalist composers easily maintain their 'monophony' for an hour or longer, whereas Bach after five minutes would go back to business as usual."

For readers who in 1976 may not have been familiar with minimalism, this must have been a very clarifying explanation, much better than the description Clive Barnes gave in *The New York Times*: "Mr. Glass's music is sensational – literally.

16 Nic Brink, "De ijzeren long van Glass en Wilson," *De Groene Amsterdammer*, October 27, 1976. Original quotes: "Ondanks het feit dat de handelingen zich in tergend traag tempo voltrekken, is er geen moment van verveling. Het lijkt alsof Wilson de schouwburg weet om te toveren in een ijzeren long, waarin alle levensfuncties zich verlangzaamd voltrekken. Het besef van tijd en van snelheid verdwijnt." "Ineens realiseerde ik me dat ik bij bepaalde, melodietjesloze muziek van andere komponisten een zelfde soort euforische sensatie onderga." "Met dien verstande dat de laatsten hun 'monofonie' rustig een uur voortzetten, waar Bach na 5 minuten weer overgaat tot de orde van de dag."

It is almost more monotonous than Bach's – yes, there are fugal elements – and, more important, at times almost as interesting."[17]

Most critics agree that it is the happy combination of Wilson's, Glass's, and De Groat's qualities that make *Einstein on the Beach* the "landmark" it is often called. The Dutch critic W. Hofman wrote:

> If ever something can be dubbed "total theater," then it is *Einstein on the Beach*. Nothing in this work has a life of its own, everything supports every-thing else. The result is really a "total theater," which is completely different from putting several elements together in one production.[18]

Hofmans's "total theater" can be considered roughly equivalent to the word *Gesamtkunstwerk*, which also appears in many reviews.

Not all critics were sensitive to this aspect. For instance, Edwin Wilson, the reviewer of the *Wall Street Journal*, disliked the music and apparently didn't under-stand the role of the composer, because he wrote: "In each section, having wound up his oversized, animated music box, Mr. Wilson lets it run on interminably, repeating the same sounds and movements over and over again, making a slight change every ten minutes or so."[19] But his view was quite an exception.

Most reviewers understandably paid attention to *Einstein*'s formal structure, maybe because it is one of the more easily describable aspects of the perfor-mance, but there were few who did better than giving a mere outline. Andrew Porter, *The New Yorker*'s esteemed music critic, made an interesting observation about the knee plays:

> At first they seem to function like the intermezzi that were played between the acts of an opera seria, [...] but they carry so much musical (and at the last, emotional) weight that they can be regarded as the main matter of the opera, and the acts themselves as extended intermezzi or developments. Although *Einstein* has been generally treated as if it were a work by Wilson with incidental music by Glass, it is very different – in tone, structure, pace, and appearance – from Wilson's earlier pieces. To describe it as a character-istic Glass score with scenic accompaniment by Wilson – and choreographic accompaniment by Andrew DeGroat – would be nearer the mark but still not quite accurate. It is a *Gesamtkunstwerk* in which Wilson's romantic profusion,

17 Clive Barnes, "'Einstein on the Beach' Transforms Boredom into Memorable Theater," *The New York Times*, November 23, 1976.
18 W. Hofman, "Einstein on the Beach, of 'Vijf uren zijn nog te kort,'" *Magazijn*, October 1976. Original quote: "Als er ooit sprake was van totaal theater, dan is het wel bij *Einstein on the Beach*. Niets leidt een eigen leven, alles is ter ondersteuning van het andere. Resultaat "werkelijk totaal theater" wat reëel iets anders is dan een aantal elementen samenstoppen in één produktie."
19 Edwin Wilson, "An Avant-Garde Production at Met," *The Wall Street Journal*, November 26, 1976.

allusiveness, and collage techniques are tempered by Glass's sharp-focus insistence on pure structure.[20]

Porter's only objection concerns the occasional loudness of Glass's music.

Several critics were puzzled by questions such as: what is the meaning of *Einstein on the Beach*? Or how to interpret it? Especially in the Dutch reviews from 1976 it is striking that several of them asked – or searched – for political meanings, which demonstrates the mood in Holland during the mid-seventies, especially among left-oriented people. Political, sociological, or educational messages were almost obligatory when staging a theatrical performance. The Dutch theater critic Max Arian perceived *Einstein* as a purely political piece, although he conceded that his impressions might be of a very personal nature. The trial scene, for instance, reminded him of the trial against Sacco and Vanzetti, or the McCarthy sessions. In the choreography he saw parallels with the revolutionary operas of Mao's China. "And is Einstein himself not, like a modern Nero, playing his fiddle while his world, the United States, is on fire?" he asked. [21]

The music critic of the Dutch daily newspaper, *De Volkskrant*, Hans Heg, did not perceive it like that, but nevertheless touched upon this angle:

> One can hardly accuse Wilson and Glass of dealing in pronounced political theater; one will neither see nor hear fists raised in this piece. But the way in which they manage to translate the fortunes and misfortunes of their own times into images and music is apparent to everyone who is willing to understand it.[22]

And he adds: "Of course it is an easy way out to get yourself lulled away by the fantastic scenery, the cleverly designed lighting effects, the fascinating slow-motion performances of the actors, the often-enthralling music or the dancers' simple and playful movements."

In the USA, the reviewers usually didn't look for a political stance, though plenty of them, prompted by Wilson, offered explanations in an Einsteinian vein, and divined associations about relativity, the atomic age, and so on. The Spaceship scene as well as the famous light-bar scene prompted several observers to notice

20 Andrew Porter, "Many-Colored Glass," *The New Yorker*, December 13, 1976, 164.
21 Max Arian, "Vormingstoneel voor intellektuelen?" *Toneel Teatraal*, November 1976. Original quote: "Zit Einstein niet zelf als een modern soort Nero viool te spelen terwijl zijn wereld, de Verenigde Staten, in brand staat?"
22 Hans Heg, "Einstein on the beach: 'n kolossale nieuwe opera," *De Volkskrant*, August 14, 1976. Original quote: "Je kunt Wilson en Glass moeilijk verwijten dat ze met geprononceerd politiek theater bezig zijn; gebalde vuisten kun je bij hen noch zien noch horen. Maar de manier waarop ze het wel en wee van hun eigen tijd in beeld en muziek weten te vertalen is duidelijk voor iedereen die het wil begrijpen. Al blijft het natuurlijk een gemakkelijke weg om lekker weg te dromen op de fantastische toneelbeelden, de uitgekiende belichtingseffecten, het fascinerende slow-motionspel van de acteurs, de vaak meeslepende muziek of het simpele en speelse bewegingsspel van de dansers."

parallels or allusions to Kubrick's *2001: A Space Odyssey* (1968), but had it been a year later they doubtlessly would have mentioned *Close Encounters of the Third Kind* (1977).

Martin Gottfried summed it up quite nicely in his *New York Post* review:

> There is no explanation that can, need or should be made or the why of this major work of Wilson's; no comparison that can be made with anything else, not really, on the stage. It is the theater of a visionary, one who knows what he is doing and can do it; one who sees things as no others see them and can materialize that so it can be seen by others. I take that to be the function of the artist.[23]

There are two elements critics universally agree upon: the admirable concentration and endurance of the performers, and the sheer beauty of Wilson's images. But several of them voice distrust about this latter quality.

The poet and critic David Shapiro, who wrote a very interesting essay with a philosophical slant for the collection *The Art of Performance*, put it like this, getting carried away a little by his own words:

> Wilson converts the opera into something as flat and usable as a map. Here opera draws attention to itself as a self-regulating whole, not by the usual thickening of language but by the deliquescence of so many seemingly central resources. While there is a little bit of the merely magical to Wilson, there is much of the necessary shamanism required to heal us in a restless universe agitated in its smallest parts. Still, one might be sceptical, because it is most wonderful in its very lack of explanatory power. Often its architecture seems merely good interior design. It is shattered as the fruit dish of Paul Cézanne. But the point of pointlessness is to be at once shattered and whole, like the fruit dish of Cézanne. We suffer through it as in its melancholy scene of the eclipse of our clock. Time, our former absolute sun, now dreamily obscured by theory. One is reminded of the trauma Einstein occasioned in his enduring witness to relativism. Yet does not a sly dice-playing God reign over this essentially collective dream theatre?'[24]

Shapiro comes across as almost too clever for his own good, but he offers plenty of perspicacious observations in just a few pages. His essay is still worth reading.

Far more severe criticism was voiced by Bonnie Maranca, who in 1977 wrote an essay about *Einstein* for the *New York Arts Journal*. She first voices her concern about the avant-garde – and especially Bob Wilson – which according to her

---

23 Martin Gottfried, "Wilson's *Einstein On the Beach* Is Awash with Visual Events," *New York Post*, November 23, 1976.
24 David Shapiro, "Notes on *Einstein on the Beach*," in *The Art of Performance: A Critical Anthology*, ed. Gregory Battcock and Robert Nickas, New York, Plume, 1984, 271–77.

is capitulating to fashion and commercialism. She then gives a quite extensive description and analysis of *Einstein on the Beach* and finally concludes:

> Wilson's recent pieces have used contemporary myths to illustrate his dis-satisfaction with the alienation of modern life. His vision is apocalyptic; he seeks a return to order and peace after the holocaust. Is this not a reflection of Romantic longing for a return to a world that we will never see again? Wilson's handling of contemporary problems is too naive to take seriously.[25]

According to Maranca, Wilson's escapism is the problematical element in his theater. The danger is that audiences, overwhelmed by the monumental settings and the beauty of the images, will be passively drawn into the spiritualistic world of his theater, which in peculiar ways mirrors the growing mass consciousness of the seventies. Critics as well as audiences have admitted that they see *Einstein on the Beach* as a work one must give oneself up to. All elements contribute to making *Einstein on the Beach* an experience of transcendental meditation in the theater:

> It is this sense of loss of time and place, the religiosity of the experience, the absorption in images that by their nature are ambiguous, simple resolutions of harsh political realities, and the acceptance of a theatre that hypnotizes its devout followers that is disturbing. It is indeed questionable whether Wilson will lead us to higher consciousness. Theatre must be more than something to gape at or lose oneself in.[26]

Her demand for a message of some sort is somehow reminiscent of the Dutch crit-ics, who searched for political meaning in *Einstein*. Nevertheless, in her dismissal of the work, Maranca is quite an exception.

In 1984–85, when *Einstein* was revived, the coverage was less intense. The dif-ferences in opinion were more extreme, though. For instance, a review by Gregory Sandow in *Voice*, headed *Einstein in the Fog*, echoes Maranca's views by saying: "More than anything else it's the beauty of *Einstein on the Beach* that keeps peo-ple from seeing how shallow it is." Sandow compares it with other theater pieces by Wilson and says: "I can easily imagine the opera with a different score," in which he disagrees with a vast majority of reviewers. As a final verdict he writes: "*Einstein on the Beach* turned out to be not a classic of the genre, but instead a creaky antique."[27]

At the other end of the spectrum in 1984 was a review by Robert Brustein in *The New Republic*, who waxed lyrical, writing:

25 B. Maranca, *Theatre Writings*, New York, PAJ Publications, 1984, 121.
26 Maranca, *Theatre Writings*, 122.
27 Gregory Sandow, "Einstein in the Fog," *Voice*, January 8, 1985.

It represents one of those rare moments in cultural history where the most gifted people at work in the performing arts combine their resources to wallop us into an oceanic perception of our relation to the cosmos. Few contemporary works have penetrated so deeply into the uncreated dream life of the race. Pulling ecstasy from boredom, finding insight through repetition, alternating mechanical rhythms with pulsing climaxes, *Einstein on the Beach* manages to burrow into your mind and work on you like a wound.[28]

Incomprehensible as Brustein's last metaphor is, these two examples serve to show that, even in 1984, *Einstein* had reached legendary status and could therefore easily lead to extreme disappointment or extreme elation.

When *Einstein* was staged again, in 2012–15, after more than 20 years, the work apparently had become such a widely acknowledged classic that in many reviews the approach was one of reverence. Once more, there was a significant amount of praise, with much use of the epithet "magical." Somehow, the beauty-argument of earlier years, be it positive or negative, hardly played a role anymore. The admiration for the stamina and the skills of the performers was, if possible, even greater than in the seventies. And, more than ever, many reviewers didn't go beyond mere descriptions.

Nevertheless, there were dissenters. The British critic Rupert Christiansen apparently hated the work and concluded his review in *The Telegraph* with these words:

I remain adamantly of the view that such stuff is flatulently pretentious in its wilful opacity and without aesthetic, intellectual or spiritual substance. It is also asphyxiatingly tedious and left me wanting to scream. Unless you are a paid-up devotee of the Glass-Wilson cult, avoid this like the plague.[29]

There were several reviewers who thought the theatrical staging showed its age. Anthony Howell wrote in the online magazine *The Fortnightly Review*:

The need to deny message – to add in red-herrings and whimsical reference in a cool, krazy New York way – ultimately begins to irritate as much as any message ever would, and when something is actually said – well, much of the text sounds dated now, especially the proto-feminist guying of feminism, the references to Mr Bojangles and the love and kissing bit at the conclusion.[30]

---

28 Robert Brustein, "Expanding Einstein's Universe," *The New Republic*, January 28, 1985, 23.
29 Rupert Christiansen, "Einstein on the Beach, Barbican, review," *The Telegraph*, May 7, 2012. www.telegraph.co.uk/culture/music/opera/9250317/Einstein-on-the-Beach-Barbi can-review.html, Accessed: May 2, 2017.
30 Anthony Howell, "Watching 'Einstein on the Beach' through a periscope," *The Fortnightly Review*, May 6, 2012. http://fortnightlyreview.co.uk/2012/05/einstein-beach/, Accessed: May 2, 2017.

His Canadian colleague Robert Everett-Green, writing for *The Globe and Mail*, said the same, albeit in a friendlier tone:

> Sometimes it seemed very fresh and strange, because it said "opera" on the program and we still expect narrative and characters and arias from that. Other times it felt very 1976. It was cool and knowing in the particular way some things were then. You could come in and see two people sitting like robots in uniform shirts and suspenders, and think of Kraftwerk. Even precision can age, like everything else.[31]

Cordelia Lynn of the British *Ceasefire Magazine* had a similar experience, but put it elegantly into perspective:

> This *Einstein* is a faithful reproduction of the original 1976 version. Despite how imaginative and daring much of the direction is, it already seems strangely outdated. You walk away with an odd, somewhat patronising feeling of "Ah yes, all that seventies experimental formalism." *Einstein on the Beach* is no longer the brave new world it once was: "those were the days." Though perhaps the fact that it feels so unoriginal at times is a testament, if nothing else, to the huge influence that both Wilson and Glass have had on theatre and music over the past three decades.[32]

The pivotal question of course is whether *Einstein* is still up-to-date, relevant to our times, and how should we assess its historical position?

"Today *Einstein on the Beach* is more revolutionary than when it was created [...] It demonstrates once again how in theatre it is not necessary to understand but get lost in the wonderful 'other' life of the stage,"[33] wrote Marinella Guatterini in the Italian newspaper *Il Sole ventiquatro ore*.

By contrast, Anthony Tomassini wrote in *The New York Times*:

> In advance of this tour many critics and devotees of the Glass operas wondered whether *Einstein* would by now come across as dated or pretentious. But the piece seems particularly suited to current musical politics and social

---

31 Robert Everett-Green, "Einstein on the Beach: A lot of numbers with stories, relatively speaking," *The Globe and Mail*, June 11, 2012. www.pressreader.com/canada/the-globe-and-mail-metro-ontario-edition/20120611/282398396484335, Accessed: May 2, 2017.

32 Cordelia Lynn, "Review: Einstein on the Beach (Barbican)," *Ceasefire Magazine*, May 9, 2012. https://ceasefiremagazine.co.uk/einstein-beach-philip-glass-robert-wilson/, Accessed: May 2, 2017.

33 Marinella Guatterini, "Einstein rivoluziona la spiaggia," *Il Sole 24 Ore*, March 25, 2012. www.ilsole24ore.com/art/cultura/2012-03-25/einstein-rivoluziona-spiaggia-081939.shtml, Accessed: May 2, 2017. Original quote: "Più rivoluzionario oggi di ieri, Einstein on the Beach [...] dimostra che a teatro non serve capire [...], ma piuttosto perdersi nella meravigliosa, quando è tale, vita 'altra' della scena."

culture. In 1976 *Einstein* was seen as a combative declaration from the boom-
ing downtown scene directed against the established uptown culture, especially the complex, intellectual styles of contemporary music sanctioned within
academia. Actually, at the time, Mr. Glass and Mr. Wilson were more interested in fulfilling their personal vision than engaging in polemics.

Even when *Einstein* was here in 1992, the scars from that contemporary
music battle were still sore. Now those bad times seem long gone. Composers
do whatever they want to. Audiences are open to everything. Performers
champion all styles.[34]

Michael Glitz argued in *The Huffington Post* that the imagery of *Einstein* tran-
scends its origins:

It was only on a second viewing this go-round I appreciated how very much
of its time *Einstein* was: the speech by a woman at a gathering of activists
demanding equal rights (and using the very 70s expression "male chauvinist
pig"), the appearance of Patty Hearst, the fear of Cold War nuclear annihilation and other seemingly random details must have made this opera seem
very timely indeed, especially when compared to say *Bluebeard's Castle* or
The Ring Cycle. But they completely transmuted those details of the 1970s
so they could breathe and live on. In 1976, Patty Hearst undoubtedly seemed
ripped from the headlines, in 1984 it might have seemed dated, in 1992 perhaps ironic and today she has a symbolic power far outweighing her historical
roots. Just as you need footnotes to place some of Shakespeare's historical
figures, but their actions on stage embody something eternal.[35]

For Zachary Woolfe, the critic of *The New York Times*, it was just the other way
around. He is a lifelong admirer of Philip Glass's *Einstein*-music, but when he
visited the performance it left him strangely unaffected. After describing this, he
pointed out parallels with reconstructions of other "original" staging, of baroque
opera for instance, and then continued:

Great works transcend time, but even the best stagings are products of their
moment. It is worth thinking about the centrality we have given these exhuma-
tions of classic productions in our cultural life, why we so value the seductive
illusion of authenticity they offer. With *Einstein*, the fantasy is the return to
that bohemian, avant-garde New York, so full of excitement and possibility.
Both those who were there and those of us who were not want badly, for our

34 Anthony Tomassini, "Time Travel with Einstein: Glass's Opera Returns to the Stage," *The New York Times*, September 16, 2012. www.nytimes.com/2012/09/17/arts/music/einstei n-on-the-beach-at-the-brooklyn-academy-of-music.html, Accessed: May 2, 2017.
35 Michael Glitz, "The Opera Einstein on the Beach Triumphs (Again)!" *The Huffington Post*, September 20, 2012. www.huffingtonpost.com/michael-giltz/theater-the-opera-einst ei_b_1901498.html, Accessed: May 2, 2017.

different reasons, to conjure an event, a moment, even an entire city that now exists only as a memory. It is Mr. Glass's music that is more than that, and it remains as close as your computer.[36]

These last words refer to the beginning of his review, where Woolfe recounts that he listened to Knee Play 1 on YouTube over and over again.

As might be expected, it is next to impossible to find a common denominator for all these opinions and perspectives. Maybe I've underplayed the many plaudits and positive reviews – because in a way they were so uniform – giving greater emphasis to reviewers who expressed doubts.

An apt conclusion is the last lines of the review by Clive Barnes in *The New York Times* – published on November 23, 1976, half a lifetime ago, but still very appropriate: "*Einstein on the Beach* is being repeated next Sunday. You will never forget it, even if you hate it. Which is a most rare attribute to a work of art. Nowadays."[37]

---

36 Zachary Woolfe, "An Opera Better Heard Than Seen," *The New York Times*, September 21, 2012. www.nytimes.com/2012/09/22/arts/music/einstein-on-the-beach-tries-to-r ecapture-a-new-york-era.html, Accessed: July 12, 2017.

37 Clive Barnes, "*Einstein on the Beach* Transforms Boredom into Memorable Theater," *The New York Times*, November 23, 1976. www.nytimes.com/1976/11/23/archives/eins tein-on-the-beach-transforms-boredom-into-memorable-theater.html, Accessed: May 2, 2017.

Appendix 1

Robert Wilson, *Einstein on the Beach*, storyboard drawings

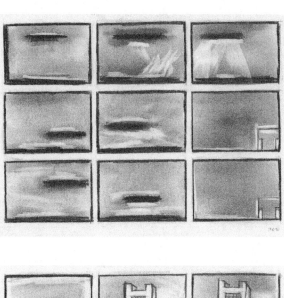

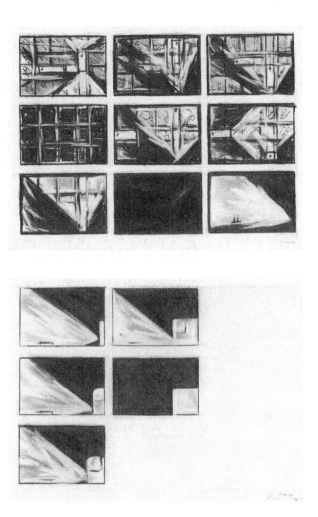

Appendix 2

Einstein on the Beach, spoken texts

EINSTEIN ON THE BEACH

KNEE PLAY 1

KNEE PLAY CHARACTER 1
(Numbers recited randomly)

KNEE PLAY CHARACTER 2
 (Text written by Christopher Knowles)

Would it get some wind for the sailboat. And it could get for it is.
It could get the railroad for these workers. And it could be were it is.
It could Franky it could be Franky it could be very fresh and clean
It could be a balloon.
All these are the days my friends and these are the days my friends..
It could get some wind for the sailboat. And it could get for it is.
It could get the railroad for these workers. It could get for it is were.
It could be a balloon. It could be Franky. It could be very fresh and clean.
All these are the days my friends and these are the days my friends.
It could be those ways.
Will it get some wind for the sailboat and it could get for it is it.
It could get the railroad for these workers workers. It could get for it is
All these are the days my friends and these are the days my friends.
Put these days of 888 cents in 100 coins of change...
These are theiidays mmy friends and these are my days my friends.
Make a tiota on thses these are theiidays loop
So if you say will it get some wind for the sailboat and it could for
It could be Franky it could be very fresh and cleann. So it could be
those ones. So if

You cash the bank of world traveler from 10 months ago.
Doo you remember! Honz the bus driver... , Well put the red
ball blue ball two black and white balls. And Honz pushed on his brakes
          and

the four balls went down to that. And Honz said. "Get those four
balls aw ay from the gearshift." All these are the days my friends and these are th
e days my friends. It could get the railroad for these workers.

                    It could

Would will it get some wind for the sailboat. And it could get for it is.

ACT I

SCENE I: TRAIN ONE

MAN CALCULATING (CRAZY EDDIE)
(Text written by Christopher Knowles)

This love could be some one
Into love
It could be some one that has been somewhere like them
It could be some like them

Tis one like into where that one has been like them
Well, it could be be some like them
Those like into where like that into this
This one has been broken like into where
But it could be some that it could be some like into like Into like into
Like into where like that

It could be be some of the lucky ones then

This has been like into where that the ones

That where that it could be some like them too
This one, the ones that it could be somewhere like them
It could be somewhere like
Let's see
Then, it could be somewhere like the one
It could be somewhere that it could be somewhere
That it could be somewhere
Like into that one has been lucky

The one it has like into where ever
The one it has like into where like into
Where like into
Where the singing of the love of them

This one has been like into where the one it has
Like into what is of that
Is where that love was
It could be somewhere like them them
Them them them
It could say where by numbers this one has
Like into it
The one is you over all the all the all the
It could be some that it could be,

Could be so like that it is the one it could be the one
It was the ones like them
It could be some like them
That one
It could be some like them
It could be *somewhere*
The ones like them
You will
The ones are
The ones are
The ones are are
The ones are like
The ones are like into where the ones are the ones
The ones
The ones are like into this
The ones are like that
It
The ones are like
The ones are like
The ones are like them
The ones are like to the Crazy Eddies
Are the are the a million
The ones are like what you do Crazy Eddies
That could be some that is into it is like what is it
What is it
What is it
What is it
What is it
Yes, come to the self service

What is it that could have some like I into it
What is it
That is it
What is it
It could be some one like them
It could be some one like them
Like them
Like that

The ones are like that
This one is not like them
I could be cry like a baby I'll be there
It could be course of that has been
The ones are like them them them them
Who
Them them them them them them them
The other ones, then, that has been
Like when it was the ones who prefer the ones
Are like them them them

These circles
The ones the th th th th th th th th th th th
You will
Crazy Eddies Crazy Eddies Crazy Eddies Crazy Eddies Crazy Eddies
Goodbye Crazy Eddies
Crazy Eddies are the most ones
Like into a coat jacket
Are into like it has the has the ever
Ever ever ever ever ever ever ever ever the

And that is the answer to your problem, handsome
Problem
Promise
The ones are like into this way
This always be
This
That it could be somewhere into where that it could be into some

SCENE 2: TRIAL ONE

JUDGES:
This court of common pleas is now in session

LAWYER: MR BOJANGLES
(Text written by Christopher Knowles)

If you see any of those baggy pants it was huge
Mr Bojangles
If you see any of those baggy pants it was huge chuck the hills
If you know it was a violin to be answer the telephone and if
any one asks you please it was trees it it it is like that
Mr Bojangles, Mr Bojangles, I reach you
So this is about the things on the table so this one could be counting up.
The scarf of where in Black and White
Mr Bojangles If you see any of those baggy pants chuck the hills
It was huge If you know it was a violin to be answer the
telephone and if anyone asks you please it was trees it it it is like that.
Mr Bojangles Mr Bojangles Mr Bojangles I reach you
The scarf of where in Black and White
This about the things on the table.
This one could be counting up.
This one has been being very American.
The scarf of where in Black and White.
If you see any of those baggy pants it was huge chuck the hills
If you know it was a violin to be answer the telephone and if
any one asks you please it was trees it it it it it it it it it
is like that
So this could be reflections for
Christopher Knowles-John Lennon
Paul McCartney-George Harrison
This has

This about the things on the table
This one has been very American
So this could be like weeeeeeee
Mr Bojangles
This could be about the things on the table This about the gun gun gun gun gun ... This has

OLD JUDGE
PARIS (IN ORIGINAL PRODUCTION)
(Text written by Mr. Samuel M. Johnson)

When considering the best liked cities on earth, Paris looms large among them. Paris is one of the world's greatest tourist attractions. And not without reason, for Paris has much to offer. Paris does not have a multiplicity of skyscrapers like New York, but it has much beauty and elegance. And Paris has an illustrious background of history.

In Paris there is a number of young men who are very beautiful, very charming and very lovable. Paris is called "the city of lights." But these young men who are very beautiful, very charming, and very lovable, prefer the darkness for their social activities.

One of the most beautiful streets of Paris is called Les Champs-Elysees, which means the Elysian Fields. It is very broad, bordered with trees, and very pleasant to look at.

One of the most beautiful things of Paris is a lady. She is not too broad, bordered with smiles, and very, very, very pleasant to look at. When a gentleman contemplates a lady of Paris, the gentleman is apt to exclaim: "Oo la la," for the ladies of Paris are very charming. And the ladies of Paris are dedicated to the classic declaration, expressed in the words: "L'amour, toujours l'amour!"

A Russian man once said that the eyes of a Paris lady are as intoxicating as good wine, and that her burning kisses are capable of melting the gold in a man's teeth.

In Germany, in Italy, in Congo, in China, and in the United States, there are men who say: "If you've never been kissed by a lady of Paris, you've never been kissed at all."

OLD JUDGE
ALL MEN ARE EQUAL (ALTERNATE SPEECH, WRITTEN FOR 1984 REVIVAL)
(Text written by Mr. Samuel M. Johnson)

"In this court, all men are equal." You have heard those words many times before. "All men are equal." But what about all women? Are women the equal of men? There are those who tell us that they are.

Last week, an auspicious meeting of women was held in Kalamazoo. The meeting was addressed by a very prominent lady who is noted for her modesty. She is so modest that she blindfolds herself when taking a bath. Modesty runs in her family. She has a nephew who is just ten years of age. Sometimes, the nephew says "I'm going to the forbidden name store." The little fellow is too modest to say "I'm going to the A & P." Well, here is what that modest lady said to the gathering of women in Kalamazoo:

"My sisters: The time has come when we must stand up and declare ourselves. For too long have we been trodden under the feet of men. For too long have we been treated as second-class citizens by men who say that we are only good for cooking their meals, mending their socks, and raising their babies.

"You have a boyfriend, and he calls you his queen. Then, when he marries you, he crowns you. These are the kind of men who, when they become romantic or, I should say, when they are in a certain mood, they want to kiss you and kiss you and kiss you again.

"My sisters, I say to you: Put your faces against it, and, if the man takes from you without your permission, look him squarely in the face, roll your eyes at him, and say to him 'How dare you, you male chauvinist pig! You put that kiss right back where you got it from.'

"My sisters, we are in bondage, and we need to be liberated. Liberation is our cry. Just yesterday, I talked with a woman who is the mother of fifteen children. She said 'Yes, I want to be liberated from the bedroom.'

"And so, my sisters, the time has come when we must let this male chauvinist understand that the hand that changes the diapers is the hand that shall rule the world.

"And now, my sisters, let us stand and sing our national song, For the benefit of you who have not yet memorized the words, here they are:

The woman's day is drawing near, it's written in the stars
The fall of men is very near, proclaim it from your cars.
Sisters, rise! Your flags unfurl! Don't be a little girl.
Say 'Down with men, their power must end: Women shall rule the world!'"

YOUNG JUDGE
(Text written by Christopher Knowles)

Would... Would it... Would it get... Would it get some... Would it get some wind... Would
it get some wind for... Would it get some wind for the... Would it get some wind for the sailboat.

KNEE PLAY 2

KNEE PLAY CHARACTER 2
(Text written by Christopher Knowles)

Would it get some wind for the sailboat. And it could get those for it is.
It could get the railroad for these workers. It could be a balloon.
It could be Franky, it could be very fresh and clean, it could be.
It could get some gasoline shortest one.
All these are the days my friends and these are the days my friends.
Could it get some wind for the sailboat. And it could get those for it is.
It could get the railroad for these workers. It could be a balloon.
It could be Franky, it could could be very fresh and clean, it could be.
It could get some gasoiine shortest one.
All these are the days my friends and these are the days my friends.
It could get a stopper. It could get the railroad for these workers.
Could it could be a balloon. It could be Franky, it could be.
Back to the rack and go back to the rack. It could be some workers so.
It could be a balloon, it could be Franky, it could be.
Which one are the ones for. So if you know. So i you take your watch off.
They're easy to lose or break. These are the days my friends and these are
the days my friends. It could be some of th ... It could be on your own.
It could be where of all. The way iron this one. So if you know you know.
this will be into where it could be. So look here.
Do you know they just don't make clothes for people who wears glasses.
There's no pockets anymore. So if you take your glasses off. They're easy
to lose or break. Well New York a Phonic Center has the answer to your
problem. Contactless lenses and the new soft lenses. The Center gives
you thirty days and see if you like them. And if you don't. They could
refunds your money. So this could be like into a satchel in the sky. A batch
of cookies was on the for these are the days. This could be into
a satchel.
It could get the railroad for these works
Do you know they just don't make clothes for people who wears glasses.
There's no pockets anymore. So if you take your glasses off They're easy
to lose or break. Well New York A Phonic Center has the answer to your
problem. Contactless lenses and
Would it get some wind for the sailboat and it could get for these workers
So all these are the days my friends and these are the days my friends.
Do you know they just don't make clothes for people who wears glasses.
There's no pockets anymore. So if you take your glasses off. They're easy
to lose or break Well New York a Phonic Center has the answer to your problem.

Contactless lenses and the new soft lenses.
The Center gives you thirty days and see if you
like them. And if you don't. They could refunds your money. (Except for
the exammination fee.) So if you're tired of glasses. Go to New York a Phonic Center on
Ele
ven West Fourty-Second Street near Fifth Avenue for sight with no hassle.
Please Call Br9-5555 ...
Would it get some wind for the sailboat. And it could get those for it is.
It could get the railroad for these workers. It could be a balloon.
It could be Franky, it could be very fresh and clean, it could be.
It could get some gasoline shortest one it could be.
All these are the days my friends and these are the days my friends.
Look .. ,. batch catch hatch latch match patch watch snatch scratch. Look.
SWEARIN TO GOD WHO LOVES YOU
FRANKIE VALLI THE FOUR SEASONS

KNEE PLAY CHARACTER I
(Numbers recited randomly and portions of *MR. BOJANGLES*)

ACT III

SCENE 1: TRIAL TWO / PRISON

LAWYER
MR BOJANGLES (TRIAL 2)
(Text written by Christopher Knowles)

The song I just heard is turning
(The song in where) ....
Tis thing
This will be the time that you come
This has been addressed to all those girls
All this one has been very American
So stop
When you see when it was it has been
When you   Hey Mr Bojangles
               Hey Mr Bojangles
               Hey Mr Bojangles

This has
This song wear a black and white then this has been
This about the things on the table
This will be counting that you allways wanted has been very very tempting
So stop
Hey Mr Bojangles
Hey Mr Bojangles
Hey Mr Bojangles
This has
This scarf of wear in black and white
That this has been.....
This about the things on the table
This will be counting
This has been addressed to the girls where
The song of (Satan) where it could be
Into where into where a
Hey Mr Bojangles
Hey Mr Bojangles
Hey Mr Bojangles
Ah this hah this scarf of wear of black and white that this about the
things on the table
This will be counting but

All this one has been very American
So stop
When you see where has been
Hey Mr Bojangles
Hey Mr Bojangles
Hey Mr Bojangles
This has red blue
Always run very quickly in a mad world
Say this
That call you Piggy in the sky
Like up in the.....
This is written
John Lennon for from Christopher Knowles' actions where that (major) star
Paul McCartney
George Harrison
The peoples
Where I this has also worked
This has been reflections Has been lucky as the sky
This has been like ...
So this one has
If you be so arrogant
It could be somewhere like to those ones
So learn what is so
So well like into a satchel like into where like a monster
If you know like gong like like a gong gong gong gong gong gong
Hey Mr Bojangles
So like if you see a little (nose) beggar with baggy pants

WITNESS
PREMATURELY AIR-CONDITIONED SUPERMARKET
(Text written by Lucinda Childs)

I was in this prematurely air-conditioned supermarket
and there were all these aisles
and there were all these bathing caps that you could buy
which had these kind of Fourth of July plumes on them
they were red and yellow and blue
I wasn't tempted to buy one
but I was reminded of the fact that I had been avoiding the beach.

LAWYER
(Text written by Christopher Knowles)

So uh this is abut the uh things on the table
so this one will be counting up
If you see any of those baggy pants, chuck the hills
And if somebody asked him, it was trees

the uh scarf of where in black and white
that this one will be sittin'
this about the uh things on the table
this will be counting up

so uh uh this is about the uh things on the table
the uh scarf of where in black and white
that this one is sittin'
this is about the uh things that were
If you see any of those, then this could be one of them
so stop here so stop this so look here
so this is written
Hey Mr Bojangles
Hey Mr Bojangles

Hey Mr Bojangles
so this could be the one that was
so if you see this one, then ...

Gun gun gun gun
Hey Mr Bojangles
Hey Mr Bojangles
Hey Mr Bojangles
Christopher Knowles bank robbery
so if you know
bank robbery bank robbery bank robbery is punishable by
20 years in federal prison so this is written
so if you know this is one so so look here
so Christopher Knowles and the Beatles
so so

WITNESS
I FEEL THE EARTH MOVE
(Text written by Christopher Knowles)

I feel the earth move ... I feel the tumbling down tumbling down ..... There was a judge who
like puts in a court. And the judge have like in what able jail what it could be a spanking. Or a
whack. Or a smack. Or a swat. Or a hit.
This could be where of judges and courts and jails. And who was it.
This will be doing the facts of David Cassidy of were in this case of feelings.
That could make you happy. That could make you sad. That could
make you mad. Or
that could make you jealous. So do you know a jail is. A court and a judge could
do this could be like in those
green Christmas Trees. So Santa Claus has about
red. And now the Einstine Trail is like in Einstein on the Beach. So this will.
So if you know that fafffffffff facts. So this what happen what I saw in. Lucy or
a kite. You raced all the
way up. This is a race. So this one will have eight in
types into a pink rink. So this way could be very magic. Sothis will be like to
Scene women comes out to grab her. So this what She grabbed her. So if you lie on
the grass. So this could be where if the earth move or not. So here
we go.
I feel the earth move under my feet. I feel tumbling down tumbling
down. I feel if
Some ostriches are a like into a satchel. Some like them. I went to the window
and wanted to draw the earth. So David Cassidy tells you when to go into this on
onto a meat. So where would a red dress. So this will get some gas. So this could
This would be some all of my friends. Cindy Jay Steve Julia Robyn Rick Kit and
Liz. So this would get any energy. So if you know what some like into were. So ...
So about one song.
I FEEL THE EARTH MOVE
CAROLE KING
So that was one song this what it could in the Einstein On The Beach with a trial
to jail. But a court were it could happen. So when David Casidy tells you all
of you to go on get going get going. So this one in like on WABC New York ...
JAY REYNOLDS from midnight to 6 00.
HARRY HARRISON
So heres what in like of WABC ..
JAY REYNOLDS from midnight to 6 AM
HARRY HARRISON from 6 AM to L
I feel the earth move from WABC ...
JAY REYNOLDS from midnight to 6 AM.
HARRY HARRISON from 6 AM to 10 AM.
RON LUNDY from 10 AM to 2 PM.
DAN INGRAM from 2 PM to
So this can misteaks try it aga9 ..
JAY REYNOLDS from midnight to 6 AM.

HARRY HARRISON from 6 AM
This could be true on WABC.
JAY REYNOLDS froj
This can be wrong.
This would WABC.
JAY REYNOLDS from midnight to 6 AM.
HARRY HARRISON from 6 AM to 10 AM.
RON LUNDY from 10 AM to 2 PM.
DAN INGRAM from 2 PM to 6 PM.
GEORGE MICHAEL from 6 PM to 10 PM.
CHUCK LEONARD from 10 PM to midnight.
JOHNNY DONOVAN from 10 PM to 3 AM.
STEVE-O-BRION from 2 PM to 6 PM.
JOHNNY ONOVAN from 6 PM to 10 PM.
CHUCK LEONARD from 3 AM to 5 AM.
JOHNNY DONOVAN from 6 PM to 1OPM.
STEVE-O-BRION from 4 30 AM to 6 AM
STEVE-O-BRION from 4 30 AM to 6 AM
JOHNNY DONOVAN from 4 30 AM to 6 AM

KNEE PLAY 5

KNEE PLAY CHARACTER 1
(Numbers and *MR. BOJANGLES*)

KNEE PLAY CHARACTER 2
(*KNEE PLAY 1*)

BUS DRIVER
TWO LOVERS
(Text written by Mr. Samuel M. Johnson)

The day with its cares and perplexities is ended and the night is now upon us. The night should be a time of peace and tranquility, a time to relax and be calm. We have need of a soothing story to banish the disturbing thoughts of the day, to set at rest our troubled minds, and put at ease our ruffled spirits.

And what sort of story shall we hear? Ah, it will be a familiar story, a story that is so very, very old, and yet it is so new. It is the old, old story of love.

Two lovers sat on a park bench, with their bodies touching each other, holding hands in the moonlight

There was silence between them. So profound was their love for each other, they needed no words to express it. And so they sat in silence, on a park bench, with their bodies touching, holding hands in the moonlight.

Finally she spoke. "Do you love me, John?" she asked. "You know I love you, darling," he replied. "I love you more than tongue can tell. You are the light of my life, my sun, moon and stars. You are my everything. Without you I have no reason for being."

Again there was silence as the two lovers sat on a park bench, their bodies touching, holding hands in the moonlight. Once more she spoke. "How much do you love me, John?" she asked. He answered:

"How much do I love you? Count the stars in the sky. Measure the waters of the oceans with a teaspoon. Number the grains of sand on the sea shore. Impossible, you say. Yes and it is just as impossible for me to say how much I love you.

"My love for you is higher than the heavens, deeper than Hades, and broader than the earth. It has no limits, no bounds. Everything must have an ending except my love for you."

There was more of silence as the two lovers sat on a park bench with their bodies touching, holding hands in the moonlight.

Once more her voice was heard. "Kiss me, John," she implored. And leaning over, he pressed his lips warmly to

hers in fervent osculation... •

Bibliography

Abbate, Carolyn. *Unsung Voices: Opera and Musical Narrative in the Nineteenth Century.* Princeton: Princeton University Press, 1991.

Abbate, Carolyn and Roger Parker. *A History of Opera: The Last 400 Years.* London: Allen Lane, 2012.

Adorno, Theodor W. *Essays on Music.* Introduction, commentary, and notes by Richard Leppert. Translated by Susan H. Gillespie, et al. Berkeley: University of California Press, 2002.

Als, Hilton. "Slow Man: Robert Wilson and his First Masterpiece." *The New Yorker*, September 17, 2012.

Als, Hilton and Anthony Elms. *"Conversation: Hilton Als and Anthony Elms on Christopher Knowles,"* October 7, 2015. Philadelphia, PA: Institute for Contemporary Art. Video accessed at https://vimeo.com/151703149, February 3, 2015.

Als, Hilton and Anthony Elms. *"Christopher Knowles: In a Word."* Gallery Guide. Philadelphia, PA: Institute for Contemporary Art. http://static.icaphila.org/pdf/gall ery-notes/2015_fall/christopher_knowles_galleryguide.pdf. Accessed: January 20, 2016.

Anker, Suzanne and Dorothy Nelkin. *The Molecular Gaze: Art in the Genetic Age.* Cold Spring, NY: Cold Spring Harbor Laboratory Press, 2004.

Aragon, Louis. "Lettre Ouverte à André Breton: sur Le Regard du Sourd. L'art, la science et la liberté." *Les Lettres Francais*, no. 1388 (2–8 June, 1971): 3–15.

Arendell, Telory D. "Thinking Spatially, Speaking Visually: Robert Wilson and Christopher Knowles." *International Journal of Music and Performing Arts* 3, no. 1 (2015), 16–24.

Arendell, Telory D. *The Autistic Stage. How Cognitive Disability Changed 20th-Century Performance.* Rotterdam: Sense, 2015.

Ashbery, John. *"Christopher Knowles,"* New York Magazine, September 19, 1978, 88–89.

Assmann, Jan. "Collective Memory and Cultural Identity." *New German Critique*, 65 (Spring–Summer 1995), 125–133.

Augé, Marc. *Non-Places: Introduction to an Anthropology of Supermodernity.* Translated by John Howe. New York: Verso Books, 1995.

Banes, Sally. *Terpsichore in Sneakers.* Boston: Houghton Mifflin Company, 1980.

Banes, Sally. *Democracy's Body: Judson Dance Theater 1962–1964.* Ann Arbor: UMI Research Press, 1983.

Banes, Sally. *Subversive Expectations: Performance Art and Paratheater in New York 1976–85.* Ann Arbor: The University of Michigan Press, 1998.

Baracks, Barbara. "Einstein on the Beach." *Artforum*, March 1977, 30–36.

Barbican Centre. Laurie Anderson, Trisha Brown, Gordon Matta-Clark: *Pioneers of the Downtown Scene, New York, 1970s*. London: Prestel Publishing Ltd., 2011.

Baron-Cohen, Simon and Sally Wheelright. "'Obsessions' in children with autism or Asperger's Syndrome: Content Analysis in Terms of Core Domains of Cognition." *British Journal of Psychiatry* 175, no. 5 (1999), 484–490.

Barthes, Roland. *Camera Lucida: Reflections on Photography*. Translated by Richard Howard. New York: Hill and Wang, 1981.

Barthes, Roland. *The Responsibility of Forms: Critical Essays on Music, Art, and Representation*. Translated by Richard Howard. New York: Hill and Wang, 1985.

Barthes, Roland. *S/Z*. Translated by Richard Miller. Oxford: Blackwell Publishing, 2000.

Barthes, Roland. *The Neutral: Lecture Course at the College de France (1977–1978)*. Translated by Rosalind Krauss and Denis Hollier. Text established, annotated, and presented by Thomas Clerc under the direction of Eric Marty. New York: Columbia University Press, 2007.

Battcock, Gregory and Robert Nickas, eds. *The Art of Performance: A Critical Anthology*. E.P. Dutton New York, (1984)..

Beckett, Samuel. *The Complete Dramatic Works of Samuel Beckett*. London: Faber & Faber, 2006.

Benhart, Walter and Lawrence Kramer, eds. *On Voice*. Amsterdam and New York: Rodopi, 2014.

Birringer, Johannes. "Postmodern Performance and Technology." *Performing Arts Journal* 9, no. 2/3. 10th Anniversary Issues: The American Theatre Condition (1985), 221–233.

Birringer, Johannes. *Performance, Technology and Science*. New York: PAJ Publications, 2009.

Birringer, Johannes. "Gestural Materialities and the Worn Dispositif." In *Digital Movement: Essays in Motion Technology and Performance*, edited by Nicolas Salazar util/Sita Popat, 162–185. Basingstoke: Palgrave Macmillan, 2015.

Blenner, Stephanie, Arathi Reddy, and Marilyn Augustyn. "Diagnosis and Management of Autism in Childhood." *BMJ: British Medical Journal* 343, no. 7829 (2011): 894–899.

Bogart, Anne. *A Director Prepares. Seven Essays on Art and Theatre*. London and New York: Routledge, 2001.

Boyles, Michael. *Beethoven: The Emergence and Evolution of Beethoven's Heroic Style*. New York: Excelsior, 1987.

Bradby, David and Clare Finburgh. Jean Genet. London: Routledge, 2012.

Brecht, Stefan. *The Theatre of Visions*: Robert Wilson. London: Methuen, 1994.

Broadhurst, Susan. *Liminal Acts: A Critical Overview of Contemporary Performance and Theory*. New York and London: Cassell, 1999.

Broadhurst, Susan. "Einstein on the Beach: A Study in Temporality." *Performance Research* 17, no. 5 (2012): 34–40.

Brustein, Robert. "Expanding Einstein's Universe." *The New Republic* 192, no. 4 (1985): 23–25.

Brustein, Robert. "Introduction." In Shyer, Laurence, *Robert Wilson and his Collaborators*. New York: Theatre Communications Group, 1990.

Bürger, Peter. "Avant-Garde and Neo-Avant-Garde: An Attempt to Answer Certain Critics of Theory of the Avant-Garde." *New Literary History* 41, no. 4 (Autumn 2010): 695–715.

Carbonneau, Suzanne. "An Art of Refusal: Lucinda Childs' Dances in Silence, 1973–78." http://danceworkbook.pcah.us/asteadypulse/dances/interior_drama.html. Accessed: March 5, 2019.

Castelvecchi, Stefano. "From 'Nina' to 'Nina': Psychodrama, Absorption and Sentiment in the 1780s." *Cambridge Opera Journal* 8, no. 2 (1996): 91–112.

Cavarero, Adriana. For More Than One Voice: *Toward a Philosophy of Vocal Expression*. Translated by Paul A. Kottman. Stanford: Stanford University Press, 2005.

Clarke, Eric F. "Subject-Position and the Specification of Invariants in Music by Frank Zappa and P. J. Harvey." *Music Analysis* 18, no. 3 (1999): 347–374.

Connor, Steven. *The Horror of Number: Can Humans Learn to Count?* The Alexander Lecture, University College, University of Toronto, October 1, 2014. http://stevenconnor.com/wp-content/uploads/2014/10/Horror-of-Number.pdf. Accessed: March 30, 2017.

Connor, Steven. *Beyond Words: Sobs, Hums, Stutters, and Other Vocalizations*. London: Reaktion Books, 2014.

Cooke, Mervyn, ed. *The Cambridge Companion to Twentieth-Century Opera*. Cambridge, UK: Cambridge University Press, 2005.

Cook, Nicholas. *Analysing Musical Multimedia*. Oxford: Clarendon Press, 1998.

Corbin, Alain. *The Lure of the Sea: Discovery of the Seaside 1750–1840*. Translated by Jocelyn Phelps. London: Penguin Books, 1995.

Cumming, Naomi. *The Sonic Self: Musical Subjectivity and Signification*. Bloomington and Indianapolis: Indiana University Press, 2001.

Davis, Lennard J. *Obsession: A History*. Chicago: University of Chicago Press, 2008.

Deleuze, Gilles. *Cinema 1: The Movement Image*. Translated by Hugh Tomlinson and Barbara Habberjam. London - New York: Continuum, 1986.

Deleuze, Gilles. *The Logic of Sense*. Translated by Mark Lester and Charles Stivale. London: Athlone Press, 1990.

Delezue, Gilles and Félix Guattari. *Anti-Oedipus: Capitalism and Schizophrenia*. Translated by Robert Hurley, Mark Seem and Helen R. Lane. London and New York: Continuum, 2004.

Delgado, Maria M. and Paul Heritage, eds. In *Contact With the Gods?: Directors Talk Theatre*. Manchester: Manchester University Press, 1996.

Di Pietro, Rocco. Dialogues with Boulez. London: The Scarecrow Press, 2001.

Dibben, Clare. "Pulp, Pornography and Spectatorship: Subject Matter and Subject Position in Pulp's This Is Hardcore." *Journal of the Royal Musical Association* 126, no. 1 (2001): 83–106.

Djordjev, Bojan. "Pozorišna (neo)avangarda pedesetih i šezdesetih godina - Atelje 212." In Istorija umentosti XX vek : Radikalne umetničke prakse, edited by Miško Šuvaković, 367–374. Belgrade: Orion Art, 2010.

Eidsheim, Nina Sun. *Sensing Sound: Singing and Listening as Vibrational Practice*. Durham, NC: Duke University Press, 2015.

Erlmann, Veit. *Reason and Resonance: A History of Modern Aurality*. New York: Zone Books, 2010.

Fatherly, Richard W. and David T. MacFarland. *The Birth of Top 40 Radio. The Storz Stations' Revolution of the 1950s and 1960s*. Jefferson, NC: MacFarland & Company, 2014.

Fearn, Raymond. *Italian Opera Since 1945*. New York and Abingdon: Routledge, 1997.

Feldman, Martha (Convener). Why Voice Now? *Journal of the American Musicological Society* 68, no. 3, 2015, 653–685.

Ffrench, Patrick and Roland-François Lack, eds. *The Tel Quel Reader*. New York and London: Routledge, 1998.

Fink, Robert. "Going Flat: Post-Hierarchical Music Theory and the Musical Surface." In *Rethinking Music*, edited by Nicholas Cook and Mark Everist. Oxford: Oxford University Press, 1999.

Fink, Robert. *Repeating Ourselves, American Minimal Music as Cultural Practice.* Berkeley: University of California Press, 2005.

Fischer, Iris S. Mabou Mines: *Making Avant-Garde Theater in the 1970s.* Ann Arbor: University of Michigan Press, 2012.

Fisher, Mark. Something in the Air: Radio, Rock, and the Revolution that Shaped a Generation. New York: Random House, 2007.

Flakes, Susan. "Robert Wilson's 'Einstein on the Beach'." *The Drama Review*: TDR 20, no. 4. Theatrical Theory Issue (1976): 69–82.

Fong-Torres, Ben. *The Hits Just Keep On Coming. The History of Top 40 Radio.* San Francisco: Backbeat Books, 1998.

Fried, Michael. *Art and Objecthood: Essays and Reviews.* Chicago: The University of Chicago Press, 1998.

Fried, Michael. *Why Photography Matters as Art as Never Before.* New Haven: Yale University Press, 2008.

Frith, Uta. *Autism: A Very Short Introduction.* Oxford: Oxford University Press, 2008.

Fuchs, Elinor and Una Chaudhuri, eds. Land/Scape/Theatre. Ann Arbor: University of Michigan Press, 2002.

Gann, Kyle. Robert Ashley. Urbana, etc.: University of Illinois Press, 2012.

Gann, Kyle, Keith Potter, and Pwyll ap Siôn. "Introduction: Experimental, Minimalist, Postminimalist? Origins, Definitions, Communities." In *The Ashgate Research Companion to Minimalist and Postminimalist Music*, edited by Kyle Gann, Keith Potter, and Pwyll ap Siôn, 1–16. London: Ashgate, 2013.

Gillis, John R. The Human Shore: Seacoasts in History. Chicago: University of Chicago Press, 2012.

Glass, Philip, Robert Wilson, and Andrew de Groat. *Einstein on the Beach: An Opera in Four Acts.* New York: EOS Enterprises, Inc., 1976.

Glass, Philip. "Notes: Einstein on the Beach." *Performing Arts Journal* 2, no. 3 (Winter 1978): 63–70.

Glass, Philip. *"Note on Einstein on the Beach."* Einstein on the Beach, Tomato Records, TOM-4-2901 (1979).

Glass, Philip. *Music by Philip Glass*, Edited by Robert T. Jones. New York: Harper & Row, 1987.

Glass, Philip and Robert T. Jones, ed. *Opera on the Beach.* London: Faber and Faber, 1988.

Glass, Philip. "Notes on Einstein on the Beach." In the CBS Masterworks recording (M4 38875), 1979.

Glass, Philip. *Words without Music: A Memoir.* New York: Liveright Publishing Company, 2015.

Grover-Haskin, Kim, ed. Dance and Gender. The Netherlands: Harwood Academic Publishers, 1998.

Gunning, Tom. "The Cinema of Attraction: Early Film, its Spectator and the Avant-Garde." *Wide Angle* 8, no. 3–4 (1986), 63–70.

Hammond, Mark. "Problems of Uncleanliness, Neglect, Fade Slowly at O.D. Heck Center." *The [Schenectady] Daily Gazette*, December 17, 1990.

Hanna, Judith Lynne. *Dance, Sex and Gender: Signs of Identity, Dominance, Defiance, and Desire.* Chicago: University of Chicago Press, 1988.

Haskins, Robert. "The Music of Philip Glass, 1965–1975: An Analysis of Two Selected Early Works and Einstein on the Beach." Master's thesis, University of Rochester, Eastman School of Music, 1996.

Hoffmann, Frank W. *WABC Weekly Music Charts, 1970–1977*. San Bernardino: Paw Press, 2015.

Holmberg, Arthur. *The Theater of Robert Wilson*. Cambridge, UK: Cambridge University Press, 1996.

Howell, John. "Forum: What A Legend Becomes." *Artforum* 23, no. 7 (1985): 90.

Hui, Alexandra. *The Psychophysical Ear: Musical Experiments, Experimental Sounds, 1840–1910*. Cambridge, MA: MIT Press, 2012.

Hutcheon, Linda. *The Politics of Postmodernism*. 2nd edition. London and New York: Routledge, 1989.

Ingold, Tim. *Lines: A Brief History*. London and New York: Routledge, 2007.

Jameson, Fredric. "Reification and Utopia in Mass Culture." *Social Text* 1 (Winter 1979): 130–148.

Jameson, Fredric. "Postmodernism and Consumer Society." In Postmodern Culture, edited by Hal Foster. London: Pluto Press, 1985.

Jameson, Fredric. Postmodernism, or, The Cultural Logic of Late Capitalism. Durham, NC: Duke University Press, 1991.

Jameson, Fredric. Brecht and Method. London: Verso, 2000.

Jensen-Moulton, Stephanie. "Disability as Postmodernism: Christopher Knowles and Einstein on the Beach." Unpublished typescript, 2012.

Johnson, Tom. "Maximalism on the Beach: Philip Glass." February 25 – March 3, 1981. http://tvonm.editions75.com/articles/1981/maximalism-on-the-beach-philip-glass.html. Accessed: August 22, 2017.

Johnson, Tom. *The Voice of New Music: New York City 1972–1982*. Eindhoven: Het Apollonhuis, 1989.

Kanner, Leo. "Autistic Disturbances of Affective Contact." *Nervous Child* 2 (1943): 217–250.

Kawashima, Takeshi. "Conjunction of the Essential and the Incidental: Fragmentation and Juxtaposition; or Samuel Beckett's Critical Writings in the 1930s." *Samuel Beckett Today* 14 (2004): 469–482.

Kerman, Joseph. *Opera as Drama*. Berkeley and Los Angeles: University of California Press, 1988.

Kessler, Frank. "The Cinema of Attractions as Dispositif." In *The Cinema of Attractions Reloaded*, edited by Wanda Strauven, 57–70. Amsterdam: Amsterdam University Press, 2006.

Key, Wilson Bryan. *Subliminal Seduction: Ad Media's Manipulation of a Not So Innocent America*. Introduction by Marshall McLuhan. New York: Prentice-Hall, 1973.

Key, Wilson Bryan. *The Clam-Plate Orgy and Other Subliminal Techniques for Manipulating Your Behavior*. New York: Signet, 1980.

Kirk, Elise K. *American Opera*. Urbana: University of Illinois Press, 2001.

Kittler, Friedrich. *Gramophone, Film*, Typewriter. Translated by Geoffrey Winthrop-Young and Michael Wutz. Stanford: Stanford University Press, 1999.

Kittler, Friedrich. *The Truth of the Technological World*. Stanford: Stanford University Press, 2013.

Kostelanetz, Richard. "A Theater of Performance, Not Literature." *Dialogue* 8, no. 2 (1975): 39–47.

Kostelanetz, Richard and Robert Flemming, eds. *Writings on Glass: Essays, Interviews, Criticism*. Berkeley and Los Angeles: University of California Press and Schirmer Books, 1997.

Krauss, Rosalind. "Sculpture in the Expanded Field." *October* 8 (Spring, 1979): 30–44.

Kuhn, Thomas S. *The Structure of Scientific Revolutions*. Chicago: University of Chicago Press, 1962.

LaBelle, Brandon. *Background Noise: Perspectives on Sound Art*. New York: Continuum, 2007.

LaBelle, Brandon. *Lexicon of Mouth: Poetics and Politics of Voice and the Oral Imaginary*. London and New York: Bloomsbury, 2014.

Lasch, Christopher. *The Minimal Self*. New York: Norton, 1985.

Lawrence, Tim. *Loves Saves the Day: A History of American Dance Music, 1970–1979*. Durham, NC: Duke University Press, 2004.

Lehmann, Hans-Thies. "Robert Wilson, szenograph." *Merkur* 437 (1985): 554–563.

Lehmann, Hans-Thies. *Postdramatic Theatre*. Translated by Karen Jürs-Munby. New York and London: Routledge, 2006.

Letzler Cole, Susan. Directors in *Rehearsal: A Hidden World*. New York: Routledge, 1992.

Lévi-Strauss, Claude. *The Savage Mind*. Chicago: University of Chicago Press, 1966.

Lipman, Samuel. "From Avant-Garde to Pop [Commentary, 1979], Reprinted in *The House of Music*. Boston: Godine, 1984.

Lipman, Samuel. "Einstein's Long March to Brooklyn [*The New Criterion*, February 1985], Reprinted in The New Criterion Reader: The First Five Years, edited by Hilton Kramer. New York: Free Press, 1988.

Lyotard, Jean Francois. *Libidinal Economy*. Translated by Iain Hamilton Grant. Bloomington, IN: Indiana University Press, 1993.

Macey, David. *The Penguin Dictionary of Critical Theory*. London, New York: Penguin Books, 2000.

Makin, Stephen. *Indifference Arguments*. Oxford: Blackwell, 1993.

Mander, Jerry. *Four Arguments for the Elimination of Television*. New York: Quill, 1978.

Manning, Erin. *Always More Than One: Individuation's Dance*. Durham, NC: Duke University Press, 2013.

Marcus, Greil. *Lipstick Traces: A Secret History of the 20th Century*. Cambridge, MA: Harvard University Press, 1989.

Marranca, Bonnie. *Theatre Writings*. New York: PAJ Publications, 1984.

Marranca, Bonnie. "The Forest as Archive: Wilson and Interculturalism." PAJ 11, no. 3 / 12, no. 1 (1989): 36–44.

Marranca, Bonnie. *The Theatre of Images*. Baltimore and London: PAJ Publications, 1996.

McClary, Susan. "Terminal Prestige: The Case of Avant-Garde Music Composition." Cultural Critique 12 (Spring 1989): 57–81.

McClary, Susan. "Rap, Minimalism, and Structures of Time in Late Twentieth-Century Culture." In *Audio Culture: Readings in Modern Music*, edited by Christoph Cox and Daniel Warner, 289–298. New York: Continuum/The Wire, 2004.

McClary, Susan. "Minima Romantica." In *Beyond the Soundtrack: Representing Music in Cinema*, edited by Richard Leppert, Lawrence Kramer, and Daniel Goldmark, 48–67. Berkeley and Los Angeles: University of California Press, 2007.

McClary, Susan. "The Lure of the Sublime: Revisiting Postwar Modernism." In Transformations of Musical Modernism, edited by Erling Guldbrandsen and Julian Johnson, 21–35. Cambridge, UK: Cambridge University Press, 2015.

Merleau-Ponty, Maurice. *Phenomenology of Perception*. Translated by Colin Smith. London and New York: Routledge, 2005.

ertens, Wim. *American Minimal Music*. Translated by J. Hautekiet. London: Kahn and Averill, 1983.

Metcalf, Sasha. "Institutions and Patrons in American Opera: The Reception of Philip Glass, 1976–1992." PhD dissertation, University of California, Santa Barbara, 2015. ProQuest (AAT 3733595).

Michaels, Bianca. "Opera for the Media Age: Composer Robert Ashley on Television Opera." *The Opera Quarterly* 22, no. 3–4 (Summer-Autumn 2006): 534–537.

Miller, Arthur I. Einstein, Picasso: *Space, Time and the Beauty that Causes Havoc*. New York: Basic Books, 2001.

Mitter, Shomit and Maria Shevtsova, eds. *Fifty Key Theatre Directors*. New York: Routledge, 2005.

Morey, Miguel and Carmen Pardo. *Robert Wilson*. Barcelona: Ediciones Polígrafa, 2002.

Murray, Stuart. *Representing Autism: Culture, Narrative, Fascination*. Liverpool: Liverpool University Press, 2008.

Murray, Stuart. *Autism*. New York: Routledge, 2012.

Neumeyer, David, ed. *The Oxford Handbook of Film Music Studies*. Oxford: Oxford University Press, 2014.

Nietzsche, Friedrich. *Richard Wagner in Bayreuth / Der Fall Wagner / Nietzsche contra Wagner*. Stuttgart: Reclam, 1986.

Novak, Jelena. "Throwing the Voice, Catching the Body: Opera and Ventriloquism in Philip Glass/Jean Cocteau's La Belle et la Bête." *Music, Sound and the Moving Image* 5, no. 2 (Autumn 2011): 137–156.

Novak, Jelena. "From Minimalist Music to Postopera: Repetition, Representation, and (Post)modernity in the Operas of Philip Glass and Louis Andriessen." In *The Ashgate Research Companion to Minimalist and Postminimalist Music*, edited by Kyle Gann, Keith Potter, and Pwyll ap Siôn, 129–140. London: Ashgate, 2013.

Novak, Jelena. *Postopera: Reinventing the Voice-Body*. London: Ashgate, 2015.

Nyman, Michael. "Minimal Music." *The Spectator*, October 11, 1968.

Oliver, Wendy and Doug Risner, eds. *Dance and Gender: an Evidence-Based Approach*. Gainesville: University Press of Florida, 2017.

Ovadija, Mladen. *Dramaturgy of Sound in the Avant-garde and Postdramatic Theatre*. Montreal, etc.: Mcgill-Queens University Press, 2013.

Owens, Craig. "Einstein on the Beach: The Primacy of Metaphor." October 4 (*Autumn 1977*): 21–32.

Page, Tim. *Einstein on the Beach, liner notes*. CD, 1993, Nonesuch 79323–2.

Piekut, Benjamin. *Experimentalism Otherwise: The New York Avant-garde and its Limits*. Berkeley: University of California Press, 2011.

Potter, Keith. *Four Musical Minimalists: La Monte Young, Terry Riley, Steve Reich, Philip Glass*. Cambridge, UK: Cambridge University Press, 2000.

Preko (beyond) Ajnštajna na plaži, TkH no. 2, Belgrade, September 2001. Available online: http://www.tkh-generator.net/portfolio/tkh-2-beyond-einstein-on-the-beach/, Accessed: September 19th, 2019.

Raickovich, Milos. "Einstein on the Beach by Philip Glass: A Musical Analysis." PhD dissertation, The City University of New York, 1994.

Read, Alan. *Theatre in the Expanded Field: Seven Approaches to Performance*. London: Bloomsbury, 2013.

Remington, Anna, John Swettenham, Ruth Campbell, and Mike Coleman. "Selective Attention and Perceptual Load in Autism Spectrum Disorder." *Psychological Science* 20, no. 11 (2009): 1388–1393.

Richardson, John. *Singing Archaeology: Philip Glass's* Akhnaten. Hanover, CT: Wesleyan University Press, 1999.

Richardson, John. "Resisting the Sublime: Loose Synchronization in La Belle et la Bête and The Dark Side of Oz." In *Musicological Identities: Essays in Honour of Susan McClary*, edited by Steven Baur, Raymond Knapp, and Jacqueline Warwick, 135–148. Aldershot: Ashgate, 2008.

Richardson, John. *An Eye for Music: Popular Music and the Audiovisual Surreal*. New York: Oxford University Press, 2012.

Ricoeur, Paul. *Time and Narrative*. Vol. 1. Translated by Kathleen McLaughlin and David Pellauer. Chicago: The University of Chicago Press, 1990.

Rigolli, Alessandro. "Einstein on the Beach di Philip Glass e Bob Wilson: caratteri de una 'non-opera.'" *Rivista Italiana di Musicologia* 36, no. 2 (2001): 351–373.

Ross, Alex. *The Rest is Noise: Listening to the Twentieth Century*. New York: Farrar, Straus and Giroux, 2007.

Rotman, Brian. "Ghost Effects." Lecture at Stanford Humanities Institute, 2004.

Salzman, Eric and Thomas Desi. *The New Music Theater: Seeing the Voice, Hearing the Body*. New York: Oxford University Press, 2008.

Scherzinger, Martin. "The Return of the Aesthetic: Musical Formalism and Its Place in Political Critique." In *Beyond Structural Listening? Postmodern Modes of Hearing*, edited by Andrew Dell'Antonio, 252–277. California: University of California Press, 2004.

Schöllhammer, Georg. "An Ontologist Observes." Springerin, no. 1 – 'Other Modernities', Vienna, 2007, http://www.springerin.at/dyn/heft_text.php?textid=1900&lang=en. Accessed: 05.09.2008.

Schwarz, David. *Listening Subjects: Music, Psychoanalysis, Culture*. Durham, NC: Duke University Press, 1997.

Schwarz, K. Robert. Minimalists. New York: Phaidon Press, 1996.

Scott, Charles. E. *Living with Indifference*. Bloomington, IN: Indiana University Press, 2007.

Sedgwick, Eve Kosofky. *Touching Feeling: Affect, Pedagogy, Performativity*. Durham, NC: Duke University Press, 2003.

Shapiro, David. "Notes on Einstein on the Beach." in *The Art of Performance: A Critical Anthology*, edited by Gregory Battcock and Robert Nickas, 271–277. New York: Plume, 1984.

Shearer, Harry. "Captain Pimple Cream's Fiendish Plot." *Cheetah Magazine*, 1967, Reprinted in Jonathan Eisen, ed. *The Age of Rock: Sounds of the American Cultural Revolution*. New York: Random House, 1969.

Shevtsova, Maria. *Robert Wilson*. New York: Routledge, 2007.

Shute, Nevil. On the Beach. New York: William Morrow and Company, 1957.

Shyer, Laurence. *Robert Wilson and his Collaborators*. New York: Theatre Communications Group, 1989.

Sidiropoulou, Avra. *Authoring Performance. The Director in Contemporary Theatre*. New York: Palgrave Macmillan, 2011.

Simmer Bill. "Robert Wilson and Therapy." *The Drama Review*: TDR 10-1, Theater and Therapy (1976): 99–110.

Sklar, Rick. *Rocking America: How the All-Hit Radio Stations Took Over*. New York: St. Martin's Press, 1984.

Sniffen, Alan. ed. http://www.musicradio77.com. Accessed: December 15, 2015 – April 17, 2016.

Stamenković, Vladimir. *Kraljevstvo eksperimenta* – 20 godina BITEF-a. Belgrade: Nova knjiga, 1987.

Steege, Benjamin. "Acoustics." In *Keywords in Sound*, edited by David Novak and Matt Sakakeeny, 23–32. Durham, NC: Duke University Press, 2015.

Stern. Daniel N.. *The Interpersonal World of the Infant: A View from Psychoanalysis and Development Psychology*. London: Karnac Books, 1985.

Stiegler, Bernard. *Technics and Time, 1. The Fault of Epimethus, [1994]*. Translated by Richard Beardsworth and George Collins. Stanford: Stanford University Press, 1998.

Stiegler, Bernard. *Technics and Time, 2: Disorientation*. Translated by Stephen Barker. Stanford: Stanford University Press, 2008.

Šuvaković, Miško. "Razoriti (ili) čitati teatar. Pisanje o pisanju o teatru – slučaj Ajnštajn na plaži." *TkH Journal*, no. 2 (2001): 79–92.

Suzuki, Dean. "Minimalism in the Time-Based Arts: Dance, Film, and Video." In *The Ashgate Research Companion to Minimalist and Postminimalist Music*, edited by Keith Potter, Kyle Gann, and Pwyll ap Siôn, 109–128. Farnham: Ashgate, 2013.

Symonds, Dominic and Pamela Karantonis, eds. *The Legacy of Opera: Reading. Music Theatre as Experience and Performance*. Amsterdam: Editions Rodopi B.V., 2013.

Szendy, Peter. *Sur écoute: Esthétique de l'espionnage*. Paris: Minuit, 2007.

Szendy, Peter. *À coups de points: La ponctuation comme expérience*. Paris: Minuit, 2013.

Tarasti, Eero. *Myth and Music: A Semiotic Approach to the Aesthetics of Myth in Music, Especially that of Wagner, Sibelius And Stravinsky*. Helsinki: Suomen Musiikkitieteellinen Seura, 1978.

Taylor, Diana. "Saving the "Live"? Re-performance and Intangible Cultural Heritage." *Etudes Anglaises* 69, 2 (2016): 149–161.

Taylor, Marvin J. *The Downtown Book: The New York Art Scene, 1974–1984*. Princeton: Princeton University Press, 2006.

Teorija koja Koda *(TkH) Journal* No. 2, 2001. Available online: http://www.tkh-generator.net/portfolio/tkh-2-beyond-einstein-on-the-beach/. Accessed: December 12, 2017.

Théberge, Paul, Kyle Devine, and Tom Everrett, eds. *Living in Stereo: Histories and Cultures of Multichannel Sound*. New York, etc.: Bloomsbury, 2015.

Thomas, Helen, ed. *Dance, Gender and Culture*. Hampshire, UK: MacMillan Press, Ltd., 1993.

Thompson, Emily. *The Soundscape of Modernity: Architectural Acoustics and the Culture of Listening in America, 1900–1933*. Cambridge, MA: MIT Press, 2004.

Turner-Brown, Lauren, et al. "Phenomenology and Measurement of Circumscribed Interests in Autism Spectrum Disorders." *Autism* 15, 4 (2011): 437–456.

Välimäki, Susanna. *Subject Strategies in Music: A Psychoanalytic Approach to Musical Signification*. Imatra: Semiotic Society of Finland, 2009.

Vagapova, Natalija. Bitef: pozorište, festival, život. Belgrade: Bitef teatar, 2010.

Van Maas, Sander, ed. *Thresholds of Listening: Sounds, Technics, Space*. New York: Fordham University Press, 2015.

Verschaffel, Bart. "Rome/Over theatraliteit." *Vlees en Beton* 16 (1990): 63.

Vujanović, Ana. " Nove pozorišne tendencije: BITEF / Beogradski internacionalni teatarski festival." In *Istorija umetnosti XX vek : Radikalne umetničke prakse*, edited by Miško Šuvaković, 375–384. Belgrade: Orion Art, 2010.

Wagner, Richard. Das Kunstwerk der Zukunft. Leipzig: Wigand, 1850.

Wagner, Richard. *Opera and Drama*. Translated by William Ashton Ellis. Lincoln: University of Nebraska Press, 1995.

Weber, William. "Did People Listen in the 18th Century?" *Early Music* 25, no. 4, 25th Anniversary Issue; Listening Practice, November 1997.

Weinberg, Leah. "Opera behind the Myth: An Archival Examination of Einstein on the Beach." PhD thesis, The University of Michigan, 2016. https://deepblue.lib.umich.edu /handle/2027.42/120839. Accessed: May 2, 2017.

Willett, John, ed. and trans. *Brecht on Theatre*. New York: Methuen, 1978.

Wilson, Robert. Review of Christopher Knowles, Typings, 1974–1979. New York: Vehicle Editions, 1986. http://www.vehicleeditions.com/Site/Robert_Wilson.html. Accessed: March 26, 2016.

Wilson, Robert and Umberto Eco. "Robert Wilson and Umberto Eco: A Conversation." *Performing Arts Journal* 15, no. 1 (1993): 87–96.

Wilson, Robert and Philip Glass. *Einstein on the Beach*. Paris: Éditions Dilecta, 2012.

Witzel, Frank. *Die Erfindung der Roten Armee Fraktion durch einen manisch-depressiven Teenager im Sommer 1969* [The Invention of the RAF by a manic depressive teenager in the summer of 1969]. Berlin: Matthes & Seitz, 2015.

Young, Miriama. Singing the Body Electric: The Human Voice and Sound Technology. Farnham: Ashgate, 2015.

Scores

Glass, Philip and Robert Wilson. *Einstein on the Beach*. New York: Dunvagen, 1976.

Glass, Philip and *Robert Wilson*. Einstein on the Beach, Opera in Four Acts. Full Score. London: Chester, 2013.

Interviews (selection)

Freyer, Achim. Interview with Achim Freyer, By Wolfgang Veit, October 20, 1988 at the occasion of the premiere of Einstein on the Beach at Wurttemberg Statsoper. Material available at the archive of Akademie der Künste in Berlin.

Glass, Philip and Robert Wilson. "Einstein at the Met (An Operatic Interview)." By Maxime de la Falaise, *Andy Warhol's Interview* 7, no. 2 (1977): 27–30.

Glass, Philip. "Phil Glass: Interview." By Sylvère Lotringer and Bill Hellermann, Semiotexte 3, no. 2 (1978): 178–191.

Glass interviewed in Cole Gagne and Tracy Caras, *Interviews with American Composers*. Metuchen, NJ: Scarecrow Press, 1982.

Glass, Philip. "Everything is Available." Conversation with Philip Glass, by Jelena Novak. *New Sound International Journal of Music* 14 (1999): 17–22.

Glass, Philip. "Philip Glass tvillingpar – Opera Och Film." Nutida Musik 1, 2008/03, 26–32. Interview by Jelena Novak. (Translation of "Opera and Film as Twins," Philip Glass interviewed by Jelena Novak, Lisbon, June 24, 2007, unpublished manuscript in English).

Glass, Philip. "The Politics of Creativity through Economy of Love and Death." Fragments of recorded phone conversation between Philip Glass and Jelena Novak that took place on September 5, 2009 on the occasion of Belgrade production of Glass's dance opera "Les Enfants Terribles," published in Les Enfants Terribles program booklet, 2009, 5–9.

Glass, Philip and Lucinda Childs. "Philip Glass and Lucinda Childs Discuss Einstein on the Beach." By Mark Swed, UC Berkeley Events, April 29, 2011. https://www.youtube. com/watch?v=e8Cx7XOYj_w.

Glass, Philip and Robert Wilson. "The Power of 2." By Anne Bogart, Penny W. Stamps Distinguished Speaker Series, University of Michigan Penny W. Stamps School of Art and Design, January 15, 2012, Ann Arbor, MI. http://playgallery.org/video/the_power_of_2/. Accessed: December 10, 2018.

Glass, Philip. "Interview with Philip Glass." In *Schizo-Culture*, 2-Vol, Semiotext(e), edited by Sylvère Lotringer and David Morris. Cambridge, MA: MIT Press, 2014.

Wilson, Robert. "Robert Wilson and 'Einstein on the Beach'." "Interview/Report by Jeff Goldberg. *New York Arts Journal* 2, no. 1 (Spring 1977): 15–18.

Wilson, Robert. "Robert Wilson: Interview." By Sylvère Lotringer. *Semiotexte* 3, no. 2 (1978): 20–27.

Wilson, Robert. "Robert Wilson: Entrevista por Erik Berganus." In *Robert Wilson [exhibition catalog, IVAM Centre del Carme]*. Valencia: Institut Valencia d'Art Modern, 1994.

Wilson, Robert and Philip Glass. "Robert Wilson and Philip Glass, 'How we made: Philip Glass and Robert Wilson on Einstein on the Beach'." Interviews by Tom Service, *The Guardian*, April 23, 2012, http://www.theguardian.com/culture/2012/apr/23/how-we-made-einstein-on-the-beach. Accessed: December 30, 2018.

Wilson, Robert, Philip Glass, and Lucinda Childs. *"Robert Wilson, Philip Glass, and Lucinda Childs discuss Einstein on the Beach."* By Matias Tarnopolsky, Cal Performances, Zellerbach Playhouse, University of California, Berkeley, October 28, 2012. https://www.youtube.com/watch?v=k8iLOGPm7AY. Accessed: January 14, 2019.

Catalogues, program booklets, performance documentation (selection)

'Ajnštajn na plaži,' BITEF 10 catalogue, Belgrade, 1976.

10e Biennale de Paris (Paris, 1977), 138–139.

Einstein on the Beach, program booklet, Oper Stuttgart, 1988.

Einstein on the Beach, Philip Glass/Robert Wilson, opera/installation at the staatsbankberlin. (Installation/staging by Berthold Schneider and Veronika Witte), August 2001, performance documentation.

Einstein on the Beach, von Philip Glass und Robert Wilson, Operninstallation von Staatsbankberlin / Operaworks, 24., 26., 27., 29., 30 July and 1., 2., 4., 5., August 2005, Parochialkirche Berlin (Installation/staging by Berthold Schneider and Veronika Witte), performance documentation.

Einstein on the Beach, program booklet, Theater Dortmund: Opernhaus, 2017.

Philip Glass Trilogy, program booklet (compiled by Lara Francis and edited by Debra Pahl), August 5–23, 2014, Her Majesty's Theatre, State Opera South Australia.

'Pismo za Kraljicu Viktoriju,' BITEF 8 catalogue, Belgrade, 1974, 42–62.

'Violine i brojke,' BITEF 10 catalogue, Belgrade, 1976.

Films and video recordings (selection)

Absolute Wilson. Directed by Katharina Otto-Bernstein. Film Manufacturers, Inc., 2007.

Baby Einstein on the Beach. Advertizing video of Brooklyn Academy of Music, April 1, 2013. https://www.youtube.com/watch?v=ipMkm1_5jf8. Accessed: May 2, 2017.

Einstein on the Beach: The Changing Image of Opera. Directed by Mark Obenhaus, 1987. Santa Monica, CA: Direct Cinema, 2007. DVD. https://www.youtube.com/watch?v=j1PxYB0wqSE. Accessed: March 8, 2017.

Einstein on the Beach. DVD, Opus Arte, 2016.

Einstein on the Beach. Directed by Achim Freyer, Oper Stuttgart, 1988. (Video recording of the performance from the archives of Oper Stuttgart.)

Einstein on the Beach. Directed by Leigh Warren, 2014. (Video recording of the performance from the archives of State Opera South Australia.)

Einstein on the Beach. Directed by Kay Voges, Theater Dortmund: Opernhaus, 2017. (Video recording of the performance from the archives of Theater Dortmund: Opernhaus.)

Glass: A Portrait of Philip in Twelve Parts. Directed by Scott Hicks. 119 min. Koch Lorber Films, 2009.

Louis Vuitton. Spring/Summer 2013, Full Fashion Show (excerpts). https://www.youtube.com/watch?v=CsuorSZEURs. Accessed: May 2, 2017.

On the Beach, film. Directed by Stanley Kramer, 1959.

On the Beach, television film. Directed by Russell Mulcahy, 2000.

Bareilles, Sara. "Brave." *The Blessed Unrest.* Epic Records, 2013, compact disc.

Rutkowski, Richard. *Sunshine Superman,* 16mm film, 1987.

Audio recordings (selection)

Glass, Philip and Robert Wilson. *Einstein on the Beach,* The Philip Glass Ensemble, Tomato Records TOM 2901, 1979, Stereo LP.

Glass, Philip and Robert Wilson. *Einstein on the Beach,* The Philip Glass Ensemble, CBS Masterworks M4K 38875, 1985, compact disc.

Glass, Philip and Robert Wilson. *Einstein on the Beach,* The Philip Glass Ensemble, Elektra Nonesuch 79323–2, 1993, compact disc.

Glass, Philip and Robert Wilson. *Einstein on the Beach*: highlights, The Philip Glass Ensemble, Orange Mountain Music OMM 0083, 2012. A CD featuring highlights from the complete Einstein on the Beach accompanied by a DVD of the documentary film "The Changing Image of Opera" (1984).

Unpublished interviews and correspondence

Berthold Schneider in conversation with Jelena Novak, Opernhaus Wuppertal, October 8, 2016 (unpublished manuscript).

Kay Voges in conversation with Jelena Novak, Theater Dortmund: Opernhaus, June 4, 2017 (unpublished manuscript).

Veronika Witte, email correspondence with Jelena Novak, March 2018.

Archives

A Steady Pulse: Restaging Lucinda Childs, 1963–78. The Pew Center for Arts & Heritage, Philadelphia, 2015. http://danceworkbook.pcah.us/asteadypulse/.

Bibliotèque nationale de France, Paris, France.

Bitef / 40 godina novih pozorišnih tendencija. Dokumenta Beogradskog internacionalnog teatarskog festivala 1967-2006, Belgrade, Istorijski arhiv Beograda, 2007.

Brooklyn Academy of Music Hamm Archives, Brooklyn, NY.

Maison Jean Vilar, Avignon, France.

Robert Wilson Papers, 1969–1995. Rare Book & Manuscript Library, Columbia University, New York, NY.

The Soho Weekly News Collection, 1976–1978. Downtown Collection, Fales Library & Special Collections, New York University, New York, NY.

Theater on Film and Tape Archive, New York Public Library for the Performing Arts, New York, NY.

Reviews (selection)

Als, Hilton. "Slow Man. Robert Wilson and his First Masterpiece." *The New Yorker*, September 17, 2012. http://www.newyorker.com/arts/critics/atlarge/2012/09/17/120 917crat_atlarge_als#ixzz2E1AiQzx9. Accessed: July 10, 2015.

Arian, Max. "Vormingstoneel voor intellektuelen?" *Toneel Teatraal*, November 1976.

Barnes, Clive. *"Einstein on the Beach* Transforms Boredom Into Memorable Theater." The New York Times, November 23, 1976. www.nytimes.com/1976/11/23/archives /einstein-on-the-beach-transforms-boredom-into-memorable-theater.html. Accessed: May 2, 2017.

Brink, Nic. "De ijzeren long van Glass en Wilson." *De Groene Amsterdammer*, October 27, 1976.

Brustein, Robert. "Expanding Einstein's Universe." *The New Republic*, January 28, 1985, 23.

Christiansen, Rupert. "Einstein on the Beach, Barbican, Review." *The Telegraph*, May 7, 2012 http://www.telegraph.co.uk/culture/music/opera/9250317/Einstein-on-the-Beac h-Barbican-review.html. Accessed: May 2, 2017.

Clements, Andrew. "Einstein on the Beach." *The Guardian*, May 6, 2012. http://www.theg uardian.com/music/2012/may/06/einstein-on-beach-glass-review. Accessed: August 4, 2015.

Coghlan, Alexandra. "Review of Einstein on the Beach." *New Statesman*, May 10, 2012. http://www.newstatesman.com/blogs/culture/2012/05/review-einstein-beach. Accessed: June 11, 2015.

Corwin, Christopher. "Back to the Beach." September 18, 2012. http://parterre.com/2012/ 09/18/back-to-the-beach-2/Back to the Beach. Accessed: December 12, 2014.

Donadio, Rachel. "Paris Embraces 'Einstein' Again." *New York Times*, January 3, 2014. https://www.nytimes.com/2014/01/04/arts/international/history-time-and-space-in-opera.html?_r=0. Accessed: February 18, 2017.

Everett-Green, Robert. "Einstein on the Beach: A Lot of Numbers with Stories, Relatively Speaking." *The Globe and Mail*, June 11, 2012. http://www.pressreader.com/canada/ the-globe-and-mail-metro-ontario-edition/20120611/282398396484335. Accessed: May 2, 2017.

Glitz, Michael. "The Opera Einstein On The Beach Triumphs (Again)!" *The Huffington Post*, September 20, 2012. http://www.huffingtonpost.com/michael-giltz/theater-the -opera-einstei_b_1901498.html. Accessed: May 2, 2017.

Gottfried, Martin. "Wilson's *Einstein On the Beach* Is Awash With Visual Events." New York Post, November 23, 1976.

Guatterini, Marinella. "Einstein rivoluziona la spiaggia." *Il Sole 24 Ore*, March 25, 2012. http://www.ilsole24ore.com/art/cultura/2012-03-25/einstein-rivoluziona-spiaggia-081939.shtml. Accessed: May 2, 2017.

Heg, Hans. "Einstein on the Beach: 'n kolossale nieuwe opera." *De Volkskrant*, August 14, 1976.

Hirsch, Lisa. "Einstein Casts its Spell." *San Francisco Classical Voice*, October 26, 2012.

Hofman, W. "Einstein on the Beach, of 'Vijf uren zijn nog te kort.'" *Magazijn*, October 1976.

Holland, Bernard. "Review/Music; An 'Einstein' in Repose (Relatively Speaking)." *New York Times*, November 21, 1992. http://www.nytimes.com/1992/11/21/arts/review -music-an-einstein-in-repose-relatively-speaking.html. Accessed: May 5, 2015.

Howell, Anthony. "Watching 'Einstein on the Beach' through a Periscope." *The Fortnightly Review*, May 6, 2012. http://fortnightlyreview.co.uk/2012/05/einstein-be ach/. Accessed: May 2, 2017.

Lynn, Cordelia. "Review: Einstein on the Beach (Barbican)." *Ceasefire Magazine*, May 9, 2012. https://ceasefiremagazine.co.uk/einstein-beach-philip-glass-robert-wilson/. Accessed: May 2, 2017.

Midgette, Anne. "A Procession of Elusive Images by the Merlin of Surreal Form." *The New York Times*, July 04, 1999.

Porter, Andrew. "Many-Colored Glass." The *New Yorker*, December 13, 1976, 164.

Rockwell, John. "Einstein Returns Briefly." *New York Times*, December 17, 1984.

Rockwell, John. "Review/Music; 3 Philip Glass Operas Become a Sort of Modern 'Ring' Cycle." *New York Times*, June 25, 1990. http://www.nytimes.com/1990/06/25/a rts/review-music-3-philip-glass-operas-become-a-sort-of-modern-ring-cycle.html. Accessed: April 17, 2019.

Rockwell, John. "Robert Wilson Tackles the French Revolution." *New York Times*, November 3, 1992.

Sandow, Gregory. "Einstein in the Fog." *Voice*, January 8, 1985.

Tomassini, Anthony. "Time Travel with Einstein: Glass's Opera Returns to the Stage." *The New York Times*, September 16, 2012. http://www.nytimes.com/2012/09/17/arts/ music/einstein-on-the-beach-at-the-brooklyn-academy-of-music.html. Accessed: May 2, 2017.

Wilson, Edwin. "An Avant-Garde Production at Met." *The Wall Street Journal*, November 26, 57 (1976): 4.

Woolfe, Zachary. "An Opera Better Heard Than Seen." *The New York Times*, September 21, 2012. http://www.nytimes.com/2012/09/22/arts/music/einstein-on-the-beach-tri es-to-recapture-a-new-york-era.html. Accessed: July 12, 2017.

Index